Genesis

Volume I

Bible Student's Commentary

Genesis

Volume I

Translated by William Heynen

G. Ch. Aalders

ZONDERVAN
PUBLISHING HOUSE
OF THE ZONDERVAN CORPORATION
GRAND RAPIDS, MICHIGAN 49506

PAIDEIA
P.O. Box 1450
St. Catharines
Ont., CANADA L2R 7 JB

THE BIBLE STUDENT'S COMMENTARY
Originally published in Dutch under the title KORTE VERKLARING DER HEILIGE SCHRIFT

Copyright © 1981 by The Zondervan Corporation
Grand Rapids, Michigan

Library of Congress Cataloging in Publication Data

Aalders, G. Charles (Gerhard Charles), 1880–
    The Book of Genesis.

    (The Bible student's commentary)
    Translation of: Het boek Genesis.
    1. Bible.   O.T. Genesis—Commentaries.   I. Title.
II.   Series: Korte verklaring der Heilige Schrift,
met nieuwe vertaling.   English.
BS1235.3.A213   222'.11077   81-4677
Zondervan: ISBN 0-310-43968-X   AACR2
Paideia: ISBN 0-88815-101-2

The translation used in THE BIBLE STUDENT'S COMMENTARY is the *Holy Bible, New International Version.* Copyright © 1978 by New York International Bible Society.

Designed and Edited by Edward Viening

Printed in the United States of America

Contents

Publisher's Foreword

Introduction to the Pentateuch   1

Introduction to Genesis   42

Commentary on Genesis

     Part One   50

     Part Two   260

Foreword

The leading evangelical commentary on the whole Bible among the Dutch-speaking people is a set of 62 volumes entitled *Korte Verklaring Der Heilige Schrift*. Unfortunately, the *Korte Verklaring* has not been widely known in the English-speaking world, although a number of the contributors and editors have made contributions to biblical and theological studies that have been acknowledged outside the Netherlands.

Publication of this highly regarded commentary began in the 1930s and 40s, with occasional additions and updating, and continued into the 60s. It was designed as a commentary for the lay reader who does not have a knowledge of Hebrew and Greek or a detailed knowledge of critical questions. It has admirably served this purpose and yet at the same time has been highly regarded and frequently used by scholars because of its exegetical insights.

The Bible Student's Commentary at last will make the *Korte Verklaring* available to the English-speaking world, beginning with the two-volume work on Genesis. Other volumes are already in translation. It is adapted for English use by incorporating the text of the New International Version into the commentary discussion. Where appropriate, the original contributor's discussion has been edited to reflect the wording of the NIV and translation issues among the other English versions. *The Bible Student's Commentary* is a work of enduring value in terms of the exegetical material that it makes available to the serious student of Scripture.

The Publishers

Introduction to the Pentateuch

I. *Name, Contents and Divisions*

The Jews divide the Hebrew Old Testament, which is their Bible, into three main sections: the Law, the Prophets, and the Writings. Our Lord Jesus had the same division in mind when He said "everything must be fulfilled that is written about me in the Law of Moses, the Prophets and the Psalms" (Luke 24:44). In this case the section which is usually known as the Writings is designated as the Psalms, which certainly constitute the most familiar part of the Writings.

The Law (Torah, in Hebrew) includes the first five books of our Bible, namely, Genesis, Exodus, Leviticus, Numbers, and Deuteronomy. Although the Law is divided into these five books, it must be seen as one definite unit. When we divide the Old Testament, as we often do in common usage, into historical, poetical, and prophetic books, this essential unity of the first five books is not preserved. Books such as Joshua, Judges, Ruth, etc., are then included with the historical books. Although we grant that the first five books have a historical character, we must nevertheless insist that they form one distinct unit just as, for instance, 1 and 2 Samuel or 1 and 2 Kings form specific units.

Genesis, Exodus, Leviticus, Numbers, and Deuteronomy together form one continuous whole—one mighty epoch of history. This epoch begins with the creation of heaven and earth. It proceeds to record the history of humanity up to the time of Abraham, describes the adventures of the patriarchs and the saga of the people of Israel born from them, and concludes with the dramatic scene of the death of Moses. Keeping this close-knit unity in proper perspective, a concise commentary such as ours cannot and should not offer a separate, extended introduction to each of the first five books of the Bible. It is imperative, rather, that we preface our treatment of the first

1

book with a general introduction to the entire Book of the Law.

Referring to these five books as "the Law" as is done, for example, in the New Testament (Matt. 12:5; Luke 10:26; John 1:46; Acts 13:15; 24:14; 1 Cor. 14:34; also, "Law of the Lord"—Luke 2:23–24; or "Law of Moses"—Acts 28:23; 1 Cor. 9:9) demands some explanation. By far the predominant element in the major historical section of the first five books of our Bible is concerned with the people of God receiving the Law of God through Moses, after their departure from Egypt. This name, "the Law," was of such paramount importance to the Jews that they frequently referred to the entire Old Testament—Law, Prophets, and Writings—simply as "the Law." There are striking examples of such usage in the New Testament as well. In John 10:34 the Lord Jesus refers to a passage from the Psalms as "written in the Law." In 1 Corinthians 14:21, the apostle Paul cites a passage from Isaiah and designates it as "in the Law it is written."

Another name that is used extensively, especially in scholarly circles, is the "Pentateuch." This is taken from the Greek and is a contraction of "pentateuchos biblios," meaning the fivefold book. Obviously this name emphasizes the unity of the five Books of the Law while it also recognizes the fact that the book falls into five sections.

Among modern scholars there are differing views regarding the origins of the Pentateuch. We will discuss these more fully later. Some scholars have suggested that the Book of Joshua should be included with the first five books and consequently they speak of the Hexateuch (sixfold book). Others go still further and have included the Books of Judges and Samuel, and even large sections of Kings. They then speak of the Heptateuch, Octateuch, and Enneateuch (sevenfold, eightfold, and ninefold book). Since we, however, reject all such views, as we will see when we examine them more closely, there is no substantial reason for combining other Old Testament books with the Law and employing nomenclature such as Hexateuch, etc.

The names of the individual books are partly of Greek and partly of Latin origin. The Jews themselves were accustomed to designating books by their opening words. Thus they called the first book *berēšît* because that was the first word (translated, "in the beginning"). The second book was called *šēmôt* (names), because it began, "These are the names of the sons of Israel." The third book they designated as *wayyigrā́* (and He called), because it opened with "the Lᴏʀᴅ called to Moses." To the fourth book they gave the name *bemidbar* (in the wilderness), in keeping with the first words, "The Lᴏʀᴅ spoke to Moses in the [wilderness] of Sinai." Finally, the fifth was named *debārîm,* (literally, "words"), since it commenced with "These are the words Moses spoke to all Israel."

The ancient Greek translation of the Old Testament, which originated in Egypt a few centuries before our era, was called the "Septuagint." In this the books were named according to their content: Genesis—origin; Exodus—departure; Leuitikon—the Levitical Book; Arithmoi—numbering, referring to the counting of the Israelites; Deuteronomion—repetition of the Law. These names were taken over by the well-known Latin translation of the Bible, known as the "Vulgate," for centuries the Bible of the Roman Church. The Vulgate substituted the Latin equivalent "Numeri" for the word "Arithmoi" and the ends of the words were all Latinized. This, then, is also the form in which the names have come down to us: Genesis, Exodus, Leviticus, Numbers, and Deuteronomy.

The content of the Law, or the Pentateuch, is, as we have already pointed out, the history of humanity from creation to Abraham. It includes the narrative of the patriarchs and the people of Israel up to and including the death of Moses. In the history of humanity up to Abraham, the following events are highlighted: the creation of heaven and earth, Paradise and the Fall, the twofold line of development after the Fall, the Flood, the new mankind after the Flood, the tower of Babel and the confusion of speech. This section ends by giving the sequence of generations from Shem to Abraham.

The history which follows disregards the rest of humanity and concentrates on the people of Israel and their forefathers. The adventures of the three patriarchs, Abraham, Isaac, and Jacob, are described in considerable detail. Here the emphasis falls on the promises God gave to them, which were to be fulfilled in the people who descended from them. This history of the patriarchs ends with the arrival of Jacob and his family in Egypt.

The period that includes their stay in Egypt, during which they grew into a great nation, is described in only a few lines. Then we are given a broad treatment of the oppression of Israel by the Egyptians and their eventual departure "out of the house of bondage," which was effected by the mighty miracles of God.

In the course of their journey toward Canaan, Israel came to Mount Sinai. There God, through the mediation of Moses, gave them the law which was to govern their entire religious and civil life. This law is extensively revealed. The record of this revelation covers more than half the Book of Exodus and the entire Book of Leviticus.

In the Book of Numbers the continuation of Israel's journey to Canaan is described. Here the spotlight falls brightly on the events that took place when they reached the borders of Canaan. The discouraging report of the spies stirred the people to fear and murmuring and consequently God condemned them to forty years of wandering in the wilderness. A few significant events out of this 40-year period are recorded. The historical account concludes with Israel again approaching the borders of Canaan, this time on the east bank of the Jordan. The East Jordan country was conquered while Moses was still in command. At Israel's request, this territory was allotted to the tribes of Reuben and Gad and half the tribe of Manasseh. Now the moment was near when the great man of God who had led his people out of Egypt was to leave this life. Because of his sin, he might bring the Israelites *to* Canaan, but not *into* it. He delivered his farewell discourse on the flat plains of Moab. This is recorded in detail in Deuteronomy, and it concludes with his psalm, his benediction, and then his death.

This historical material can basically be divided in accordance with the division of the books. The Book of Genesis begins with creation and ends with the arrival of Jacob and his family in Egypt. Numbers has a suitable starting point in the futher history of Israel, after the Law had been given at Sinai. It ends, fittingly, when they arrive at the plains of Moab. The Book of Deuteronomy, as it were, stands by itself as the last will and testament of Moses. It ends with the account of his death. There is no clear and marked division between Exodus and Leviticus. The last half of Exodus and the entire Book of Leviticus contain the giving of the Law. Numbers, however, includes some detailed legal prescriptions for special occasions. There is, moreover, a certain obvious distinction between Exodus and Leviticus. Exodus provides specific details for building and establishing the tabernacle, while Leviticus outlines the prescriptions for the worship services which were to be held in that holy place.

Within the overall compass of these books we can then distinguish the following main divisions:

Genesis 1:1–11:26 — The history of mankind.
Genesis 11:27–50:26 — The history of the elect lineage from which the people of Israel would descend.
Exodus 1:1–15:21 — The description of the departure from Egypt.
Exodus 15:22–40:38, plus Leviticus — God establishing His covenant with His people Israel at Mt. Sinai, embodied in the giving of the Law.
Numbers 1:1–14:45 — The wilderness journey and God's judgment on Israel at the borders of Canaan.
Numbers 15:1–26:13 — The wilderness wanderings, to the time of their arrival at the Jordan.
Deuteronomy — No clear divisions can be made but a rough outline would be somewhat as follows:

Ch. 1-4 — Moses' introductory message;
5-26 — Moses' great farewell address;
27-34 — Conclusion

II. *The Question of Origin and Date*

The magnificent historical book that we have as the Pentateuch is an anonymous document. Nowhere does the author mention his name. Within its pages we are given no indication as to who composed this carefully designed book.

From the outset the Jews ascribed it to the man who played such a significant role in this history—Moses. He was Israel's great leader and law-giver. Several centuries before the Christian era the Mosaic authorship was already firmly established for the Jews. Admittedly the closing passage of Deuteronomy, in which the death and burial of Moses is recorded, gave them some difficulty. Some of the Jewish scholars, such as Philo and the historian Flavius Josephus, considered this to be no problem. They believed that Moses himself wrote this passage by prophetic foreknowledge of future events. The Talmud, on the contrary, ascribes the last eight verses of the Torah (Deut. 34:5-12) to Joshua's pen.

The opinion of the Jews regarding Mosaic authorship was, in turn, taken over by the early Christian church. From time to time there were those who questioned this, such as the second-century pagan adversary of Christianity, Celsus; the English free-thinker, Thomas Hobbes (d. 1679); and the pantheistic Jewish philosopher, Spinoza (d. 1677). Even so, until the second half of the eighteenth century this remained the generally accepted position.

The man who paved the way for the great change was the French physician, Jean Astruc (1684-1766), personal physician to Louis XV, and professor on the medical faculty of the University of Paris. Although he still held to Mosaic authorship, his views laid the groundwork for all later criticism of the Pentateuch. In 1753 he wrote *Conjectures sur les mémoires originaux, dont il paroit que Moyse s'est servi pour composer le livre de la Génèse*. In this book he pointed out, as some of his predecessors had done, what he considered to be the repetitions and the contradictions included in the Pentateuch. He tried to explain these by the supposition that Moses had used various "sources." He suggested that Moses used four sources which he arranged in parallel columns. Later copiers, then, supposedly blended these together into one record. Astruc thought this theory would resolve the difficulties in the text of the Pentateuch.

The key Astruc introduced for distinguishing these sources was the fact that in distinct portions, especially of Genesis, the name "Lord"

(Hebrew—*Jahweh*) is consistently used, while in other sections the name "God" (Hebrew—*Elohim*) is used with the same regularity. In this way he came to the conclusion that originally there were two main sources. He called these the Jahwistic and the Elohistic sources. In addition to these, Astruc claimed, another 10 sources of lesser significance could be distinguished. It was especially this criterion of "source splitting" which established Astruc as the father of all later Pentateuch criticism. To this day the different use of names for God is the chief characteristic of source splitting. Later studies pointed out other differences between the sources, such as differences in the use of language, narrative style, and religious outlook. Even so, these distinctions are based on the original splitting of the sources according to the use of the names of God. Thus we can say with certainty that the use of the names of God formed the foundation for Pentateuch criticism.

Astruc's followers took the next step and decided that Moses was not involved in writing the Pentateuch. They dated the sources much later. Successively various theories developed which may be outlined as follows:

1) The older documentary hypothesis of Eichhorn and Illgen. They joined Astruc in accepting two primary sources plus a few secondary sources.

2) The fragment hypothesis of Geddes, later taken over by Vater and others. According to them the Pentateuch was written at about the time of the Babylonian captivity and consisted of the stringing together of a large number of fragments taken from older "sources."

3) The supplementary hypothesis, especially propagated by Tuch. He held that one Elohistic primary source was completed by Jahwistic elements.

4) The newer documentary hypothesis of Hupfeld and others. They distinguished between four sources, namely, two Elohistic, one Jahwistic, and one Deuteronomistic. This often has been called the "four-source theory."

Generally this division into four sources has continued, but a remarkable shift of opinions took place regarding the age and the order of these sources. Originally they were arranged as follows: the first Elohist, the second Elohist, the Jahwist, and the Deuteronomist. This last source was then dated in the year 620 B.C., the eighteenth year of the reign of King Josiah. This was the time when the well-known "reformation" of Israel's worship services took place. It was assumed that the "Book of the Law," which was the basis for this reformation (2 Kings 22:8ff.), was none other than the gathering of the laws which constitute the core of the Book of Deuteronomy. Supposedly, this Book of the Law was first produced at that time in order to support and effect the reformation. The "finding" of the Book of the Law was considered to have been a clever comedy which was played in order to put the good cause into effect. It is even suggested that Hilkiah, the high priest, who was one of the players, may have been the first sacrificial offering.

Still another opinion broke upon the scene under the influence of three scholars. They were the German, Graf, the modern Old Testament scholar, Kuenen, of Leyden, and especially the German professor, Julius Wellhausen. This theory held that the source which had been considered the earliest, the first Elohist, was actually the latest, even later than Deuteronomy. This source, they contended, was formulated at the time of Ezra, who himself had a leading hand in the project, and was dated about 450 B.C. This was called the Priestly Codex. They also changed the order of the two pre-Deuteronomy sources. By the end of the 19th century this was considered to be the most substantial result of Old Testament scholarship and a brilliant success on the part of erudite critical genius. What has usually been called the Graf-Wellhausen school taught, in short, that the Pentateuch consisted of the following four elements:

1) The Jahwist, indicated by the letter "J," dated about 850 B.C.

2) The Elohist, indicated by the letter "E," from about 750 B.C.

3) Deuteronomy, indicated by the letter "D," dated 620 B.C.

4) The Priestly Codex, signified by the letter "P," and dated about 450 B.C.

When Pentateuch criticism, since Astruc, constantly uses the term "sources," it is imperative that we understand what is meant by that term. We must not think of sources of a historical record as we would use the term. We think of written or unwritten records from which the historian draws his material. But in biblical criticism "sources" refers to independent, separate historical narratives which deal primarily with the same period. Furthermore, it is not as though the author of the Pentateuch drew from these sources, but rather that he cut them in pieces and then fit them together like a mosaic. Thus he formed a new composition.

It goes without saying, then, that when we think of the Pentateuch as being composed from four sources, we must also leave room for a number of persons, from various periods of time, who busied themselves with the task of dividing the material into pieces, often small fragments, and then fitting them all together again. Such persons are called "redactors." Thus, in addition to the four sources, we must also take into account a number of redactors.

In the first quarter of the twentieth century, the dream of scientific certainty, which was claimed for these word studies in the Pentateuch, was

7

shaken by bitter disillusionment. Naturally these theories had always been opposed by strict Bible believers who never were able to accept the results of Pentateuch criticism because they made the testimony of God's Word untrue. But now serious opposition arose also within the circle of negative criticism itself. Not only was the "four-source theory" called in question, but the entire concept of splitting sources came under attack. Furthermore, the opposition focused on the basis of source splitting, the primary characteristic according to which the sources were divided, namely, the use of the different names of God.

What really happened? Astruc and all his followers proceeded from the assumption that the Hebrew text of the Pentateuch, as we presently have it, gives us the original names, exactly as they were written down by the authors of the sources. But now, a more careful study of the history of the text such as was pursued in the first part of this century, and is still being carried on, has revealed that this was a serious mistake. We are not at all sure that the present Hebrew text is the same as the original text. Rather, we are sure that this is not the case in all parts of the text. And, specifically, it is evident that with respect to the names used for God, there is great uncertainty regarding the accuracy of the text.

Studies in the Septuagint especially have indicated that at this time, in several instances, it is absolutely impossible to determine whether the original text used the name Jahweh or the name Elohim. Obviously, then, to ascribe a given section to a Jahwistic or Elohistic source on the basis of the appearance of the name Jahweh or Elohim in the Hebrew text is a totally gratuitous assumption. As a consequence the whole basis for source splitting has collapsed. It is not surprising, then, that in the first part of this century the number of scholars who questioned the results of source splitting constantly grew.

As early as 1908, Professor Eerdmans, who succeeded Professor Kuenen in the chair of Old Testament at Leyden, openly denied the four-source theory. In Germany a powerful opponent of the theory appeared in the preacher, John Dahse. In England, the Jewish lawyer, Harold M. Wiener, attacked the negative Pentateuch criticism with an endless series of publications. Unfortunately, he was killed in an uprising in Palestine in 1929.

Besides this textual critical objection to the foundation on which the source splitting theory rested, this position is no less culpable from another direction. The whole idea that the use of different names for God, in itself, indicates different authors for the related passages, is indefensible. This can be clearly seen in the Muslim Koran. There we have the same phenomenon, with different sections being characterized by the use of specific names for the divine being. Some portions consistently use the name Rab (Lord) and others with equal regularity use the name Allah (God). But here there can be no possibility of different sources. That the work has a single author is beyond doubt.

As we have already observed, after the theory of source splitting had once been conceived on the basis of the criterion of the names of God, other distinguishing characteristics for the different sources were also adduced. Scholars pointed out all kinds of differences in the use of words, word forms, and expressions. They also referred to different styles of narrative and even to a diversity in religious views. To mention just one instance, the Jahwist supposedly is characterized by an especially naive, realistic manner of presentation and a captivating narrative style. At the same time there were indications of strong anthropomorphism with respect to God. The Elohist was considered to have a definite reflective and devotional element predominating. The Priestly Codex was then characterized as having an unadorned style with a predilection for the schematic. Here we would find numbers, names, and legal designations.

We will not, at this point, enter into a detailed study of all of these supposed differences. In our interpretation of the individual books such matters will repeatedly be considered in detail. Here we want to make only two remarks of a more general nature.

In the first place, we point out that the differences of language use, even if the theory of source splitting is accepted, are not at all clear. Jonathan Kraütlein, a confirmed adherent of the four-source theory, conducted a detailed study, using the customary division of sources as a basis for his research. He compared the language use in the four sources and came up with negative results. He concluded that the number of actual characteristic peculiarities of each of the sources is very limited. In the Priestly Codex he found 17; in Deuteronomy, 14, and in Jahwist and Elohist combined, 13 characteristic expressions. It is striking that in following this method it was impossible to distinguish between Jahwist and Elohist. Even so the results were so limited that the man who conducted the research himself admitted that the differences in language which he found could as well be explained by purely accidental causes. He, however, was of the opinion that they did support the customary source-splitting theory.

Our second remark refers to the supposed differences in narrative style and religious views. With regard to this we are not dealing with objective, verifiable, positive data. The evaluation of the ''character'' of the sources depends entirely on the subjective insights of those conducting this research. As long as one holds to the four-source theory, great importance is attached to these things. But as soon as the theory is abandoned, it is recognized, as was the case with Professor Eerdmans, that the sources are of a "highly problematic nature."

There have been other attempts to prove that the Pentateuch could not have been written by one author but was the product of the joining of different, originally independent parts. It has been pointed out, for instance, that it contains doublets and contradictions. The term "doublets" refers to a repetition of the same narrative. Examples of this are, then, two creation accounts (Gen. 1 and 2), two appearances of God to Abraham (Gen. 15 and 17), two abductions of Sarah (Gen. 12 and 20), two expulsions of Hagar (Gen. 16 and 21), two changes of name for Jacob (Gen. 32:28 and 35:10), two records of the call of Moses (Exod. 3 and 6), two reports about the events at Meribah (Exod. 17 and Num. 20), etc.

In this introduction we cannot treat each of these supposed doublets specifically. Naturally, we will do this in our interpretation of the related passages. We should, however, at this point explain what we actually are to understand by a doublet. All reports or records which reveal a certain similarity are not actually doublets.

When a striking diversity of detail is indicated, in addition to a general similarity, we may well be dealing with essentially different, although similar, events. Moreover, it should be noted that an author may have definite reasons for referring again to an event which has already been recorded. These reasons may lie in the overall plan of the writer or may pertain to the context in which the incident is reported. Actual doublets, then, are only those in which both the principal matter and the details involved clearly indicate that the same event was intended. At the same time there must be no reasonable basis evident for the writer to return to something already recorded.

It must be seriously questioned, moreover, whether the presence of actual doublets establishes the concept of more than one source, either in the sense that the source-splitting school speaks of these, or, for that matter, in any sense at all. Two sources or two authors is not the only viable explanation. Such actual doublets could also be explained by one author producing the major historical work of the Pentateuch and including in this work older documents he used in the process.

The contradictions which have supposedly been found in the Pentateuch are the following: According to Genesis 6:19 and 20, one pair of all animals, and according to Genesis 7:2 and 3, seven pair of the clean animals and birds, were to be taken into the ark. In Genesis 35:19 the death of Rachel is recorded, while in Genesis 37:10 she is still alive. According to Genesis 37:28 Joseph was sold to Midianite tradesmen, but in Genesis 40:15 Joseph says he was stolen from the land of the Hebrews. According to Exodus 4:20, Moses took his wife and children along to Egypt, while Exodus 18:2 implies that he left them in Midian. Numbers 2 locates the tabernacle in the midst of the camp, and Exodus 33:7 and Numbers 11:26 have it located outside the camp. According to Numbers 20:22ff., Aaron died on Mt. Hor, while Deuteronomy 10:6 says it was in Mosera. And there are more of a similar nature.

Attention is called especially, however, to different prescriptions of the laws which are difficult to harmonize with each other. For example, Exodus 20:24 seems to allow sacrifices anywhere while Deuteronomy 12:11 requires that sacrifices be restricted to one specified place; the two redactions of the Ten Commandments (Exod. 20; Deut. 5), etc.

Now it is obvious that the presence of contradictions, if indeed there be such, would have a far deeper and more serious implication than merely to establish the possibility of more than one source. For us the Bible is the Word of God and therefore cannot contain essential contradictions. If there really were contradictions in the Pentateuch this would not merely imply that there was a possible basis for the four-source theory, but it would actually call into question the divine authority of the Pentateuch.

Meanwhile, closer study reveals that the supposed contradictions are not all that serious. Several of the examples offered become obviously insignificant if they are given a second look. To give just one illustration, the reports regarding the number of animals in the ark are easily reconciled (see our commentary regarding these passages). This is true of other examples also. In the various volumes of this series all of these apparent contradictions will be given ample consideration. This does not imply that all these contradictions will be cleared up in a completely natural and simple way. In most instances we will be able to do so, but we must acknowledge that we are not yet in a position where we are able to overcome the difficulty in every instance. In those instances we will calmly await more light. We certainly are not going to allow a few problems, which we are not yet able to resolve, to shake our faith in the divine aspect of the Pentateuch. We are wholly committed to the authority of the Holy Scripture and of the Pentateuch as part of that Scripture, regardless of the difficulties that may be adduced. Naturally, we will do our best to resolve these difficulties. If, however, a few instances remain which we are unable to resolve, we will simply confess our own lack of knowledge and wait until the Lord enables us to find a solution to that difficulty.

It should be noted that the charge that there are contradictions is not limited to the Pentateuch. A serious discrepancy has allegedly been discovered between the laws given in the Pentateuch and the actual practices in the life of the Israelites as revealed in the rest of the books of the Old

Testament. The entire later history of Israel, it is charged, is absolutely irreconcilable with the presentation given in the Pentateuch, that Moses was entrusted with a developed structure for the exercise of worship. It is alleged that there is not a trace of the tabernacle and its ceremonies to be found in the period of the Judges and the Kings. Even godfearing leaders of the people, kings and prophets, supposedly did all kinds of things which in no way were concerned with the structure prescribed in the Pentateuch. Not until the days of King Josiah was a beginning made to carry out many of the requirements specified in the giving of the Law.

This argument appears more formidable than it actually is. In the first place, the silence about these matters, which supposedly characterizes the later books, is, as we will see later, not as total as is claimed. But even if it were true, we cannot deduce from this silence that the Pentateuchal giving of the Law did not exist. Even if a certain matter or institution is not specifically mentioned, this is no proof for its nonexistence. The argument from silence (the so-called *argumentum silentio*) has merit only if in a given instance it can be proved that certain things, if they existed, *must* have been mentioned. Whether anyone has succeeded in pointing out passages in the Old Testament where some reference out of the Pentateuch must be mentioned, but is not included, is open to reasonable doubt. Likewise, we cannot conclude from the violation of certain Pentateuchal laws and prescriptions that these did not exist. There have always been and still are many laws that are not observed. Some are even constantly transgressed without penalty. We could mention the practice of cremation, for instance, which was forbidden by law in certain countries, but for many years has been practiced without interference. Even when godfearing leaders of their people transgress a given law, this is no evidence for the nonexistence of that precept. There could be all kinds of circumstances which conditioned such behavior. It certainly must be remembered that Israel entered a period of general spiritual decline and degeneration as soon as it entered the land of Canaan. In such a time it is more than likely that even the noblest and best of the people would do things that did not comply with the strict demands of the Law. Moreover, unusual circumstances require the use of unusual measures. And such a practice might be considered proper which in normal times would be unauthorized.

Having said all this, it is of utmost importance to declare it simply is not true that the alleged gap between the testimony of the later historical books and the contents of the Pentateuch is as enormous as it is claimed to be. It is possible to compile an extensive list of passages from the entire Old Testament which indicates an obvious acquaintance with the laws given in the Pentateuch. In fact, these passages actually prove that these laws did exist.

This list of references, going back to the time of Joshua, immediately after Moses, establishes that the Law already had a significant place in the national life of Israel. This introduction would become much too extensive if we were to include all these references. Moreover, delving into these passages would uncover all kinds of new problems which we should then also discuss. Thus, for instance, there are many references to the laws given in the Pentateuch in the Books of Chronicles. But negative biblical criticism has, at best, a low regard for the historical trustworthiness of the writer of the Chronicles. It is charged that he simply transferred situations from his own time (long after the Captivity) to the earlier history. As a consequence, if we were to offer texts from Chronicles to prove our point, we would immediately be faced with the added problem of the historical trustworthiness of the writer of Chronicles. (Anyone who is interested in that particular issue should consult this author's article on Chronicles in the *Christelijke Encyclopaedie*.) If we were to cite passages from Daniel or from part of Isaiah (chs. 40–66) we would face a similar difficulty. (These problems will be discussed in the respective volumes in this commentary series.) Consequently we will limit ourselves to a few references to illustrate our position in this matter.

The prophet Ezekiel offers numerous evidences of his acquaintance with the laws of the Pentateuch. This is actually not too surprising since we know that he was a priest. In Ezekiel 4:14 he testifies that he had never eaten "carrion" or "what was born of beasts" nor "foul flesh." These terms clearly refer, respectively, to Deuteronomy 14:21; Exodus 22:31; and Leviticus 7:18 and 19:7. In Ezekiel 18:6–8, a number of sins are listed. Among them are several that are direct violations of specific laws given in the Pentateuch. To "have intercourse with your neighbor's wife" was forbidden in Leviticus 18:20 and 20:10. To "approach a woman . . . during the uncleanness of her monthly period" is a reference to Leviticus 18:19. To "take advantage of" refers back to Leviticus 25:17. Withholding "a debtor's pledge" is found in Exodus 22:26 and Deuteronomy 24:13. To "commit robbery" was forbidden in Leviticus 6:4. To "lend at interest" and "take any increase" are mentioned in Exodus 22:25; Leviticus 25:36–37; Deuteronomy 23:19. At the close of Ezekiel 18:13 we read, "his blood will be on his own head." This is mentioned repeatedly in Leviticus 29:9ff. The statement in Ezekiel 18:20, "The soul who sins is the one who will die. The son will not share the guilt of the father, nor will the father share the guilt of the son," refers back to Deuteronomy 24:16. In Ezekiel 20:26 we find a typical departure from the Pentateuchal law structure. "The first offspring of every womb" was the term used only in the Law for "firstborn" (Exod. 13:2, 12, 15; 34:19; Num. 3:12; 18:15). Again in Ezekiel 22:7, 10–12, a number of sins are mentioned which are violations of specific laws. Also, Ezekiel 40–48 constitutes Ezekiel's vision of restoration in which a new temple and a new law are extensively described. In this message there are numerous references which obviously relate to the Pentateuch so that details need not be indicated.

Ezekiel's older contemporary, Jeremiah, also clearly reveals acquaintance with the Pentateuchal laws. In Jeremiah 2:3 Israel is compared with the first fruits which were exclusively dedicated to the Lord. This is an obvious reference to Leviticus 22:10–16. In Jeremiah 3:1, the example of the divorced and remarried woman who could not return to her first husband clearly reminds us of Deuteronomy 24:1–4. Jeremiah 7:6 records a list of sins taken from Exodus 22:20–22. The reference to "redemption" in Jeremiah 37:7–8 points to Leviticus 25:25. Jeremiah 32:18 is a quotation of the promise and penalty of the second commandment in Exodus 20:5–6. Jeremiah 34:14 appeals to the provision for freeing Hebrew slaves in the seventh year according to Exodus 21:2 and Deuteronomy 15:12.

In sections of the Book of Isaiah which are accepted as genuine also by negative criticism, we find the following data: Isaiah 1:11–14 contains a summary of several aspects of the ceremonial worship as this was prescribed in the Pentateuch. Mention is made of "sacrifices" as distinguished from "burnt offerings," which suggests acquaintance with this distinction as made in Leviticus 1 and 6:9ff. Elements of the sacrifice acceptable to God are listed as "fat" and "blood" as in Leviticus 3:14–17; 7:23–27; 17:10–12; etc. Animals for the sacrifices are listed as "rams," "bulls," "lambs," and "he-goats," in keeping with consistent usage in the Pentateuch. The one bringing the offering appeared before the Lord "at the entrance to the Tent of Meeting," which reminds us of such references as Leviticus 1:3; 4:4, etc.; and especially 17:1–6. There are also references to "the new moon," "sabbath," and "feasts," taken from Numbers 28. In Isaiah 1:17, 23 we have a reference to Exodus 22:22 regarding the orphans and widows. Even more, the combination of accepting a "bribe" and neglecting the "fatherless and the widow" is a direct reference to Deuteronomy 10:17–18. Isaiah 19:21 again refers to two kinds of offerings (cf. Lev. 2) and joins this with "the vows," which clearly refers to Deuteronomy 23:21–23.

Isaiah's older contemporary, Micah, also speaks about the ceremonial worship in Micah 6:6–7. He mentions burnt offerings, the sacrificial animals—calves and rams. He also speaks of "oil," which according to Leviticus 2:14–15 and Numbers 28:5, was an essential element in the "grain offering."

Turning to an even earlier prophet, Hosea, we find in 2:11 mention made of "New Moons," "Sabbath," and "appointed feasts." Hosea, in 5:10, uses the term "move boundary stones" taken from Deuteronomy 19:14. In 8:11 mention is made of a multiplication of altars which was a violation of the command in Deuteronomy 12:13. In Hosea 9:4, "wine offerings" and the idea of being defiled by "bread of mourners" originated with being defiled by a dead body (Num. 19:14–22). In Hosea 12:14, "the guilt of his bloodshed" refers to the repeated legal formula of Leviticus 20:9ff.

In the somewhat older Book of Amos we read in 2:7 "profane my holy name," which sounds like Leviticus 20:3. In Amos 2:8 there is a reference to lying "down beside every altar on garments taken in pledge." This refers to a commandment in Exodus 22:26–27, and Deuteronomy 24:12–13. According to Amos 2:12 the Nazirites' requirement of drinking no wine relates to Numbers 6:3–4. In Amos 5:21–22 we again meet various details about the laws of offerings, "feasts," and even the solemn "assemblies." The latter reference is to Leviticus 23:36; Numbers 29:35; and Deuteronomy 16:8. The three kinds of offerings—"burnt offerings," "grain offerings," and "fellowship offerings"—are, of course, based directly on the Pentateuch. In Amos 8:5 there is again reference to "New Moon" and "Sabbath." In the same verse "skimping the measure" by the use of "dishonest scales," is a clear reference to Leviticus 19:36 and Deuteronomy 25:13–15.

In the Books of Kings we read about "burnt offerings" and "fellowship offerings" brought by Solomon (1 Kings 3:15). The entire layout of Solomon's temple reveals the closest possible association with the tabernacle and its furnishings, described in the Pentateuch. We can point specifically to holy objects described in 1 Kings 7:48ff. When the temple was dedicated (1 Kings 8:64) we again find "burnt offerings," "grain offerings," and "fellowship offerings." Also, special mention is made of "fat," which was of special import. First Kings 11:2 contains a reference to Exodus 34:16 and Deuteronomy 7:3–4. In the narrative about Elijah on Mt. Carmel (1 Kings 18:29), we find the "evening sacrifice." First Kings 21:13 presupposes the regulations of Leviticus 24:11ff. Second Kings 3:20 mentions the "morning sacrifice," and 2 Kings 4:23 again points to "New Moon" and "Sabbath." The lepers at the "entrance of the city gate," in 2 Kings 7:3, is an application of Leviticus 13:46. Second Kings 12:4 refers to various requirements regarding money for the temple service and clearly points back to Exodus 30:12–16 and Leviticus 27:1–8. Second Kings 12:16 distinguishes between "guilt offerings" and "sin offerings," and these meet the requirements of Leviticus 5:16 and Numbers 5:8. The isolation of the leprous King Uzziah in 2 Kings 15:5 was based on Leviticus 13:46.

15

Second Kings 16:13-15 again gives details from the Law for "burnt offerings," "grain offerings," "drink offerings," and "blood sacrifices." Special mention is made of "blood" as an element of the sacrifices. Also there is another reference to "morning offering" and "evening offering." The "bronze altar" is a clear reference to Exodus 27:1-8. In 2 Kings 17:35-39 there is a clear reminder of the giving of the laws in the Pentateuch. It is striking that in 2 Kings 12:10; 22:4, 8; and 23:4, mention is made of the "high priest," based on Leviticus 21:10 and Numbers 35:25, 28. This name does not appear in Deuteronomy. According to the critical view of the Pentateuch both the name and the position supposedly are dated after the Captivity. The earlier appearance of the term "high" (in Heb. "great") is then explained as an insertion by a later glossator. It is, of course, not explained why this supposed glossator did not consistently use the same term.

We will not discuss the relationship between Josiah's reformation and the laws of the Pentateuch at this time. We therefore move on to a consideration of the Books of Samuel. There we find Elkanah making regular visits to the house of the Lord (1 Sam. 1:3, 21). This was in keeping with the law of Exodus 34:23. When the sins of Eli's sons are exposed, we again meet various details of the Law: 1 Samuel 2:28—"altar," "incense," and "ephod"; 1 Samuel 2:29—"offering" and "sacrifice." In 1 Samuel 3:3 we have a reference to "the lamp of God" which goes back to Exodus 27:20-21, and Leviticus 24:2-3. The "ark" is discussed at length in chapters 4-7. To be sure, in the negative, critical circles, this ark is considered to be completely different from the one described in the Pentateuch. First Samuel 4:4 (see also 2 Sam. 6:2) speaks of the "cherubim," while what happened to the men of Beth Shemesh (1 Sam. 6:19) points back to Numbers 4:15, 20. Writing "the regulations of the kingship" in a book and "depositing it before the Lord" (1 Sam. 10:25) reminds us of Moses doing the same thing with the Law. First Samuel 15, the defeat of Amalek, goes back to Deuteronomy 25:19. First Samuel 15:22 again refers to "burnt offerings," "sacrifices," and the "fat" of the sacrificial animals. First Samuel 26:19 speaks about an offering, and of special interest is the mention of a pleasing "aroma." This refers back to Leviticus 2:2, 9, 12, where there is mention of the "aroma" of the cereal offering. In 1 Samuel 23:9 and 20:7 the priestly "ephod" is mentioned, used specifically for inquiring of the Lord, in keeping with Numbers 27:21. In 1 Samuel 28:3 we note that Saul had the mediums and wizards put to death. This points back to Leviticus 19:31; 20:6; Deuteronomy 18:11.

Moving on to 2 Samuel, we have the account of the death of Uzzah in 6:6-7. This is in accord with Numbers 4:15. Second Samuel 6:17-18 again refers to "burnt offerings" and "fellowship offerings." The reference to God dwelling in a "tent" or "tabernacle" in 2 Samuel 7:6 fits with the sanctuary, which is described in the Pentateuch. Significant here is the use of both words side by side. The first word refers to the wooden frame and the other to the tent cloth that covered it. David's action in 2 Samuel 8:4 was based on Deuteronomy 17:16. Bathsheba's rite of being "purified . . . from her uncleanness" (2 Sam. 11:4) was based on Leviticus 15:19ff. David's response to Nathan's parable that the ewe lamb should be paid for "four times over" (2 Sam. 12:6) agrees with Exodus 22:1. The distinction between Zadok the priest and the Levites in 2 Samuel 15:24 is in full accord with the Law. That the Levites carried the ark was based on Numbers 4:15. In 2 Samuel 24:25 there is another reference to "burnt offerings" and "fellowship offerings."

Finally, we want to mention a few facts about the Book of Judges. We will not discuss the Book of Joshua because the critical views group this with the Pentateuch and thus do not consider it as an independent historical source alongside the Pentateuch. In Judges 1:17 there is mention of "totally destroying" the Canaanites. This is in accord with Deuteronomy 7:2. In Judges 2:1–5 the message of the Angel of the Lord in Bochim includes various reminders of laws given in the Pentateuch. Verse 2a points to Exodus 34:12–13; Deuteronomy 7:2, 5; and 12:3. Verse 2b points to Exodus 23:21. Verse 3 points to Exodus 23:33; 34:12; Numbers 33:55; and Deuteronomy 7:16. "Prostituting themselves to other gods," Judges 2:17, brings to mind Exodus 34:15, 16. The marriages with the Canaanites must be seen in the light of the prohibition of Exodus 34:16 and Deuteronomy 7:3–4. Judges 6:8 is almost a literal citation of the introduction to the decalogue in Exodus 20:2. Judges 6:10 includes a response to the main emphasis of the Law. Judges 13:4, 14 gives us the requirement of the angel to Samson's mother not to eat anything unclean. This suggests that the distinction between clean and unclean foods was well-known, in keeping with Leviticus 11 and Deuteronomy 14. Samson's Nazarite vow conformed to Numbers 6:2–5. The Levite, who received no inheritance of land, is mentioned in Judges 17:7ff., and 19:1, in complete accord with Numbers 18:24 and Deuteronomy 10:9. Moreover, in Judges 20:1 and 21:10, 13, 16, the gathering of the Israelites is called the "assembly," a term that is repeatedly used in the Pentateuch, especially in that section which the source splitters ascribe to "P." Likewise, Judges 20:6 uses the expression "they committed this lewd and disgraceful act in Israel," taken from Deuteronomy 22:21. Judges 20:13, "purge the evil from Israel," is also found in Deuteronomy 17:12. And, once again, Judges 20:26 and 21:4 mention "burnt offerings" and "fellowship offerings," an application of Deuteronomy 25:6.

This overview is only an abbreviated anthology of all the available material. However, it clearly indicates that the claim that in the later books of the Old Testament no trace of the Pentateuchal giving of the Law can be found, is completely unsubstantiated. On the contrary, throughout all the books of the Old Testament there is scattered a mass of data which definitely proves that this giving of the Law did exist and that it was well known to the people of Israel.

To this we must add that in spite of all of this textual evidence, the splitting of sources digs its own grave by pursuing the splitting further and further with more and more sources being alleged. Since Karl Budde wrote his *Die Biblische Urgeschichte* in 1883, it has become general practice to divide the Jahwist into two sources. These are then called J^1 and J^2. Eissfeldt has identified this as a fifth source to which he gave the name "L" (Laienquelle). Furthermore, Kuenen was of the opinion that the Priestly Codex consisted of three separate sections which should be distinguished. These are then identified as P^1, P^2, and P^3. Likewise, the Elohist is considered to be without true unity. Moreover, Deuteronomy was divided in two different ways. One was an attempt to divide the main body of the book (chs. 5–26) into two sections. This then became D^1 (chs. 12–26) and D^2 (chs. 5–11). The other was an attempt to divide the book lengthwise. This resulted in trying to distinguish two sources mixed through this entire complex (chs. 5–26). The one source was known as "singularistic" since the people of Israel are referred to in the singular, and the other is "pluralistic" because it uses the plural for Israel. And these are only the most common divisions. Others go to far greater extremes.

When we study the literature which relates to the Pentateuch, it becomes apparent that the theory of splitting sources leads to an almost unending exercise in making new distinctions and recognizing portions. It has been correctly pointed out that the extremes to which the application of this approach has led have finally caused the entire method of splitting sources to appear absurd. Every sober, scholarly researcher must ask himself the question whether we are actually dealing with valuable reality or nothing more than a display of sharp ingenuity. It would be easy to give examples of those who have driven this theory to such extremes that they have lost touch with simple and obvious realities. The intent of this introduction does not, however, permit extending this list any further.

(Translator's Note: Aalders refers to several other scholars who were his contemporaries in the '20s and '30s. These are, however, of little interest to our present studies and have been deleted.)

We do want to point out that among those who question the genuineness of the Pentateuch, two general trends can be distinguished. The first of these takes an evolutionistic approach and the latter the approach of the history of religion.

According to the evolutionistic approach, any religion of long standing must have developed from step to step toward higher forms and beliefs. Those who hold to this theory, then, cannot accept what the Holy Scripture teaches, namely, that from the beginning of human history there was a true and pure knowledge of God, and that the early patriarchs stood at a very high level of religious faith and worship. They also deny that Israel could have started with such a highly developed system of laws and ritual. This view, however, has been increasingly forced to yield the field to the second approach, that of history of religion.

The history of religion school was strongly influenced by the unlocking of the ancient cultural world as a result of the excavation of old ruins, especially in Mesopotamia. The discoveries that were made opened the eyes of many scholars to the fact that the people of Israel in the time of Moses could not possibly have been as primitive as the evolutionistic view had assumed. A careful study of the religious phenomena of all great cultural nations in their earliest periods reveals that there is movement in the reverse direction from that which the evolutionists would have us believe. When we go back as far as possible into the history of Babylon, Egypt, India, and China (increasingly there is more data available in this regard), we do not discover the rise of polytheism, nor even animism and fetishism. On the contrary, we find an approach to monotheism. For this reason scholars have increasingly been inclined in the direction of the history of religion approach. This leads to the conclusion that there is a principal difference between the religious ideas of Israel and those of other nations of the same time period. There has then also been a conscious effort to establish a relationship between these ideas.

It must be admitted that the facts indicate that the narratives of Genesis rank far above those of Babylon, for example. Likewise, the Mosaic laws, from a humanitarian point of view, far surpass the laws of the Hittites, Babylonians, and Assyrians. These scholars insist, however, that this is a difference in degree and not in essence. Therefore, they never tire of explaining the laws of Israel by ascribing them to foreign sources.

We must take a position opposing this religious-history school because it totally denies the reality of special revelation. Some scholars challenge this assertion by claiming that they also believe in ''revelation.'' But what they understand by the term is radically different from the traditional view. They accept as fact that the various authors who contributed to the Pentateuch availed themselves of materials taken from pagan sagas and myths and that laws which had previously been enacted by other nations were

19

taken over by Israel. These materials were then reworked and brought to a higher level. All of this, it was claimed, was done under a special leading of God who "revealed" the element of truth in the borrowed materials. Certainly, when this is called "revelation," the term is used with a completely different meaning than has historically been the intent of the word. It also is understood in a radically different sense than the biblical teaching on revelation.

For detailed studies comparing the narratives and laws of the Pentateuch with those of other nations, we must refer to the explanations given in the various books in this series.

Old Testament scholarship is by no means unanimous in giving a late date to the Pentateuch material. There have been many strong voices, even among those who do not accept the Mosaic authorship of the Pentateuch, confirming the early date which remains firmly established for us on the basis of the testimony of Holy Scripture.

III. *The Solution to the Problem on the Basis of Scriptural Data*

We have observed that the Pentateuch is an anonymous document. Nowhere does it indicate who must be considered to be the author of this major work of history, that is, in its entirety, as it lies before us.

We do have a few indications with respect to specific sections. We are specifically told that various portions were recorded by Moses.

The first instance of this is in Exodus 17:14. Here we read that God commanded Moses to prepare a written record of the battle with the Amalekites. Two questions have been raised in this connection: (1) Does the command of God apply to the entire event, or only to the announcement that God would "completely erase the memory of the Amalekites from under heaven"? (2) Does the book mentioned here refer to an already existing book or was this to be a newly constituted book?

We need not discuss these questions at length. We can say that, concerning 1, the command of God included recording the entire event as well as the actual announcement. Regarding 2, we plan to return to this when we discuss Numbers 33:2.

Another passage that calls for our attention is Exodus 24:4–8. Here mention is made of Moses writing down "everything the LORD had said." This written record was then called "The book of the Covenant." If we inquire what is meant by "everything the LORD had said," then it is obvious that we must go back to Exodus 21:1, and thus take the section 21:1–23:33. This has been commonly referred to as "The book of the Covenant." It is possible to add the close of chapter 20 and possibly even the law of the Ten Commandments, but that is not a matter of concern at this point.

When we turn to Exodus 34:27, we read, "Write down these words," obviously referring to what immediately preceded (vv. 11–26).

Of special note is the reference in Numbers 33:2, where we read that "Moses recorded the stages in their journey." Here there is mention of a travel journal which Moses prepared. It is possible to think of this travel journal as a brief list of the places through which Israel marched from point to point. But it is more likely that Moses included the more significant happenings at each location in his record. This is all the more plausible in view of Moses' early training at the Egyptian court. He must have been well acquainted with the Egyptian annals in which day-to-day events of significance were recorded. That travel journal could have been the "book" referred to in Exodus 17:14.

We should also mention Deuteronomy 31:9–24, in which mention is made of the "law" written by Moses. There can be no doubt that this "law" refers to the Deuteronomic law, that is, the entire exhorting and legislating address which Moses delivered in the plains of Moab. It certainly included the core of Deuteronomy, chapters 5–26, and also the preceding introduction in 1:6–4:40.

Finally we have Deuteronomy 31:22, in which mention is made of a "song" Moses wrote. That song is found in Deuteronomy 32.

Thus we have data which establishes the fact that Moses actually wrote history, laws, and songs. One of the proponents of source splitting has concluded that these passages of the Pentateuch are the only ones that are of Mosaic authorship. This is, of course, an unwarranted conclusion. It would likewise be unwarranted to conclude, on this basis, that the rest of the Pentateuch must then also be written by Moses. The only proper conclusions we can make on the basis of this data are these. First, that Moses kept a travel journal in which he recorded, among other things, the battle and God's pronouncement against the Amalekites, and a complete record of all the stopping places during Israel's wilderness journey. Second, that Moses prepared two "books" of laws, the so-called book of the Covenant and the main part of our present Book of Deuteronomy. The portion in Exodus 34:11–26 was also included. And finally, Moses put the hymn of Deuteronomy 32 in writing.

Thus far we have mentioned only the data in the Pentateuch itself. When we consult the rest of the books of the Old Testament, we find that Joshua refers to the "book of the Law" written by Moses in three passages: 1:7–8; 8:31–32; 23:6–7. These passages shed little light on the nature and content of Moses' Book of the Law. The only thing we can say with certainty is that Joshua 8:31 refers back to the command recorded in Deuteronomy 27:5–7, and that in Joshua 23:7 we find the expression, "do not invoke the names of their gods,'' which is taken from Exodus 23:13. This implies that in any case these two passages appeared in the Book of the Law.

But there are strong generic reasons for going beyond this. Since the Pentateuch itself informs us about Moses' activity as an author of a book of law, it would appear to be evident that the Book of the Law to which Joshua refers included, at the least, those passages which are specifically ascribed to Moses in the Pentateuch. It is certainly more than likely, however, that the entire complex of Mosaic laws which existed in Joshua's day was included. The reference to Deuteronomy 27:5–7, which was not part of Moses' address in the plains of Moab, offers strong support for this assumption. It would be extremely unlikely that the expression, ''the Book of the Law of Moses,'' would be used in Joshua 8:31 and 23:6 if there were available several collections of laws ascribed to Moses. The objection has been raised that, since the Mosaic law was written on tables of stone, it therefore must have been of very limited compass. To this we respond that the famous Code of Hammurabi, which comes from the same period, included 282 paragraphs. This indicates that the argument which tries to limit Moses' writing potential is rather ridiculous.

In the Books of Kings we meet two more passages which refer to the written law of Moses. In 1 Kings 2:3 mention is made of ''the Law of Moses,'' although it does not specifically say that it was written. In the second instance, however, we read in 2 Kings 14:6, ''the Book of the Law of Moses.'' Here a citation from this Book of the Law is given, namely, Deuteronomy 24:16. This confirms, then, that the Book of the Law included, among other things, the core of Deuteronomy. Moreover, we may repeat what we pointed out in considering the passages from Joshua, that ''the Book of the Law of Moses'' most likely included the entire complex of the Mosaic laws.

In the Book of Daniel we find one reference to the written Mosaic Law. In Daniel 9:11 and 13 the great statesman-prophet, Daniel, in his prayer, recalls the curse which fell upon Israel because of their sins ''as it is written in the Law of Moses.'' Here, as in 1 Kings 2:3, the Law of Moses is mentioned but there is no specific reference to the *Book* of the Law. It is obvious that Daniel thought especially of Leviticus 26:14ff. and Deuteronomy 28:15ff. This confirms, as we have already pointed out, that the written law included more than those portions which the Pentateuch specifically ascribes to Moses. Deuteronomy 28 falls outside the core of Deuteronomy, and Leviticus 26 is part of a significant section of the Mosaic laws regarding which the Pentateuch makes no mention of being *written*.

In the Books of Chronicles, Ezra, and Nehemiah, we finally find several references to the written Mosaic Law. There we find the less specific term "Law of Moses" in 2 Chronicles 23:18 and Ezra 3:2 and 7:6. We also have the term "the Book of the Law of Moses" in Nehemiah 8:1. In addition, we find the term, "Book of Moses" in 2 Chronicles 35:12; Ezra 6:18; and Nehemiah 13:1. Also, the "Book of the Law" in Nehemiah 8:3, "the Law" in Nehemiah 8:14, and "the book" in Nehemiah 8:5. There are two places where the terms "the Law" or "the Book" are further described as "the Book of Moses" by an appositive, 2 Chronicles 25:4 (a parallel to 2 Kings 14:6), or as "the Book of the Law of God," Nehemiah 8:8.

As far as the content and compass of this Book of the Law is concerned, some of these passages give us further data. Second Chronicles 23:18 refers to one portion of it as the directions for the burnt offering. In 2 Chronicles 35:12 reference is made to setting aside burnt offerings "as it is written in the Book of Moses." This is found in Leviticus 3. In Ezra 3:2 mention is made of the rebuilding of the "altar" for the "burnt offerings." Thus the Law that is intended here must have included either Deuteronomy 12:5–6 or Leviticus 1:3ff., or both. In Ezra 6:18 we read about the distinctions between priests and Levites. This points directly to Numbers 3. Nehemiah 8:14 points out the fact that during the Feast of Tabernacles the people were required to live in booths. This refers directly to Leviticus 23:34–43. Nehemiah 13:1–2 contains what is in essence a repetition of Deuteronomy 23:3–5.

All of these passages confirm our view that the terms "Book of the Law" and "Law of Moses" definitely refer to the entire complex of the Mosaic laws. Moreover, this is almost said in precise words in Ezra 7:6 where Ezra, the priest and scribe, is described as "well versed in the Law of Moses." This can be understood only as referring to the entire Law.

There is still one passage that requires our attention and that is 2 Chronicles 34:14. There the book that was found by Hilkiah the priest was called "the Book of the Law of the Lord that had been *given* through Moses." This would imply that the book as it was found by Hilkiah had come directly from the hand of Moses and was not gathered by someone else after his death. This is almost certainly what the passage means. The specific designation "through Moses" could apply only to "the Law of the Lord." The actual meaning would then be, "the book which contains the Law of the Lord, which was given by Moses." This would be most in keeping with the Hebrew language usage.

The conclusion to which we come on the basis of these references in the remainder of the Old Testament is this. In the various periods of Israel's history from the days of Joshua until far after the Exile, there are frequent references to a written Mosaic Law, more specifically designated as "the

Book of the Law of Moses.'' We may rightly consider that this Book of Law incorporated the entire collection of laws in the Pentateuch. It is evident, however, that this ''Book of the law of Moses,'' without anything else, cannot be identified with the Pentateuch as such. The Pentateuch includes much more than a collection of laws. From the passages mentioned above, it appears that the book referred to included only the collection of Mosaic laws.

It must also be taken into account that, unquestionably, various copies of this collection of laws were existent. Likewise, it should be noted that the legislative sections incorporated in the great historical work, the Pentateuch, were by no means the only available copy of the laws of Moses. Joshua 8:32 refers to a copy of the Law which was inscribed on tables of stone on Mt. Ebal. Second, according to Deuteronomy 17:18, the future king was required to ''write for himself on a scroll a copy of this law.'' The term ''this law'' used here must have referred to that which Moses at that moment was declaring, that is, the core of Deuteronomy. Even so, it can be assumed that the God-fearing kings who later acted on this mandate would have included the entire collection of Mosaic laws. Finally, it must be noted that the priests, who daily dealt with the law (Jer. 2:8, et al.), must have had at least one copy and probably more.

It must have been such a copy that had been relegated to a rubbish corner during a time of deterioration. Then it was found by the priest Hilkiah when the temple was being cleaned and repaired during the reign of Josiah (2 Kings 22:3-8).

Thus, although it is obvious that the ''Book of the Law'' and the ''Law'' cannot, as such, be identified with the Pentateuch as we have it today, it is possible that, especially in the later times, these terms were used to designate the entire Pentateuch. This would be in harmony with using the term ''Pentateuch'' as part for the whole, to refer to the entire Old Testament, as was sometimes done. This, of course would not establish the Mosaic authorship of the entire Pentateuch any more than referring to the entire Old Testament as ''the Law'' says anything about the source of the rest of the books of the Old Testament. Although we do not have the data to prove that the terms ''Law'' and ''Book of the Law'' refer to the entire Pentateuch, we must certainly maintain that as a reasonable possibility.

However, there is one place in the Old Testament where the entire Pentateuch probably is mentioned but this passage says nothing about origin or date. The passage is Psalm 40:7: ''It is written about me in the scroll,'' or according to a better translation, ''In the roll of the book it is prescribed concerning me.'' If we inquire what kind of book this could have been, it is obvious that it was a document which included definite prescriptions and thus was of a legal character. But that this book contained more than the Pentateuchal laws is evident from the context in Psalm 40. In verse 6 mention is made of the prescriptions for the sacrifices and in verse 5 the psalmist sings the praises of God's "wondrous deeds and thoughts." Here we would be apt to think of such wondrous deeds as Creation and the Flood. God's "thoughts" would include His plan of salvation as it developed through the ages and was revealed in His covenant with the patriarchs and His deliverance of Israel. Although we cannot speak with absolute certainty, there is a strong probability that we have a reference here to the entire Pentateuch.

We now move to the data given in the New Testament.

The New Testament in several places refers to "Moses and the Prophets" (Luke 16:31; 24:27; Acts 26:22). This is an obvious reference to the entire Old Testament, with "Moses" referring to the entire Pentateuch. That is also the case with terms like "Law of Moses" (Luke 24:44; Acts 28:23; 1 Cor. 9:9); "book of Moses" (Mark 12:26); or merely "Moses" (Acts 15:21). In this respect the New Testament conforms to the usual way of speaking among the Jews. It simply calls the Pentateuch by the term commonly used at that time.

May we then conclude on this basis that Jesus and the apostles expressed themselves in favor of the Mosaic authorship of the entire Pentateuch? Definitely not. The use of a common manner of speaking without any careful scholarship being involved says nothing about the personal judgment of those using these forms of speech. All we can conclude is that Jesus and His disciples saw no reason for objecting to or departing from the designation commonly used by the Jews in their day. What we have learned from the Old Testament data that we have considered, and what will become clear from our consideration of New Testament data as well, is that the Pentateuch, in any case, included some significant Mosaic material. Moses included in a book the history of the people of Israel of his day and the entire giving of the Law. These combine to form at least four-fifths of the entire Pentateuch. In view of this, it is not at all surprising that Jesus and His disciples took over the common way of referring to the Pentateuch. In the same way, we need not be surprised when Jesus quotes from the Psalms and refers to it as found in "the Law," and Paul uses a quotation from the prophet Isaiah as being "written in the Law."

At this point a discussion of 2 Corinthians 3:15 is in order. The expression, "when Moses is read," which appears there, at first glance suggests the Mosaic authorship of the Pentateuch. The preceding verse, however, in a parallel situation, speaks of "when the Old Covenant is read." Since we certainly cannot ascribe the entire Old Testament to the pen of Moses, we undoubtedly have here another example of a reference to the entire Old Testament by a figurative use of the name "Moses." We find similar usage in John 10:34 and 1 Corinthians 14:21. None of these passages offers any substantial data on Mosaic authorship.

There are also a number of passages in the New Testament where explicit appeal is made to the authority of Moses. We find a more general appeal of this nature in John 1:45; 5:45; and Hebrews 7:14. More specific quotations from the Pentateuch are found in Matthew 22:24; Mark 7:10; 12:19; Luke 20:28; Acts 3:22; and Romans 10:5, 19. The fact that in some of these passages the speakers are Jews does not detract from their significance. Since they appealed to Moses in opposition to Jesus, Christ certainly would have challenged their quotations if He had questioned their authenticity. In Mark 12:19; Luke 20:28; John 1:45; 5:45; and Romans 10:5, Moses is designated as the spokesman or writer of statements considered to be from the Pentateuch. All of these statements, however, are limited to those portions of the Pentateuch that record the history of Israel contemporary with Moses, and the giving of the Law. Thus, although these passages confirm the Mosaic authorship of those two major sections of the Pentateuch, they do not establish his authorship of the *entire* Pentateuch.

Even general references from the Pentateuch which include predictions of the coming of Christ, such as John 1:45 and 5:45, do not establish Mosaic authorship of the entire Pentateuch because those portions definitely ascribed to Moses include ample reference to the coming Messiah.

One question which probably could be debated is whether the Greek word *grammata,* used in John 5:47, should be translated "books." If this proves to be the correct translation, these books must have included the entire Pentateuch since we know of nothing else that Moses wrote. This would then characterize the Pentateuch as a writing of Moses. But the use of the Greek word *grammata,* standing by itself, does not warrant this conclusion. When the word is used to designate books of the Bible, as in 2 Timothy 3:15, it is always accompanied by the word "holy." Our conclusion, then, is that the word *grammata* in John 5:47 simply refers to the "writings" of Moses. What we have then is the spoken words of Christ compared with the writings of Moses.

Thus the data found in the New Testament leads to the same conclusion as that found in the Old Testament. The Pentateuch includes a significant legacy of Mosaic writings, specifically in the record of the history of Moses' time, and the giving of the laws. Beyond this we find no direct evidence that would ascribe the rest of the Pentateuch to Moses' pen. At the same time it must be acknowledged that this does not prove that the entire Pentateuch is *not* of Mosaic authorship. Even though the direct data given in the Old and New Testaments establishes Moses as the author of only certain portions of the Pentateuch, it would still be altogether reasonable and possible, in the light of the received data, to accept the Mosaic authorship of the entire Pentateuch.

It must be admitted that we find in the Pentateuch itself a number of indirect references which militate against the Mosaic authorship of the entire work as we find it in our Bibles. Among these we can immediately refer to that part of Deuteronomy 34 in which the death and burial of Moses are recorded. Some of the Jews ascribed the last eight verses not to Moses, but to Joshua. We do not want to exclude the possibility of a prophetic prediction of such events, but we do not consider that likely in this case. The Pentateuch is not a prophetic book but rather a historical work. The historical books of the Bible generally are characterized by describing events of the past. Unless there are compelling reasons for insisting on the Mosaic authorship of the Pentateuch from the first word to the last, which there are not, we will simply accept the fact that these verses also were written after the events took place by someone who lived after Moses' death.

There are also other passages that demand consideration in this connection. In Genesis 14:14 mention is made of a place called "Dan." This place could be so designated only after Israel had occupied Canaan. In Genesis 36:31 we read about kings of the Edomites who reigned "before any Israelite king reigned." This would imply that it was written after Israel actually had kings. In Exodus 16:35 we are told that the Israelites ate manna "until they reached the border of Canaan." This suggests that it was written after Canaan had been occupied. In Numbers 21:14–15 a quotation is given from the "Book of the Wars of the LORD." This is an unknown book and would be difficult to consider as a record of wars other than the conquest of Canaan. In Numbers 32:34ff. there is a reference to the building of cities in the land east of the Jordan. These cities could not have been built until the tribes that settled there had fulfilled their promise to help in the conquest of the rest of Canaan west of the Jordan. We read in Deuteronomy 2:12 that the Edomites drove out the former dwellers of Seir, and then there is added, "as Israel did in the land the LORD gave them as their possession." This implies that Canaan had already been occupied by Israel. In several passages the term "near the Jordan" (NIV) is used to designate the land east of the Jordan (Gen. 50:10–11; Numbers 22:1; etc.). This could not have been Moses' designation because he was not permitted to cross to the west of the Jordan. It must have come from the pen of someone who lived west of the Jordan after Canaan was occupied.

27

In addition to these passages, which appear to have been written after the time of Moses, there are also statements that can be ascribed to Moses only with great difficulty. We think of Exodus 11:3 where we read, "Moses himself was highly regarded in Egypt by Pharaoh's officials and by the people." Numbers 12:3 tells us, "Now Moses was a very humble man, more humble than anyone else on the face of the earth." It is difficult to conceive of Moses speaking about himself in this manner, especially the latter statement, which would have made him guilty of an alarming conceit.

An attempt has been made to explain all of these statements which cannot be harmonized with Mosaic authorship by proposing that they are insertions and interpolations by a later author. This was the same theory that some of the Jews adopted regarding Deuteronomy 34:5–12. We would not deny that something like this is possible. But we must also recognize that this explanation for the appearance of non-Mosaic passages in the Pentateuch seriously detracts from the unity of this powerful work. It also allows later editors and authors a certain freedom with the text as originally written which we find difficult to accept. From our point of view, we could resort to such an explanation only if there were strong, compelling reasons for maintaining the Mosaic authorship of the entire Pentateuch. Since, in our judgment, such compelling reasons do not exist, we consider it inadvisable to resort to this hypothesis.

We are of the opinion, moreover, that the Pentateuch itself gives some clear direction with respect to this whole issue. We believe that the genesis of the Pentateuch took place in a way that differs from the view of those who hold to the interpolation theory. It is indeed striking that the portion that deals specifically with the history of Moses' own time, which is by far the major part of the work, was put together as follows: The extensive sections in which Moses speaks in the first person, as lawgiver, are embodied within a narrative framework which speaks of him in the third person. It is precisely in that narrative framework, moreover, that the above-listed passages, which plead against Mosaic authorship, appear. What should especially draw our attention is the fact that in the "I" sections the term "beyond the Jordan" definitely refers to the land west of the Jordan. This, of course, concurs with Moses' location since he did not cross the Jordan with the rest of Israel (see Deut. 3:20, 25; 11:30). At the same time, in the narrative section the term refers to the land east of the Jordan. When we consider these facts it is altogether acceptable to conceive of the genesis of the Pentateuch as follows: An author who lived after Moses made use of the material left by Moses, namely his travel journal and his laws. He also availed himself of other documents, and thus created the great work of history we now possess in the Pentateuch.

If this idea of the way the Pentateuch originated is correct, we must face a further question. Is it possible to establish anything further regarding the materials that the author used in addition to the Mosaic legacy of history and laws?

First of all we should consider the "Book of the Wars of the LORD" to which the author himself refers in Numbers 21:14. As we have observed above, this book must be considered as a record of the wars Israel waged in conquering the land of Canaan. Numbers 21:14 and 15 offer only a fragmentary quotation from this book. It reads, "Waheb in Suphah and the ravines, the Arnon, and the slopes of the ravines that lead to the site of Ar and lie along the border of Moab." The fragmentary character of this quotation becomes clear when we note that the name "Waheb" and the word used for "ravines" have beside them the Hebrew symbol for the fourth case, while there is no verb form present to which these words could form the object. We may assume with much certainty that this "book" included the narrative of the conquest of that part of Canaan which lay east of the Jordan. There is a strong possibility, therefore, that those sections of the Pentateuch which give the details concerning this part of the conquest of Canaan were also taken from this book.

Second, in Numbers 21:17–18, we have "The song of the well." This took place at Beer (well) which received its name because there God commanded that a well be dug to provide water for the people. Nothing is said about the source of this song. All we are told is that Israel sang this song. The fact that the name of the composer of the song is not mentioned strongly suggests that it was composed by someone other than Moses.

Third, in the same chapter there is another reference that deserves mention (Num. 21:27–30). This is introduced with the formula, "This is why the poets say." What must we understand by this? In Hebrew the present participle is used which is based on a verb that sometimes serves to signify the "making of a proverb" (Ezek. 16:44). More often, however, the word denotes "the reciting of a proverb" (Ezek. 12:23; 17:2; 18:2, 3; 24:3). It is conceivable we should think of these composers of proverbs as people whose task it was to present proverbs and songs. They may have been traveling singers, as was common among the Greeks, known as minstrels during the Middle Ages. These singers probably transmitted their songs by oral tradition. It is also possible that these traditional songs and proverbs in the course of time were written down by someone who made a collection of them. Thus the song referred to in our passage was likely a part of such a collection that was transmitted either by oral tradition or as a written collection.

29

Among the non-Mosaic sections, which the editor of the Pentateuch used, we should mention, fourthly, the Proverbs of Balaam. These consist of four proverbs or parables of some length (Num. 23:7–10, 18–24; 24:3–9, 15–19). Then there are three shorter ones (Num. 24:20, 21, 22, and 23–24). It is of course obvious that these are not the words of Moses. Balaam, the mysterious fortuneteller from Pethor in Mesopotamia, is apparently literally quoted in the text. It should also be observed that these words were not spoken to Israel but were spoken in the presence of Balak, king of Moab. Nowhere are we told how the author of the Pentateuch obtained this material. It has been suggested that the victorious Israelites found a copy of these predictions on the body of the fortuneteller himself. It was then supposed that Balaam preserved this material in the hope of gaining a reward from the Israelites or of saving his own threatened life. But all of such conjecture lacks evidence and even likelihood.

These few suggestions, then, are all we have been able to discover to indicate the possible sources of the material that served to supplement the writings ascribed to the pen of Moses. It is possible that the editor had access to other materials, either written documents or oral traditions, but this cannot be established with certainty. Another difficulty we face is that we do not know precisely what was included in Moses' travel journal. Because of the nature of the material, we can be reasonably certain that the section giving the laws of Moses was literally copied by the author. But we cannot say how faithful the section on the history of the Mosaic period was to the manuscript that Moses wrote.

When we turn to that part of the Pentateuch which presents the pre-Moses history, that is, the Book of Genesis and the first and possibly the second chapter of Exodus, we must acknowledge that we have no direct information available. We may, however, accept on good grounds that the writing of the pre-Moses history also was based on written documents that were available to the author. Although it is true that oral tradition played a far more important role at that time than it does today, it is unlikely that the entire pre-Moses history was based exclusively on such oral tradition. Undoubtedly, the rapid development of the nation of Israel in Egypt fostered a sense of urgency for preserving an accurate record of their past history. The traditions regarding the antediluvial period and the history of the patriarchs, insofar as they had not yet been put in writing, certainly would have been carefully recorded at this time. This legacy of literature which the people of Israel most certainly had preserved, would have been an essential part of the national treasures that were carried out of the land of bondage into the Promised Land.

That there were written records before Israel's sojourn in Egypt is obvious from the genealogies that appear in the Book of Genesis. Unless we want to brand these as products of sheer fantasy, they must certainly be based on old documents that were available to the author. Genesis 5:1 gives incontestable evidence that such documents indeed existed, since the title of the specific document that was used is given.

Besides the genealogies, we must take note of Genesis 14, a chapter that has long commanded the attention of scholars. To be sure, opinions regarding this biblical material differ widely. Some ascribe a very late date to it, even later than the Priestly Codex. Others consider it to be a very early source. The evidence for the latter is so convincing that it really cannot be questioned that we are dealing here with a section of an old archive. It is possible that this record was of non-Israelite origin. We note the reference to Abram as "the Hebrew" in verse 13.

There are also other brief passages that may have been put in writing at an early date. We think of the Song of Lamech in Genesis 4:23–24, the curse and the blessing of Noah in Genesis 9:25–27, the blessing of Isaac in Genesis 27:27–29 and 39–40, and the blessing of Jacob upon Ephraim and Manasseh in Genesis 48:20. In each case it is difficult to determine whether these were based on written records or, because of the brevity, had been orally transmitted.

Somewhat different is Jacob's deathbed address to his sons in Genesis 49:1–27. Although we can conceive of this being perserved via a long-lasting oral transmission, its considerable length would suggest that it may well have been put in writing at a very early date. Some modern scholars, however, have ascribed a very late date to this source passage. We will not discuss this further here since it will be considered in the body of the commentary on this passage.

Professor Yahuda, a well-known Semitic scholar at Heidelberg, proposed that much of the material in the Pentateuch evidences a strong Egyptian influence both in thought patterns and language usage. In a book published in 1929 he advanced the theory that the Pentateuch must have been written during the time of Israel's sojourn in Egypt or shortly thereafter. The results of our research in the biblical data would lead us to the same conclusion. Our position then would be that this work of history, for the major part, came into being during Israel's stay in Egypt or shortly after Israel left Egypt. We have concluded that the pre-Mosaic history was put into writing during Israel's stay in Egypt. The history of Moses' own time, furthermore, with the giving of the Law which is incorporated in it, is based on a significant and extensive literary legacy received from Moses.

More than this we cannot say with any degree of certainty. That Moses wrote the entire Pentateuch with his own hand cannot be established. At the same time, fixing the sources which are used in the preparation of the Pentateuch in an Egyptian setting all but eliminates the usual four-source theory and the theories which date the Pentateuch many centuries after Moses' time.

The question remaining for us to consider is the identity of the author who brought the entire Pentateuch into existence. We will not attempt to discover his name because that will probably always remain hidden from us. We will, however, try to determine the approximate time when this mighty work of history was formulated.

Naturally, we get some direction in this regard from the post-Mosaic expressions and manner of speech we have discovered in the Pentateuch. Deuteronomy 34 informs us, for instance, that the Pentateuch was completed after the death of Moses. Moreover, the statement in verse 6, "to this day no one knows where his grave is," suggests that it probably was quite some time after his death.

The time is more closely designated by passages such as Exodus 16:35: "They ate manna until they came to the border of Canaan," and Deuteronomy 2:12: "The descendants of Esau drove them out . . . as Israel did in the land the LORD gave them as their possession." Also worthy of note is the quotation from the "Book of the Wars of the LORD" in Numbers 21:14–15, and the expression, "near the Jordan," used to designate the land east of the Jordan (Gen. 50:10–11; etc.). All of these passages seem to indicate a time after the conquest of Canaan had been completed.

We also should discuss, briefly, the reference to a city called Dan, in Genesis 14:14. An attempt had been made to prove that this name could have been used prior to the conquest of Canaan. The evidence that has been adduced is based on the use of a similar name in the Amarna tablets. Since these tablets are dated 1411–1360 B.C., it is argued that this name was in use prior to the conquest of Canaan. The reference to Dan in Genesis 14:14 could then refer to the same person or place as that designated in the tablets, rather than the city of Dan in the northern part of Palestine. We are convinced that much of the reasoning in this regard is, at best, dubious. Just what is designated by the name in the tablets and where it is located is not at all clear. Moreover, the time factor is also not convincing. A plausible theory holds that Israel left Egypt during the regin of Pharaoh Amenophis II, which would place the date of the Exodus at approximately 1445 B.C. This has been confirmed by excavations which have revealed that the cities of Jericho, Ai, Hazor, and Bethel were destroyed about 1400 B.C. This could then predate the Amarna tablets and make the appearance of a name which is somewhat similar to Dan quite irrelevant. We are, therefore, convinced that the name Dan in Genesis 14:14 refers to none other than the familiar city of Dan in northern Palestine, "from Dan to Beersheba" (Judg. 20:1; etc.).

That Genesis 14:14 refers to this familiar city is also confirmed by the context. We read that Abram pursued the invaders to Dan. After defeating them there he chased them as far as Hobah, north of Damascus. This would have been the natural route of escape for an army defeated in the area of Dan, the northern city.

We learn from Joshua 19:47 and Judges 18:29 that this city was formerly called Leshem or Laish. Only after the area was assigned to the tribe of Dan was the name of the city changed to Dan. It follows, therefore, that the completion of the Pentateuch must be dated after the conquest of Laish. Just when this occurred is not known. The entire context in the Book of Judges suggests that a period of decline had already set in after the death of Joshua and his contemporaries (Josh. 24:31; Judg. 2:7-13).

We are compelled to consider even a later date by the reference in Genesis 36:31, "These were the kings who reigned in Edom, before any Israelite king reigned" This assumes that Israel already had kings. In that case the date of the Pentateuch cannot be placed before the reign of King Saul.

Once again, we should consult the rest of the books of the Old Testament. Earlier we inquired whether there were traces of the laws given in the Pentateuch in these other books of the Bible. Our inquiry now is directed toward finding references to the Pentateuch as such. A careful search reveals that throughout the Old Testament there are references which indeed do place the Pentateuch at a point in time that is prior to all the other books of the Old Testament. We want to demonstrate this with a number of examples.

Before we do this we want to point out, however, that the mere recollection of a historical event which is mentioned in the Pentateuch offers no clear evidence. Undoubtedly the Israelites had a body of oral tradition concerning their early history, and a mere reference to some event in the past could very well be drawn from that. This is frequently done in the Psalms, for example.[1] The only substantial evidence for the prior existence of the Pentateuch as such, would be the presence of literal quotations from the Pentateuch. Moreover, these quotations should be taken from the historical sections and not from the giving of the laws, since there were plenty of separate copies of the laws available. Greatest weight must be given to

---

[1] See Dr. W. H. Gispen, "Indirecte gegevens voor het bestaan van den Pentateuch in de Psalmen," Zutphen, 1928 (especially Pss. 74; 77; 78; 81; 105; and 136). Also, "Mondelinge overlevering in het Oude Testament," Meppel, 1932, p. 180.

references that are clearly taken from the pre-Mosaic history or from the general framework, which is obviously the work of the editor of the Pentateuch.

There is still another guideline which should be set for this research in the other books of the Old Testament. In one sense, there is no need to cite quotations from the Pentateuch which are found in the later books, such as Chronicles, Ezra, and Nehemiah. No one questions that the Pentateuch was already in existence when these books were written. Even so, it is especially significant when we discover statements in these later books, taken from the Pentateuch, which are also found in the earlier books. It must be admitted that the presence of one single quotation in a given book offers no substantial evidence. When we discover, however, that such data from the Pentateuch (which appears in the earlier books), reappears in identically the same form in the later books (when the Pentateuch definitely did exist), this gives strong evidence for the existence of the Pentateuch. This, of course, goes without saying in the case of the genealogies which appear in almost the same form in Chronicles as they do in Genesis, strongly suggesting that the writer of the Book of Chronicles had Genesis before him.

We now want to place a number of these passages before our readers in order that our conclusions may be carefully evaluated.

We turn, first of all, to Nehemiah 9:7, where we read that God brought Abraham out of "Ur of the Chaldeans." This name appears nowhere else except for three references in the Pentateuch (Gen. 11:28, 31 and 15:7). Further, in Nehemiah 9:9 we read that God heard the "cry" of the Israelites at the Red Sea. In Nehemiah 9:11, the miracle that God wrought at the Red Sea is described with the same word as that used in Exodus 14:21, the verb "cleaved" or "split." The sinking of the Egyptians "into the depths" and also "like a stone" concurs with Exodus 15:5. Also, Nehemiah 9:12 refers to God "leading" His people with a "pillar of cloud" and a "pillar of fire," to give them light, all expressions taken from Exodus 13:21. Also in Nehemiah 9:13, "You came down on Mt. Sinai," is a recalling of Exodus 19:20. Nehemiah 9:17, they "appointed a leader in order to return to their slavery," points back to Numbers 14:4. In the same verse God is described as a "forgiving God, gracious and compassionate, slow to anger and abounding in love," which is like Exodus 34:6. Recalling the sin with the golden calf, in Nehemiah 9:18, reminds us of Exodus 32:4 and 8. Multiplying "as the stars in the sky" in Nehemiah 9:23 points back to God's promise to Abraham in Genesis 22:17.

The Books of Chronicles include, besides the genealogies, many references to events that are recorded in the Pentateuch. Seldom do these references appear in the same terms that are used in the Pentateuch, however, and consequently they do not give evidence of an acquaintance with the Pentateuch. The few passages which do merit mention are the following: In 1 Chronicles 24:1 there is a reference to the four sons of Aaron. Of special note is the way the death of Nadab and Abihu and the priesthood of Eleazar and Ithamar is recorded. "But Nadab and Abihu died before their father . . . so Eleazar and Ithamar served as the priests" (v. 2). When this is compared with Numbers 3:4 we find that almost the identical words are used. Also of some significance is the reference to Bezalel the son of Uri, the son of Hur, in 2 Chronicles 1:5. This is the same as Exodus 31:2; 35:30; and 38:22. This is even more significant because this information is given nowhere else than in these two passages.

In Malachi we have only one reference of any importance. In Malachi 4:4 there is an admonition to keep the "law" of Moses, which is then further designated by the words "decrees and laws." This same combination of words, "decrees and laws" is found in Leviticus 26:46, which is considered to be in that section of the Pentateuch written by the "editor." However, since the same designations are also used in other parts of the Pentateuch, this passage is of little evidential value.

When we move to a somewhat earlier time, we find in Daniel 12:1 the expression, "everyone whose name is found written in the book." This bears a strong resemblance to the way Exodus 32:32 speaks of God's Book, "The book you have written." In Ezekiel 20:5–6, the expression, "I swore to them (literally, 'I lifted up my hand') that I would bring them out of Egypt," reminds us of Exodus 6:7. In Ezekiel 38:22 there is the prediction that God would "pour down . . . rain, hailstones, and burning sulphur" on Gog. This is literally the same as God's judgment on Sodom and Gomorrah in Genesis 19:24. In Jeremiah 4:23 we find the familiar *tōhû wābōhû* of Genesis 1:2. (For the meaning of these words see our commentary on Gen. 1:2).

We are told in Jeremiah 20:16; 49:18; and 50:40, that Sodom and Gomorrah were "overthrown." This is also found in Isaiah 13:19 and Amos 4:11, and this expression must have been taken from Genesis 19:25. Jeremiah 48:45–46 is taken from Numbers 21:28–29. Zephaniah 2:11 uses the expression "the nations on every shore" and the only other place this appears is in Genesis 10:5. Nahum 1:10 speaks of those who were "consumed like dry stubble," and this probably is taken from Exodus 15:7.

It is generally conceded that the Books of Kings received their final editing at the time of the Exile. Much of the essential content of these books, however, is based on earlier material. Thus we find in 1 Kings 12:28 a citation from Exodus 32:4, "Here are your gods, O Israel, who

35

brought you up out of Egypt.'' In the Hebrew the phrases are identical. In 2 Kings 18:4 the ''bronze snake'' is described in the same words used in Numbers 21:9.

In Isaiah 12:2 we find a literal citation from Exodus 15:2, ''The LORD the LORD, is my strength and my song; he has become my salvation.'' Micah, Isaiah's contemporary, refers to Assyria as ''the land of Nimrod'' in 5:6, as does Genesis 10:9–11. Hosea 1:10 uses the expression, ''like the sand on the seashore, which cannot be measured or counted.'' This makes us think of the promise to Abraham in Genesis 22:17, and, even more strongly, of the words in which Jacob repeats that promise in Genesis 32:12. In Hosea 12:4 the same verbs, ''struggled'' and ''overcame,'' are used as those in the description of Jacob's wrestling at Peniel in Genesis 32:28. This is the more significant because the first verb is used nowhere else. In Hosea 12:5, the expression that the ''LORD'' (Jahweh) is God's name undoubtedly refers to Exodus 3:15.

Finally, we come to the oldest historical books, the two Books of Samuel and the Book of Judges. We are bypassing the Book of Joshua since the Pentateuch critics include this in their theory of the genesis of the Pentateuch. The Books of Samuel offer only two evidences. In 1 Samuel 12:3, Samuel defends his office as Judge in the same words that Moses had used when he defended his position against the rebellion of Korah, Dathan, and Abiram, Numbers 16:15: ''I have not taken so much as a donkey from them.'' First Samuel 15:29 almost literally quotes the words of Balaam in Numbers 23:19, ''God is not a man . . . that he should change his mind.''

The Book of Judges gives more significant data. In 2:1 we have an expression that is parallel to Genesis 50:24. The messenger of the Lord said, ''I brought you up out of Egypt, and led you into the land that I swore to give to your forefathers.'' On his deathbed Joseph used the same expression, ''God will take you . . . to the land which he promised on oath to Abraham, Isaac and Jacob.'' When we look at this text in the original, there is a similarity of language that is so striking that it is almost certain that the author of the Book of Judges had a copy of Genesis before him when he wrote. A careful study of the verb forms used makes this practically incontestable.

Another passage in Judges that seems to echo the Pentateuch is 2:10. In Exodus 1:8 we read, ''Then a new King, who did not know about Joseph, came to power in Egypt.'' In Judges we read, ''Another generation grew up, who knew neither the LORD. . . .'' The identical use of words, word order, and verb forms in the Hebrew can hardly be explained as a happenstance. The author of Judges must have been well-acquainted with the passage from Exodus.

We find another striking echo from the Pentateuch in the message of Jephthah to the Ammonites in Judges 11:15–27. Here there is not only a similarity of subject matter, even to specific details, but there is also a similarity of manner of expression that can be explained only by a thorough knowledge of the text of the Pentateuch. Thus, in verse 17 we find the expression, ''Give us permission to go through your country.'' In Numbers 20:17 we have identically the same expression. In Judges 11:18 we read that Israel ''skirted the land of Edom and Moab.'' Numbers 21:4 uses the same words. In Judges 11:18 is the phrase ''and camped on the other side of the Arnon,'' and the same statement appears in Numbers 21:13. The statement ''for the Arnon was its border,'' appears in verse 18 of our passage and also in Numbers 21:13. The inclusion of this geographic detail in Jepthah's message clearly indicates that the writer directly consulted the text of Numbers. In Judges 11:19 we have, ''Israel sent messengers to Sihon king of the Amorites.'' This is a literal repetition of Numbers 21:22. So also Judges 11:20, ''Sihon, however, did not trust Israel to pass through his territory. He mustered all his men and encamped at Jahaz and fought with Israel,'' is, with a few small changes, the equivalent of Numbers 21:23. Finally, in Judges 11:22 we read that Israel took possession of all the territory of the Amorites, ''from the Arnon to the Jabbok,'' and this is also found in Numbers 21:24, in the same words.

Strong evidence that the writer of Judges was well-acquainted with the Pentateuch is the expression used in Judges 13:5 and 7, ''You will conceive and give birth to a son.'' In the original Hebrew this is a literal transcription from Genesis 16:11. The striking thing about this expression is that the verb ''give birth to'' is used in an altogether unique form which appears nowhere else in the entire Old Testament. It was such an unusual usage that even the old rabbinical scholars had serious problems interpreting it. Now the fact that this totally unique verb, in identically the same phrase, is used both in Judges 13:5, 7 and in Genesis 16:11 could not have been accidental. It offers conclusive evidence that the two passages are closely related.

Still another passage that provides data for our consideration is Judges 13:18. Here the reply of the angel to Manoah's question, ''What is your name?'' begins with identically the same words (in Hebrew) as the answer Jacob received at Peniel, in Genesis 32:29, ''Why do you ask my name?''

Finally, let us consider the narrative of the stranger and his concubine at Gibeah, in Judges 19. Here there are such remarkable similarities to the narrative of the visit of the angels to Lot's house in Sodom, in Genesis 19, that it demands our careful attention. In Judges 19:22 we read, ''the wicked men of the city surrounded the house.'' In Genesis 19:4 we have ''the men from every part of the city of Sodom . . . surrounded the house." Further, in Judges 19 we are told that they said, "Bring out the man who came to your house so we can have sex with him." In Genesis 19:5 are found these words, "Where are the men who came to you tonight? Bring them out to us so we can have sex with them." In the Judges passage, the host said, "No, my friends, don't be so vile." In the Genesis passage Lot says essentially the same words to his fellow citizens. In the narrative in Judges, the host resorted to the shocking tactic of offering his virgin daughter and his guest's concubine. Lot resorts to the same extreme recourse when he offers his virgin daughters. In each case we find exactly the same words used, "Look"; "I will bring them out"; "You can do what you like with them." This accumulation of exact parallels cannot possibly be explained as mere coincidence. The conclusion cannot be avoided that the writer of the Judges narrative was thoroughly acquainted with Genesis 19.

We believe that the data we have listed above simply demonstrates the fact that traces of the Pentateuch appear, as such, in all the varied periods of time covered by the Old Testament. Moreover, these indications build up to the time in which the Book of Judges was written. We can also point out that the evidence for acquaintance with the Pentateuch is fully as strong in Judges as it is in the postexilic books (leaving aside the genealogies in Chronicles). We should then try to establish when the Book of Judges originated. We will then have, besides the earliest date that the Pentateuch could have been written, which we established above, also the latest date that can be considered.

In considering the date of the origin of Judges, we are going to set aside the "supplement" to the book, chapters 17–21, which probably is of a later date than the main narrative of chapters 1–16. For our present study this is of no consequence because the main body of the book offers ample evidence of acquaintance with the Pentateuch.

When we consider chapters 1–16 we find that this section could have existed during the reign of King Saul, and in any case, no later than the first part of David's reign. According to Judges 1:2 the Fortress of Zion had not yet been conquered from the Jebusites. David accomplished this (2 Sam. 5:3–9) shortly after he was acknowledged as king by all Israel. (This is developed in an earlier study on the Old Testament canon by the author.) Thus we have found that the latest date for the completion of the Pentateuch would be during the first seven years of David's reign. Then let us recall that the earliest possible date we arrived at was during the reign of Saul. Thus the date for the formation of this mighty work of history, which includes a mass of earlier material as well, is fixed with considerable accuracy.

Now we must still give our attention to another related issue. Although the Pentateuch as a whole obviously received its present form some time between the first year of Saul's reign and the seventh year of David's reign, there could have been certain alterations or additions that were introduced at a later time. In our judgment, we should not accept this possibility too quickly, for the same reason that we could not accept all post-Mosaic material as later additions. In the circles of negative criticism it is assumed that there was a great deal of freedom and arbitrariness in dealing with the literary resources that were available during the time the Old Testament was being formed. We consider this assumption to be completely untenable. Factual evidence for such arbitrary handling of the sources of sacred literature has never been adduced. It was merely assumed in order to support a preconceived hypothesis regarding the origins of the books of the Bible. The knowledge we have of the ancient Oriental cultural world lends no support to this assumption of the critics. Just one illustration will suffice. Thanks to the discovery of the Amarna tablets and the Archives of Boghazkay, we know that cuneiform writing developed throughout the Near East about 1400 B.C. The material that was used consisted of clay tablets in which the letters were inscribed with a stylus. Then they were baked in an oven. This laborious method of writing, especially in the case of sacred materials, caused these tablets to be treated with utmost respect and vigilance. It is inconceivable that anyone would be free to make arbitrary changes in these documents, even if this were possible.

In spite of all of this, we are willing to allow the possibility of a few isolated changes in the text of the Pentateuch after its final redaction under Saul and David. But such minor isolated changes in the text can be granted only on the basis of the most binding evidence that they must have been written at a later date.

We are willing to make this concession because there is an instance of this kind of later supplement in another historical book of the Bible. We are referring to a marginal note in 1 Samuel 9:9. This indicates that the name "seer," which was used in Samuel's time, later was changed to "prophet." This marginal note must have been written at a time when the name "seer" was no longer in common usage. A careful study of the later books of the Old Testament establishes that this note must have been added after the time of Isaiah. Because the role of the prophet was always a significant factor in the life of the people of Israel, it probably stems from the last period of the kingdom of Judah before the Babylonian Captivity. Since there is every reason to date the Books of Samuel no later than during the reigns of the first kings after the division of the kingdoms, we will grant a later addition in this isolated instance of 1 Samuel 9:9. This is confirmed by the nature of this marginal note, which is actually an explanation of what is written in verse 11.

It should be clearly understood, however, that such an addition which became part of the text before the closing of the canon, is accepted as being just as inspired as the passage in which it appears. The possibility of such inspired alterations in the Pentateuch should not be excluded in advance. Just to mention one instance, Professor van Gelderen, one of the authors of this series, has developed some material regarding the "Table of Nations" found in Genesis 10. It is his conviction that these tables have been edited from time to time and that the last change was made during the reign of King Hezekiah, or shortly after his death. Details of this study will be included in our treatment of Genesis 10. It is mentioned here only to illustrate the fact that there is no principial objection to such a conclusion. Whether the conclusion is justified in a given instance, however, depends entirely on the evidence which the Scripture itself provides.

We have dwelt at some considerable length on the history of the genesis of the Pentateuch. And this is, indeed, a very significant matter, especially in view of the ideas that have been developed in this regard by the school of negative criticism. There is far more at issue than merely a historical problem. If the usual views of Pentateuchal criticism are correct, the truth of this part of the Holy Scriptures would be affected. The Pentateuch repeatedly and specifically states that the laws that are contained in it were given by Moses. But negative criticism, no matter how much variation there may be within its ranks, unanimously agrees that the giving of the laws of the Pentateuch did not take place until long after Moses disappeared from the scene. Criticism of the Pentateuch, moreover, not only comes into conflict with the testimony of Scripture with respect to the giving of the laws, but it also calls into question the accuracy of the historical record, especially with respect to the oldest history of mankind. When scholars proceed from the position that the historical record must be dated at a time which is separated by many centuries from the actual events, it is not surprising that they also have a tendency to question the trustworthiness of that historical record to a greater or lesser degree.

Over against all such attacks on the trustworthiness of the Pentateuch we maintain, with the greatest earnestness and emphasis, that this great work of history is a part of the very Word of God. We insist that this Word of God is infallibly true, and that we can believe, without any doubt, all that it says. Our entire explanation of the origin of the Pentateuch, on the basis of the biblical data we have considered, aims at remaining faithful to this principle. We have tried to stand exclusively and unconditionally on what Scripture says. Certainly, the authority and truth of a given book of the

Bible does not depend on the correct answer to the question of authorship. It depends solely on the fact that it was breathed by the Holy Spirit. Our primary concern is that the divine inspiration of the entire Pentateuch, as it now lies before us, as the fruit of the work of Moses and others, be acknowledged fully and without reservations. Therefore, all that is recorded in it is to be accepted as infallible truth. Any presentation regarding the origin of the Pentateuch which is in conflict with this position we cannot, in good faith, accept.

Introduction to Genesis

I. *The Name of the Book*

As we have already mentioned in the General Introduction to the five books of the Law, the name of the book that we know as Genesis was "In the beginning" *(Berēšît)* among the Jews. This was based on the first word of the book. We owe the name "Genesis" to the Septuagint and it came down to us via the Vulgate.

Genesis means "becoming." The book was given this name because it contains the description of the "becoming" of the world, the human race, and the chosen people of Israel. The commentary by J. C. Sikkel calls it by the name, "The book of births," based on the Hebrew word *tôledôt* which appears in Genesis 2:4 and in other passages. This is, however, not correct. *Tôledôt* in Hebrew language usage does not refer to the "birth" itself, but rather to the product of the "bearing," that is, "posterity" or "descendants." In a few instances the word has an even broader meaning and refers to what happened to these descendants, or "history." If we were going to name the book according to the word *tôledôt* because it is used repeatedly in the book, we would have to call it the "Book of Histories" or "The Book of the Generations." It is far better, however, to stay with the name "Genesis," which has become rooted by centuries of usage.

II. *Content and Outline of the Book*

The Book of Genesis begins with the description of the creation of heaven and earth. It continues with the history of that created world (see Gen. 2:4), a history which primarily becomes the history of humanity. This history is given on the broadest possible basis. Up to a certain point in time, it embraces the whole of mankind. Thereafter it limits itself exclusively to the history of one family. That point is in Genesis 11. The line of division is between verses 26 and 27. In Genesis 11:10-26 the genealogy of Shem is given, up to Terah. This then concludes with the names of Terah's three sons, Abram, Nahor, and Haran. In verse 27 a new section is introduced with the words, "This is the account of Terah." Then, first of all, the names of the three sons of Terah are repeated. Thereafter, the narrative is limited primarily to Terah's son, Abram. It then continues with the children born to Abraham, especially Isaac. It then goes on with Isaac's twin sons, Jacob and Esau, but the emphasis falls on Jacob. Following that it moves on with Jacob's twelve sons, among whom Joseph appears in the foreground. In great detail it describes how Joseph came to Egypt and how he became the occasion for the entire family of Jacob to move to Egypt. It concludes with the death of Jacob and then, finally, also of Joseph.

From the above it becomes apparent that the book falls into two main divisions. The first section gives the history of mankind from creation to Terah, the father of Abram. The second main section gives the history of God's specially chosen family, from which the people of Israel were to come forth. The following books then give the history of the people of Israel.

The division we must make does not lend itself to a distinct division of chapters, then, but falls between verses 26 and 27 of chapter 11. The first section consists of Genesis 1:1-11:26, and the second section, Genesis 11:27-50:26.

Narrower subdivisions of the first main section are readily determined by the subjects that are treated. The Creation of the world—Genesis 1:1-2:3; Paradise and the Fall—Genesis 2:4-3:24; Cain and Abel—Genesis 4; Adam's genealogy—Genesis 5; the Flood—Genesis 6:1-9:17; after the Flood—Genesis 9:28-29; the Table of Nations—Genesis 10; the Tower of Babel—Genesis 11:1-9; and the genealogy from Shem to Abram—Genesis 11:10-26.

In the second main section, seemingly, we should be able to delineate subdivisions with equal facility. Here we have successively the histories of the three partriarchs, Abraham, Isaac, and Jacob, and then we can allot a special section to Joseph. The difficulty with such a division is that these sections overlap to a considerable degree. Thus the account of the life of Abraham begins in Genesis 11:27 and we would be inclined to let this end with his death in Genesis 25:8. But this section also includes one of the most significant chapters of the life of Isaac, namely, the acquiring of his bride, Rebekah. This is recorded in Genesis 24, certainly in proper chronological order since it precedes Abraham's death. But it does confuse a distinctly outlined division of that part of the book. We face an even greater difficulty in the case of Isaac, since his death is not recorded until Genesis

35:28–29. The section from chapter 27 to 35, however, deals with the story of Jacob. Furthermore, in chapter 36, we have a brief review of the story of Esau or Edom. When the story of Jacob is resumed in chapter 37, this is interrupted with the episode of Judah and Tamar, chapters 38–41, and then Joseph is brought into such prominence that it actually is his story, rather than that of Jacob. In chapters 42–49 we return to the narrative of Jacob, but Joseph remains prominent throughout this section. In Genesis 49:33 the death of Jacob is recorded and in chapter 50 we read of his funeral. Following this there are a few words about Joseph's later history and then the book closes with the account of his death in Genesis 50:26. Because the narratives of the three patriarchs overlap the way they do, we will not attempt a division of this part of the book into neatly delineated sections.

We had intended to devote one volume of this commentary to each of the two main divisions of Genesis. The treatment of the first eleven chapters, however, of necessity must deal with many significant questions of interpretation which come to the surface when this portion is carefully considered. We also wanted to include a general introduction to the entire Pentateuch. Consequently this first volume actually extended to the middle point of our entire treatment of Genesis. Even though our treatment of the second main division of the book is far more brief, it contains so much material that it was considered wiser to divide this material into two small volumes.

III. *Character and Subject Matter of the Book*

The entire Pentateuch is a work of history. So also the Book of Genesis gives clear indications of being intended as a description of history.

That we are dealing with history in Genesis, that is, that the events which are treated happened exactly as they are described in the book, is almost universally denied. The manner in which this is done varies widely.

Radical modern scholars insist that, although what is recorded in Genesis is intended to be history, and this is exegetically undeniable, this must be ascribed to the naiveté of the ancient narrators. For the enlightened and scientifically educated person of the present, it is completely obvious that this narration cannot be considered to be actual history.

A more moderate and therefore also more half-hearted view holds that the writers themselves did not pretend to be recording actual history. The first eleven chapters of Genesis especially indicate that the writers were simply trying to set forth their own ideas. They were offering their own answers to questions people were raising, such as, How did the world come into being? Why is man mortal? What is the source of strife and wars? etc.

A third position holds that the writers recorded old human traditions regarding real events, but that these traditions had become mixed with various mythological embellishments and therefore cannot be considered as present historical truth.

A fourth view must be mentioned, which considers the historical narratives of Genesis to be nothing more than poetry, symbolic compositions, and allegories, which seek to give expression to certain truths.

We cannot accept the first three theories because they essentially deny the authority of Scripture. That is the only objection we have to the view of the radical modern scholars, but it is an insurmountable objection. Exegetically we agree with them that Genesis intends to be history. This they acknowledge. This intent of the book is, at the same time, the main problem we have with the last three views. This is the only objection, but again a formidable one, that we hold to the view that considers the book to be made up of poetry, symbol, and allegory. As such, it cannot be denied that there is poetry, symbol, and allegory in Scripture. But this does not warrant arbitrarily relegating a given portion of Scripture to the level of poetry, symbol, or allegory. The real issue is, What did the sacred text itself intend? When the Scripture intends to record history, we may not simply declare it to be poetic or symbolic or allegorical.

That Genesis intended to give history is not difficult to establish. There is not one substantial argument which can be advanced that would prove the contrary. All the reasons that have been given from time to time for questioning this intent of the book are, at best, tenuous. The entire design of the book indicates that the positive intent was to present actual history. This is in keeping with the nature of the entire Pentateuch, of which Genesis is a part, and which is unmistakably a work of history. This is confirmed by its own self-designation as *tôledôt*—"history" or "account" in Genesis 2:4; 6:9; 11:27; 37:2. This is in keeping with the general impression the entire book gives. Also, there is a constant use of a verb form which, in Hebrew, serves to describe historical events.

It is claimed that serious objections can be raised against the genuine historicity of Genesis. The radical modern scholars insist that, although Genesis intends to portray history, it does not succeed in presenting authentic history. As a result, many scholars have sought out ways in which the biblical narrative can be given another purpose.

We cannot just ignore these claims or deny them without giving them serious consideration. We believe we can do this more effectively, however, when we take up the individual passages in the body of this commentary. Most of these objections are not of a general nature. They are more apt to flow from a specific point. They usually go something like this:

When modern scholars discover something in Genesis which they consider to be in conflict with what is generally assumed to be scientific fact, they conclude that it cannot be true. Objections of this nature which are based on Genesis 1–11 will be taken up when we discuss the specific references later in this volume. One exception to this is the objection that deals with the creation narrative. The author has discussed this at some length in his book, *De Goddelijke Openbaring in de Eerste Drie Hoofdstukken van Genesis*. Moreover, the objections that have been raised against the historicity of the patriarchs, which are not as common as those advanced against the "prehistory," will be taken up later in this commentary.

Closely related to this is the question regarding the source of this material. Since the critics will not acknowledge that Genesis is genuine history, they ascribe the materials of the book either to pure myth and legend or to human traditions that have been corrupted by mythological and legendary elements. It is claimed that often the narrator would present his own ideas but would clothe them in the form of myth and allegory.

To pursue this further we must then inquire into the source of these myths and legends. Naturally they could be ascribed to Israel itself because they certainly could have originated there as well as with other nations. But when they are compared with the myths and legends that have been discovered from other nations, the researchers tend to ascribe them to non-Israelite sources. Here we see the influence of the history of religions school to which we referred in our Introduction to the Pentateuch. Most of the scholars in this school consider Babylon to be the most likely source. Thus the material in Genesis 1–11 would be considered of Babylonian origin. There was a time when some scholars boldly declared that the entire prehistory, in fact the entire Old Testament, and, according to a few, also the New Testament, was simply a copy of Babylonian materials. However, these views have long since been abandoned and scholars have become much more cautious in their judgments. Today they dare go no further than to declare that the narrators independently reworked these materials and as a result they produced something that stands on a far higher level.

These positions are defended by the discovery of traces of Babylonian influences which are evident in the biblical narratives.

We are not going to test the reliability of these claims of the critics at this time. Because they invariably involve specific details in the biblical text, we will consider them, in each case, when they arise in the course of this commentary. Again, we will exclude a treatment of these details as they appear in Genesis 1–3 because the author has treated these materials in his *De Goddelijke Openbaring*.

Other scholars insist that the sources are more apt to be Egyptian rather than Babylonian. Among these is Professor Yahuda, to whom we referred earlier. In fact, Yahuda was the first to develop the theory of Egyptian sources. Since they also speak openly of myths and legends, however, their theories are open to the same careful examination as those who opt for all Babylonian sources.

Whether the materials of Genesis are ascribed to Babylonian sources, Egyptian sources, or, as a few believe, to Egyptianized Babylonian sources, makes little difference. As long as these sources are considered to be merely legend and myth, we principally brand all such presentations as wholly objectionable. Each passage to which these theories relate will be treated in the course of this commentary and the claims of the critics will be carefully examined. These detailed studies will make it clearly obvious that these theories have no substantial basis in fact. Furthermore, it will become evident that they add nothing to the understanding of the subject matter of the biblical narrative as it has come down to us.

IV. *Text, Translation and Commentary*

Regarding the Hebrew text of Genesis, on which our translation is based, there are a few matters that must be clearly understood. As has been noted elsewhere, we must be aware of the process of "vocalization," which was effected by the Masoretic scholars.

The original text of the Hebrew Old Testament consisted only of consonants. There were no vowels. When the text was read aloud the vowels were supplied by the reader. Although we do not know all the details about the process by which the standard vocalization of the Hebrew text came about, we do have enough information to warrant drawing certain conclusions and setting certain guidelines.

The Masoretes were Jewish scholars of the sixth and seventh centuries, A.D., who obviously intended to provide uniformity in the reading of the Hebrew Scriptures. They therefore inserted into the Hebrew words symbols or "points" which represented vowel sounds. We will grant that these "points" were based on traditional pronunciations used by the Jews in their formal readings in the synagogues. Even so, it must be remembered that they were not formally and generally introduced into the Hebrew text of the Old Testament until the sixth and seventh centuries A.D., thus many centuries after the Old Testament had been written.

It should be understood, therefore, that we are not bound by these guides to pronunciation because they were definitely not a part of the original Old Testament Scripture. All they are is an indication of how scholarly Jews read the Old Testament during the sixth and seventh centuries A.D. In those instances where an alternative reading is possible, it is altogether permissible and, in some instances, necessary to depart from these Jewish vocalizations. There are instances where an alternate vocalization makes the words of Scripture more intelligible and meaningful.

Naturally, we should not make such changes arbitrarily. The Jewish pronunciations that were based on centuries of usage have real value. But when we can provide an alternate reading of a word or phrase of Scripture by changing the vowel points, while maintaining the original consonants, such a reading should not be rejected merely because it does not follow the Masoretic vocalizations. As Bible-believing Christians we must always ask the overarching question, "What saith the Scripture?" We may never be bound by purely human deliverances, even though these may originate with the ancient Jews.

Today every reliable translation of the Old Testament assumes the freedom to depart from the Masoretic vocalizations, where this proves to be necessary or preferable. The pointings of the Masoretes, although of great value, remain human deliverances and, as such, have no divine authority. They are therefore not binding for our understanding of the true meaning of Scripture.

In actual fact, the traditional text of Genesis is amazingly reliable and there are very few passages in which we find it necessary to depart from the Jewish reading of the text.

Now, finally, a word about this commentary. It has already been observed that, especially with respect to the first 11 chapters of Genesis, we have not adhered too strictly to the demand for a *brief* or concise commentary. We believe we have, however, avoided excess verbiage as much as possible.

It can be understood that a thorough treatment of this book of the Bible has required extensive review of a vast body of literature. Much of this is not purely exegetical. A word of appreciation goes to all who have assisted in this background study. Many of the fruits of their labors are included in this book.

One general comment should be added. The Book of Genesis is a book of history, but this history is not simply a reproduction of human tradition. Even though this tradition may be based on documents which go back far into the past and have been preserved by a special divine providence, the Book of Genesis is more than this. Genesis is divine revelation. It is this, not only in the sense that God has revealed Himself in the events communicated here, but also in the sense that this communication itself is divine revelation. This communication, just as it now lies before us in this book as a result of various factors working together, all under God's guidance, has been put into writing by a special inspiration of God, because He wanted to reveal to us everything that is written in this book. This also determined the choice of material and its meaning. It was not intended to fully satisfy our desire for knowledge, or, perhaps, our curiosity. Many things happened that are not communicated to us. In the events that are revealed to us, there remain countless questions to which we are not given answers.

The purpose of divine revelation is to reveal to us God's plan of redemption for fallen humanity. In keeping this purpose, Genesis begins with creation, in order that we might know that the God who prepares deliverance for us is, first of all, our Creator and the Creator of all things. From there it moves immediately to the glorious state in which humanity dwelt in Paradise. Then follows the dreadful fall into sin, but at the same time we hear the first gospel promise. It continues with the division of mankind between the unholy line in which we see evil develop and the holy line in which God's work of grace becomes manifest. Then comes the decadent flowing together of both lines and the resulting deluge which brings an almost total destruction of humanity. But God's plan of redemption is carried forward in righteous Noah. From Noah a new humanity descended, but, once again, sin got the upper hand. Now it becomes manifest how God again marks off His own limited domain, in which He carries forward the preparation for His great work of redemption. The promise of the gospel is repeated, with a more restricted line that runs forward to the promised "seed of the woman": Abraham, Isaac, Jacob, Judah. Thus the entire Book of Genesis is a revelation of Jesus Christ. The whole history points forward to Him. That is its purpose. That is its value. This history unveils for us the unfathomable mercies of God who through Jesus Christ seeks to deliver fallen humanity out of the misery into which they have cast themselves by their own sin and guilt.

Genesis
Commentary

Part One

The History of the World From the Creation to Abram
(1:1–11:26)

1. *The Creation of the World* (1:1–2:3)

The first words of the Bible are a revelation from God regarding the creation of the world. There are those who suggest that this revelation is given in the form of a vision. Others suppose that we are dealing with a poem, and it certainly does evidence an exalted style. We do not accept these theories, however, but insist that God's revelation regarding the Creation comes to us as a historical message.

1:1 *In the beginning God created the heavens and the earth.*

The first words of the first verse immediately confront us with a question that has caused interpreters to give a number of answers. The question is this: Are we to accept the words "in the beginning" as absolute and then bind them into one unified concept with the succeeding verb so that we read, as we have done, "In the beginning God created . . ."? Or are we to translate it, "When God began creating"? The translation we accept will also influence the connection we establish between verse 1 and the following verses. If we adopt the first reading, verse 1 forms an independent sentence and verses 2 and 3 follow as independent sentences. If, on the other hand, we adopt the second reading, verse 1 becomes a dependent clause, verse 2 becomes a transitional statement, and verse 3 forms the conclusion which verse 1 modifies and to which it relates.

50

The issue of the translation of these words thrusts upon us the entire critical question of whether Genesis 1 teaches the creation of a world which did not previously exist, or teaches that the "creation" described in Genesis 1 was merely the process of transforming a preexistent world. If we take the words "in the beginning" as absolute, we immediately declare that the world owes its existence solely to God. If, on the other hand, we follow the other concept, verse 1 gives us no more than a designation of time when God began "creating" the heaven and the earth. Then verse 2, the transitional statement, speaks of a world which was already in existence and describes the condition of that preexistent world when God began His "creative" work. It is obvious, then, that this question is of critical significance.

In making our decision on this issue, let it be stated without any equivocation that the words "in the beginning" must be taken in their absolute sense. First of all, this is the most natural and obvious interpretation. Furthermore, this is the rendition that is found in every ancient translation, without any exception. Finally, although the alternative interpretation is linguistically possible, it does not reflect common Hebrew usage. We may safely affirm that if such a construction was intended here it would have been expressed in such a way that any possible ambiguity would be avoided. There is no other instance in the entire Old Testament where a similar connection is made where it could possibly allow for an ambiguous interpretation. Although this other interpretation is preferred by a few modern scholars, it is rejected by a vast majority of exegetes from widely differing persuasions.

If, then, the expression "in the beginning" is taken in its absolute sense, we thereby, at the outset, point back to the beginning of everything that exists. It is not possible to go back beyond that designated point in time. We have reached the ultimate limits of the past which are conceivable to us as human beings.

That beginning, then, was formed by God's act of creation. What are we now to understand by "creation"? In the Old Testament the verb is used exclusively regarding God and His activity. It is never ascribed to a human person. The word is used not only to designate the activity of God which brings the world into being, but also to describe His mighty works in upholding or renewing the world. Thus it is used with a regularly reappearing natural phenomenon such as the wind (Amos 4:13), for disasters sent by God (Isa. 45:7), for miracles in behalf of Israel (Exod. 34:10), especially for the return from captivity (Isa. 41:20 and Jer. 31:22), for the destruction of Korah, Dathan, and Abiram (Num. 16:30), for the renewal of the sinful human heart (Ps. 51:12), for the fruit of the lips, that is,

51

praising God with human lips (Isa. 57:19), and also for the new heaven and the new earth (Isa. 65:17). It should be noted that, as a rule, it is used with activities or events that are new or unusual. Furthermore, it is never combined with the fourth case of any material as is done with verbs such as "make," "form," and "manufacture." This would indicate that "creating" actually is more definitely an act of God. It is God giving existence to something that did not previously exist so that it is not formed from materials already at hand.

This concept of the word "create" is confirmed by the interesting circumstance that the act of creating is ascribed to the *Word* of God (Pss. 148:5; 33:9; Isa. 48:13; and in the New Testament, Rom. 4:17 and Heb. 11:3).

Thus it is determined that in the beginning creation was an act of God. The first words of Scripture purposely lift our hearts on high to God. In this way it becomes apparent from the outset that Holy Scripture, in its very nature, is the revelation of God. And first of all, the revelation of God as Creator. This is the first reality we must recognize and acknowledge, that God is Creator and that everything that exists, in all of its diversity and multiformity, with all of its power to amaze and enrapture us, exists only through an act of God which brought it into being.

Finally, verse 1 tells us that the object of God's creative work was "heaven and earth." In the Old Testament, and to some extent also in the New Testament, this is a definition of everything that exists. It has the same connotation as our word "universe," for which the Hebrew language did not have a specific word. To give an inclusive designation of everything that exists they would, as a rule, speak of "heaven and earth" (Gen. 14:19, 22; Exod. 31:17; 2 Kings 19:15; 1 Chron. 29:11; 2 Chron. 2:12; Pss. 115:15; 121:2; 124:8; 134:3; Jer. 23:24; 32:17; 51:48). In a few instances the word "sea" is added (Exod. 20:11; Neh. 9:6; Pss. 69:34; 146:6). In the New Testament we find it in this form in Matthew 24:35 and Ephesians 1:10.

It has been claimed that since the expression "heaven and earth" normally designates the present, organized world, this must also have been the case here. Genesis 1:1, it is argued, is a kind of heading and verse 2 then begins the actual creation narrative. This cannot be the case, however, because of the way verse 2 starts. The words "and the earth," which refer back to verse 1, clearly indicate that this is not the beginning of the creation narrative and therefore verse 1 cannot be considered to be a formal heading for what is to follow.

Since verse 1 is not just a heading, it is likewise true beyond doubt that "the heavens and the earth" do not there refer to the present, organized universe as it appeared after the creative work described in Genesis 1 was completed. How the universe became what it is today is described in detail in verses 3–31. "The heavens and the earth" in verse 1 are thus a designation of the essence of the world before the detailed forming and ordering, which is described in the rest of the chapter, took place.

We can conclude then that the term "the heavens and the earth" in verse 1 refers to the *substance* of the universe. We can also say it this way, that Genesis 1:1 describes the creation of the substance from which the entire universe was formed. We are fully aware that the text itself does not use that terminology. We are simply attempting to verbalize what the Word of God itself says in order that we may, to some extent, approach its meaning.

1:2 *Now the earth was formless and empty, darkness was over the surface of the deep, and the Spirit of God was hovering over the waters.*

In verse 2 we are given a more detailed description of one part of the whole, as it was brought into being by the creative act revealed in verse 1. This verse speaks only of the "earth," and the word "earth" is placed in a position of emphasis. Now with respect to the earth, it "was formless and empty, darknes was over the surface of the deep."

That the "earth" is given a place of emphasis here need not surprise us. This is where we human beings dwell, where we live, suffer, and die. Genesis 1:1 informs us that there is more in God's creation than only this earth. But the earth is more particularly our domain.

In explaining the words "formless and empty, darkness was over the servace of the deep" we must take note that three nouns are used. This is not without a reason. In Hebrew, as in other languages, the characteristics and qualities of an object can be expressed by using adjectives, and this is normal usage. It is also possible, however, to express these by the use of nouns, and then the effect is to strengthen the concepts that are being expressed. Thus, for example, in Psalm 23:5 we read, "My cup is 'abundance' or literally, 'a flood.'" This is stronger than "overflowing" or "flows over." It should be noted, however, that it is difficult to translate these nouns in Genesis 1:2 as nouns and still maintain a smooth reading of the verse. For this present study we will, however, treat them as nouns.

The first word so used to describe the condition of the earth as it first came from the Creator's hand is literally translated "emptiness." The word appears in other places in the Old Testament also. Sometimes it is translated "vanity" or "vain things" (1 Sam. 12:21; Isa. 40:17, 23; 59:4). In other passages it is used of "chaos" or a "trackless waste" (Job 12:24; Ps. 107:40). Obviously the basic idea of the word is a state of wildness because there is nothing there. Thus it depicts the loneliness and forsakenness of the barren desert. That this is correct is confirmed by the use of the word in Job 26:7, "He suspends the earth over nothing," and the first part of that verse, which correctly translated says, "He spreads out the northern sky over empty space." From this we can conclude that the meaning in Genesis 1:2 is that the earth was still devoid of all the countless living creatures which now occupy it in all of their colorful multiplicity. It was still one expanse of emptiness.

The second descriptive word is used in two other places in the Old Testament—Isaiah 34:11 and Jeremiah 4:23. Jeremiah 4:23 clearly refers back to Genesis 1:2. The prophet sees the earth brought back to its original condition. In verse 11 of this chapter mention is made of a judgment that would befall the land. The meaning seems to be that God would break down and destroy everything until only chaos remained. However, this translation could suggest that the earth had previously had a more ordered condition which had somehow been destroyed. This is certainly not the intent of Genesis 1:2. Therefore, the preferable translation is "formlessness." The meaning it conveys is that the earth still had not been given the ordered form it now has.

With respect to the third term, we must point out that we do not concur with the common idea that this forms a separate independent sentence and thus is to be translated "and darkness was over the deep." The following weighty reasons militate against this rendering. In the first place, in the Hebrew text the verb "was" appears only once. The logical reading then is that which joins "darkness over the deep" with that verb in the first part of the verse. In the second place, the usual reading suddenly introduces "the deep" as a separate entity, while there is no reference to the creation of such an entity in verse 1. The question that must be faced, then, is where this "deep" came from. We have therefore been led to consider the three noun forms, "emptiness," "formlessness," and "darkness over a deep," as all being dependent on the one verb "was." The three together constitute a composite description of the condition of the earth after the initial creative act of verse 1.

Just what is intended by the term "darkness over a deep" can be clarified as follows: Two things are conveyed by this statement: (1) That there was no light on the earth; (2) That the earth was not constituted as a firm body. This is confirmed by the next statement, which we will consider shortly, "The Spirit of God was hovering over the waters." It would be logical to assume that the term "waters" refers to the same substance as "the deep." This, then, confirms the idea that we must not think of the earth in its original state as being in a firm or solid condition.

It is doubtful, however, that we must think of the earth only as a water mass. The word "water," as it is used in Scripture, is not limited to designating the substance we usually think of as water—drinking water, rivers, and seas. It is used to designate anything that is in a fluid state. Thus the term "bread and water" may refer to any kind of food and any kind of drink. So too the term "poisoned water" in Jeremiah 8:14, et al., likely refers to the sap of a poisonous plant. When Joshua 7:5 says in symbolical language that "the hearts of the people melted and became like water," it means that the heart, which usually is considered to be a firm object, was turned into a fluid condition. In view of this, it is better to think of the earth in its original form, not as actually consisting of literal water, but rather as being of a fluid, unsolid consistency.

We now come to the statement "And the Spirit of God was hovering over the waters." The Hebrew words for "wind" and "spirit" are the same. An old Jewish exposition, therefore, describes this as God causing a wind or a movement of air. This interpretation has found adherents at various times in history. We do not accept this view, however, because "of God" has a far deeper implication than merely being caused by God. In the first two verses of Genesis everything that takes place is described as being effected by God. If all that was intended here was that God caused an air current it certainly would not be described as being an "air current of God." If this was intended to portray a new creation of God, it most certainly would have been expressed in a way similar to all the other creative acts of God as presented throughout this chapter. There is no mention here of a creative act of God or some new created object. There is mention only of a presence and a working of God, Himself. Thus there can be no real doubt that we must translate this "the Spirit of God."

Although most interpreters agree on this translation, there is no agreement as to what is to be understood by the term "the Spirit of God." Neither the text itself nor the immediate context can offer an answer to this question. This must be determined on the basis of the entire Scripture. Many interpreters object to making the Holy Spirit, as mentioned here, the Third Person of the Holy Trinity. This is, however, a consequence of their view of Scripture. They do not accept the unity and the authority of the Holy Scripture as the Word of God. For those who do accept this, there is no doubt that here, in the first verses of the Bible, there is a reference to the Holy Spirit.

We are told that this Spirit of God "hovered over the waters." Many believe that the word "hovered" should read "brooded," and then various other conclusions follow from this alternative reading. We believe, however, that there is no basis for translating the word as "brooded." The Hebrew word used here appears in two other places in the Old Testament.

In Jeremiah 23:9 it means to shake or to tremble. In Deuteronomy 32:11 it is used of a bird. This is claimed as a basis for the "brooding" translation. But when the word is used in Deuteronomy it refers to the action of a mother bird with regard to her young. The word "brooding" just does not fit once the eggs have been hatched and the mother is involved in training her young. Thus it is more likely that the word here refers to the mother bird watching over her young as they learn to fly. When they falter in flight she swoops beneath them and rescues them from falling. When all is considered the translation "hovered" still has the preference.

What then is the purpose of this hovering of the Spirit of God over the waters? It is obvious that it does not indicate a mere presence of the Holy Spirit. The purpose apparently is that an active power goes forth from the Spirit of God to the earth substance that has already been created. This activity has a direct relationship to God's creative work. Perhaps we can say that the Spirit preserves this created material and prepares it for the further creative activity of God by which the then disordered world would become a well-ordered whole, as the further creative acts unfold for our view in the rest of this chapter.

1:3 *And God said, "Let there be light," and there was light.*

The first special creative work of God, we are told, is the formation of light. "And God said, 'Let there be light,' and there was light." When mention is made, here and in the following verses, about God *speaking* in order to bring the organized world into being, this must be carefully understood. This does not mean that God merely made certain sounds and that as a result the desired thing came into being. The fact that in several instances this speaking of God is accompanied by an action on God's part (vv. 7, 16, 21, 25, 27) clearly indicates that we are dealing with a manifestation of divine power. In His speaking, God's effective will comes into expression. This speaking must then be understood as an anthropomorphic expression. This indicates that God's creative work was accomplished in such a way that it can best be described by our human concept of speaking. Just exactly how this creative work of God actually was accomplished we are not told. It is such an unfathomable demonstration of God's almighty power that it is far beyond our ability to comprehend its full reality.

Many questions have been asked about the nature of this *light* which God created in the beginning and how it was produced. The holy text gives no answers to these questions. We simply must reverently bow before this unfathomable act of the majesty of God since He has not disclosed this secret to us. It is enough for us to know that the first step in the process by which God brought order into the substance of the world was the formation of light. Unquestionably this points back to one of the elements that was ascribed to the earth in its original state, in verse 2, which was darkness. This is now changed by the creation of light.

1:4 *God saw that the light was good, and he separated the light from the darkness.*

"God saw that the light was good." Here also we have an expression that is anthropomorphic. This expression, just as the one that says God speaks, is repeated several times (vv. 10, 12, 18, 21, 25, 31). It is used to convey to us the fact that in each part of God's creative work there was a perfection which completely fulfilled God's will. As human beings we step back to examine something we have made to determine whether it meets our intended purpose. In the same way the almighty God ascertains that the results of His creative work fully conform to His plan and purpose.

We read further, "And he separated the light from the darkness." This teaches us that the formation of light did not mean that there was no more darkness. In verse 2 there was only darkness. Now a change has taken place. Light has penetrated the darkness and exists alongside darkness. They are distinguished from each other as two separate created factors which alternate. When there was light there was no darkness, and vice versa.

1:5 *God called the light "day" and the darkness he called "night." And there was evening, and there was morning – the first day.*

God gave names to "light" and "darkness." He called the light "day" and the darkness He called "night." In the Babylonian account of the origins of the world the naming of things was equivalent to calling them into being. Some have claimed that the Genesis account is simply a copy of the Babylonian record. That this is not the case is evident here since the light and the darkness already existed when God gave them their names.

Some have insisted that the naming of the created phenomena indicated no more than that God was supreme Ruler over all things He had created. We find this difficult to accept in the light of other instances in Scripture where God gave "names." God gave Abram the name of Abraham. This was done, we are told in Genesis 17, because God made Abraham what his new name implied, a "Father of many nations" (Gen. 17:5). The same was true of Sarah in Genesis 17:15. When the prophet Jeremiah, in the name of the Lord, had to give the name Magor-missabib, meaning "terror on every side," to Pashhur, this implied that God had made Pashhur just that, a terror both to himself and to everyone else (Jer. 20:3, 4). In the same way, when God named "night" and "day" this implied that God made the light day and He made the darkness night. By separating light from darkness God ordained day and night as alternating sequences of radiant light and a withholding of that light.

The next statement is, "and there was evening, and there was morning." The "evening" came when God withheld the beaming light He had created, and the darkness once again took over. The commencement of the beaming light was called "morning." Morning dawned with God's creation of light.

These two, evening and morning, establish the boundaries of "one day," as the Hebrew has it. Because more of such days follow, however, the best translation is "the first day." Now one day had been brought into existence by God's act of setting limits to the beaming light. "Evening" is mentioned first since it was not until the evening arrived that the light became day. This concurs well with the way the Jews customarily figured their calendar days. They started a new day at sunset. Consequently the order of evening and morning is maintained in the rest of the account also. It should be noted that in the rest of the days of creation, the morning which is mentioned does not follow the evening, but is the morning which precedes it. Referring to the parts of the day in this reverse order is not uncommon in the rest of the Old Testament either. The psalmist utters his complaint in Psalm 55:17, "evening, morning and noon," that is, all the day long.

There have been many attempts to measure the creation day which God first established in terms of our standard of measuring time. There are still those today who are convinced that the creation days were simply 24-hour days. This is certainly without any substantiation in Scripture. It is obvious that the creation day was limited by morning and evening, by the beginning and ending of the beaming light. Our 24-hour day includes the night and as such is a different concept in itself. But beyond that, when the first day (actually the first three days) was established, the standard by which we measure our days had not yet been created. The solar system by which we measure time was not created until the fourth day. In addition to all that, when we speak of the "days of creation" we are not talking about days in relationship to human beings because they had not yet been created. We are speaking rather about a day of God. It should be obvious that the standard by which we currently try to measure our days, namely the turning of the earth on its axis, in no way was a limiting standard for God the Creator of it all.

It will always remain an idle effort to measure the length of the creation days. It behooves us to humbly limit ourselves to the data given in the text of Scripture. All we can do, on that basis, is to accept the fact that God established the first day by setting limits to the beaming of the light He had created. How these limits were set and how long the interval was between these boundaries of the beginning and the ending of the beaming light, we are not told in Scripture. We should therefore not presume to say anything further about this.

1:6 *And God said, "Let there be an expanse between the waters to separate water from water."*

We now come to the second of the specific acts of creation by God, the forming of an "expanse." The Hebrew word that is used here comes from a verb form which means to strike or stamp. In this connection we could think of a firmly stamped-down floor, or, as in Job 37:18, of a molten mirror. However, the meaning of the verb form that is used does not lend itself to that translation. The stamping to which the word points refers only to stamping of the feet in vexation. The striking it could indicate refers to the working of metal, which by continual hammering is beaten out to something very thin to be used, for example, as a covering for a wooden image. This latter meaning suggests a basis for the use of this word for the expanse. It portrays something that is thin, that is stretched out in order to bind something else together. When we consult all the passages in the Old Testament where the word expanse appears there is not a single designation of something that looks like a massive dome as some have suggested. Even Job 37:18 does not intend to ascribe to the clouds (that is what is referred to) the firmness of actual metal. The old Israelites, who were far better acquainted with open nature than we are, could not have been unaware of the inner mobility of the clouds. The "molten mirror" could not possibly have been considered a suitable object for comparison with a closely-packed covering of clouds.

Just what, then, does the text tell us about the "expanse"? The first statement that draws our attention is that it appeared "between the waters." The water that is mentioned here is, of course, the same water referred to in verse 2. The expanse then, which is here effected by God's creative act, must be formed in that fluid mass which was the condition in which the earth was originally created. At the same time the purpose of the expanse is given in that it "separated water from water." It must have divided into two what had until now been one fluid mass. Just how this was accomplished is not mentioned. There is certainly no indication that the expanse must be considered as a firm substance in itself.

59

1:7 *So God made the expanse and separated the water under the expanse from the water above it. And it was so.*

In the seventh verse we are told about the actual carrying out, in the creative act, of what had been expressed in verse 6 as a creative word. God made the expanse and thereby effected a separation between two kinds of water. Thus what had been declared in verse 6 was accomplished. "And it was so."

Here we notice something further about the separation between the two waters. We are told that there was a separation of the water "under" the expanse and the water "above" the expanse. This is usually translated "under" and "above" the expanse. But in the original it literally says, "the lower side with respect to the expanse, and the upper side with respect to the expanse." This does not necessarily imply that part of the water was above the expanse itself but rather that part was at a lower level and part at a higher level, and the latter could have been at the level of (by or at) the expanse itself. That this can be considered a correct translation is clear from 2 Chronicles 26:19, where the same mode of expression is used. King Uzziah was struck with leprosy "by" the altar of incense.

1:8 *God called the expanse "sky." And there was evening, and there was morning —the second day.*

The question as to what we are to understand by the expanse, and, in this connection, what we are to understand by the two kinds of water, is answered in verse 8 where the expanse is called "sky." The word we have translated "sky" is the same word used in verse 1, but here it has a more limited meaning. There "the heavens and the earth" referred to the entire universe. Here the word "heaven" refers to that which meets our eye as we look up and therefore our word "sky" is more correct.

The water that is above "at" the expanse is, then, the water in the clouds and the atmosphere, from which the rain and snow come down. (Although this was not understood fully until later, it certainly was well known to the Jews when Genesis was written.) Many of the critics claim that this verse portrays an ancient legendary view that the sky was a vast dome made of some solid substance. This legend was, then, supposedly borrowed from the Babylonians. Such views find no basis in the text of Scripture. They are no more than arbitrary eisegesis of the sacred text. The Genesis account says nothing more than that God created the sky or its constituent elements. The creation narrative is completely and consistently silent on all such details. All it does is reveal to us that the sky that we daily see above us owes its existence to our Creator God.

The verse closes with the declaration that the creation of the sky concluded the second day: "And there was evening, and there was morning —the second day." After the beaming light of the first day was extinguished, the darkness of evening introduced the second day. Another morning dawned with a renewal of beaming light and it continued until evening darkness once again descended. Thus the second day of creation became a reality.

1:9 *And God said, "Let the water under the sky be gathered to one place, and let dry ground appear." And it was so.*

The third special work of creation was the separation of the water from the dry land. In verses 6–8 we are told that part of the waters (the fluid mass of which the earth consisted) were separated and took their place "above" to form the clouds and the sky. Now we learn of another separation by which fluid and solid materials are placed side by side. The earth was no longer to be a "deep," a water mass. The water under the expanse, or sky, now was brought together within designated boundaries which separated it from the dry land. This occurred just as God had planned and as He had proclaimed by His word of creative power.

1:10 *God called the dry ground "land," and the gathered waters he called "seas." And God saw that it was good.*

Thereupon we have another instance of "naming" (vv. 5, 8), as God "called" the dry ground "land," and the gathered waters "seas." The word we have translated "land" is the same as the word "earth" in verses 1 and 2. Here it has a different meaning, however. There it referred to the earth in its entirety. Here it refers to that part of the earth which is not covered with water, thus, dry land.

The word "sea" is used in the plural form in the text, "seas." This is the so-called extensive plural and includes the enormous area covered by the sea.

Again it should be noted how sober and simple the account of God's creative acts is. Not a single word is said about how this was all accomplished. The enormous transformation of the earth from a fluid mass to its present form of land and seas is reported without one detail of how this was brought about. All we have is the revelation that land and sea as we know them did not develop by themselves but that they were formed by the sovereign power of God.

And just as we heard in verse 4 about light, so we are told here, "And God saw that it was good." This anthropomorphic way of speaking reminds us that also this work of divine creation was perfect and completely fulfilled God's plan and purpose.

1:11 *Then God said, "Let the land produce vegetation: seed-bearing plants and trees on the land that bear fruit with seed in it, according to their various kinds." And it was so.*

Now that the dry land has been separated from the water, a new divine creative word is issued. God now calls forth all plant life to cover the earth with green things. This plant life is divided into two categories. This division, of course, is not intended to be a scientific classification and should not be evaluated as such. Plants are distinguished as "seed-bearing" and "fruit-bearing." The obvious distinction was whether the seed was inside a fruit or not.

Of special note here is the expression "according to their various kinds." It is extremely difficult to determine precisely what the Hebrew word "kinds" connotes. In the Old Testament it is applied only to living organisms and then usually to animal life. This is the only place it is used to denote plant life. If we examine the passages in which the word occurs, no clearly defined meaning of the word comes through. In verse 21 of this chapter it is used to distinguish such broad groups as water creatures and birds. In verses 24–25 it likewise applies to broad groups such as cattle and creeping things. In Genesis 6:20 and 7:14 it is used of birds, cattle, and creeping things, and in Ezekiel 47:10 of fish. Over against this, in Leviticus 11:13–19, and in Deuteronomy 14:12–18, the word is used to designate specific kinds of birds. In Leviticus 11:29–30 it refers to all kinds of lizards, while in Leviticus 11:22 only certain kinds of edible grasshoppers are designated. It is obvious, therefore, that there is no justification for concluding that the word indicates a certain definite classification that would meet the standards of botanists or biologists. These are not "species" as they are generally understood in these sciences. All that we can say is that the word "kind" indicates that, from the day of creation, an abundance of variety was displayed in the world of plants. This fact, that there was an abundance of variety in the plant life that came from the hand of the Creator, is a significant revelation.

1:12 *The land produced vegetation: plants bearing seed according to their kinds and trees bearing fruit with seed in it according to their kinds. And God saw that it was good.*

Whatever God's creative word commands happens. The earth produced vegetation, plants bearing seeds and trees bearing fruit, after their kind. It should be noted that it is expressly stated that the seed of each fruit tree accorded with the nature of that tree. This clearly indicates that from the beginning there was a great variety of plants.

When it is stated that the earth "produced" these plants, this does not mean that the power for this lay within the earth itself. It merely indicates that the divine will caused plants to sprout forth from the earth.

Once again, we are assured that God saw "that it was good" (cf. v. 4).

1:13 *And there was evening, and there was morning–the third day.*

Not until this point are we told that another day has ended. Again there was an evening after a new morning had dawned. This was the third day. It is worthy of note that the third day was distinguished by having two major special acts of creation by God. These were the forming of land and sea, and the creation of the plant world.

1:14, 15 *And God said, "Let there be lights in the expanse of the sky to separate the day from the night, and let them serve as signs to mark seasons and days and years, and let them be lights in the expanse of the sky to give light on the earth." And it was so.*

We now move on to the record of another new creative act of God. Before us now is the creation of the "lights in the expanse of the sky." The question we face immediately is whether the heavenly bodies now, for the first time, came into existence. The answer to this question seems to be rather obvious. In verse 1 we are told that God created "the heavens and the earth." Verse 2 then goes on to speak specifically about the earth, as distinguished from the heavens. It would be reasonable to conclude that "the heavens" mentioned in verse 1 included the heavenly bodies. We may then assume that the heavenly bodies already existed when the creative acts of verses 14 and 15 took place.

When God then says, "Let there be lights in the expanse of the sky," this implies that although these bodies did exist, as far as their substance was concerned, they were now established as "lights" to "give light on the earth." The emphasis here is placed on the *function* of certain heavenly bodies to give light on the earth. It is therefore also stated that they were to serve to divide day from night and to mark off seasons, days, and years. All of these functions are aspects of the role of these heavenly bodies as "lights" on the earth.

It is evident that here the separating of the day from the night stands in relationship to the function of the heavenly bodies. This is by no means the same as that which is expressed in verses 4 and 5. There it was the separation between the divine day of creation from the following night. Here it is the rotation of day and night here on earth. This confirms what we have already pointed out, that there is no justification for making those divine creation days equivalent to our earthly days. We are dealing with two different levels of existence and reality. Genesis 1 teaches us to maintain that distinction carefully.

Besides the reference to day and night mention is also made of "signs" and "seasons" and "days and years." There is little agreement regarding how these various functions must be related to each other. Some are of the opinion that "signs" must be taken as a general designation which includes the other two special functions. Then we would read, "signs both of seasons and of days and years." Others are convinced that the three concepts must be placed side by side. Then we would have "lights" serving as "signs," as "seasons," and as "days and years." Either of these interpretations is textually acceptable.

There is also considerable difference of opinion regarding the meaning of these three concepts. There are those who feel that "signs" refers to astrology. When we take into account, however, how strongly the entire Old Testament opposes all forms of fortune telling, this interpretation is questionable. We would do better to think of the use of the stars for determining geographic location and as navigational aids, especially for travel by sea.

The term that is translated "seasons" can also be read "times." The word probably does not refer to the calendar seasons, since that is more likely to be included in the concept of "days and years." Many think it refers to the Jewish feast days but this is also a doubtful interpretation. It is far more reasonable to think of these designations in a more general way as referring to seedtime and harvest time, which were, of course, determined by the heavenly bodies.

Finally, we come to the term "days and years." This definitely refers to the arrangement of the calendar, which is also dependent on the movement of the heavenly bodies. It is more than interesting that this presentation anticipates the appearance of the human person as a creature of God. This description of the "lights" in the heavens presupposes the presence of intelligent, human persons on the earth. The earth is being prepared to receive humanity as the crown of God's creative work.

We must pause briefly at this point to deal with the relationship between the "expanse" and the "heavens." The two words are used side by side in this verse. Critics have seized upon this and have charged that Genesis assumes that the heavenly bodies were located in the earth's atmosphere. Actually there is nothing in the text that even suggests this. This is another example of reading something into the text of Scripture for the purpose of trying to discredit the biblical narrative. As it stands, the expression is no more than an adaptation to our human perspective. When we look up we see the blue sky—the "expanse," But we also see the heavenly bodies and they appear to be located in that sky, and so we speak of the "stars in the sky." But this says nothing about precisely where these heavenly bodies are located, and what their relationship is to each other and to the earth. The text has no intention of specifying these factors. What the Word of God teaches us here is that myriads of "lights of heaven," as we see them in all of their grandeur against the vault of heaven and as they benefit us in countless ways, have been ordained and created by God.

After the creative word we read, "And it was so." As in verses 3 and 9, it happened just as God willed it and as He had declared by His word of power.

1:16 *God made two great lights—the greater light to govern the day and the lesser light to govern the night. He also made the stars.*

In this verse, as in verse 7, the statement is added that God "made" the objects described. It was so because God made it so. This word "made" is not in conflict with what we suggested in our interpretation of verses 14 and 15. We observed that the heavenly bodies were brought into existence when the "heavens" were created (v. 1). That this causes no conflict is obvious when we compare it with the creation of man. In verse 26 the verb "made" is used and in verse 27 we read that man was "created." Meanwhile, 2:7 tells us that man was "formed" out of an already existing substance.

In verses 14 and 15 the creation of the heavenly bodies is described only in general as "lights." Now, in verse 16 these lights are more specifically defined. First, mention is made of the two "great" lights. Here again we should point out that this is spoken from a human perspective. There is no attempt here to scientifically gauge the relative size of the heavenly bodies. These are the two lights which we see as great from our perspective. These two great lights are, then, further delineated as the "greater light to govern the day,'' the sun, and the ''lesser light to govern the night,'' the moon. That the latter is described as ''lesser'' undoubtedly refers to the fact that its light is less brilliant. Then the stars are also mentioned.

A word must be said about the use of the term ''to govern.'' There are interpreters who insist that this points to the pagan belief that the heavenly bodies are ''rulers'' or ''gods.'' This certainly is not the meaning here because the entire Old Testament strongly opposes worship of the heavenly bodies. If there had been any hint that this term would have been interpreted this way, another term would most certainly have been used. The term used here simply points out the period or time when each of the two bodies provide the light for the earth.

1:17, 18 *God set them in the expanse of the sky to give light on the earth, to govern the day and the night, and to separate light from darkness. And God saw that it was good.*

What follows relates closely to the creative act just mentioned. The created lights were set in their respective places and courses in the heavens by God's creative word. In other words, they did not acidentally fall into their designated positions. The whole system was effectively established by God with a view to controlling the orderly rotation of days and nights, years and seasons. Again, as in verse 4, we are told that God saw that it was good.

1:19 *And there was evening, and there was morning–the fourth day.*

This concludes another day of creation. Again it was evening after the morning, the fourth day. The manner in which this ''day'' is designated is exactly the same as that of the first three days. Although the measuring of time on the earth, as we know it, had now been established, this has no bearing on God's ''creation day'' as we discussed this in our treatment of verse 5. There is no indication that the creation days now underwent a radical change. We should consider all of God's creation days alike.

1:20 *And God said, ''Let the water teem with living creatures, and let birds fly above the earth across the expanse of the sky.''*

The next creative act pertains to the multitude of living creatures that live in the water, and to the birds that fly in the air. Once again we begin with the creative word of God, ''Let the water teem with living creatures.'' This is expressed in a general way, for the word includes all kinds of creatures that populate the waters. ''And let the birds fly above the earth across the expanse of the sky." Here also all of the varied winged creatures that move through the air are included. We should note again that the way of expressing this accords with the perspective from which we see it, namely, that the birds fly "against the sky." Regarding the relationship between "sky" and "heavens" see our interpretation of verses 14–15.

1:21 *So God created the great creatures of the sea and every living and moving thing with which the water teems, according to their kinds, and every winged bird according to its kind. And God saw that it was good.*

Following the divine creative word we again have the divine creative act. In this case, slightly more specific details are given than in previous instances. Side by side we are told about "the great creatures of the sea" and "every living and moving thing with which the water teems." The word we have translated "creatures of the sea" has various meanings in the Old Testament. In Exodus 7:9–12; Deuteronomy 32:33; and Psalm 91:13 it refers to a kind of serpent. In Jeremiah 51:34 it can be translated "dragon." In Ezekiel 29:3 and 32:2 the word probably means "crocodile." Here, as in Psalm 148:7 and Job 7:12, we must think of it in a more general sense as referring to all the enormous creatures that have their habitat in the sea. Some have translated it "whales," but that is too narrow. Included in the expression "living and moving things" which follows are then all the rest of the sea creatures—fish, crustaceans, etc.

No further classification is given for the birds. The only characteristic that is mentioned is that they were "winged."

With respect to both the sea creatures and the birds we are told that they were created "according to their kinds," and we have discussed this expression in connection with verse 11. Thus we see that also among the creatures of the sea and the birds there was great variety from the outset.

Finally, we are once again told that God saw "that it was good."

1:22 *God blessed them and said, "Be fruitful and increase in number and fill the water in the seas, and let the birds increase on the earth."*

God blessed the creatures of the seas and of the air which He had created and He said, "Be fruitful and increase in number and fill the waters in the seas, and let the birds increase on the earth." We should not understand this as though God was speaking directly to these creatures as such. It is rather that God pronounced His blessing over these creatures. This is equivalent to a creative word whereby He bestows fruitfulness upon them and enables them to multiply.

1:23 *And there was evening, and there was morning—the fifth day.*

With this another creation day comes to an end. Again, as before, evening arrives after the morning, this time of the fifth day.

1:24 *And God said, "Let the land produce living creatures according to their kinds: livestock, creatures that move along the ground, and wild animals, each according to its kind." And it was so.*

Now another creation act is announced. God calls forth the animals that live on the land. Again, we first hear the creative word. "Let the land produce living creatures according to their kinds." It goes without saying that we must not think of this as though the power to produce these creatures lay within the earth itself. (See v. 12.) The animals came forth from the earth by God's creative power. There is an indication here that the bodies of the animals were formed out of materials that were present in the earth. This is in agreement with the entire presentation in the creation narrative. The substance, the materials of heaven and earth, were created in the beginning. All the further creative acts in the six days of creation consisted of forming and organizing the world into its completed form out of the materials created at the outset.

For a discussion of "according to their kinds" see our interpretation of verse 11. Among land animals also there was a wealth of forms.

This variety is described in the text in just a few words. Three distinct groups are mentioned. As was the case with the world of plants, these groups must not be considered as scientific classifications. The first group mentioned consisted of cattle or livestock. This would include our familiar domestic animals. Second, we have creeping things or, as our translation has it, "creatures that move along the ground." Finally, there are the wild animals. These are the animals that roam in the wide open fields. It should be noted that the term "wild animals" is not a literal translation of the Hebrew, for the term "wild" does not appear in the Hebrew at all. The concept of carnivorous beasts of prey is not included here. The Hebrew term actually says, "those living on the earth." Throughout the Old Testament, however, the term is used to distinguish animals, many of them large, that live in the wilderness, from those that are domesticated. Thus the threefold distinction of the animal world does no more than describe the animals in accordance with the way the average person looks at these creatures. At the same time it is obvious that the intent is to include all the various kinds of land animals. Again, the expression "after their kinds"

68

does not denote biological species but only indicates that within each group there was great variety from the outset.

1:25 *God made the wild animals according to their kinds, the livestock according to their kinds, and all the creatures that move along the ground according to their kinds. And God saw that it was good.*

After the creative word we read, "And it was so." But, just as in verses 15–16, it immediately follows that God "made" what He had called forth. In other words, it was so because God effectively made it so. This act of creation is described in words that are in close accord with those God used in the creative word. Thus the three groups—cattle, creeping things, and animals—are mentioned, but now in a different sequence. In each case it is also mentioned that God made them "according to their kinds."

Again we read, "God saw that it was good" (see v. 4).

1:26 *Then God said, "Let us make man in our image, in our likeness, and let them rule over the fish of the sea and the birds of the air, over the livestock, over all the earth, and over all the creatures that move along the ground."*

Now we come to the last of God's special acts of creation—the creation of humanity. This is introduced by a report of the divine "taking counsel," which preceded this act of creation. We read, "Let us make man in our image, in our likeness." The fact that this introduction is found only here and not before any of the other acts of creation is an indication that a special significance is attached to the creation of humanity. Special attention is focused on this creative act.

For years there has been much discussion about how we must understand the plural in "Let *us* make man." Some scholars have interpreted this as a remaining vestige of an original polytheism. But this is certainly incorrect. The entire creation account is strongly monotheistic. This is recognized by all. It is unthinkable that such a vestige, if it did indeed exist, would not have been carefully removed when this could so easily be done. The fact that it was allowed to stand clearly indicates that some other meaning was definitely intended.

There are also other explanations that have been offered for the use of the plural "us" and "our." Because of the importance of these words for one of our cardinal biblical doctrines, it would be well to review some of these interpretations.

Some have argued that God took counsel with the angels. This must be rejected because nowhere else in the Bible is it suggested that man was created in the image of the angels. Others have suggested that this is the plural of majesty or honor. This is impossible because the Hebrew does not have such a use of the plural. There are a few references in Ezra where we may have a use of this kind of plural (Ezra 4:18; 7:24), but these are written in Aramaic and not in Hebrew.

Only slightly more likely is the view that the word "God" in Hebrew is itself a plural word, even when it is used in a singular sense, because it is modified by plural adjectives and used with plural verb forms. For that reason, it is argued, the plural form "us" is used here. In reply it must be said that this plural form of the word "God" is used only when people speak about God. This would not explain why God would use a plural form when speaking about Himself. Even more likely would be the interpretation that when a person talks to himself and, as it were, consults with himself, he would have a tendency to use the plural "us" and "we," as though he were dividing his personality. But even this explanation has a serious objection in that the Bible never uses the plural form when a person seemingly consults with himself. The only time this plural form is used is when it is God who is speaking. (See Gen. 11:7.)

In the light of all this, it would seem most acceptable to hold to the interpretation advanced by the ancient church fathers and universally accepted by scholars of the past, that this is a reference to the Triune God. It goes without saying that this passage, standing by itself, would not constitute a clear proof of the Trinity. There is, for instance, no mention of three here. But what is clearly indicated here is that God, in His unity, has a certain plurality. This can also be related to verse 2 where the Spirit of God is mentioned. Thus, the first chapter of the Bible already gives a significant signal which points to the mighty mystery of the Tri-unity of God which is more clearly revealed in the rest of the pages of the Book of books.

"Let us make man in our image, in our likeness." The special significance of the human person as created by God is revealed here in that this person is created in the image of God. Now there is considerable difference of opinion regarding the meaning of the prepositions "in" or "after" which are used here. The Hebrew uses two different prepositions. This interpreter is convinced that the preposition "in," which is used exclusively in verse 27, must be read in the light of the other preposition which can only mean "as" or "after." It would then not have the usual meaning of "in" or "through" or "with," but rather means, as is often the case, "in the quality of," or "in the manner of," or, to put it briefly, "as" or "after." This portrays the significant fact that the human person "is" God's image. When the preposition is translated with the meaning of "as," it serves to indicate essential and characteristic qualities. It expresses the fact that the person or matter referred to indeed is what "as" points to. For example, in Exodus 6:2 God says, "I appeared to Abraham, to Isaac and to Jacob *as* God Almighty." Any presentation which makes the human person only something to be compared with the image of God, or the image of God something outside of the person, according to which he was created, does not do justice to the text. That is why we read in the New Testament (1 Cor. 11:7) that man "*is* the image and glory of God."

Now we turn to the words "image" and "likeness." There is no apparent difference between these two terms. Thus in verse 27, where God's purpose to create man is announced, only the word "image" is used. In Genesis 5:1 where the creation of man is again referred to, we have only the word "likeness." We can, however, define these words more carefully. "Image" implies that there is the same similarity between the human person and the person of God as there is between a person and a picture of that person. The word "likeness" strengthens this by giving the impression that the resemblance is exact. This, however, does not exclude the fact that there is a profound difference between the infinite God, the Creator, and the finite human person, the creature of His hand. Here the emphasis falls on the similarity rather than the difference, in order that, from the outset, the high position of the human person may be clearly seen and, in consequence, the awfulness of the fall into sin and the misery that resulted from it may be the more sharply perceived.

From this high position, which the Creator gives to humanity by creating them in His own image, it follows that humanity is given dominion over the whole earth and over all living creatures, fish, birds, and land animals. It is rather striking that the "wild animals" are omitted here. Many interpreters say that since this word is included in the Syriac translation, it must have been erroneously lost from our versions. If this is true, it is hard to understand that the true reading has been nowhere preserved in the Hebrew text. It probably would be more reasonable to assume that the Syrian version has inserted the word in an effort to make this passage conform to the summary given in verses 24-25. What is declared here, in short, is that in subjection to God, humanity is given dominion over the works of His hands (Ps. 8:7-9).

1:27 *So God created man in his own image, in the image of God he created him; male and female he created them.*

After God takes counsel, the carrying out of that counsel is revealed. "So God created man in his own image, in the image of God he created him." It is worthy of note that here the singular form is used. The use of the plural in verse 26 expresses the reality that in His unity God also has plurality, and the use of the singular emphasizes that this plurality in no way detracts from God's unity.

A new element introduced in the execution of God's creative purpose is the distinction of the human sexes—"male and female he created them." These words are not the usual Hebrew words for "man" and "woman." The words seem to specifically designate the distinction of the sexes— male and female. In verse 22 we are told that God blessed the animals and made them fruitful. This implies that the two sexes were also created among the animals, but there it is not specifically mentioned. That this is specifically pointed out in the case of humanity must have a definite reason. This must be found in the fact that the distinction of the sexes in humanity was to develop into a completely unique relationship, namely, holy marriage. Thus we have here a preparation for the revelation of the beautiful mystery of marriage which will be given in chapter 2.

1:28 *God blessed them and said to them, "Be fruitful and increase in number; fill the earth and subdue it. Rule over the fish of the sea and the birds of the air and over every living creature that moves on the ground."*

By the creative word human beings were blessed and given fruitfulness and the ability to multiply. Even so, there is a difference between animals and people. The blessing is merely spoken over the animal world. In the case of humans it is addressed to them. In the latter case we specifically read, "And God . . . said to them." That is the first revelation of God to humanity.

This revelation also included the instruction about man's task and appointment to rule over the works of the Creator's hands (v. 26). There is a close connection here with the divine "taking counsel." Here again, there is mention of subduing the earth and having dominion over the animals. The animals are divided into three groups—fish, birds, and every living creature that moves on the ground. The term "livestock," which is used in verse 26, is omitted here. This indicates how precarious it would be to insert the term "wild animals" in verse 26. It is interesting that both the Syriac version and the Septuagint have inserted the word "livestock" here, after the "birds of the heavens." This insertion must be seen in the same light as the Syriac insertion in verse 26 and therefore should not be adopted.

1:29, 30 *Then God said, "I give you every seed-bearing plant on the face of the whole earth and every tree that has fruit with seed in it. They will be yours for food.*

And to all the beasts of the earth and all the birds of the air and all the creatures that move on the ground–everything that has the breath of life in it–I give every green plant for food." And it was so.

To this twofold revelation there is now added a third. This one deals specifically with how human and animal life was to be maintained. As far as human beings were concerned, their food was to consist of both types of plant life described in verses 11–12, herbs bearing seed and trees bearing fruit. Animals were to limit their food to the first type of plants, and they were assigned all green plants for food.

There are those who divide plant life into three groups in verses 11 and 12—grass, herbs, and trees. This presents difficulty in our present verse because then man would be allotted two groups of plants for food, and animals would be allotted the third group. Animals, however, also eat the herbs that are allotted to man. This suggests that limiting the division to two groups in verses 11–12 is more accurate.

It should be noted that in this passage the animals are arranged in three groups—wild animals, birds, and all the living creatures that move on the ground. The fish are not mentioned here since, from their very nature, they are not involved at this point. It is strange that "livestock" are omitted here also. It becomes abundantly clear from the various ways in which these summaries are arranged in verses 26, 28, and 30, that there is no attempt here at careful and complete classification, but only a general inclusion of all animal life.

Once again, regarding the provision of food for animals and human beings, it is declared that "it was so." It happened just as God willed it and ordained it. The fact that a change took place later, in that man was also permitted to eat meat (Gen. 9:3), does not alter the fact that the original provision was ordained by God as it is described in verses 29–30.

1:31 *God saw all that he had made, and it was very good. And there was evening, and there was morning–the sixth day.*

This concludes the series of God's special creation acts. It has been repeatedly said that "God saw that it was good." Now all of God's creative work is included when it is declared, "God saw all that he had made, and it was very good." The entire work of creation that had now been completed was perfect, fully conformed to God's will in every respect. Indeed, "it was very good."

Again we have the end of a creation day; evening followed the morning of that day and this concluded the sixth day.

2:1 *Thus the heavens and the earth were completed in all their vast array.*

"Thus the heavens and the earth were completed in all their vast array," or "and all their hosts." With these words our attention is called to the results of God's entire work of creation. The words "the heavens and the earth and all their hosts" include the entire organized world, the world in the condition in which we know it today. Undoubtedly, the text intends to turn our attention once again to Genesis 1:1. There we were told that in the beginning God created the heavens and the earth. But as is immediately evident from verse 2, this was not the world in its organized state as we know it today. At that point the world was still "formless," "darkness," and "empty." The results of the six days of God's creative work changed this completely. This change is expressed by the addition of the words "and all their hosts." In these hosts we are to include everything that made and makes the unorganized world of Genesis 1:1 into the organized world in which we live. In short, it includes everything that is in and on the world.

Genesis 2:1, then, portrays the result of God's entire creative work. It encompasses the initial creation of heaven and earth as far as their substance was concerned, and also the work of the six days. In this way, as is described in the entire first chapter, the present world was brought into existence by God's almighty will.

This expression in 2:1 also implies that the created world came into being as a fully developed whole, as a finished product. God's creative power did not merely produce a phenomenon with vast possibilities and potentials which, in turn, would develop in the course of eons of time. The world was finished, complete, a product of God's workmanship that was fully done.

This is also indicated by the fact that plants, in 1:11-12, were created as full-grown plants able to produce seed and fruit. In 1:20 we observe that the birds were created as adult creatures, able to fly from the outset. Man was also created in an adult state so that it was possible for God to communicate with him (1:28-30). Even the light beams which radiated from the heavenly bodies reached and illuminated the earth from the beginning (1:14-18).

At the same time it must be maintained that this does not imply that the created world had no potential for growth and development. This is clearly revealed by God's word of power by which He endowed man and the animals with the ability and the responsibility to be fruitful and multiply (22, 28). The created world was to move forward into history and God intended it to follow a definite course of growth and development. The unfolding of this process would be revealed in the rest of Scripture.

2:2 *By the seventh day God had finished the work he had been doing; so on the seventh day he rested from all his work.*

The first half of verse 2 presents a problem in interpretation. God's creative work was completed on the sixth day. It seems strange that we should now read (as is found in some translations) that the completion of that work came on the seventh day. In the Samaritan Pentateuch, in the Septuagint, and in the Syrian version this has been made to read "the sixth day" instead of "the seventh day." Many translators and interpreters have accepted this as the correct reading. We, however, consider this to be incorrect. It should be noted that if the original text had used "the sixth day" there would have been no problem and there would have been no conceivable reason for anyone to change this to the "seventh day." On the other hand, it would have been plausible for someone to change the word to "the sixth day," precisely to avoid the apparent difficulty that appears here. One interpreter has taken a radical approach and has decided to just scratch the first half of verse 2 since he considered it to be nothing more than a variant of the last half of the verse.

Others have tried, in various ways, to explain how it could be said that the work of creation was actually completed on the seventh day. Some have translated it "ceased creating." Others have used "rested from creating." Still others have suggested that on the seventh day God declared that His work of creation was complete. We believe that the simplest and most satisfactory answer is to read the verb form which is used here as a past perfect. This is permissible in Hebrew usage. It would then read, "God *had finished* the work of creation." In other words, the work had been completed by the last creative act on the sixth day. This reading satisfactorily resolves the difficulty.

Another question that must be faced is, "What kind of *day* was this seventh day?" Is this to be looked upon as a day similar to the six divine days on which God performed His work of creation? (See our interpretation of v. 5.) It would seem apparent to us that this divine day of rest was analogous to the six divine days in which God performed His work of creation. It would be difficult to conceive of this "seventh day" as an ordinary 24-hour day, as many claim, or as a day from sunup to sundown. This immediately raises the problem of whether God's rest continued for only one 24-hour day. Certainly, we must consider the possibility that this rest of God still continues. For us humans a day of rest is always followed by another series of work days. But this is not the case with God's creation days. With Him we have six days of creation and then one day of rest. But His day of rest is then not followed by more days of creation work. Our attention should also be called to the omission of any reference to "evening" and "morning" with respect to this day of rest. In the light of what has been said above, this is understandable. This seventh day began with a morning but it had no evening because it still continues.

The resting described here is, moreover, not to be understood as complete emptiness. The text makes it clear that this "rest" stands opposed to the work of creation only. God rested on the seventh day "from all the work He had done in creating." The entire passage concentrates on the work of creation and, therefore, other kinds of activity in which God was involved are not mentioned. Scripture makes it clear, for instance, that from moment to moment God sustains and governs that which He created. This we call God's providence. Continuing this work of providence certainly is not in conflict with the concept of God's "rest" on the seventh day. "Resting" simply says "not creating." There is, therefore, also no conflict between Genesis 2:2 and the words of Jesus in John 5:17, "My Father is always at his work to this very day, and I, too, am working."

2:3 *And God blessed the seventh day and made it holy, because on it he rested from all the work of creating that he had done.*

At this point a statement is inserted about the human day of rest. In the fourth commandment the motivation for observing the Sabbath Day is closely related to the creation of the world in six days and God resting on the seventh day. So also here, it is declared that God's "blessed and hallowed the seventh day" for us as human beings, because He rested from His work of creation on the seventh day.

This statement, "God blessed the seventh day and hallowed it," obviously refers to the *human* day of rest in distinction from the *divine* day of rest. "Blessing and hallowing" are activities that fall within the realm of human experience. Thus God makes this weekly day of rest a day of sacredness and blessing for humanity. He sets this day apart from the regular, everyday routine in order to give it a special purpose. It is this purpose that gives this day its holy character because it promotes a special relationship to God and to His service.

Some have raised the objection that if the seventh day in verse 3 refers to the human week, the seventh day in verse 2 should not be defined as a divine day. They argue that then the seventh day in verse 2 should also be counted as part of the human week. To this we reply that the use of the same word does not, in every case, imply that the meaning is the same. Thus, for example, the word "heavens" in 1:8 obviously does not mean the same as the word "heavens" in 1:1. The word "earth" in 1:10 has a different connotation than the same word in 1:1-2. In each case the context in which the word appears determines its meaning. When the context clearly indicates that the word is used in a different sense this must be honestly recognized and accepted. Thus, in our present passage it is unmistakably clear that in verse 2 the text is speaking about God's day of rest, while in verse 3 the same word refers to the human day of rest. The two concepts are as far apart as an infinite God is exalted above a finite human being. The connection between the two is identical to that which is manifest in the fourth commandment. Because God, on His seventh day, rested from His work of creation, He ordains for mankind our seventh day as a blessed and holy day. It should be noted that there is no mention here of its being a day of *rest* for mankind, although this concept of a weekly day of rest is clearly in the background. It should be remembered that the inspired writer is dealing with a concept that was familiar to his readers. There was, therefore, no need for him to stress the importance of a day of rest since this was part of the entire structure of their life. All he does here, under the guidance of the Holy Spirit, is to relate this blessed institution to creation.

Before we conclude this section we should say a word about the "creation narratives" that have appeared among many other ancient peoples. These actually should not be called "creation" narratives because these tales about the origin of the world are poles distant from the account of creation which is given in Holy Scripture. Even so, it cannot be denied that certain similarities can be observed between these other accounts and the biblical narrative.

Offering a satisfactory explanation for these similarities has caused much discussion and has provoked many different theories. Basically, the presence of traditions and legends about the origin of the world among most ancient peoples is not at all surprising. It must be assumed that from the beginning God gave man a basic revelation about the origin of the world. The memory of this original revelation, in spite of the astounding distortions which obviously corrupted it, was preserved to some extent among all peoples.

Many are of the opinion that the similarities that have been discovered indicate that these other accounts had a marked influence on the biblical narrative of creation. The account that is usually singled out is the Babylonian record of the creation of the world. Later the Egyptian account was also considered to have exerted a strong influence on the biblical account.

It is of considerable importance that the points of similarity upon which these conclusions have been based be carefully examined. Whether the facts actually warrant the conclusions that have been drawn must be thoroughly reviewed. We do not, however, intend to pursue this detailed study in this volume. I have devoted an exhaustive study to this in my work, *De Goddelijke Openbaring in de Eerste Drie Hoofdstukken van Genesis*. Those who are interested in such a detailed study should consult this work or a similar source. Suffice it to say here that, on the basis of this detailed, exhaustive study, I have firmly established that there is no substantial, objective ground for ascribing either a Babylonian or an Egyptian influence to the biblical narrative.

Another matter, no less important, is the relationship of the biblical narrative to the positions which "natural science" (we use this designation in its broadest sense) has advanced. It is not a question of whether the theories advanced by natural science can be harmonized with biblical data or not. It is rather a question of whether there are any incontestible "scientific" facts which present serious difficulties to the believer's conscience when they are placed side by side with the revelation of Holy Scripture. Once again, we are going to omit from this volume a broader discussion of this whole area of research. We would again refer the reader to the book mentioned above and similar studies undertaken by reputable biblical scholars. Let it be said here, in summary only, that no substantial or demonstrable facts have been adduced that should disturb our faith in the truth of the biblical narrative, provided, of course, that the biblical text is faithfully and properly interpreted.

2. *Paradise and the Fall Into Sin* (2:4–3:24)

The revelation about the creation of the world is followed by a description of the history of that created world. The first scene portrayed in that history is Paradise and the events associated with it, primarily the Fall into sin.

Many interpreters are of the opinion that this section, especially 2:4b–3:24 (2:4a is then included with the preceding section), must be seen as a second creation narrative. This is then ascribed to a different writer. It is also generally assumed that this second narrative is considerably older than the first. Those who hold to the source-splitting theory ascribe the first narrative to the Priestly Codex (P) which is dated at about the fifth century B.C. The second narrative is ascribed to the Jahwist source (J), which is dated in the ninth century B.C., and thus is supposedly five centuries older.

Our basic objections to the theory of source splitting have been discussed at length in our Introduction to the Pentateuch. We now want to make some observations more specifically about the application of that theory to the creation narrative.

In the first place, it is certainly incorrect to call Genesis 2:4b-3:24 a second creation narrative. The contents of this section clearly belie such a designation. It is granted that chapter 2 includes a few matters that relate to creation, and that the creation of woman is given a broader treatment than it received in chapter 1. Even so, it cannot be denied that the major purpose of chapter 2 is to prepare the way for what is revealed in chapter 3, namely, the Fall into sin. This explains the contents of chapter 2. This explains the extensive description of the Garden of Eden (vv. 4-18), in which the persons who were created by God were placed. This also explains why the commandment, which was transgressed in chapter 3, is spelled out in the words of God (vv. 16-17). This even explains the detailed account of the creation of woman (vv. 18-24), since she was destined to play such a significant role in the tragic event of the Fall. It also explains the contents of verse 25 since this prepares the reader for what is recorded in 3:7-11.

It should also be noted that the heading given in 2:4a indicates that we are not dealing with a repetition of the creation narrative. It serves, rather, to introduce the history of that created world. It is true that 2:4a has commonly been considered as a conclusion to 1:1-2:3, rather than a heading for 2:4b-3:24. However, the Hebrew pronoun "this," which is used here, normally refers to something that is to follow. For this reason 2:4a can more correctly be considered to point ahead rather than to point back to what preceded.

Some have suggested that, although this is a heading, it is actually a heading for 1:1-2:3. They have then arbitrarily moved this statement and placed it before 1:1. There is no basis for such a maneuver except, perhaps, to support a preconceived notion that this statement cannot be considered to be the heading for 2:4b-3:24. Even the word "history," which is used, makes it obvious that this cannot be tied to 1:1-2:3. "History" cannot be used to describe the origin and the formation of the world. Wherever it appears in the Old Testament it has the meaning of something that comes forth from, as in our word *generation* or *descendants*. It then receives the broader meaning of what happens to these descendants, and thus it denotes their "history." This is what it obviously means here also. It announces what now happened to this world which was created by God (and did not originate some other way) and as such, the history of that created world.

In the second place, the evidences that are used to support ascribing the creation narrative (1:1-2:3) and the first chapter in the history of the created world (2:4-3:24) to two different authors are wholly unconvincing. The argument based on form in distinction from the material emphasizes that in the first section the name "God" is used exclusively, while in the

79

second section the name "the Lord God" is used with considerable regularity, although not exclusively.

In the Introduction to this volume, we observed that the use of the names of God plays a vital role in the whole process of splitting sources. We would then also refer our readers to the Introduction for our refutation of this argument, but we do want to add one comment here, and that with some emphasis.

It is in this section, 2:4–3:24, that the combined name "the Lord God" (Jahweh Elohim) appears exclusively. Consequently, if the source splitters were consistent with their own presuppositions, they should ascribe this section to a completely distinctive source. But none of the scholars of this school has ever ventured to support such a thesis. In other words, they shrink from their own theory precisely with this passage. How then can they expect others to ascribe any merit to their theory?

It has usually been held by the critics that the names "God" and "Lord" have been combined by adding the name "God" to the original name "Lord." But there is just as much basis for assuming that the opposite is true and that the original name was "God" and that this was later supplemented by the name "Lord." If this assumption is correct, and we believe it is, then Genesis 2:4–3:24 uses the same name "God," which was used in 1:1–2:3, and as a result the whole argument based on the use of the different names of God is a fantasy.

The other arguments which are based on a few differences in choices of words and expressions are even less significant. They will not be treated here, but readers who are interested in pursuing these matters further are again referred to the author's book on the first chapters of Genesis, which treats these matters in detail.

Moving now to the material argument, its main contention is that Genesis 2:4–3:24 gives a presentation of creation that is essentially different from that given in Genesis 1:1–2:3. The former account, it is argued, gives the order of creation as first plants, then animals, and finally humanity. The latter account, it is claimed, gives a different order with man first, then plants, then animals, and finally woman. Now it is true that Genesis 2:9 refers to the formation of various kinds of plants after the creation of human beings. But when we consult the context, it immediately becomes clear that 2:9 is not referring to the formation of plants in general, but only to the plants which were used to adorn the Garden of Eden (v. 8). And if our interpretation of verse 6 is correct (see below), the creation of plants is mentioned before the creation of man here, just as it was in chapter 1. As far as the creation of the animal world is concerned, the whole question of when this took place depends on how 2:19 is translated. It is possible to translate it either as "when the LORD God had formed" or as "then the LORD God formed." The Hebrew permits either translation. How it must be translated in this specific instance depends entirely on the context. Maybe we should say that it depends on what presupposition we make before we approach the text. Our translation will be determined by whether we consider Genesis 1:1–2:3 and Genesis 2:4–3:24 to be in agreement with each other or in conflict with each other. There is then no substance to the claim that the latter passage clearly presents a different order of creation and therefore disagrees with chapter 1.

Let us assume for a moment that we accept the theory of source splitting and then assume also that two creation narratives, which originally gave conflicting accounts of the order of creation, were combined by a later redactor. This redactor certainly would have spared no effort to make these two accounts agree. In order to accomplish this harmony of the two accounts, he certainly must have intended to say in 2:19, "when the LORD God *had* formed." Thus, even assuming the validity of the source-splitting theory, the translation of 2:19 we have adopted must be considered the more acceptable one. As a result the alleged conflict with chapter 1 is a fantasy.

There have also been repeated attempts to split Genesis 2:4–3:24 into two or three different sections, which originally, supposedly, existed independently. Then, it is claimed, a later hand brought them together to form our present text. These efforts depend entirely on subjective insights with no substantial evidence and as such we will not discuss them further here.

The account of Paradise and the Fall, just as was the case in the account of creation, bears the character of a historical message. There is no basis for considering this to be a symbolic presentation or an allegory, as some have tried to do. This historical message is distinguished from that of creation as follows: While the event of creation primarily occurred outside the realm of human experience, Paradise and the Fall were events in which humanity was personally involved. Even so, we are not dealing in this document with a mere human composition (be that purified by divine inspiration). But, as in all of the ensuing history of the created world of which we here receive the first episode, we are dealing with a revelation given by God.

2:4a *This is the account of the heavens and the earth when they were created.*

We begin our exposition, then, with the heading that designates what will follow. It must be seen that this heading points beyond the immediate pericope in which Paradise and the Fall are treated. The history of the heavens and the earth extends far beyond the events in Paradise, also in Genesis. This heading actually makes an incision which divides Genesis 1:1–2:3, the creation narrative, and everything that follows as the history of the created world. But this history also has definite turning points and demarcations which set designated events or epochs apart from the rest of the narrative. (See, for example, Gen. 6:9; 11:10, 27; 25:19.) The phrase, ''When they were created,'' indicates that the history of the world commenced at the moment creation became an accomplished fact.

2:4b, 5 *When the LORD God made the earth and the heavens, no shrub of the field had yet appeared on the earth and no plant of the field had yet sprung up; the LORD God had not sent rain on the earth and there was no man to work the ground.*

The second half of verse 4, as well as the succeeding verses, raises the question of how the connection between the various sections was established. Interpreters are by no means agreed on this.

First of all, it must be determined whether the last half of verse 4 is a parallel phrase, offering further information about 4a, ''when they were created.'' If this is the case, verse 5 begins an entirely new independent sentence. It should then be translated something like this, ''Now there was as yet no shrub of the field on the earth, and as yet there was no plant of the field, because the LORD God had not sent rain on the earth,'' etc. We believe, however, that this reading must be rejected. In the Hebrew, verse 5 begins with a conjunction that can be translated ''now.'' But this is badly misplaced if we take verse 4 in its entirety as a heading, and start the actual history with verse 5.

If the actual starting point of the history is 4b, we face another problem, for 4b is a subordinate clause which designates time and it must modify a main clause which follows. Just where do we find this main clause to which the time factor in 4b refers? Some have argued that this follows immediately in verse 5. Others place it in verse 7. The former designation can hardly be correct because we would then have the translation, ''At the time that the LORD God made the heavens and the earth, there was as yet no shrub on the earth nor did any plant sprout on the earth, because the LORD God had not sent rain on the earth and there was no man to work the ground, but a 'mist' came up from the earth to water the whole surface of the ground.'' What we are then saying is that when the creation was established there were no plants. We would be inclined to say, naturally, when the earth was created there were no plants. But this becomes critical when we add that there were no plants because it had not rained and because there was no person to work the ground. In other words, we are saying that before the earth was created there were no plants because there was no rain and no one to till the ground. To avoid this impossible reading, we are compelled to relate this time factor to what is stated in verse 7.

This, in turn, raises another problem. How then must verses 5 and 6 be related to their context? The usual interpretation says that they are simply a parenthesis—the two verses taken together. But this presents other difficulties because it would make both verses 5 and 6 negative statements.

It is our conviction that only verse 6 must be considered as a parenthesis and this is also the way we have translated the passage. What we are saying then is, "at the time of creation," when the following conditions prevailed —including 4b and 5—then verse 6 is a parenthesis and verse 7 goes on with the actual event.

If it should be asked why there is such a strong emphasis here on plant life, this can be explained by the fact that the first episode takes place in Paradise and the outstanding characteristic of the garden was its prolific and varied plant life.

Verse 5 distinguishes two kinds of plant life, which we have designated as "shrubs" and "plants." The distinction seems to be between more wooden plants that continue from year to year and the green plants that spring up anew each year. This is confirmed by what is said about each of them. The shrubs are characterized as "being on the earth," while the green plants are those which "spring up." Of special note is what is said about the latter group, that they spring up as the consequence of two factors, the rain and the tilling of the ground by man. Here we have a further distinction between the wild plants that spring up naturally out of the Palestinian soil after the rains, and those plants that need the sowing and tending of human hands. Thus we are reminded here that all of these varieties of plants were created by God. They were made by Him *before* that process, which now is regularly observed, became a reality. The process is that there are plants that are stable and continue from year to year, and those which annually spring up anew, either as the result of the rains or of being sown by the hand of man. This is why we prefer the translation "before" rather than "not yet."

We must add a few words about the use of the name "The LORD God." The name "God" is used exclusively in Genesis 1:1–2:3. To this is now joined the proper name "The LORD," in Hebrew *Jahweh*. We recognize some difficulty in designating the use of this proper name of God adequately in English translation. Some translations simply use the transliterated name *Jahweh*. There is also the danger that the word might be looked upon as an attribute of God rather than His proper name. Further attention will be given to this name later in this series of commentaries. At this point we want to emphasize the fact that the word designates one of the names which reveals the very essence of God, and this must always be borne in mind. Later this name became very significant as God revealed Himself to His people as their God in a special redemptive relationship. Why it is suddenly introduced here remains an open question to which no ready answer has been given. As we have already observed, the reasoning of the source splitters regarding this question offers no help either.

2:6 *But streams came up from the earth and watered the whole surface of the ground.*

As we have already pointed out, we consider verse 6 to be a parenthesis. Here we are informed that moisture came up to water the earth. There are various translations of this and there is considerable difference of opinion as to the exact meaning of the word ''moisture.'' Some translators have chosen the word ''streams.'' Others have used the word ''mist.'' Whatever form it may take, the text indicates that this moisture came up from the earth rather than having descended from the sky.

The reference evidently describes a phenomenon which relates to the newly created plant life. A specific detail not recorded in chapter 1 is added here, namely, that God provided for the watering of the first plants that were created. The way this is inserted indicates that plants were created before the creation of man, and this is also in harmony with chapter 1.

2:7 *And the LORD God formed man from the dust of the ground and breathed into his nostrils the breath of life, and man became a living being.*

Now, finally, comes the statement referred to in 4b. This is really the focal point of this passage, namely, the creation of man. It is described as follows, ''And the LORD God formed man from the dust of the ground.'' There are those who have stressed the fact that here the word ''formed'' is used. This is the same word that is used of the workmanship of the potter. It is then argued that the formation of man was like the modeling of a clay doll, precisely as it is presented by the Babylonian and Egyptian accounts.

In reply to this it should be observed that this word ''formed'' has a broader, more common meaning than merely to describe the work of the potter. Examples of this broader use of the word can be found in Isaiah 43:1; 44:2; 45:7, 18.

It should be noted, further, that the Hebrew expression does not specifically state that man was formed *out of* the dust of the ground. In the Hebrew the word translated ''dust'' does not mean clay or earth. It rather means any given material or substance broken down to its basic elements or parts. Thus in Leviticus 14:41 it refers to the scrapings from the stones of a house; in Deuteronomy 9:21 to the grindings of the golden calf when it was destroyed; in 2 Kings 23:12 to the broken pieces of the altars of idols that were broken to pieces. In general it also refers to the substance of the earth (Gen. 3:14; Josh. 7:6; Job 2:12; 7:21; 21:26; Pss. 7:5; 22:15; Isa. 65:25; Lam. 2:10; Ezek. 27:30; Dan. 12:2; Mic. 7:17). In view of this it is definitely not necessary to hold that, on the basis of this passage, man was formed out of dust or clay into some kind of clay doll. It is far more likely that these words must be understood in such a way that the body of man is entirely built up of basic substances similar to those found in the earth.

To this is added, "and breathed into his nostrils the breath of life." Naturally, the first question here is what are we to understand by the term "the breath of life"? By studying the use of the word "breath" in the Old Testament, we discover that the word is used, first of all, to describe the audible or visible effects of breathing. (See Dan. 10:17.) Further, the word is used in a broader sense to indicate *life*. It is used to indicate human life in Genesis 7:22; Deuteronomy 20:16; Joshua 10:40; 11:11, 14; 1 Kings 15:29; 17:17; Job 27:3; Psalm 150:6; Isaiah 42:5; 57:16. In Genesis 7:22 it is used of animal life. It is clear then that the translation "breath of life" is well within the scope of the use of the word elsewhere in the Old Testament. God gave to man breath and thereby gave him life.

Another question that is raised concerns the manner in which this happened—"breathed into his nostrils." We would do well not to take this expression too literally, as though God physically breathed into the nostrils of a lifeless body. "Nostrils" are mentioned because these are the passages through which breath normally passes. What we are told here is that the human being received life-breath by a direct act of God's creative power.

"And man became a living being." The word which our translation has rendered "being" has traditionally been translated "soul." Thereupon all kinds of deductions have been drawn from this reading. The word, however, does not mean *soul* as we usually understand that term. It is better, therefore, to avoid the use of this term altogether. Here it is combined with "living"—"living being"—and in this form it appears various times in the Old Testament. In most instances it refers to animals (Gen. 1:20, 21, 24; 2:19; 9:10, 12, 15; Lev. 11:10, 46; Ezek. 47:9). In Genesis 9:16 it is used of human beings and animals together. This does not mean, of course, that human life is placed on a level with animal life. Precisely because the giving of life to human beings is specifically described as the result of a special work of God's creative power, in distinction from the creation of all other forms of life, clearly indicates that human life stands on a far higher

85

level than animal life and all other forms of life. When this is related to Genesis 1:26–27, where we are told that man was created "in the image and likeness of God," we receive a clear picture of the uniqueness of human life as created by God.

Although it is hardly justifiable to develop carefully defined concepts regarding the constitutional nature of man exclusively on the basis of this passage, Christian theology has generally found a basis here for the two-sided nature of human beings. We are told with considerable clarity that man is related to the physical world by virtue of his formation from the substance of the earth. At the same time it is clear that man is related to the non-physical world. There is something about human life which distinguishes it from animal life and all other forms of life. This distinguishing factor has its source directly and immediately from God. Thus man is the image and likeness of God. Even though these terms are not used here in chapter 2, we can properly speak of human beings as being both physical and spiritual, or, more simply, as being body and soul.

2:8 *Now the LORD God had planted a garden in the east, in Eden; and there he put the man he had formed.*

From the creation of mankind, which is given the most prominent place in the creation narrative, we now move to a description of the stage on which man makes his first appearance. God Himself prepared a garden for man. It is customary to refer to this "garden" as Paradise, but this word does not appear in this entire pericope. The term Paradise is actually of Persian origin and simply means "garden." It is used in a few places in the Old Testament (Neh. 2:8; Eccl. 2:5; Song of Sol. 4:13). In these instances, however, it does not refer to the garden described in Genesis 2 and 3. The word Paradise is first used to describe this garden in the Septuagint translation and its general usage has been taken from that.

God planted this garden in Eden. It is obvious that Eden was the name of the country where the garden was located. It is, therefore, improper to refer to the garden itself by the name "Eden." Just where the land of Eden was located remains completely unknown. It has been assumed that it can be located on the west bank of the lower Euphrates and this would place it in the area of the familiar Ur of the Chaldees. But this is purely a matter of conjecture.

We are told, further, that it was "in the east." This is the only designation of the location of Eden that we are given. There have been attempts to make something mystical out of this by suggesting that it relates to the Babylonian belief that the "dwelling of life" lay in the east. All the expression actually says is that for the writer of the Pentateuch Eden lay in an easterly direction. This is, at best, a very vague designation.

2:9 *And the LORD God made all kinds of trees grow out of the ground—trees that were pleasing to the eye and good for food. In the middle of the garden were the tree of life and the tree of the knowledge of good and evil.*

We are told also that the Lord God adorned the garden with all kinds of trees that were pleasing to the sight and exceptionally good for food. Among these trees two were singled out for special attention and given names. There was ''the tree of life'' and ''the tree of the knowledge of good and evil.'' These were located in the middle of the garden. Since the word order of this sentence is a bit unusual, some have concluded that the text has been altered. It is claimed that originally there was only one tree singled out and that the reference to the second tree was added later. Among those who hold this view there are again differing opinions as to which was the original reference and which was added later. Based merely on the word order, there is, however, no justification for this position. There are other examples in the Old Testament of a similar word order. Although this word order may appear strange to us, it obviously was acceptable Hebrew usage. To give one example, Genesis 12:17 reads, ''the LORD inflicted serious diseases on Pharaoh and his household.'' Other examples of the same usage are listed in the author's book, *De Goddelijke Openbaring in de Eerste Drie Hoofdstukken van Genesis.*

Some have argued that it is impossible for two trees to be located in the middle of the garden. This is a rather childish argument since the passage certainly does not pretend to deal with such facts with geometric precision.

The names given to these two trees are of considerable importance. In each case the word ''tree'' is placed in conjunction with an abstract concept—''Life'' and ''knowledge.'' This, of course, does not imply that we should not think of actual trees since similar expressions are common in Scripture. Note, ''the ark of the covenant,'' ''the rock of strength,'' ''the blood of atonement,'' etc. Besides, it is specifically stated that God caused these trees to grow ''out of the ground'' with all the other trees in the garden.

''The tree of life'' is mentioned first. In keeping with Hebrew usage, the word ''life'' appears in a plural form. This is called the plural of abstraction. Moreover, it is accompanied by the definite article ''the,'' which indicates that this tree relates to this specific concept of ''life.''

It is obvious that the term reveals that this tree was intended to serve a special function related to the maintenance of life. But this is not the whole story. The other trees in the garden also were good for food and thus also served to maintain life. When this one tree is singled out as ''the tree of life'' it is obvious that this tree served a unique function, above all others, in providing and maintaining life. This is further confirmed by 3:22, where the tree of life is related to *eternal* life.

The second tree is called ''the tree of the knowledge of good and evil.'' Here it must be observed that the definite article is placed with ''knowledge'' but is not used with ''good and evil.'' This can be easily explained by pointing out that these latter concepts are used in a general sense. No specific kind of good and evil is intended but good and evil in general. The use of the definite article with ''knowledge'' presents some difficulty, but the apparent intent is that the entire expression, ''the knowledge of good and evil,'' must be taken as a unit and placed parallel to ''the life,'' which also has the definite article. Thus it refers to the whole realm of knowledge of good and evil.

To understand the purport of this expression we must consult other passages in the Old Testament where the verb ''to know'' or synonyms of it are used in conjunction with the concepts of ''good'' and ''evil.'' Such references can be found in Deuteronomy 1:39; 2 Samuel 14:17; 19:35; 1 Kings 3:9; Isaiah 7:15–16. In these passages it is evident that the idea of knowing involves having the ability to distinguish or discriminate (see especially Isa. 7:15–16).

With respect to good and evil it should be noted that these terms are not always narrowly restricted in their meaning. In 2 Samuel 14:17 and 1 Kings 3:9 they are practically the same as justice and injustice. In other passages, however, the meaning is much broader. The terms evidently indicate that which is morally good or evil, but they are also used to designate what is beneficial and harmful, worthy and unworthy, attractive and unattractive. Thus, just as the tree of life is related in a special sense to the possession of life, so also the tree of the knowledge of good and evil is related in a special sense to the ability to discriminate between good and evil.

But this is not the whole story either. We certainly cannot conclude that human beings in their paradise state were devoid of all knowledge of good and evil. In 2:15 we are told that man was commanded to ''take care of'' the Garden. This certainly required a certain ability to discriminate between what was good and evil, beneficial or harmful. We must therefore think of a specific kind of discrimination between good and evil as it relates to this tree. Just what that specific sense of the term was will become clear when we treat 2:16–17, where we will consider God's specific command not to eat of this tree.

2:10 *A river watering the garden flowed from Eden, and from there it divided; it had four headstreams.*

In addition to what has already been said about the Garden, a more detailed geographic description is now provided. This encompasses verses 10–14. Although much effort has been spent on interpreting this passage, most of the results have been less than acceptable.

First of all, we note that a great river found its source in the land of Eden, where the Garden was located. This served to water the Garden. This river, in turn, divided into four streams. There are those who insist that this division into four streams occurred before the river reached the Garden and that it was these four streams that irrigated the Garden.[1] We are confident, however, that the word we have translated "from there" modifies the word "garden" and that consequently the divison was located at a point after the river had passed through the Garden.

The four side streams are now identified. It is not the intent of the passage to indicate that the names given to these four streams, the countries through which they passed, and the products which these countries produced, were identified as such at the time of the Paradise event. These are, rather, names and identifications that were common at the time when the writer of this book prepared his record. They are mentioned here only to indicate that these four streams had their source from that one great river that flowed through Paradise.

2:11, 12 *The name of the first is the Pishon; it winds through the entire land of Havilah, where there is gold. (The gold of that land is good; aromatic resin and onyx are also there.)*

The name of the first river was "Pishon." Although no river by that name is known today, the details that are given about it do give some help in determining which river is referred to. We are told that the river flowed through the land of Havilah, where there was gold. In seeking to locate the land of Havilah we note that this name appears in other passages (Gen. 10:7 and 1 Chron. 1:9). There, however, it is used as the name of one of the sons of Cush. These names are not primarily the names of persons but of peoples who lived in specified areas. Then in Genesis 10:29 and in 1 Chronicles 1:23 the name Havilah is given to one of the sons of Joktan. This also designated a people or a country. Further, in Genesis 25:18 and in

[1]A. Noordzij: *God's Woord en der Eeuwen Getuigenis* (Kampen 1931), p. 156. Also the article "Eden" in *Christelijke Encyclopaedie* (Vol. II), p. 19.

1 Samuel 15:7 we read the phrase "from Havilah to Shur." This data, however, gives no specific information about the exact location of Havilah. The name Joktan points to Arabia. Cush, on the other hand, usually refers to Ethiopia, but in a few places it may also refer to another location (see our interpretation of v. 13). It is doubtful, in fact, whether it can refer to Ethiopia in Genesis 10:7. There Cush is presented as the father of certain Arabian tribes such as Scheba (the Sabaeans) and Dedan. In verse 8 Nimrod is included and this people occupied certain kingdoms in Babylon— Babel, Erech, and Accad (v. 10). Shur, on the other hand, lies near the Egyptian border. Thus the expression "from Havilah to Shur" is used in Genesis 25:18 to designate the land of the Ishmaelites, and in 1 Samuel 15:17 the territory of the Amalekites. Even the expression that Havilah "produced much fine gold" gives us little help. Some have identified Havilah with Ophir, the famous land of gold (1 Kings 9:28; 10:11; 22:49; etc.). But this also offers no help because the exact location of Ophir is not known either.

Besides gold, two other products of Havilah are mentioned, namely, "aromatic resin," which was a sweet-smelling resin from a type of palm tree native to certain areas in southern Arabia, Babylonia, and India. Onyx is mentioned, which was obviously a highly valued precious stone, and is also mentioned in Exodus 25:7; 28:9; etc. We know absolutely nothing, however, about the actual nature of this stone. Thus these two products of Havilah also offer us no help in determining the precise location of Havilah, and consequently, of the Pishon River mentioned in our text.

2:13 *The name of the second river is the Gihon; it winds through the entire land of Cush.*

The name of the second river is Gihon. Again, a river by this name is wholly unknown today. We are told that this river flowed through the entire land of Cush. As we indicated earlier, Cush is the name usually given to Ethiopia. Thus we would have a fairly definite disignation. However, there are a number of passages where it has another meaning. Genesis 10:7 and 2 Chronicles 14:9ff. make it rather difficult to make Cush refer to Ethiopia. In the latter passage we have a description of a battle between the Cushite (rsv incorrectly translates Ethiopian) Zerah and King Asa of Judah. It is impossible to think of this as an Ethiopian army because they would have had to pass directly through Egypt to reach Judah. In later years the Ethiopian kings did have control over Egypt but that was not the case at the time of King Asa. Thus the Cushite Zerah must be considered to have been an Arabian prince.

There is another reason why the land of Cush, through which the Gihon River flowed, could not have been Ethiopia. If it were, the Gihon could have been none other than the Nile River, which flows through Ethiopia first and then through Egypt. It would have been unthinkable, however, for the Nile not to be called by its own name which was so well known among the Jews. Moreover, if the Nile was meant, it would have been described as flowing through Egypt rather than through Ethiopia. Thus, also regarding the Gihon, we are not able to make any definite identification.

2:14 *The name of the third river is the Tigris; it runs along the east side of Asshur. And the fourth river is the Euphrates.*

The name of the third river is "Hiddekel." This name also appears in Daniel 10:4. There is no doubt that this refers to the Tigris River. Linguistically the identity of the two names is clearly evident. The Hebrew *hiddegel* is the same as the Assyrian "Idiglat." This was shortened to Diglat and in Persian this became Tigras, from which we get our Tigris. That this is correct is confirmed by the added comment that it "runs along the east side of Asshur." This refers to Assur, the ancient capital from which both the land and the people of Assyria got their name. Later this was replaced by Nineveh.

Finally, the fourth stream is the Euphrates. Regarding this there is no question.

In the light of the information presently available to us, the data given in verses 10–14 is not sufficient to give us a clearly specified location for the district of Eden. It is, of course, possible that we will discover more information pertaining to these geographic areas.

2:15 *The LORD God took the man and put him in the Garden of Eden to work it and take care of it.*

Verse 15 returns to the narrative of the human experience. The Lord God placed man in this Garden to work it and to take care of it. The word "to work" strongly contradicts the notion some have, that in Paradise, before the Fall, man enjoyed a glorious state of inactivity. Genesis 1:28 already indicated that God had given man tasks to perform. These responsibilities are now more clearly defined, as they pertained to the Garden in which man was placed.

This "working" of the Garden also implies that the perfection of creation (1:31) did not preclude responsible work on man's part. The Garden of Eden with all its precious trees required tending. Man had to devote his

91

physical and spiritual powers to this task. Here we are dealing with what we might well call the beginning of "agriculture."

Furthermore, the need for "caring for" the Garden in the sense of guarding it implies that there were hostile forces against which man was to be on guard. That such destructive forces existed becomes clearly evident, of course, in chapter 3.

2:16, 17 *And the LORD God commanded the man, "You are free to eat from any tree in the garden; but you must not eat from the tree of the knowledge of good and evil, for when you eat of it you will surely die."*

To His general order with respect to the Garden, God now added a very specific command. This command related to one of the two special trees in the middle of the Garden, introduced in verse 9. It was permissible to eat the fruit of all the trees in the Garden without any restrictions, with one exception. Eating the fruit of this one tree, the tree of the knowledge of good and evil, was emphatically forbidden. This, of course, casts more light on the significance of that specific tree.

It should be carefully noted that the ability to distinguish between good and evil was not to be acquired by *eating* of that tree, but precisely by *not eating* of it. How must this be understood? The prohibition against eating clearly impressed on the human conscience the contrast between good and evil. By His prohibition God declared that eating of that tree was "evil" in sharp distinction from *not* eating, which was "good." It is our opinion, then, that the way in which this tree specifically taught man the difference between good and evil was by forcing man into a deliberate, conscious choice between good and evil.

We observed, in our treatment of verse 9, that the idea that man was completely devoid of any ability to distinguish good from evil is not acceptable. The responsibility to "guard" the Garden, for one example, clearly involved a capacity for making such distinctions. It should be noted, however, that this distinction between good and evil was not yet in clear, sharp focus for man. He did the good of his own accord, naturally, without having to make a conscious judgment to do the good instead of evil. By the divine prohibition with respect to the fruit of this one tree, this now was to change. Man was to be placed before a conscious, deliberate choice of the good in contrast to the evil. Thus, if man obeyed the prohibition of God, he would acquire a clear, conscious capability to distinguish good from evil.

The question has been raised whether the fruit of this tree in itself was harmful. Are we to look upon the eating of that fruit as being inherently morally wrong? Our answer to that question is an emphatic negative. The Paradise narrative does not offer the slightest evidence that eating this fruit was, in and of itself, harmful. In fact, the opposite was true. This tree also was good for food. If man were to eat of it, nothing would happen to harm him physically in any way. Moreover, there is nothing here that suggests that the fruit of this tree possessed some quality that made it inherently morally objectionable to partake of it. It is unmistakably clear that eating of this fruit became evil only because God prohibited it.

We might even say that partaking or not partaking of the fruit of that tree belonged to the "indifferent" things. It is understandable that the command of God should be applied precisely to a matter which in itself was indifferent. In that way the true conflict between good and evil was to be impressed upon the human consciousness. Evil was not something which man in himself and by himself discovered to be harmful, unacceptable, or morally objectionable. Evil was, in its very essence, a matter of being in conflict with the will of God. Only thus could its true nature be understood.

The Christian church has correctly designated this prohibition of God as God's "trial command." It placed man before a choice, a decision. Clearly and consciously man was placed before the conflict between good and evil and thus he was put on trial. This trial was what God intended when He announced His prohibition with respect to this one tree and placed the human person before this critical choice.

Accompanying God's prohibition was the pronouncement of a serious penalty, "When you eat of it you will surely die." With a view to the subsequent history, the purport of these words should not be weakened. The meaning is definitely that in the day when this command of God is transgressed, man will become the victim of death. This penalty is understandable if we recognize the true intent of the command. The decision before which man was placed involved the basic principle of human morality. Man was placed before a clear-cut choice—either a conscious acceptance of the good by completely submitting to the will of God, or a conscious choice of evil by declaring his complete independence from the will of God. It is unmistakably clear that this latter choice, to sever oneself from the living God who is the source of all life, would have the inevitable consequence of death.

2:18 *The Lord God said, "It is not good for the man to be alone. I will make a helper suitable for him."*

The narrative now moves to the forming of woman. This is introduced by the announcement that God decided to provide man with a life's companion. Undoubtedly we must understand this announcement as being similar to God's decision in 1:26 to create man. In that connection we explained that the creation of man was of special significance. Similarly, here special attention is focused on the importance of the creation of woman. This passage, then, places full emphasis on the significant position of woman as a life's companion for man.

2:19, 20 *Now the Lord God had formed out of the ground all the beasts of the field and all the birds of the air. He brought them to the man to see what he would name them; and whatever the man called each living creature, that was its name. So the man gave names to all the livestock, the birds of the air and all the beasts of the field.*
But for Adam no suitable helper was found.

Verses 19 and 20 often are interpreted as though they portray various futile attempts on the part of God to find a suitable companion for man. The animals, then, are introduced as some kind of misfits for the role of woman. This view follows from an idea, which we discussed in the introduction to this pericope, that this section constitutes a second creation narrative. It is claimed, then, that this narrative follows an entirely different order than the Genesis 1 account, with the creation of animals following the creation of man. With respect to this view we would refer the reader back to our comments in the Introduction to this section.

Besides this, we want to point out the fact that the suggestion that the creation of the animals must be seen as a series of abortive attempts to fulfill the divine purpose expressed in verse 18 is in conflict with the entire context. What stupidity we would have to ascribe to the author of Genesis 2:4–3:24 to reach this conclusion. How could the same author who describes God as the almighty Creator of man in verse 7, now describe this same God as being unable to create a companion for man without going through a series of blundering, unsuccessful attempts. This is unthinkable.

But if we proceed from the position that the animals were created before man, as we have done in our translation (*had* formed), we face the question of why the animals were first brought to man in connection with God's purpose to create woman as a companion for man. In order that the creation of woman might fulfill its true purpose, a sense of need first had to be awakened in man. This need would then be satisfied by God's forming of woman. This sense of need became a reality as man, with his superior intelligence, looked at the animals and recognized his own uniqueness. At the same time he must have realized that many of the animals had a certain social companionship among themselves that he lacked. These social needs on the part of man the animals could not satisfy because of his superiority over them. Thus there developed within man a longing for social companionship with a being who was his equal in every respect. That longing the Almighty satisfied by forming the woman as human life's companion for man.

In this connection we read about the naming of the animals. This task, which God assigned to man, proved that man completely understood the natures of the animals. The closing statement of verse 19 must then also be read as indicating that the names man gave to the various animals expressed the true nature of the respective animals.

We should mention here that there is no justification for the conclusion that man made up his own language in connection with the naming of the animals. On the contrary, man made use of a language that was already present. We need only refer to God's communication with man from the beginning, as in Genesis 1:28–30; 2:16–17. We will simply have to accept the fact that this language was given when man himself was created as a communicating being.

2:21 *So the LORD God caused the man to fall into a deep sleep; and while he was sleeping, he took one of the man's ribs and closed up the place with flesh.*

No suitable creature was found among the animals to satisfy man's need for social companionship. So God caused a deep sleep to fall upon the man as an initial step in the creation of woman. This "deep sleep" must be considered as something akin to an anesthesia which the medical profession can induce by various means. In fact, the operation that God performed on the man is not wholly unlike medical surgery. God took away one of his ribs and filled the empty place with flesh. The Hebrew word translated "rib" appears nowhere else in the Old Testament with this meaning. The usual meaning is "side." Thus it is used of the "side" of the ark (Exod. 25:12, 14), the "side" of the tabernacle (Exod. 26:20), the "side" of the altar (Exod. 27:7) and even of the slope on the side of a mountain (2 Sam. 16:13). It is also used in the sense of a side room, as of the temple (1 Kings 6:5).

It has been suggested that this should not be considered as a literal rib but that it refers rather to the space or cavity of the body. To this then are added all kinds of peculiar speculations that man originally was bisexual. Proceeding from this idea of the bisexual nature of man, some have even used the word for female sex organs in the place of "rib." Against all of this speculation is the clear statement that God took *"one* of his ribs." The other readings have to assume then that man originally had a number of body cavities or female sex organs of which God then took one. All of this

95

becomes completely absurd with no basis in the text of Scripture. The old translation of "rib" can be logically related to "side" since the ribs do form the side of the human body.

2:22 *Then the L*ORD *God made a woman from the rib he had taken out of the man, and he brought her to the man.*

From the rib God took from man, He now formed the woman. As a consequence of this reference in Scripture, the question has often been asked whether man has one more rib than woman has. Then when research in the human anatomy reveals that men and women have precisely the same number of ribs, this whole passage has been called into question and made a matter of ridicule. But there is no reason for such questions and ridicule. Regarding just how God intervened in the body of man and precisely how the woman was formed from the rib taken from the man, the Scripture gives no information. We should not then try to satisfy our idle curiosity about such matters. Let no one be so foolish as to try to make certain conclusions about the miracle of the creation of woman on the basis of the present body structure of man and woman. If we truly have respect for the Word of God, let us simply accept what is recorded here. Further details that are not revealed to us are of no consequence. God has revealed that woman was created from man and that is enough to cause us to recognize the complete and inherent unity of man and woman. Thus we are brought to the vital realization of that wonderful mystery that the two are one.

2:23 *The man said, "This is now bone of my bones and flesh of my flesh; she shall be called 'woman,' for she was taken out of man."*

After God had created the woman, He brought her to the man, who meanwhile had been awakened from his deep sleep. Man immediately recognized her as the life's companion who was the complete fulfillment of the longing that had been awakened in him. She was his equal and he knew, by divine revelation, that she had been taken out of his own body. He recognized the contrast between her and the animals and he cried out, "This is now bone of my bones and flesh of my flesh; she shall be called 'woman,' for she was taken out of man."

This was a poetic exultation with which he broke forth. The divine miracle he witnessed and experienced filled him with inexpressible joy and inspired him to a poetic outburst. The Hebrew word "woman" is formed by adding a feminine ending to the word for "man." This is commonly done by adding a feminine suffix to the masculine word to denote the female of the species, as in lioness, tigress, etc. In English this is evident in our word "woman," which includes the word "man."

2:24 *For this reason a man will leave his father and mother and be united to his wife, and they will become one flesh.*

Some Roman Catholic exegetes include verse 24 in the words of Adam recorded in verse 23. However, this is not correct. These are the words of the inspired author of the Book of Genesis, who injects a statement about the character and the responsibilities of marriage. Many deny that this statement is intended as a sacred precept. They consider it to be no more than a statement of fact regarding the nature of marriage. They translate it, "Therefore a man leaves his father and mother and clings to his wife and thus the two become one flesh." Although this translation is linguistically possible, it makes the statement very dull. It should also be remembered that Jesus calls on this passage to establish the fact that marriage is an ordinance of God (Matt. 19:5–6). It is our conviction, therefore, that in these lines the sacred writer gives us the basic ordinance which establishes the close binding unity of man and woman in the marriage bond.

2:25 *The man and his wife were both naked, and they felt no shame.*

Verse 25 tells us that the first man and woman were naked. This nakedness, which people today cannot conceive of without a sense of shame, had no such effect on the first human couple. Some have interpreted this, "They were not ashamed before each other." Although the verb form that is used can be translated in this way, this does not establish the correctness of this translation. In any case it is not acceptable to draw the conclusion, on the basis of that translation, that the sacred writer implies a certain moral shortcoming on the part of the first couple. It is not until 3:7–10ff. that we are told that the sense of shame was awakened in people, and that as the result of their transgression of God's command. If it had been the intent of the writer to indicate that the lack of a sense of shame was a moral failing, he should then have presented the awakening of that sense of shame as a step of moral progress. All we have here is a simple statement of fact that at this time man and woman did not feel a sense of shame because of their nakedness. There is no judgment passed on this fact. From chapter 3 we learn that the development of a sense of shame accompanied their consciousness of guilt resulting from their transgression. Thus when we are told that they were not ashamed, this can be read as one of the marks of their state of sinlessness.

97

3:1 *Now the serpent was more crafty than any of the wild animals the L*ord *God had made. He said to the woman, "Did God really say, 'You must not eat from any tree in the garden'?"*

We now are introduced to a new figure, the "serpent." As will become apparent, in the course of the history of the world created by God, the serpent exerted a strong and destructive influence.

This figure is introduced as the most crafty of all the beasts of the field, which the Lord God had made. This certainly indicates that the serpent belonged to the animal world. In the course of history many have tried to describe the serpent as not being an animal at all. These attempts must be emphatically rejected.

There has been much conflict about the meaning of the word we have translated "crafty." Should this be understood in a favorable or an unfavorable sense? The use of the word in Scripture indicates that it is usually used in a favorable sense (Prov. 12:16, 23; 13:16; 14:8, 15, 18; 22:3; 27:12). It is then translated "prudent" or "wise." It does appear in a few references in an unfavorable sense as "crafty" in Job 5:12; 15:5. I am therefore convinced that the word should be taken in its most obvious meaning and this would be a favorable quality. It should thus be translated "discerning" or "sagacious." This is also confirmed by the context.

It has been argued that what is told us about the serpent's activity in chapter 3 seems to dictate that the unfavorable sense of the word should be used. The intent of the first verse then would be to prepare us for the evil that this creature was to bring about. No wonder that the serpent tempted the woman since this was the nature of the beast to act in this fashion. However, we are not convinced that this is the context we should consider.

Mention is made here of "any of the wild animals the Lord God had made." This points directly to the creation of the animals in 1:25, and of the animals it is said, as it was of the entire creation, "And God saw that it was good." When we establish this context we have no choice except to declare that the serpent also was good and that the favorable intent of the word was intended. If we choose the other reading we would face the question, "From where did one of God's good creatures receive such an evil quality?"

As far as the connection with what follows is concerned, we do not question that what is said about the serpent prepares the way for this. This should not, however, be related to the actual temptation, but rather to what immediately follows, namely, what the serpent "said to the woman." The quality ascribed to the serpent should explain why it was precisely this animal that began to speak to the woman. Further, it should indicate why the woman was not surprised when the serpent spoke to her, for the serpent was the most prudent of all the animals.

This "speaking" on the part of the serpent has been a rock of offense for many through the ages. Rationalistic unbelief has insisted that animals simply do not speak and consequently what is recorded here cannot be accepted as literally true. But even among those who accept the Bible there have been frequent attempts to circumvent the rational objections to the speaking serpent. Hoberg, a strong Roman Catholic exegete, suggests that this "speaking" must be understood as follows: When the woman saw the serpent she felt the temptation rising within her to transgress the command of God, and this temptation became so strong that it was as though the serpent spoke to her. But the following verses record a formal, two-sided conversation between the serpent and the woman. Exegetically every arbitrary explanation is excluded. According to the text it is obvious that the serpent actually spoke. Whoever accepts the Scripture as the Word of God, then, will not be swayed by any objections. When God's Word says that the serpent spoke we accept this as a fact without further argument.

Now, what did the serpent say? "Did God really say, 'You must not eat from any tree in the garden?'" This is a question which appears to be fairly innocent. But obviously it concealed a malicious craftiness. In the Hebrew the words are so arranged that the statement can be understood in two ways. It can read, "not from every tree," or "not from any tree." There has been much discussion on the part of interpreters as to which reading is the correct one. This is all unnecessary since the statement no doubt was meant to be ambiguous. The duplicity of the question was intended in order to be most effective in arousing suspicion in the mind of the woman. Could it be possible that God would deny to human beings the pleasure of eating all the fruit of the garden? Even if the question was understood in its narrower sense, "not of every tree," it still opens the way for overthrowing the command of God. Could there be various trees from which God had forbidden them to eat?

The intent is evident. It was directed toward instilling doubt in the heart of the woman, doubt with respect to the exact wording and the precise purpose of the divine command. It served to raise a question about the fairness and justice of the trial command.

3:2, 3 *The woman said to the serpent, "We may eat fruit from the trees in the garden, but God did say, 'You must not eat fruit from the tree that is in the middle of the garden, and you must not touch it, or you will die.'"*

The answer the woman gave revealed that the arrow had found a target. Doubt had actually risen in her heart. She gave evidence of this in the way she repeated the command of God. Her wording of this command, on the one hand, made the command itself more severe, while, on the other hand, it made the penalty for disobedience less severe than the words God had originally spoken. The command itself was sharpened by adding the words, "You must not touch it," which are not included in the command as God gave it (Gen. 2:16–17). The weakening of the penalty comes out in the words "or you will die." What she actually says is that it was possible that they would die, rather than God's positive declaration that they would surely die.

It is interesting also that she does not refer to the forbidden tree with the name God had given to it, but only as "the tree that is in the middle of the garden." There is no reason to assume that she did not know the name of the tree. Although the original command was given to the man before the creation of woman, she obviously knew the command. Undoubtedly the man told her about the command precisely as he had received it grom God, including the name of the tree. Therefore, we must assume that she intentionally omitted the name of the tree. This name, which reveals the true character of the tree, is omitted in favor of a designation which places the tree on a level with all the trees in the garden. It is described only by its location, not by its true nature and significance. This is also a symptom of the doubt that had been awakened in her. The woman did not acknowledge the fairness of God's command without some reservations.

It has been remarked, in this connection, that the comment of the woman indicates that there was only one tree in the middle of the garden instead of the two special trees mentioned in 2:9. This is hardly a warranted conclusion to be drawn from her remarks. Her conversation with the serpent dealt exclusively with the one tree. The other tree was in no sense within her purview at that time. It is not at all surprising, then, that she made no mention of the second tree. No conclusions can properly be drawn from this omission.

3:4, 5 *"You will not surely die," the serpent said to the woman. "For God knows that when you eat of it your eyes will be opened, and you will be like God, knowing good and evil."*

After the doubts that had been planted had sprouted, as is evidenced by the answer the woman gave, the serpent continued his attack. He assured the woman that they should not fear death, but rather that if they eat of the tree would result in "your eyes will be opened, and you will be like God, knowing good and evil."

The tactics the serpent used must be carefully observed. He then revealed a knowledge regarding the trial command he pretended not to have when he asked his first question. He knew very well what the trial command included. Even though the woman departed from the words of God, the serpent now reviewed some of the words in which God had given the command, only giving them his own deceptive interpretation. Instead of the weak "or you will die," he used the original "you will surely die," but he denied that this would really happen. He used *"when* (in the day that) you eat of it" but he distorted the meaning of these words. The woman had not named the tree, but he included the term "knowledge of good and evil" again, giving it his own meaning.

The serpent's insinuation, "God knows," should especially be noted. Here he put the purposes of God in an ugly light. He suggested that God's purpose was to prevent man from enjoying something of greatest value. The threat of death was, according to the serpent, no more than a scare tactic on God's part to keep man from becoming like God. Thus it was really an expression of jealousy on God's part. Moreover, while God had told man that the way to achieve the knowledge of good and evil was to *not* eat of the tree, the serpent claimed that this was intentionally misleading on God's part since God knew that the opposite was true and that this knowledge would be gained by eating of the tree.

This entire presentation by the serpent raises the legitimate question, "What was the actual source of all of this?" Here there is evidence of a knowledge and a deliberate argument which far surpasses the level of animal life. How did such evil and deceptive tendencies enter into a creature that had been created good by God? Are we not compelled to recognize that behind this serpent there was concealed an evil, spiritual force which used this animal to pursue its godless purposes? The Lord Jesus gives us the identity of that evil spiritual force when He says that the devil was "a murderer from the beginning, not holding to the truth, for there is no truth in him. When he lies, he speaks his native language, for he is a liar and the father of lies" (John 8:44). For this reason, some have argued that the serpent was no real animal at all and that the name "serpent" was no more than a pseudonym for the devil. This, however, conflicts with verse 1 where the serpent is specifically called an animal. Reference has also been made to a few places in the Book of Revelation where the devil is called "that ancient serpent" (Rev. 12:9; 20:2). Although these references probably do point back to the Paradise scene, this is symbolic, figurative language, and thus cannot serve as proof that the serpent was not an actual animal in the Genesis account. The best interpretation seems to be that the devil used the serpent as an instrument to tempt mankind.

3:6 *When the woman saw that the fruit of the tree was good for food and pleasing to the eye, and also desirable for gaining wisdom, she took some and ate it. She also gave some to her husband, who was with her, and he ate it.*

The words of the serpent, or rather of the devil through the serpent, found acceptance with the woman. After doubts had risen in her soul, she also became receptive to the blasphemous charge that God had intentionally misled man with an idle threat in order to prevent man from becoming like God. "The woman saw that the fruit of the tree was good for food and pleasing to the eye, and also desirable for gaining wisdom." When she looked at the tree she, in her heart, began to agree with the serpent. Truly, the fruit of the tree was suitable for food and it was attractive in appearance. She failed to see why she should not eat it. Nothing seemed to substantiate the divine command. Probably it was true that the fruit of the tree would not produce death but would rather produce new insights and understanding. This knowledge of good and evil, about which the serpent had spoken, strongly appealed to her. Then she would be like God, stand on an equal level with Him, and no longer be subject to Him. She would no longer be restricted to God's delineation between good and evil, but independent of God, equal with God, she would autonomously distinguish what was good from what was evil. That ideal of sovereign independence, which had been presented to her by the serpent, lured her on, "and she took some [of the fruit] and ate it." Thus the deed of taking and eating followed as a realization and confirmation of the principal decision at which the woman had arrived.

After she had acted she turned to the man in order to have him join her in her disobedience. He also made the decision to eat—"She also gave some to her husband, who was with her, and he ate it." The biblical narrative gives no details at this point. We are not told whether the man was present during the conversation between the serpent and the woman and thus was led into the same path of temptation, or that, in the course of his tending of the garden, he approached the scene after the woman had eaten of the tree. We do not know whether the women actually approached the man and urged him to eat or what effort she expended in this direction. First Timothy 2:14 suggests that the man was not present during the conversation with the serpent but later was influenced by the woman to participate in the fatal eating of the tree.

3:7 *Then the eyes of both of them were opened, and they realized they were naked; so they sewed fig leaves together and made coverings for themselves.*

And now comes the disillusioning experience which followed the transgression. What became of the attractive predictions the serpent had made to them? To be sure, "the eyes of both of them were opened," but only to a sudden realization that they were naked. That was the only knowledge they acquired. Undoubtedly this must be understood as a sudden recognition that their nakedness, which previously was wholly proper and comfortable (2:25), now was something unpleasant and distasteful. Their nakedness now disturbed them. Therefore they tried to cover their nakedness by sewing fig leaves together to cover themselves. Fig leaves were used because these were large and were best suited for this purpose.

Many have tried to portray this as a sense of shame associated with their sexual differences, and have concluded that the fall into sin actually consisted of the sex act. We need not devote much time to deny this presentation. Not only does the preceding context make it abundantly clear what the nature of the first transgression was, but, as the narrative progresses, it is evident that the sense of shame was not related to sexuality. Verse 10 tells us about man being called to account by God and there it is evident that their nakedness caused them to be afraid before God. And this must not be seen as a pretext on the part of man. The consciousness of his nakedness actually caused him to be afraid before God. Thus it is clear that the awareness of Adam and Eve's nakedness was more than a consciousness of their sexuality. It was definitely a matter of their spiritual, inner sense of guilt before God that caused them to feel naked. The transgression immediately brought the realization that the original wholeness they had enjoyed had been shattered. This awareness, that man no longer was what he was intended to be, finds its first expression in the feeling that they were naked. But this was only an outward manifestation of the inner sense of guilt that caused them to be afraid of God.

3:8 *Then the man and his wife heard the sound of the LORD God as he was walking in the garden in the cool of the day, and they hid from the LORD God among the trees of the garden.*

"Then the man and his wife heard the sound of the LORD God as he was walking in the garden in the cool of the day, and they hid from the LORD God among the trees of the garden." This deals with the awareness of the presence of God, and this presence of God filled the man and his wife with fear. No longer did they enjoy the right relationship with God, and their confidential communion with Him had turned into anxious fear of Him. This, in turn, led to their attempt to hide from God among the thick foliage of the garden.

"The sound of the LORD God as he was walking in the garden," is, of course, an anthropomorphic manner of speaking. It was as though our first parents heard God's footsteps. The intent of the figure is that they became aware of the presence of the Most High through a specific movement in nature. This movement or activity is designated as the "cool of the day" or "the day-wind." This must be understood as a certain type of wind which blew during the middle of the day. It has often been thought of as the coolness of the evening but the Hebrew word strongly suggests that this phenomenon occurred during the day.

3:9, 10 *But the LORD God called to the man, "Where are you?"*
He answered, "I heard you in the garden, and I was afraid because I was naked; so I hid."

Naturally, the attempt to hide from God was wholly futile. The Almighty calls Adam and Eve out of their hiding place—"Where are you?" To this the guilty Adam answers, "I heard you in the garden, and I was afraid because I was naked; so I hid." As we observed in our consideration of verse 7, this was an expression of their sense of guilt. The consciousness of their nakedness as something unacceptable flows from their awareness that their original harmonious relationship had been disturbed. And from this also resulted their fear of God and the realization that, in their present state, they could not stand in His holy presence.

3:11–13 *And he said, "Who told you that you were naked? Have you eaten from the tree that I commanded you not to eat from?"*
The man said, "The woman you put here with me—she gave me some fruit from the tree, and I ate it."
Then the LORD God said to the woman, "What is this you have done?"
The woman said, "The serpent deceived me, and I ate."

By speaking of his nakedness, man actually betrayed himself. How could he have come to this awareness unless he had sinned and transgressed the command of God. Thus the admission that came in response to the examining question of the Judge could not be delayed; but this admission came in the form of an excuse. The woman whom God had given him as a companion was, he charged, the guilty one. Thus, in a way, he even blamed God, who had placed such a dangerous creature at his side. When the woman was called to give an account, she also had her excuse ready and accused the serpent of deceiving her.

3:14 *So the LORD God said to the serpent, Because you have done this, "Cursed are you above all the livestock and all the wild animals! You will crawl on your belly and you will eat dust all the days of your life.*

Now we are told about the sentencing of the guilty ones. First, a heavy curse was pronounced upon the serpent, which would set it apart from all the other animals. The serpent would always move about by crawling on its belly and would eat dust. This "eating" of dust does not imply that dust would be the main food supply for the serpent, but rather that in the process of crawling around on its belly it would get dust in its mouth.

There have been many attempts to understand both of these expressions as being figurative and then to apply them to the devil. It is true that the statement "lick the dust" is used figuratively in passages such as Psalm 72:9; Isaiah 49:23; Micah 7:17. In Lamentations 3:29 we have "let him bury his face in the dust." These passages do not indicate, however, that the reference in our verse must also be taken figuratively. In Micah 7:17 we read "They will lick dust like the snake," and thus the figurative use is compared with the literal meaning. This would seem to prove that in the case of the serpent it must be considered to be a literal description.

Undoubtedly we must understand this as indicating that a radical change was brought about in the method of locomotion on the part of the serpent. Although Calvin insists that nothing was changed in the natural structure and habits of the serpent and that the serpent crawled on its belly from the beginning, this claim is doubtful. The present method of locomotion of the serpent is the direct consequence of the curse God pronounced on it. This does not mean that the whole appearance of the serpent changed. It is possible that the serpent kept its general appearance while changing its means of getting about.

3:15 *And I will put enmity between you and the woman, and between your off-spring and hers; he will crush your head, and you will strike his heel."*

To this curse on the serpent there is then added what has often been called the "maternal promise." It would be well for us to first consider the immediate and obvious meaning of this statement. It must first be applied directly to the serpent to whom it is spoken. Although it obviously also has a deeper meaning, which has always been accepted by the Christian church, it would be a completely arbitrary exegesis to apply the first part of the sentence of punishment to the serpent and then apply the second part to someone, or something, else.

Obviously we are told something about the relationship between serpents and people. Between the two there is a deadly hostility. Thus there are places in the world where ten times as many people are killed by snakes as by all other kinds of animal life put together. And from the other side, how many of us do not have a deep hatred and revulsion for snakes. There are some expositors who feel that is all we have here, a reference to the enmity between serpents and people. No reference is then made to the triumph of the ''seed of the woman'' that is pronounced in the further words of the text. They simply conclude that as long as there are serpents and people the two will live in mutual hostility to each other, hating and killing each other.

To ''crush the head'' of the serpent certainly indicates that the serpent is going to be defeated in the conflict. At the same time to ''strike the heel'' of a human being need not have fatal results. Even if we think of poisonous serpents, to which the text seems to refer, the venom injected by the serpent need not prove fatal or harmful if it can be promptly removed from the wound.

There is some difficulty with the fact that the Hebrew uses the same word ''crush'' in both instances. This word seems to be altogether suitable when we think of killing a snake by crushing its head, but it doesn't seem to fit the bite of a snake. The Hebrew language is fond of using a play on words and this is obviously what we have here, with the euphonious repetition of the word ''crush.'' When the word is used of the bite of a poisonous snake we must simply translate it in keeping with the nature of such an attack. Since a snake, with its head raised up, lashes out at its victim with great speed and power in order to drive its fang into the flesh and deposit the deadly venom, our word ''strike'' constitutes an accurate translation. The triumph on the part of the woman and her descendants is also indicated by the order in which the statements are placed, with the ''striking of the heel'' being given a secondary place in the order of the sentence. This word order definitely indicates that the final triumph would be on the part of the seed of the woman while in the process of gaining that victory that seed of the woman would be wounded by the serpent.

It is precisely this victory on the part of the human race that suggests that this passage has a deeper meaning. There is more here than a victory of people over snakes. In verses 1–5 we observed that behind the serpent was concealed an evil, spiritual force. This evil, spiritual force we learn to know, from the words of Jesus, as the devil. It is worthy of note that in the pronouncement of the penalty the object—the woman—changes to the ''seed'' of the woman. However, in the case of the ''serpent'' the object remains the same ''you'' which is addressed throughout. This ''you'' who had tempted the woman, with whom the woman had struck up a conversation, against whom there would be enmity on the part of the woman and her seed, is the same "you" who in the end will have his head crushed by the seed of the woman. Thus it is evident that in the "serpent" we are dealing with one definite personal being, here represented by the serpent, but who would continue to be one of the contestants in the battle which would rage on through the ages.

And now we take the next step. If the enemy, whose ultimate defeat is announced here, is a personal being, then the force which would ultimately gain the victory over him must also be a personal being. In the use of the words "head" and "heel," both in the singular, we have a further indication that the conflict would ultimately be settled between two contestants. Also the reference to the "seed of the woman" by the singular preposition "it" demands that the victor would be one single contestant. This "it" refers back to the noun "seed" and, being in the singular, strongly suggests that the ultimate victory would be gained by one individual among that seed of the woman. This triumphant victor, of course, is our Lord Jesus Christ. Here in Paradise God gives the first revelation of His eventual victory. Thus Genesis 3:15 has been rightly called the "maternal promise," the "protevangelium," the first proclamation of the gospel of grace.

We would not want to claim that this "maternal promise," in its deeper application, refers exclusively to the Christ. It is obvious that in the first part of the verse the terms "the seed of the woman" and the "seed of the serpent" are collective nouns. Thus, unless we want to separate the second part of the verse completely from the first part and apply the deeper meaning only to the second part while taking the first part strictly literally, we cannot escape the conclusion that the first part of the verse announces the ongoing spiritual conflict between the seed of the woman and the seed of the serpent. In other words, what we have portrayed here is the constant conflict between the children of the devil and the children of the kingdom. Even so, in the actual conflict between these two forces, the seed of the woman will gain the ultimate victory and thus the Mediator takes the prominent place. The victory in that conflict is not won by the collective seed of the woman, but by that one unique seed of the woman, our Lord Jesus Christ, and by Him alone.

Thus we see that in the sentence that is pronounced upon the serpent the ultimate annihilation of the wicked instigator of evil is clearly announced. For fallen humanity this same pronouncement reveals the glorious light of God's grace for sinners. That light of grace is revealed already in the enmity between the serpent and the woman in their respective seeds. Friendship with the evil tempter became evident as a curse for mankind. Enmity against him is a blessing. In this God evidences His mercy in that He turns this chosen friendship into enmity. But this light shines even more brightly in the promise of the Conqueror who will ultimately fully destroy that enemy. This is the gospel announced by God Himself to our first parents.

3:16 *To the woman he said, "I will greatly increase your pains in childbearing; with pain you will give birth to children. Your desire will be for your husband, and he will rule over you."*

The second part of the sentencing is applied to the woman. The word "pains" or "heaviness" reappears in verse 17 in the penalty pronounced upon the man, "through painful toil you will eat of it." The word has as its root the verb which means to injure, to cause pain, to grieve. Thus it refers to something that brings a person great difficulty and grief. The "grief" of childbirth is further amplified with the words, "with pain you will give birth to children." This latter term refers to physical pain. It should be noted that the punishment did not lie in childbirth as such, but in the agony of it, not the bearing of children but the grief which would accompany this. Bearing children is in itself a blessing as was evident from the word of God at the time of creation, "Be fruitful and increase in number; fill the earth and subdue it" (Gen. 1:28). Thus also in the punishment pronounced on the serpent, the having of seed on the part of the woman was an element in God's program of grace.

The second part of this penalty for the woman says that the desire of the woman will be for her husband. This "desire" is actually a tendency or an inclination. We have a reference here to the tendency of the woman to seek sexual relationships with her husband. In other words, all the pain associated with childbearing would not restrain her from desiring sexual fulfillment with her husband. The basis of this punishment can be seen in that the woman will not be able to escape the pain and agony of childbirth by simply refraining from sexual intercourse. Even though she knows full well the pain that results from such intercourse, she will be impelled by an irresistible urge to seek precisely what produces this pain. Thus she herself will contribute to the fulfilling of her own punishment.

Finally, we are told that the man would "rule over" the woman. This refers to the place of subjection that the woman would be given. In 2:18 the woman was described as a suitable companion for man, and she stood on a level of equality with man. Now she is sentenced to a position of subjection. The word "rule" is the same word that is used of a ruler over his subjects. By the Fall the harmonious relationship between man and woman was disturbed. Instead of the proper relationship in which, although the husband is the head and gives the leadership, the wife stands beside him as an equal, she now is penalized by being given a position of subjection to the man. This has been sharply demonstrated in many of the ancient Eastern cultures where women were relegated to a place of slavery or considered as chattel. It should be noted that this degradation of women was a punishment for sin and that the original position of equality as companion and helper instituted by the Creator remains the ideal relationship.

3:17–19 *To Adam he said, "Because you listened to your wife and ate from the tree about which I commanded you, 'You must not eat of it,' "Cursed is the ground because of you; through painful toil you will eat of it all the days of your life. It will produce thorns and thistles for you, and you will eat the plants of the field.*

By the sweat of your brow you will eat your food until you return to the ground, since from it you were taken; for dust you are and to dust you will return."

Finally, we have the announcement of the sentence on the man. It commences with, "Because you listened to your wife and ate from the tree about which I commanded you, 'You must not eat of it'." Then the punishment follows and it includes three aspects. In the first place, "pain" or "heaviness" in the cultivation of the ground. The ground is cursed as a consequence of man's sin. The word "pain" is the same word that is used in connection with woman and the pain of childbirth. Here we must think of the tiresome labor that must be exerted in order to harvest the fruits of the soil.

The second aspect is the impairment of the fruits of the soil by pernicious weeds—thorns and thistles. The third part is that there will be no rest from these burdens but they will plague the man all his life. He will eat bread in the sweat of his brow until he himself returns to the earth from which he was taken.

It is striking that the only pain and toil that is mentioned is that which is associated with agricultural work. Man's pain and toil is, however, certainly not limited to this. What is said here about agricultural work applies to all the work involved in human culture, with certain necessary adaptations. There is always pain and toil involved when man seeks to achieve productive results. And there are always counteracting forces that tend to restrict those results. In every instance man is faced with painful, laborious toil until the day of his death. Just as was the case with the woman, the actual punishment lies in the accompanying circumstances. Work as such is not a punishment. The punishment lies in the difficulties that are involved in performing the work and the opposing forces that tend to curtail the anticipated results.

Of special note here is the fact that it is not until all of this has been said that there is any direct mention of death as punishment for sin. When the original command was given by God, He announced, "When you eat of it you will surely die" (2:17). It would then be expected that when the man and the woman ate of that forbidden tree they would immediately be struck dead. Or, certainly, the pronouncement of judgment should have started with this, "Because you have eaten of the tree of which I commanded you not to eat, you will die this very day." This is, however, obviously not what happened. The penalty pronounced upon the woman does not even mention death. In the case of man, only at the end of the judgment pronounced is the subject of death brought in—"until you return to the ground." Then there is added, "for dust you are and to dust you will return."

Some interpreters understand this only as a recognition of the natural end of human life. In their view, then, the entire threat issued at the time of the trial command was no more than idle words. They hold that all we have here is that human mortality was assumed in the Paradise narrative. It has no connection with a penalty for sin. The original pronouncement had threatened immediate death as soon as man transgressed the command of God. This never materialized. Instead of immediate death, the guilty pair was sentenced to other punishments. In response it should be observed that the statement, "Dust you are and to dust you will return," does not refer to the natural termination of man's life. It is a direct reference to the original command. Here man is told that the penalty that had been pronounced at that time would definitely be carried out. It is striking, however, that this statement comes here at the end of the sentencing and that it obviously does not imply immediate death. Man would surely die, but the timing of the execution of that sentence was relegated to an undetermined future.

Others have claimed that the threat of the original command did go into immediate effect and they have then pointed to the "spiritual death" to which man and woman immediately were subjected. Although the latter is true, we seriously question whether this was the intent of the pronouncement made at the time of the command. This pronouncement certainly must have included physical death also; in fact, it seems most likely that its primary intent was to condemn the sinner to physical death. Thus it is difficult to deny that what God had threatened was not immediately put into effect.

The only conclusion that can be drawn from this delay in the execution of the sentence is that a merciful God immediately evidenced His grace to fallen humanity. Those who object to the use of the term "grace" in this connection can call it by another name if they wish, but the fact remains that God did not immediately execute the full punishment He had pronounced against the guilty. Even so, this evidence of grace does not cancel the pronouncement of punishment. There is delay, but the punishment is not cancelled. Moreover, such an expression of God's grace does not indicate that His original pronouncement was idle words. The grace that was extended in no way diminishes the integrity of the pronouncement and the seriousness of its ultimate execution.

3:20 *Adam named his wife Eve, because she would become the mother of all the living.*

After the announcement of the punishment, we are told about the name the man gave to his wife. This account seems to be somewhat out of place at this point. We would expect the narrative to continue with what is recorded in verses 22–24. Even so, this does not give adequate reason to insist that verses 20–21 were taken from another source and then inserted here. The name given to the woman relates closely to statements made in the announced punishment. There we are told that she would have "seed" and that she would "bear children." The fact that the giving of the name is placed here does not mean that this occurred at this time. It is possible that this took place later. But the inspired writer included it here because it relates to the "bearing of children," which is mentioned in the sentence of punishment that had just been recorded.

The name given to the first mother reads *hawwā* in Hebrew. The word means "life" or "living." She is given this name because she is the source of life, the mother of all human life. This Hebrew word is translated "Eua" in the Septuagint and it is from this Greek word that we get our "Eve."

Admittedly, there is a linguistic problem here. These names were given during the period of the language of Paradise, before the confusion of languages at Babel. Thus, this was before the advent of the Hebrew language. Perhaps the most acceptable position in this regard is to hold that the Hebrew names should not be considered as translations from this original language, but, rather, as Hebraized renditions of the original names. It is interesting to note that Assyrian, Babylonian, Egyptian, and Persian accounts also did not translate these names into their own languages. Instead, they took over the Hebraized forms with some slight variations to adapt to their own way of speaking. It should also be noted that some of these words used as names are difficult to explain in terms of correct Hebrew form.

3:21 *The Lord God made garments of skin for Adam and his wife and clothed them.*

111

Here we are told that God Himself provided the man and the woman with suitable clothes to cover their nakedness to replace the loincloths they had sewn together from fig leaves. Although this need to be clothed was one of the consequences of sin, God does not disapprove of this. It was obviously in accord with the will of God that fallen man should be clothed.

In providing these clothes, God, in His mercy, gave man a more suitable material for making clothing. In the process He gave man the authority to slaughter animals for the purpose of making clothing. When we read the words "God made garments" and "clothed them," we must understand these statements as anthropomorphisms. As Calvin suggests, it would be entirely in conflict with the spiritual nature of God to envision Him coming down to slaughter animals, skinning them, converting their skins into clothes, and then putting these garments on the man and the woman, all with His own hands. Just how this was all accomplished we do not know, but the fact is that God provided clothes of skins of animals for the first human beings.

3:22 *And the Lord God said, "The man has now become like one of us, knowing good and evil. He must not be allowed to reach out his hand and take also from the tree of life and eat, and live forever."*

In this verse, as in 1:26, God speaks of Himself in the plural, "And the Lord God said, 'The man has now become like one of us'." As we observed in our discussion of 1:26, the only interpretation that can be posited against the traditional Christian view is that God, in consulting with Himself, divides His own personality. But we have already determined that this is in conflict with biblical usage. Therefore the only acceptable interpretation of this plural form is the traditional Christian view and, thus, we have in this passage another reference to the Trinity.

The statement, "the man has now become like one of us, knowing good and evil," needs some careful consideration. Was the serpent right after all? Among some ancient scholars the statement was considered to be irony. A few more recent interpreters have also taken this position. The second part of the statement makes it difficult to defend this position, however. The fact presented in the first part of the verse now leads to a corrective measure which is mentioned in the last part of the verse. At the same time, it is difficult to conceive of God expressing agreement with the words of the serpent which were used to lead the woman into sin.

How are we then to understand these words? We will have to accept the fact that eating the forbidden fruit could not give the knowledge of good and evil to which God had referred at the outset. This knowledge was to be gained only by *not* eating of the fruit of the tree. Still we can grant that eating of the tree did give a certain kind of knowledge of good and evil. To this extent the serpent was not altogether incorrect. That was precisely the subtlety of his deception. It had a certain resemblance to the truth. The serpent had told the woman that they would be equal to God, not dependent on God but independently distinguishing good from evil. In a certain sense this was the result of man's transgression. Man emancipated himself from God and became a law unto himself instead of submitting to the will of God. Man had judged between good and evil on the basis of his own findings. Complete independence from God is of course not possible for man. He can never liberate himself absolutely from God. But after the Fall he is a law unto himself. He is like an anarchist in a country where there is respectable government who actually is outside the control of that government. By his own efforts and intentions man knew good and evil. But, even so, he could never free himself completely from the divine norm for good and evil.

Now that man has come to this state, God declares, "He must not be allowed to reach out his hand, and take also from the tree of life and eat, and live forever." After the initial reference in 2:9, this is the first detail we are given about the "tree of life." Several interpreters have suggested that this expresses an actual concern on the part of God. It is argued that since man has now achieved one divine quality in his knowledge of good and evil, God is worried lest man should also acquire the futher quality of immortality. So God decides to restrict man. These scholars, then, see in this an evidence of the jealousy of the gods which plays such a big role in Greek mythology. But this is certainly not in harmony with the entire presentation of the Paradise narrative as we have considered it. This would be more in line with the deceptive claims of the serpent. The meaning of the statement is simply that God clearly prohibits man from eating of the "tree of life." That man, previous to this, had been free to eat of this tree is obvious. God said, "You are free to eat of any tree in the garden." The only exception was the tree of the knowledge of good and evil. Thus, eating of the "tree of life" had been permissible. But now this was no longer the case. By God's specific command it was forbidden.

There has been much conjecture as to whether man had actually eaten of the tree of life prior to this. The language in which the prohibition is phrased suggests that he had not eaten of it. If he had, the command of God would have used words such as "no longer" or "no more." Our attention is also called to the use of the word "also." Now, lest he *also* eat of this other specially designated tree, God sets up the prohibition.

In seeking an answer to the question why man might not eat of the "tree of life,'' it should be noted that this prohibition was given as a necessary consequence of the fall into sin. Human beings had eaten of the tree of the knowledge of good and evil and, as a consequence of this act, they had become subject to death. Thus it was only natural that they should be prevented from eating of the tree which represented life. Because they had eaten the forbidden fruit they now were forbidden to eat of the tree of life.

From this it is evident that the two specially designated trees in the Garden stood in a definite relationship to each other. Eating of the one precluded eating of the other. In this connection, it cannot be considered a matter of accident that man had not previously eaten of the tree of life. We could consider that, through a special guidance of God's providence, man was kept from eating of this tree. But even this interpretation is not wholly satisfying. There must have been some intrinsic reason why man ate of the one tree and not of the other. This intrinsic reason can probably be found in that the two trees represent two sides of the command. If man chose the path of obedience he would not eat of the tree of the knowledge of good and evil, but would eat of the tree of life and live forever. If, on the other hand, he chose the path of disobedience, he would leave the fruit of the tree of life untouched but would eat of the tree of the knowledge of good and evil and become the victim of death. It is clear that the Paradise narrative portrays man as standing before a twofold possibility. Either he would acquire eternal life, which he did not yet have, or he would be subjected to death, to which he had not previously been subjected.

3:23 *So the Lᴏʀᴅ God banished him from the Garden of Eden to work the ground from which he had been taken.*

In the prohibition against eating of the tree of life we see the direction which the execution of the sentence was to take. This is further evidenced in man's being driven out of Paradise. He was sent away from the beautiful garden with its precious trees to till the ground from which he was taken. This is what the divine sentence had pronounced. Henceforth man was to toil with ''pain'' and ''by the sweat of your brow.'' There is a sharp contrast between the work of tending the garden, which had been his responsibility, and the work of tilling the ground, to which he is now sentenced. The contrast consisted of the hardships and reverses which characterized the labor to which man was subjected as a consequence of the Fall.

3:24 *After he drove the man out, he placed on the east side of the Garden of Eden cherubim and a flaming sword flashing back and forth to guard the way to the tree of life.*

The dismissal from Paradise was irrevocable. There could be no thought of returning. A heavenly armed guard was placed at the entrance to make reentry impossible.

There is the added detail that the guard was placed on the "east side" of the garden. This is difficult to explain. It is possible that the first people made their home to the east of the area where the garden was located. Thus we see in Genesis 4:16 that Cain lived in the land of Nod, to the east of Eden.

The heavenly guard consisted of cherubim. These must be seen as spiritual beings who belong to the world of angels. They appear at various times in the Old Testament. In 2 Samuel 22:11 and Psalm 18:10 we read that God "mounted the cherubim." In Ezekiel 9:3 and 10 they appear in the visionary appearance of God to the prophet. Images of cherubim were placed above the "mercy-seat," which was above the ark (Exod. 25: 19–22). In this connection we read that God was "enthroned between the cherubim" (1 Sam. 4:4; 2 Sam. 6:2; 2 Kings 19:15; 1 Chron. 13:6; Pss. 80:1; 99:1; Isa. 37:16).

Later, the temple of Solomon included cherubim overshadowing the ark with their wings, within the Holy of Holies (1 Kings 6:23–28; 8:6–8). Cherubim were used also to decorate the walls of the temple (1 Kings 6:29; 7:29, 36). It is impossible for us to determine the exact nature of these heavenly beings and how they differed from other classes of angels. Of course, they had no real physical form. It is not surprising, then, that the presentation the Bible gives of them is not always the same. There is also considerable difference of opinion regarding their specific importance and function. It is obvious that in the religious thinking of ancient Israel they were very familiar. The sacred writer, therefore, refers to them without conisdering it necessary to give any further description of them.

It is also evident from this entire passage that a possible return to the earthly Paradise was not included in the promised triumph of the Seed of the woman. The way to the tree of life which God had placed in the Garden was to be forever closed. That way was guarded by cherubim with flashing swords. When the "seed of the woman" achieves the victory, the fruits of that victory will include something else than a renewal of the Garden of Eden. Jesus Christ opens the way to eternal life in the glories of heaven.

Just as we find accounts of "creation" among many other nations, even though these accounts are grossly degenerated, so we also find traces of a Paradise tradition among other peoples. Though a complete rendering of the biblical Paradise narrative is not found among any other people, various aspects of the story can be discovered. Thus we find a tradition about an original state of bliss and righteousness and then a moral breach or sin causing the termination of that happy state. Also, several peoples have traditions that portray death as not being part of man's original condition but as coming on man at a later time. There are also many other similarities that can be pointed out. Some have a tradition about a garden and even of a designated tree in that garden. This is, however, always presented as the tree of life. Some also have a narrative about a serpent who played a significant role as an evil, disruptive, spiritual force. Although these traditions are largely corrupted, they do give evidence of recollections of the tragic adventures of our first parents.

With respect to the Paradise narrative, as was the case with the creation narrative, some scholars find so much similarity between the biblical account and other accounts that they are convinced that the writer of Genesis simply copied from these other narratives. Once again, to respond to these claims, we would refer to my book, *De Goddelijke Openbaring in de Eerste Drie Hoofdstukken van Genesis*. There this claim that the account in Scripture is copied from Babylonian and Egyptian sources is carefully examined and thoroughly refuted.

3. *Cain and Abel* (4:1–26)

The history of heaven and earth now moves forward with a description of the first development of the human race from the fallen man and his wife. Emphasis is placed on the frightening fratricide that sets the destructive consequences of the Fall in such clear focus. The godless quest to be liberated from the authority of the highest Lawgiver leads to horrible licentiousness, also in the area of mutual human relationships. It was this licentiousness or rebellion against authority that was manifest in Cain's murder of his brother Abel. It was even more blatantly expressed in Lamech's boastful speech.

Genesis 4 follows logically on 2:4–3:24. This is even acknowledged by those who support the source-splitting theory. They acknowledge both passages as being from the same source—"J." They do have a problem since the name for God is now changed to the name Jahweh only, while in the former passage the name Jahweh Elohim was used. The critics give no explanation for this rather radical change. It is interesting, moreover, that in the Septuagint the name "Lord God" is retained in verses 6, 15, and 26. All of this only goes to confirm what we have pointed out in the Introduction, that dividing the sources on the basis of the names used for God has no substantial basis in the biblical text.

Many have expressed doubts about the unity of Genesis 4. The following problems have been raised. In verse 12 Cain is described as a "restless wanderer,'' while in verse 17 he is credited with building a city. Further, if Abel was a herder of sheep, Jabal cannot correctly be called, in verse 20, the father of those "who . . . raise livestock.'' Again, if Cain built a city, Jabal could not have developed the life of living in tents and raising livestock. The order should be reversed, it is claimed. First, the nomadic life of living in tents would have been developed and then, much later, the building of cities. These apparent problems, however, do not prove that Genesis 4 was drawn from more than one source. As we proceed with our interpretation of this chapter we will treat each of these objections in greater detail.

Let it be said here that the curse on Cain, which made him a fugitive and a nomad, does not preclude that he could have built a city where he would have felt more secure from pursuit. Also, nomads and city dwellers could well have lived in close proximity to each other. Later history clearly describes situations in which these two cultures were closely related to each other.

Further, it becomes immediately clear that Abel's role as a sheepherder and the broad-scale raising of livestock on the part of nomads such as Jabal were not at all similar. As a result of the shakiness of the evidence, many who support the theory of source splitting in general have little sympathy with the attempts to divide chapter 4.

That Genesis 4 is intended to be a historical message cannot be questioned. Whether we actually accept it as historical is, of course, a different matter. That is not a matter of interpretation of the text but rather depends on one's view of Scripture. It is striking that the history of Cain and Abel is memorialized a number of times in the New Testament (Matt. 23:35; Luke 11:50–51; Heb. 11:4; 12:24; 1 John 3:12; Jude 11).

4:1 *Adam lay with his wife Eve, and she conceived and gave birth to Cain. She said, "With the help of the LORD I have brought forth a man."*

In verse 1 the connection with what precedes is very clear. The history recorded here is tied to the Paradise narrative with the conjunctive phrase "and the man.'' This "man'' is presented as being familiar to us from the preceding events, with no further introduction necessary. Also, his wife is simply presented by her name, Eve, which name, according to 3:20, she had been given by her husband.

We are told that the man "knew'' (NIV, "lay with'') his wife. The word that is used is the usual Hebrew word which means "to know'' or "to become aware of.'' Here, as in many other places, it is used for sexual intercourse. It should be noted that the word is thus used only in the case of human beings. Sexual intercourse among people is not just a physical function, as it is among animals, but is a conscious act. The fact that this is the first time this relationship is mentioned does not mean that there was no sexual intercourse in Paradise. Neither should it be inferred that sexual intercourse was a consequence of the sinful eating of the forbidden tree. Sexual relationships are not wrong or sinful in themselves. They are grounded in the creation of humans as male and female. As such this is part of God's creation ordinance, "Be fruitful and increase in number." We refer also to what has been said in connection with Genesis 3:7. The account of this relationship at this point serves only as an introduction to the birth of a child to Adam and Eve. This is a common mode of expression throughout the Old Testament (vv. 17, 25; 1 Sam. 1:19; etc.). The idea that this verb "knew" is used only for the first sexual relationship between a man and his wife is untenable. This is evident from the use of the same verb with "again" in verse 25, and also from 1 Samuel 1:19.

Of some interest here is the naming of the child—"Cain," Hebrew *qayin*. Eve said that this name had been selected because of its meaning—"brought forth," which is the Hebrew word *qānâ*. As far as we can determine, there is no etymological connection between *qayin* and *qānâ*. Nor was it Eve's intention to establish this derivation. It should be borne in mind that Eve did not speak Hebrew. Once again we have an instance similar to that which we pointed out in 3:20. Apparently the inspired writer was able to find a Hebrew word that had a similar sound to the name given by Eve and the word on which Eve based her selection of a name in her own language.

There have been those who have concluded, from the fact that it was the mother who named this child, that this first society was a matriarchy. Opposing this conclusion is the fact that in this same chapter, verse 26, we already have an instance of a father naming a child.

In Hebrew Eve's statement presents some problems in translation. It would be possible to translate her statement, "I have received the Lord as a man." This must be decisively rejected. Another translation which was rather generally accepted in the ancient church and during the Middle Ages was, "I have received a man, namely, the Lord." This was then understood in such a way that Eve saw in Cain the fulfillment of the maternal promise in Genesis 3:15. She then, supposedly, looked on her child as God Himself, and thus had a preview of the deity of the Mediator. Opposing this view is the fact that Genesis 3:15 gives no hint that the "seed of the woman" was to be divine. The deity of the Messiah was not revealed until much later.

A Jewish Targum by Onkelos translates the line, "I have received a man from the Lord." This does assume a slightly different Hebrew text, including the preposition "from." Many later translations follow this suggested translation. Probably the best solution is to translate the preposition "with" in the sense of "with the help of." Thus our translation reads, "With the help of the Lord I have brought forth a man."

Unquestionably, there was much truth in the old view that Eve saw in the birth of Cain a fulfillment of the maternal promise. Certainly she did not have a developed concept of the nature of the coming Mediator. But it can be assumed that she saw in this man, whom she brought into the world with the help of the Lord, a glimpse of the "seed" that would conquer the serpent and the spiritual force which lurked behind the serpent. But how tragically Cain failed to measure up to that expectation.

4:2 *Later she gave birth to his brother Abel.*
Now Abel kept flocks, and Cain worked the soil.

It has been observed that, in the case of Eve's second son, his birth is announced without mention of a sexual relationship on the part of the man and his wife. Some have assumed from this omission that Cain and Abel were twins. However, this is reading into the text what is not there. The omission of a reference to the conception of this child can readily be explained by asserting that such a reference would have been superfluous in this context. Also, the introduction of Abel as Cain's brother does not require any fanciful interpretation. This did no more than set the stage for the gruesome event that was about to be recorded. The emphasis falls on the fact that it was his own brother whom Cain murdered. (See also v. 8.) In short, the biblical narrative, as we have received it, gives no solid evidence for Cain and Abel being twins. We should simply recognize the fact that the account does not include this information, and leave it at that.

There has been much conjecture regarding the name "Abel," in Hebrew *Habel* or *Hebel*. The Hebrew word means "futility" or "nullity." There is, however, no way of knowing just what Eve had in mind with this name. Again, we must be reminded that Eve did not speak Hebrew. Therefore, conclusions drawn from the meaning of a Hebrew word which sounds similar to the name Eve gave her son are really quite meaningless.

The two brothers chose different occupations. Cain became a tiller of the soil. It should be noted that the expression, "worked the soil," was used also in 3:23. Abel, on the other hand, became a herder of sheep, or, literally, of "small cattle." These undoubtedly included sheep but possibly also goats. Thus we see a broadening of the culture in that in addition to tilling the soil, there was also the raising of flocks.

4:3, 4a *In the course of time Cain brought some of the fruits of the soil as an offering to the LORD. But Abel brought fat portions from some of the firstborn of his flock.*

In the course of time, both brothers brought an offering to the Lord. The word that is used for "offering" became the term used for the "wheat offering" when later the sacrifices were introduced during the Mosaic period. Originally the word simply meant "a gift" or "present." More specifically, it took on the meaning of a "gift to God." And that is the sense in which it is used here.

The brothers brought offerings that were in keeping with their respective occupations. Cain brought some of his agricultural products and Abel some of his cattle. In the latter case we are told that he brought the "firstborn" of his flock. There is no basis for concluding that Cain's offering did not consist of the "firstfruits" of his harvest. This is not the significant distinction between the two offerings. Hebrews 11:4 teaches that the difference lay in the inner attitudes of the two brothers. Abel brought his offering in "faith" while Cain did not. All efforts to find the distinction in some external factor are bound to flounder because the text does not indicate this data. Mention could be made that Abel brought of "the fat" and that this was later considered to be the best part of the animal. Thus he definitely brought the best he had as an offering to the Lord. Even so, there is no indication that Cain did not do the same.

4:4b, 5 *The LORD looked with favor on Abel and his offering, but on Cain and his offering he did not look with favor. So Cain was very angry, and his face was downcast.*

We read that God looked with favor on Abel and his offering, but not with respect to Cain and his offering. The reason for this is revealed to us in Hebrews 11:4. Several other supposed reasons have been suggested. Some have insisted that the offering of animals had been instituted by God Himself in 3:21, and therefore was the only sacrifice that was acceptable to God. Although Genesis 3:21 did give warrant to kill animals, it certainly made no mention of using animals for sacrifices. Others have suggested that animal sacrifices were more acceptable to God, or that sheepherders were more acceptable than tillers of the soil, etc. There is, however, no biblical basis for any of these theories.

Even more objectionable is the ancient Jewish interpretation that Cain failed to observe the proper ritual in bringing his offering. This idea rests on a wholly unwarranted predating of the Mosaic laws for sacrifices to the time immediately after the Paradise events.

It has been correctly observed that the text in no way mentions the reason or reasons for the acceptance of the one offering and the rejection of the other. It is a serious error, moreover, to charge the text with a deficiency on this score. It is obviously with intent that the narrative is given as it is. Here were two brothers who *outwardly* did the same thing. The only difference between their acts of worship was one which only God could discern, because He knew their hearts. The difference was exclusively one of the inner attitudes of the heart. What we have here then, is the first presentation of a burning message which runs throughout Scripture. The most high God has no pleasure in mere outward forms of worship but demands the sincere offerings of the heart.

A second problem that presents itself is how Cain and Abel could determine that the one offering was accepted and the other was not. That this was immediately evident to them is obvious. It was this that stirred Cain to wrath. How then did he know that God had rejected his offering and accepted the one brought by his brother Abel?

A favorite answer to this has been that God sent fire from heaven in the one case but not in the other. This is based on references such as Leviticus 9:24; 1 Kings 18:38; etc. There have been those, moreover, who prefer to find the answer in the way the smoke ascended upward. Calvin suggests that it was a matter of the way God blessed Abel in his business while withholding His blessing from Cain's endeavors. When all have been heard, the obvious fact remains that the text does not tell us how the acceptable from the unacceptable sacrifice was discerned. It behooves us then to honestly and humbly admit that the text of Scripture does not give us this information and consequently we do not know.

4:6, 7 *Then the LORD said to Cain, "Why are you angry? Why is your face downcast? If you do what is right, will you not be accepted? But if you do not do what is right, sin is crouching at your door; it desires to have you, but you must master it."*

Because Cain became so angry, God came to him with a stern warning. The wording of this warning presents some difficulties. One recent scholar declared that verse 7 is the most obscure verse, not only of this chapter, but of the entire Book of Genesis. Some have concluded that the verse cannot be interpreted because it has been hopelessly corrupted.

The question, "Why are you angry? Why is your face downcast?" presents no serious difficulty. The purpose of the question seems to be to point out the impropriety of Cain's anger. If God did not accept his offering there certainly must have been good reasons for this. Therefore, he had no reason to be angry.

The first difficulty we face is determining the meaning of the term which our translators have rendered, "You will be accepted." The literal meaning of the term is "there is exaltation" or "lifting up." Some have translated it "forgiveness" or "acceptance" (our translation). We think then of the acceptance of the offering and the one bringing the offering. If Cain would do right, another offering would be acceptable. Among the various other interpretations there is one which our authors consider to be the most natural. This view holds that the word "exalt" or "lift up" refers to Cain's face or facial expression. This would, then, be in contrast to the statement in verse 6 that says Cain's face was downcast. In Hebrew this literally says that Cain's face "fell." The intent would be, then, that if Cain would change his ways he would be able to remove the depression from his countenance and be able to face the world with a happy face. What this amounts to is a call to repentance and change of life for Cain.

The next difficulty we have to face is the statement which our translators have worded, "If you do not do what is right, sin is crouching at your door." This is probably the most widely accepted reading. It presents sin as a dangerous animal stalking its prey. Some even think of it as a demon. If Cain does not repent of his bad attitude there is real danger that he will fall into even greater evil. This is the curse of sin when it is not confessed. It constantly leads to other and greater sins.

Our difficulty with this reading is that the text does not indicate what is intended with the word "door." It has been suggested that it must refer to the door of the heart. But if this was the intent, why is it then not stated? We certainly cannot think of the door of a house. We feel that the word probably should be used in its primary meaning, which is "opening." We can then think of the opening of the lair in which the beast is hiding. The animal lies poised at the opening of his den, ready to pounce on any hapless victim that passes that way. Obviously, in any case we are dealing with a figurative expression. The figure, moreover, is intended to warn that danger lies near. We can then simply translate it "sin lies in wait."

It should be noted that the Septuagint gives a translation of this part of verse 7 which departs radically from the Hebrew text. That translation assumed the existence of the whole Mosaic structure of the sacrifices. This is certainly a false assumption, since that structure was completely unknown at the time of Cain and Abel. This obviously biased translation serves to emphasize the fact that this verse has always presented serious difficulties for translators.

Finally, the concluding words of the verse confront us with an even greater difficulty. Our translators have rendered it, "it desires to have you, but you must master it." There is one translation that says this refers to Abel. What we have then is that Abel is favorably inclined to Cain and is willing to let Cain have the ruling rights of the firstborn. Others have turned this around and have suggested that what it means is that Cain need not be jealous of Abel because, as long as Cain did the right thing, Abel would look up to him and submit to his authority.

It is striking that the words used here are similar to those used in the penalty pronounced on Eve in 3:16, "Your desire will be for your husband, and he will rule over you." The words translated "desire" and "rule" are identically the same words used here in 4:7. Some have concluded, therefore, that this is nothing but a corruption of the original text which was caused by a copyist allowing his eye to stray into the wrong column. Genesis 3:16 just happened to be at that point and was erroneously re-copied. This explanation is a bit too radical for us to accept.

Most modern scholars agree that the sentence refers back to the preceding one in which sin is portrayed as a poised animal. The desire to sin reaches out to Cain, but he must strive against it and rule over it. There is an interesting bit of theological prejudice which has crept in at this point on the part of some translators. They make the passage read, "you *can* rule over it." This would then fortify their denial of man's natural inclination to sin. But this is not what the Hebrew text says. There is nothing more here than "you *shall* rule over it" and this must be considered as a command and not as a promise or a prophecy of human success in the battle against sin.

The fact that some have applied these words to Abel, rather than to sin, is partially explained by the masculine form of the personal pronoun used here. The Hebrew word for sin is, however, feminine and thus would require the feminine personal pronoun if this is what it referred to. Various attempts have been made to get around this linguistic obstacle. The most plausible is that the pronoun refers back to the figure of the beast which represents sin in the first part of the verse. This can properly be indentified by a masculine pronoun.

4:8 *Now Cain said to his brother Abel, "Let's go out to the field." And while they were in the field, Cain attacked his brother Abel and killed him.*

The divine warning is in vain, however. Cain cannot be dissuaded. In his hostility he invites his brother Abel out into the open field. There he beats him to death, and we have the first bloodshed of one person by another person—a ghastly fratricide. What a terrible expression of the corruption the fall into sin brought on the human race!

4:9 *Then the Lord said to Cain, "Where is your brother Abel?"*
"I don't know," he replied. "Am I my brother's keeper?"

Just as in 3:9ff., the guilty one is called to give an account before the supreme Judge. Cain's answer to the Lord's question was, however, not an acknowledgment and an excuse like that of the first human pair. On the contrary, he boldly denied all responsibility. He claimed that he knew nothing about the affair. He added the defiant question, "Am I my brother's keeper?" Some have claimed that Cain indulged in a play on words here. Just as Abel was a keeper of sheep he now mockingly rejects the idea that he should be a keeper for his brother. This is, however, pushing the text beyond what it actually says. Cain simply said that, in his judgment, he was not responsible for taking care of his brother or looking out for his well-being. Thus he defied the heavenly Judge.

4:10 *The Lord said, "What have you done? Listen! Your brother's blood cries out to me from the ground.*

But the supreme Judge will not be misled by bold denials. He openly exposes the sin of the murderer. The question, "What have you done?" brings no response. Thereby the all-knowing God declares, "You know very well what you have done." He then proceeds to spell out with painful emphasis the heinous nature of Cain's crime. He graphically portrays the blood of his slain brother crying to heaven for judgment on the one who has committed this wanton crime.

4:11, 12 *Now you are under a curse and driven from the ground, which opened its mouth to receive your brother's blood from your hand. When you work the ground, it will no longer yield its crops for you. You will be a restless wanderer on the earth."*

The murderer receives a harsh sentence. He is literally "cursed" by God. It is worthy of note that this is the first instance in which a curse is pronounced on a person. In Genesis 3 we read of the curse on the serpent and on the ground. Now God pronounces His curse on a human person.

In the Hebrew there is added, "from the ground." Some have interpreted this as meaning that Cain was banished from the "ground," that is the fruitful, tillable land. We believe the interpretation must be found in another direction. As becomes apparent from verse 12, the curse consisted, in part, in that the ground would no longer yield a harvest for Cain, no matter how hard he worked at it. Thus we have, in essence, a sharpening of the curse mentioned earlier in 3:17–19. For Cain there would not only be a curtailed yield of the crops that were tilled, but there would be no yield at all. In other words, this curse established an unbridgeable chasm between Cain and the ground. The ground which drank the blood of his brother would no longer yield a harvest for Cain. It would actually become hostile to him. This, it seems to us, is indicated by the term "from the ground"—a separation or cleavage between Cain and the ground.

Another consequence of the curse would be that Cain would become a fugitive and a wanderer in the earth. No longer would he be able to gain sustenance from the ground. He would be compelled to look elsewhere for his livelihood. And failing to find it there he would move elsewhere again. Thus he would roam from place to place without finding rest anywhere.

4:13, 14 *Cain said to the* LORD, *"My punishment is more than I can bear. Today you are driving me from the land, and I will be hidden from your presence; I will be a restless wanderer on the earth, and whoever finds me will kill me."*

God's stern sentence of judgment obviously made its impression on the guilty Cain. Some read, "My guilt is more than I can bear." Our translators have rendered it, "My punishment is more than I can bear." In either case, it is obvious that Cain no longer denies his guilt. He now turns to complaining about the severity of his punishment. This complaint must not be construed as an evidence of sincere repentance. True repentance does not complain about the severity of the punishment.

"Today you are driving me from the land." Many have interpreted this as indicating that Cain was driven from the productive, cultivated land (see v. 7). In this connection, some have suggested that Cain's further statement, "I will be hidden from your presence," indicates that it was Cain's belief that God dwells in the productive land and that all other land is deprived of His presence. This is, however, in direct conflict with what the text says further. We read in verse 15 of a sevenfold curse pronounced on anyone who would kill Cain. This revenge certainly would be executed by God. It is evident, then, that the territory covered by God's dominion extended wherever Cain might possibly wander in his life as a fugitive. Moreover, the land from which Cain is banished cannot be seen as the entire earth, since then there could be no mention of being "driven out."

What we actually have here is God punishing Cain by condemning him to the life of a fugitive and a wanderer across the face of the earth. He must leave the land which had been his home. Verse 16 suggests that this was the area in which Eden was located. Cain's statement, "I will be hidden from your presence," did not appear, as such, as part of his sentence that was pronounced by God. Just as Adam and Eve had "hidden" from God out of a sense of guilt and shame for their sin, so Cain realized that his crime had placed a barrier between him and God. He would have to hide from the presence of God, his Judge.

One other matter was of immediate concern to Cain. He, as a murderer, knew that his own life could also be taken. His natural sense of justice told him that the one shedding man's blood may have his own blood shed as punishment. Thus he sensed that his own life would henceforth be in constant danger. Whoever met him would want to kill him.

Here we face the question of whom Cain could be afraid. Where did these other people come from? Modern critics have had a heyday with this statement. On the basis of this complaint of Cain they have called the entire narrative of the origin of man in Genesis 1–3 into question. They have concluded that the account of the murder of Abel by his brother Cain is no more than a saga which came from a much later period when the human race was already well developed. When it was incorporated into the Book of Genesis, the redactor ignored the fact that it was completely incongruous with the context in which it appears. From this perspective the redactor who gathered these materials is presented as nothing more than an ignorant blunderer.

But how must this problem then be resolved? Certainly not by presupposing a race of human beings which was in existence before Adam. It should not be forgotten that, although the biblical narrative up to this point mentions only the birth of Cain and Abel, there is nothing that says that Adam and Eve did not have more children who are not mentioned. Verse 17 tells us that Cain had a wife. This clearly indicates that there were also daughters in the family. In this first family, the total number of which we are not told, brothers must have married sisters. By the time Cain and Abel were adults and Abel was murdered, there could well have been additional families with children and even grandchildren. Thus when Cain speaks about the threat to his life he obviously took into account this natural increase of the human race. Considering the great age which people reached during this period of history, the expansion of the human race could have been extensive during Cain's life span.

Again, it must be remembered that the revelation we are given does not include all the details that we might like to know, nor does it give answers to all the question we might like to ask. It tells us what we, in God's purpose, need to know.

4:15 *But the LORD said to him, "Not so; if anyone kills Cain, he will suffer vengeance seven times over." Then the LORD put a mark on Cain so that no one who found him would kill him.*

God meets Cain's fear by assuring him that he will not be an easy victim for murder attempts wherever he goes. The verse opens with a word that has caused some difficulty. The literal meaning of the Hebrew word which is used is "very well." However, the Septuagint and several other early translations have rendered this as a strong negative. This can only be considered as a facilitating of the original text. Our translators have followed this lead and have used the term, "Not so!"

Sevenfold vengeance does not imply that if Cain was killed seven members of the murderer's family would be killed. The number seven is used here in the sense of "fullness" or "completeness." Thus God assures Cain that his murder would be definitely and fully avenged.

Besides this assurance, God gave Cain a mark or sign to confirm His promise. Some read this as a mark which Cain himself wore. There are many opinions regarding the nature of that mark. One ancient Jewish view was that Cain became a leper. Others believed that he was given a wild, foreboding appearance which frightened his would-be assailants on sight of him. Others have suggested that he was branded with some identifying mark on his face—what some have called "The sign of the murderer." A favorite view among the critics was that Cain adopted an identifying tattoo on his forehead. This, it is suggested, was the same mark which the nomadic tribe of the Kenites used as a mark of identification. There is a basic objection, however, to all theories which make this "mark" something Cain himself wore on his person. Such a mark would make him readily recognizable to his enemies and as such would put him in constant danger, rather than secure his safety.

The words can also be understood as a sign given to Cain to confirm God's promise to him. The sign would then be a guarantee or pledge on God's part to Cain, assuring him of the promise that he would not be killed. Such signs were common in Old Testament times (see Exod. 3:12; 1 Sam. 10:7; 2 Kings 19:29; Isa. 7:11, 14; and Jer. 44:29). Precisely what this sign was we are not told. Once again, here is a matter on which the Scripture is silent and all conjecture is simply guesswork.

It has often been said that this assurance and its accompanying sign were a softening of the penalty pronounced on Cain. It should be remembered, however, that Cain was not sentenced to death. This protection of his life, which God provided, in no way altered the penalty that had been pronounced. The fact that Cain was not given the death sentence was indeed an evidence of the mercy of God. The punishment of being made a lifelong fugitive and vagabond in the earth was a heavy one. Even so, the sparing of his life was an evidence of God's grace. It reminds us of Genesis 3 where we are informed that Adam and Eve did not die on the day they ate of the forbidden tree. Even so, the punishment for their sin was real and serious. The grace shown to Cain is further evidenced by the assurance and the accompanying sign that his life would be protected.

4:16 *So Cain went out from the LORD's presence and lived in the land of Nod, east of Eden.*

Thereupon Cain left the presence of God and began his life as a wanderer. Many interpreters read this as indicating a complete departure from God, a total estrangement from God's presence. Some tie this in with the concept we mentioned in our study of verse 13, that the domain of the Lord (Jahweh) was restricted to the cultivated lands. Since Cain left these tillable lands, it is argued, he also cut himself loose from the gracious manifestation of the presence of God. It is our contention that this is reading far more into the text than is actually there. It is our view that these words simply indicate that Cain's immediate confrontation with God had ended (vv. 9–15) and he goes out to live his life. The passage says nothing about Cain's later religious life.

Then we are told that he settled in the land of Nod. Establishing his home in a given area is not in conflict with his life as a fugitive and a vagabond. Nomads also have a homeland, even though it may encompass a wide area. Thus Cain chose the land of Nod as the territory in which he would move about in his nomadic life style.

We do not know exactly where the land of Nod was located. No research or excavation has, to date, produced any solid evidence on which to base a precise geographic location. The text indicates that it was east of Eden. This would seem to imply that Adam and Eve and their family remained in the general area where the Garden of Eden had been located. Cain, the fugitive, could not stay there and so he moved eastward.

There have been some attempts to make a determination on the basis of the word "Nod," and even on the letters of that word. It should be pointed out that there is a basic objection to that kind of word study when it applies to names and places involved in this period. As we have repeatedly observed, we are dealing with the period before the "confusion of languages" at Babel. As such, the Hebrew language was not yet in existence.

4:17 *Cain lay with his wife, and she became pregnant and gave birth to Enoch. Cain was then building a city, and he named it after his son Enoch.*

The narrative now gives us a few details about Cain's further life, and that of his family. We immediately face the question of the origin of Cain's wife. As we observed in verse 14, she must have been his sister. That we have no previous record of the birth of this sister is of no importance. Genesis 5:4 tells us specifically that, besides the three children that are singled out by name, "Adam bore sons and daughters." Any faithful interpreter certainly recognizes the fact that the narrative before us is no official record or "family tree" giving all of the details of times and places. Thus the presence of sisters, and even of nieces and grandnieces, at this time in no way conflicts with the biblical record.

The marriage of blood relatives, in this instance, need cause no serious problem. Nor should it be used to justify such a relationship in subsequent history, since all generations of mankind stemmed "from one blood" (Acts 17:26). It was imperative, therefore, that in the beginning there should be marriages between close blood relatives. But when this necessity no longer existed, this practice was forbidden by specific command of God. The laws against consanguinity were spelled out in the Mosaic laws which came much later.

Something can be said for the fact that Cain was already married before he murdered his brother Abel. Some have even placed the birth of his son and the building of the city prior to his sentencing as a fugitive and a vagabond. But this is really unnecessary. Many of the arguments used to defend these theories are rather unrealistic.

It is not impossible that Cain's efforts toward building a city were an attempt on his part to thwart the penalty God had imposed on him, and to establish a single place of residence. Even so, the effort was doomed to failure. It should be noted that the record states that Cain "was then building a city." There is no mention of the completion of this venture. It is also possible that this city was intended as a place of safety for his tribal family while he moved about as a nomad and a wanderer. We are given some hint in this direction in that the city was named after his son and not after the builder himself. We should be rather cautious in drawing too many conclusions from the building of this city. We should not, for instance, conceive of this city as some elaborate, carefully designed metropolis. It probably was little more than a "base camp" with a few natural fortifications which were then strengthened by the erection of stone boundaries or walls which could be defended in case of an enemy attack. This would offer a greater sense of safety than camping in the open fields. Thus this represents another step in the development of culture.

The name of Cain's son and of the city that was erected was the Hebrew word *hanôk*. This has been variously translated throughout history. Our translators have used the most common translation, "Enoch." Attempts have been made to relate this name to similar names that appear later, but we should remember that Cain did not speak Hebrew.

Efforts to geographically locate the "city" built by Cain have proved futile. Naturally, the changes brought about on the face of the earth by the later deluge cannot be left out of consideration.

4:18 *To Enoch was born Irad, and Irad was the father of Mehujael, and Mehujael was the father of Methushael, and Methushael was the father of Lamech.*

Verse 18 gives us the genealogy of Cain. All attempts to discover meanings for the names which are listed here on the basis of similarity to various Hebrew words end in complete failure. Once again, we point to the linguistic problems of the period before the confusion of languages. (See our discussion under 3:20.) One interesting phenomenon is that some of the names mentioned here also appear in the register of families given in Genesis 5. Others have a striking similarity to names that appear there. These similarities will be discussed when we consider Genesis 5.

4:19 *Lamech married two women, one named Adah and the other Zillah.*

We are told that Lamech married two women. The intent of this record is obviously to indicate that he was the first to do so. Instead of the monogamous marriage which was instituted in Paradise (Gen. 2:21–23), the practice of polygamy was now introduced. This was a further evidence of the tendencies which resulted from man's fall into sin.

The name of Lamech's one wife was "Adah." This name appears later as the name of one of Esau's wives (36:2ff.). It is claimed that this is derived from a Hebrew word which means "to adorn oneself." Lamech's other wife was named "Zillah." Even though this name does not appear in the later Old Testament, it has been suggested that it is a form of the Hebrew word which means "shadow." Once again, we caution against treating these names as being Hebrew before the Hebrew language was a reality.

4:20, 21 *Adah gave birth to Jabal; he was the father of those who live in tents and raise livestock. His brother's name was Jubal; he was the father of all who play the harp and flute.*

We now have a further description of the family of Lamech. Adah bore him two sons, Jabal and Jubal. Both of these names appear only here and are difficult to define as to their meaning. Various suggestions have been made but none can be established with any certainty.

When these men are described as being "the father of" some trade or profession, it should not be concluded that these designations fail to take the Deluge into account. Certainly, no one would insist that all musicians, for instance, were related by strict genealogical connections. The intent is only to designate this individual as the first to excel in a particular skill or trade. Moreover, it goes without saying that all knowledge of such a skill or trade did not terminate at the time of the Deluge. This knowledge could well have been continued within the family of Noah.

Jabal, then, was "the father" of all who live in tents and raise livestock. There is a difficulty in translation here because there is no verb accompanying the word "livestock." Some have even translated this, "those who live in livestock tents." We have a similar expression in 2 Chronicles 14:15. We consider it better to use the word "dwell" with both nouns, only giving it a slightly different meaning when it refers to cattle. We would then get something like "Those who live in tents and by cattle." In other words, these were nomads who lived in tents and made their livelihood by raising cattle which they moved with them wherever they wandered.

It should also be noted that we have a different word used here for "cattle" than was used in the case of Abel, in verse 2. There the reference was to small cattle, sheep, and goats. The word used here can also include cows, camels, and mules. It is for that reason that Jabal can rightly be called the "father" of this industry. He carried it on in a far broader way than Abel had done.

Jubal was the "father" of all who play the harp and flute. It goes without saying that these instruments were still very primitive. Although these were greatly refined in later times, Jubal was the first to employ musical instruments for the purpose of making music.

4:22 *Zillah also had a son, Tubal-Cain, who forged all kinds of tools out of bronze and iron. Tubal-Cain's sister was Naamah.*

Zillah also bore a son, who was named Tubal-Cain. It has been suggested that he was the ancestor (or possibly the legendary figure which a tribe claimed as their founder) of a tribe by the name of Tubal. These people are mentioned at various times in the Old Testament (Gen. 10:2; 1 Chron. 1:5; Isa. 66:19; Ezek. 27:13; 32:26; 38:2–3; 39:1). The name

"Cain," which is added (omitted in the Septuagint), is then translated "the smith," or simply "of the family of Cain." Another interpretation of the name Tubal is that it meant "iron filings," and thus designated the man who worked with iron. Most of these attempts to pour meaning into these names are, however, pure conjecture.

We are told that Tubal-Cain "forged all kinds of tools out of bronze and iron." Although some different translations have been suggested, this appears to be the most faithful to the original text. One objection that has been raised is that this description of Tubal-Cain is in conflict with the historical development of the human race as this is generally understood. The simultaneous development of copper (or bronze) and iron tools does not square, we are told, with scientific discoveries regarding the ancient civilizations. The order of development started with the "stone age," then moved into the "bronze age," and not until much later do we find the "iron age." The fact that the stone age is not even mentioned in Genesis and that bronze and iron are thrown together, it is claimed, casts a dubious light on the historicity of the entire narrative.

In reply to this objection, it should be observed that this neat development of human civilization, passing through such clearly defined "ages," is scientifically open to serious question. There have been evidences that iron tools were used during the so-called "stone age." There are those scientists who question whether the "bronze age" actually existed outside the theories of certain scientists. There are, moreover, certain sections of the world where archaeological research has found no evidence of the use of stone tools at all but the use of iron tools goes back to the earliest civilizations. In view of all this, we need not be too concerned about a conflict with historical data. Nor need we resort to various exegetical contortions in order to try to square the biblical text with someone's favorite scientific theories.

It certainly is clear that the three sons of Lamech made enormous strides in the development of human culture. But it was a culture that was deprived of all awareness of man's need to serve God. Whether this godlessness is evidenced by the name Naamah, which was given to Tubal-Cain's sister, is, however, doubtful. Some have claimed that the name means "to be lovely," on the basis of a possible connection with a Hebrew word with that meaning. This would then be interpreted as an indication of a glorification of physical beauty. Just why Naamah is mentioned here is not clear. There is an old Jewish tradition that she became the wife of Noah, but there is no basis for this. It is possible that she was well known in the tradition of those for whom this record was first written. But for us today there is no information available which would indicate what her significance was.

4:23, 24 *Lamech said to his wives, "Adah and Zillah, listen to me; wives of Lamech, hear my words. I have killed a man for wounding me, a young man for injuring me. If Cain is avenged seven times, then Lamech seventy-seven times."*

The lack of reverence for God on the part of the Cainitish culture is further evidenced by the "song of Lamech." That we are here dealing with a song is evident both from its content and its form. The form includes the characteristic rhythm of poetry. It also uses the familiar parallelism, with both halves of the passage using similar modes of expression. Even in its content a poetic style is unmistakable. It is a song, however, which rings with boastful presumption and bloodthirsty violence. The discovery of tools by his son, Tubal-Cain, had provided him with weapons which gave him a feeling of strength, which, in turn, led him to defy boldly everything and everyone. Boiling up within him was an unbridled spirit of revenge at the slightest affront to his honor. Thus he boasts to his two wives. He will kill any man who wounds him. He will slaughter any child who strikes him. God may have promsied Cain that he would be avenged seven times, but he, Lamech, would avenge himself seventy times seven times. This does not indicate an exact number but, rather, speaks of excessive and unlimited execution of revenge.

There are some who believe that this song of Lamech has another origin and should not be placed in its present context. According to this theory, Lamech was not a descendant of Cain but rather the leader of a rival tribe that was known for its vicious and extreme revenge toward all who offended them. There is, however, no textual basis for this theory.

At this point the record of the genealogy of Cain ends. Some have claimed that the author of this section did not know about the Deluge. They argue that the genealogy given in chapter 5 continues right up to the Deluge. This then, we are told, indicates that chapter 4 comes from a different source. The question might well be asked of those holding this position, "Just why must the genealogy of Cain be carried up to the Deluge?" There may be good reasons for ending it with the record of Lamech and his sons. The context clearly suggests such a reason. If we compare Lamech's boastful outburst with the words of God to Cain in verse 15 the connection is clearly evident. The author establishes the relationship between Cain and Lamech. He vividly portrays the development of the brutality and violence which characterized the Cainites. When this has been achieved, the author's purpose has been realized and the genealogy is ended at that point. Whether the Deluge is brought into consideration or not has no significance in determining the authorship of Genesis 4 in distinction from Genesis 5. There is no conflict between these two chapters. Both chapters give significant background material for the narrative of the Flood.

4:25 *Adam lay with his wife again, and she gave birth to a son and named him Seth, saying, "God has granted me another child in place of Abel, since Cain killed him."*

In the Hebrew text there is no statement such as, "She said." The text moves directly into the words of Eve. It is striking that she uses the name "God" (Elohim), while the rest of the chapter consistently uses the name "LORD" (Jahweh). Some try to explain this by referring to verse 26. They then hold that the name "Jahweh" was not used until after the birth of Enosh. They insist, then, that Eve could not have used this name at this point. Naturally, they then also ascribe verses 25 and 26 to another source.

Let us respond to these interpretations by pointing out, first of all, that Eve does use the name "Jahweh" in verse 1 of this chapter. There she says, "With the help of the LORD (Jahweh) I have brought forth a man." Further, we consider the above-mentioned interpretation of verse 26 to be incorrect, as will become evident when we discuss this verse below. In general, it should be pointed out again that we need not conjure up fanciful explanations every time a specific name of God is used. The use of different names can well be wholly unintentional. If we compare our own use of the name of God in our prayers, for example, do we find it necessary to offer an explanation each time we address Him as "God" or "Lord" or "Father"? For this reason, we are convinced that there is no basis for using the names ascribed to God as grounds for dividing the sources. There is, furthermore, no call for various elaborate explanations each time a specific name of God is employed. To be sure, there are certain passages where there are obvious reasons for the use of specific names for the divine. In most instances, however, such reasons cannot and need not be determined.

The phrase, "since Cain killed him," belongs to the statement by Eve. Some have ascribed this phrase to the biblical writer. If we consider what was already said in verse 8, however, this would be superfluous here. On the other hand, it makes good sense when these words are put into the mouth of Eve, as she recalls what had been taken away from her and what had been given to her in return.

4:26 *Seth also had a son, and he named him Enosh.*
At that time men began to call on the name of the LORD.

Seth also bore a son and gave him the name "Enosh." This name is formally the same as a Hebrew word which means "man" or "humanity." We may not conclude from this, however, that this is the meaning of the name Enosh. We are reminded, once again, that prior to the confusion of speech there was no Hebrew language. The similarity between the name given by Seth and the similar Hebrew word must be explained by the existence of a Hebrew word which happens to have the same sound.

The closing words of this chapter present certain difficulties which we will consider with some care. The Vulgate gives a different translation, "and he began to call on the name of the Lord." Thus it makes Enosh the subject of the sentence. This translation, however, resulted from a faulty reading in the Septuagint. It must be recognized that the verb in this sentence has an impersonal form. It should then probably be translated "then was begun" or "men began." But, even so, there are differences of opinion regarding the meaning of the statement.

A few scholars have rendered it, "men began to call the Sethites by the name of the Lord." The problem with this reading is that the word "Sethites" is not even mentioned in the text. Thus there really is no other possible translation than, "men began to call on the name of the Lord."

The primary question, of course, is, "What does this mean?" Some place all emphasis on the name "Jahweh," which is used here. They insist that this simply says that men began to call God by the name Jahweh. This is, as we have already observed, in conflict with verse 1 of this chapter where Eve uses the name Jahweh. Again we have the basic problem that the name Jahweh is a Hebrew word and the Hebrew language did not even exist at this time. So what we come up with is that it was at this time that people began to "call on the name" of the God whom the Hebrews later called "Jahweh."

What are we to understand by this "calling on the name" of? Certainly this means more than just using the name of someone. It must, moreover, also mean more than prayer as such. It is quite unthinkable that no one had prayed to God before this time. It should be noted, for instance, that Cain and Abel brought sacrifices to God prior to this time, and this certainly must have included prayer. In the Old Testament "calling on the name of the Lord" frequently refers to public worship (note 2 Sam. 6:2; 1 Chron. 13:6; Pss. 79:6; 116:17; Jer. 10:25; Zeph. 3:9). This is also, most likely, what we must think of in the statement before us. The emphasis must fall on the public character of this worship. What was initiated at this time, the time of Enosh, was communal worship. Naturally we are not to think of a highly developed liturgy such as was established by the Mosaic laws. It was something far more simple and elementary. This development of

135

communal worship was, moreover, also a further indication of the advance of culture. But among the Sethites this cultural development took an entirely different direction than it did among the Cainites.

Although it has been possible to do much theorizing about the relationship between the biblical narratives about creation and Paradise to similar narratives among other peoples of ancient times, this is not possible in the case of the story of Cain and Abel. Not a trace of such a story is found among early Babylonian and Egyptian traditions. Attention has been called to a Phoenician tradition which has some resemblance to the biblical narrative about the development of culture among the descendants of Cain. In the Phoenician presentation there are also two brothers who are singled out. One of these established the city of Tyre and made huts from reeds and sticks. The other fabricated clothing from skins of animals, and was the first to venture out to sea in a log canoe. From the first of these brothers six other pairs of brothers descended. The first pair developed hunting and fishing; the second worked with iron, also witchcraft and fortune-telling and even the use of fishing tackle and travel by sea. The third pair developed the making of bricks for building walls and tiles for houses. The fourth pair was credited with developing gardens and yards about their homes. The fifth pair developed villages with adjoining pastures. The sixth pair discovered the use of salt. Even a casual review of these Phoenician traditions indicates that the similarity to the biblical narrative is meager indeed. All this demonstrates is that among other peoples also there was a tendency to ascribe certain cultural developments to specific historical or legendary persons. This, however, gives no basis for concluding that all of these traditions had a common origin.

It should be noted, further, that just because there may be certain similarities between a few of the crafts or skills mentioned in the Phoenician account and those included in the biblical narrative, it proves nothing. At the same time, it can be pointed out that even where there are similarities there are also basic differences. Thus, for example, while the Phoenicians also mention the development of working with iron, they make no mention of working with copper, as does the Bible in Genesis 4:22. Likewise, the Phoenician reference to raising cattle makes no mention of the "dwelling in tents" which accompanied this occupation in the biblical narrative. Our conclusion, then, is that there is no genuine parallel between the Phoenician tradition and the biblical narrative.

4. *Adam's Genealogy* (5:1–32)

There is a material connection between chapter 5 and what immediately precedes it. In 4:25–26 we have an introduction to Adam's genealogy in the line of Seth. Formally, however, the actual genealogy is presented as a separate section of the narrative in chapter 5. As such, it is clearly announced by a special heading or title. Let it be said at the outset that, in our view, we are dealing here with part of a written tradition which was available to the inspired writer of Genesis. We must accept what appears to us to be completely obvious, that the author of this history, under the guidance of the Holy Spirit, made use of written genealogies that were handed down from generation to generation. Unless we want to view these genealogies as products of fantasy we must assume that the author had these before him in written form. The heading placed above this section makes it clear that an old document was incorporated in its entirety into the biblical text.

Even those who insist on dividing the sources of the Pentateuch acknowledge that this passage comes from a specific source and in this we are agreed. However, when they ascribe chapter 5 to the same source (the so-called "P") to which they ascribe 1:1–2:4a, we strongly disagree. And 2:4–4:26 they ascribe to another source, namely, the "J" source. As we have observed in our Introduction to the Pentateuch, the basis for ascribing these passages to different sources is, first of all, the use of different names for God: in the one case, Jahweh, and in the other, Elohim. We have considered the merits of this theory at some length in our Introduction, and there is no need for further discussion here. We do want to point out, however, that although chapter 5 is classed as "P" because of the use of "Elohim," verse 29 uses the name "Jahweh." To escape this difficulty the source splitters make verse 29 an insertion from another source. Other arguments have been added to try to prove that verse 29 is not in accord with the rest of the chapter. None of these arguments is convincing, however, and they do not merit further consideration.

We do want to make one comment about the style of this chapter. In essence we have nothing more here than a list of names and numbers that are presented in a format which is consistently repeated. The critics claim that this is a characteristic of the Priestly Codex. These critics admit, however, that we are dealing with an old document which is incorporated into the text in its entirety. In order to maintain their arbitrary theory about the four sources, they have resorted to the expedient of suggesting that this old document first was incorporated in its entirety into "P" and then the redactor of Genesis took it from "P" and incorporated it in its entirety into the biblical text. Such textual gymnastics really require no refutation. Certainly the logical and natural explanation is that the inspired author of Genesis had this old document before him. The same would also be true of similar genealogies that appear later in Genesis.

5:1a *This is the written account of Adam's line.*

The first statement to draw our attention is the "heading." In Hebrew this literally reads, "This is the book of Adam's generation (or descendants)." The Hebrew word "book," however, does not mean exactly what we understand by that word. It is any written document, whether it be large or small in compass. Thus, in Deuteronomy 24:1 and Jeremiah 3:8, it is used of a divorce decree. In Jeremiah 32:10–12, it indicates a purchase contract or deed. Since the heading does not indicate that this was part of a larger document, we have good reason to believe that the entire document is included here. We can then correctly translate this heading, "This is the genealogy of Adam." It should be noted that Adam is here called by his personal name as was done in 4:25.

5:1b, 2 *When God created man, he made him in the likeness of God. He created them male and female; at the time they were created, he blessed them and called them "man."*

The record begins with a brief reference to the creation of man, which is in complete accord with Genesis 1:26–28. What we have here, then, is an instance of the use of a "doublet." A record of the same event is repeated for no apparent reason. This matter of the use of "doublets" was discussed in our introduction. Those who hold to the source-splitting theory use the presence of doublets as a basis for determining that there was more than one source for the material in the text. In this instance, however, where we have a clear-cut use of a doublet, the two passages—Genesis 1:26–28 and 5:1—are ascribed to the same source, namely the Priestly Codex. Since this is true in this case, there can be no basis for using the presence of doublets as evidence for multiple sources. On the other hand, if we adopt the position that the one inspired writer of Genesis incorporated an existing ancient document into the text of Genesis, the appearance of this doublet presents no problems. The writer simply took the document in its entirety without deletions and as a result an event which had already been recorded is simply repeated.

The Hebrew word *Adam* which is Adam's personal name, actually means "man." At times it is used to designate "humanity" or "mankind" as a whole, including both sexes. This is the sense in which the word is used in verse 1b because it is obvious from verse 2 that both sexes are included. It is unfortunate that our English word "man" does not express this well. It would probably be more correct, then, to translate this as "humanity" or "human beings," since it is doubtful whether the word "humans" can correctly be used as a noun.

It is interesting that human beings are described as created in God's "likeness" only, with the word "image" not included. The meaning of the two terms is essentially the same, however. (See our interpretation of 1:26–27.)

5:3–5 *When Adam had lived 130 years, he had a son in his own likeness, in his own image; and he named him Seth. After Seth was born, Adam lived 800 years and had other sons and daughters. Altogether, Adam lived 930 years, and then he died.*

We now begin the actual genealogy with the announcement of the birth of Seth. This is essentially the same as 4:25. Here we are given the added information that Adam was 130 years old when Seth was born. Adam then lived another 800 years for a total life span of 930 years. Then we read the significant "and then he died." This statement appears in connection with each of Adam's descendants except Enoch. In the original document it probably was no more than a formal statement. As it is used here in Genesis it stands as a vivid and constantly repeated reminder of the penalty for sin announced by God in 2:17. Although the intervening grace of God had allowed a delay in the execution of that sentence, and a lengthy delay at that, death inevitably did come.

In a reference to verse 2, we are told that Adam, who was created in God's image, had a son in his own likeness, in his own image. It is interesting that the two terms "likeness" and "image" are used in reverse order from their use in 1:26. This is a further indication that the two words essentially convey the same meaning.

5:6–8 *When Seth had lived 105 years, he became the father of Enosh. And after he became the father of Enosh, Seth lived 807 years and had other sons and daughters. Altogether, Seth lived 912 years, and then he died.*

In much the same format as was used in the case of Adam, we are now told that Seth had a son, Enosh. This is also mentioned in 4:26. Seth's age at the time of the birth of his son is also recorded as is his total life span.

5:9–20 *When Enosh had lived 90 years, he became the father of Kenan. And after he became the father of Kenan, Enosh lived 815 years and had other sons and daughters. Altogether, Enosh lived 905 years, and then he died.*

When Kenan had lived 70 years, he became the father of Mahalalel. And after he became the father of Mahalalel, Kenan lived 840 years and had other sons and daughters. Altogether, Kenan lived 910 years, and then he died.

When Mahalalel had lived 65 years, he became the father of Jared. And after he became the father of Jared, Mahalalel lived 830 years and had other sons and daughters. Altogether, Mahalalel lived 895 years, and then he died.

When Jared had lived 162 years, he became the father of Enoch. And after he became the father of Enoch, Jared lived 800 years and had other sons and daughters. Altogether, Jared lived 962 years, and then he died.

The genealogy now proceeds in precisely the same words as were used in the case of Seth. There is no variation in the basic format.

It would be difficult to explain the various names as they appear in their Hebrew form. We should remember our observation, in this connection, in our interpretation of 3:20. The name "Kenan" appears only here. Some have given it the meaning of "son," while others think it means "smith." "Mahalalel" is also the name of a man in Judea after the Exile (Neh. 11:4). It has been given the meaning, "praise of God." "Jared" (Jered) is also found among the family of Judah (1 Chron. 4:18). Some have related this to the Hebrew word *jarad,* which means "to descend." The name "Enoch" was discussed under 4:17.

5:21–24 *When Enoch had lived 65 years, he became the father of Methuselah. And after he became the father of Methuselah, Enoch walked with God 300 years and had other sons and daughters. Altogether, Enoch lived 365 years. Enoch walked with God; then he was no more, because God took him away.*

When the genealogy comes to Enoch, the monotony of the format is broken. We are given the name of his son, Methuselah, and a few other facts common to the entire list. Then two new statements are introduced with considerable abruptness. First, we are told that Enoch "walked with God." Second, the statement "and he died" does not appear but in its place we read, "he was no more, because God took him away."

What are we to understand by the statement that he "walked with God"? It is obvious that this cannot be taken literally but must be interpreted metaphorically. Some want to interpret this as a confidential relationship with God by means of which all kinds of secrets were revealed to Enoch. This is the view that was held in the Jewish tradition as was set forth in the book *Jubilees,* which dates from the second century before Christ. According to this, Enoch learned about writing and astronomy and had special knowledge about many things. It also claimed that, by way of a close communion with the angels, he was informed about everything in heaven and on earth (Jub. 4:17–21). This presentation is developed in the Book of Enoch, which also dates from the second century B.C. According to this book, Enoch not only was informed about the coming Deluge but also about the entire history of Israel up to the time of the coming of the Messiah. We do not feel that this view can be substantiated.

The term "walked with God" is also used of Noah in Genesis 6:9. The way it is used there indicates that it refers to the religious and moral attitude of the man. It portrays a life lived in spiritual communion with God and which was well-pleasing to God. The translation of the Septuagint, "that he pleased God," is essentially correct. This is also confirmed by Hebrews 11:5 where the same words appear. The Targum of Onquelos renders it, "he walked in the fear of God." The Palestinian Targum has, "he served God in truth." It should be observed that Enoch was not an ascetic who withdrew from the world and normal human relationships. He lived a normal family life as is evident from the fact that "he bore sons and daughters."

As a reward for his godliness he was treated differently than the rest of his family. We read, "He was no more, because God took him away." With respect to all the others in this genealogy we are told that "he died." Therefore, we cannot escape the conclusion that Enoch did not die. Hebrews 11:5 confirms this when it says, "Enoch was taken from this life so that he did not experience death." There are some who have suggested that he died an untimely or early death. The Jewish expositor Rasji (1040–1105) was of the opinion that Enoch was indeed pious, but that he also was very weak and easily tempted. Therefore God took him away early in life. A similar idea is expressed in the apocryphal book, "The Book of Wisdom" (4:11), where we read, "he was taken away in order that evil would not change his heart and temptation would not deceive him." Once again, this cannot be the meaning of the original text. We simply must accept the reality of an ascension into heaven without death, as later was the case with Elijah (2 Kings 2:9–12).

The verb has been variously translated. Our translators have rendered it "God took him away," although I prefer the reading, "God took him to Himself." The word certainly implies that the object taken is separated from its prior environment. It also implies a being brought near to the subject doing the taking. Thus, whether we express this in our translation or not, it is obvious that Enoch was removed from this present world and brought into the presence of God.

As an example of interpretations which deal in fantasy we can mention one view that holds that, since Enoch lived 365 years, we are dealing here with a sun myth since this is the length of the solar year in number of days. This needs no response.

5:25–27 *When Methuselah had lived 187 years, he became the father of Lamech. And after he became the father of Lamech, Methuselah lived 782 years and had*

---

other sons and daughters. Altogether, Methuselah lived 969 years, and then he died.

With Enoch's son, Methuselah, we return to the stereotyped format of the genealogy. The name Methuselah has been given the meaning of "spear," based on a Hebrew word that has some similarity to this name. This is the only place in the Old Testament where the name appears. Regarding the name of his son, Lamech, we have commented under 4:18.

One point of interest is that Methuselah lived 782 years after the birth of Lamech. Noah was born when Lamech was 182 years old. The Deluge came when Noah was 600 years old, which would have been the year in which Methuselah died. Some have tried to prove that Methuselah died in the Flood, but this cannot be established. It is just as reasonable to assume that he died a natural death before the Flood actually came on the earth.

5:28–31 *When Lamech had lived 182 years, he had a son. He named him Noah and said, "He will comfort us in the labor and painful toil of our hands caused by the ground the Lord has cursed." After Noah was born, Lamech lived 595 years and had other sons and daughters. Altogether, Lamech lived 777 years, and then he died.*

When we come to Lamech the regular format of the genealogy is again broken. The difference here is that an explanation is given for the name Lamech chose for his son, Noah. Lamech said, "He will comfort us in the labor and painful toil of our hands caused by the ground the Lord has cursed." This is, of course, a reference to 3:17. Just what is the meaning of this statement in this context and what did Lamech expect from this son?

Various answers have been given to these questions. One rather widely accepted view is that Lamech refers to the grapevine (Gen. 9:20) which, by providing wine would "gladden the heart of man" (Ps. 104:15). In this way Noah would provide respite from the "painful toil" caused by the cursed ground. Some have even added the idea that this was practically a restoration of the "tree of life," which the Israelites thought of as the grapevine.

Other answers that have been suggested are as follows: some have said that a new period in the history of mankind began with Noah. Since God gave him the promise that He would not again destroy the earth (8:21), this constitutes a cancelling of the curse of 3:17. By destroying every living creature by the Flood, the curse has been purged from the earth. Others think of Noah's sacrifice as removing the curse (8:20–21). The Jewish expositor, Rasji, decided that Noah invented the plow and by means of this tool the painful toil was lightened.

All of these views go on the assumption that Lamech spoke an actual prophecy or, at least, that the inspired writer wanted to establish an actual connection between these words and later events. But is this correct? The text gives us no reason for making such an assumption. It would be far better to determine what these words meant to Lamech at the time he spoke them. Then we can consider whether his expectations were actually fulfilled.

There are two possibilities. These words must be understood as an expression either of godlessness or of godliness.

If these words were an expression of godlessness, they could be understood as indicating that Lamech thought the curse would remain in force only during the lifetime of Adam. Noah was born in the year 1056 after the Creation, according to this genealogy. Adam lived to be 930 years old. Thus Noah was the first person listed in this genealogy who was born after the death of Adam. Consequently his father was rejoicing in the fact that the curse spoken to Adam had come to an end.

A second view is that Lamech, in a spirit of proud self-exaltation, anticipated that human skills and powers would soon be able to nullify the effects of the curse of God. One source that is offered for such an unsavory evaluation of Lamech is taken from the Samaritan Pentateuch. Following the text of this document, it is believed that Lamech lived 600 years after the birth of Noah, not 595 years as the biblical text reads. If this was the case, Lamech would have been among the unbelieving people destroyed by the Flood. It should be noted here that even if the figure of the Samaritan Pentateuch is adopted, this does not yet prove that Lamech died in the Deluge. (See our comments regarding Methuselah.)

A more natural view is that Lamech saw in the birth of his son a promise of an easing of his own toil and pain and this comforted him. This view is, however, too general to be credible.

Much can be said for taking these words as an expression of god-fearing piety. They can then be interpreted as expressing Lamech's hope that his son would bring a better life to mankind, that a new and better period in the history of mankind would be introduced. Others have suggested that Lamech lived in the faith that some day deliverance from the curse would come. This faith, moreover, became specific in that he had the conviction that his son would be instrumental in bringing that deliverance. When we ask how Lamech could have come to such a conviction, we must call to mind the promise of 3:15. Just as Eve, at the birth of Cain, fancied that this son might be the promised "seed," so now Lamech assumed that his son would finally provide the fulfillment of the promise. Of course, Lamech was just as mistaken on this score as Eve had been. His disillusionment was not characterized by the deep grief that she experienced, however.

To be sure, Noah was an example of righteousness and piety. Even so, the fulfillment of the "protevangelium," the first proclamation of the gospel, was a long way from being realized through Noah. During his life the entire world of humanity would be wiped out. But Noah was spared by a special provision of God's grace, and thus the "seed of the woman" was preserved for the future birth of that promised "Seed" who was to come.

The name "Noah" is explained by Lamech as referring to a "comforter." The Hebrew word that carries this meaning is *niham* and this has no etymological connection with the word "Noah." With respect to its Hebrew meaning, the closest we can come would be that it means "rest." However, Lamech makes no mention of rest in explaining the name of his son. Once again, we must be reminded that no Hebrew was spoken before the confusion of languages. We will have to accept the fact that, in the original language, the name Noah meant what Lamech expressed concerning his son. The inspired writer obviously could not find a suitable Hebrew word which sounded similar, so he left it as it had originally been given. Some have tried to change Lamech's words so that they would conform to the Hebrew meaning of the word but there is no justification for such a change.

5:32 *After Noah was 500 years old, he became the father of Shem, Ham and Japheth.*

Some have claimed that what we are told in verse 32 indicates that Shem, Ham, and Japheth were triplets. But it is not the intent of the statement that all three sons were born when Noah was precisely 500 years old. What is indicated here is that after Noah reached the age of 500 he bore three sons. Nor should the 500 figure be taken with mathematical precision. It must be seen, rather, as the approximate time in Noah's life when his three sons were born. In Genesis 11:10 we read that Shem was 100 years old when his son Arphaxad was born, and that this happened two years after the Flood. Since Noah was 600 years old when the Flood came, it would follow that Shem could not have been born when Noah was exactly 500 years old. It must have been a few years later. Whether Shem was the oldest of the three sons, based on the order in which the names are given, will be discussed when we treat 9:24.

The following can be observed regarding the names of these three sons of Noah:

Shem—There is a Hebrew word which sounds exactly like this but means "name." It is extremely unlikely that a father would give his son a name which means "name."

Ham—There is a like-sounding Hebrew word which means "father-in-law." This also seems like an unlikely choice for a name for a newborn son. Other attempts to relate this name to existing Hebrew words meet with no more success.

Japheth—Attempt has been made to relate his name to a Hebrew word which means "wide" or "broad."

Once again we must point out that these names must be seen as being given in the original language that was spoken before the confusion of speech while the Hebrew language was still nonexistent.

As we pointed out in our treatment of 4:18, some of the names in the Cainite and Sethite genealogies are the same and some are similar. This has led to the idea that these two genealogies are variations of one and the same original source. This idea must be emphatically rejected for the following reasons:

(1) There are names in each of these genealogies that do not appear in the other. In the Sethite genealogy—Seth, Jabal, Jubal, and Tubal-Cain.

(2) Among the names that apparently are similar, significant differences must be noted. Irad and Jared cannot be identified. Their Hebrew spelling clearly indicates that they are completely different words. So also, it is difficult to accept the fact that Cain and Kenan refer to the same name. Even Mehujael and Mahalalel, and Methushael and Methuselah have little in common.

(3) In the two instances in which the same names appear in both genealogies (Enoch and Lamech), certain distinguishing characteristics of these men are presented in each genealogy and these factors make it almost impossible to identify these men as the same persons.

(4) The sequence in which the identical names appear in each genealogy also makes it difficult to identify them as the same person. Thus, for example, Enoch is the third from Adam in the Cainite genealogy but is the seventh in the Sethite. Lamech is the seventh in the Cainite and the ninth in the Sethite. With one exception the same discrepancy of sequence also applies to those names that have some similarity.

(5) When we place the two genealogies side by side, we cannot avoid the conclusion that the Cainite list is very incomplete. The Cainite list includes only eight generations while the Sethite list includes seven. Add to this the fact that Cain was full grown when Seth was born, so the Cainite list should actually include at least one more generation than that of Seth.

In view of all of this evidence many scholars, including some who belong to the critical school, believe that we have two distinct genealogies included in this part of Genesis. The similarity of the names need not surprise us. Later history gives abundant evidence that families that have no relationship to each other often have similar names among their family members. How much more likely this would be in this case where two genealogies represent families that were closely related to each other, and both spoke the one and only language that was spoken at the time.

Holy Scripture portrays the Cainites and the Sethites as being distinguished from each other by increasing godlessness on the one hand, and evident godliness on the other. We need but compare what is said about Cain and Lamech in one line and about Enosh, Enoch, and Noah in another line. Thus the division between the "seed of the serpent" and the "seed of the woman" within humanity becomes clearly evident.

Some scholars have attempted to prove that this distinction is not tenable. They insist that Enoch's godliness was an exception in the line of Seth. Although this may be true, there is no evidence to indicate that the rest of the Sethites were godless people. It has also been argued that, by borrowing numbers regarding ages from the Samaritan Pentateuch, it can be established that three of the Sethites died in the Flood. This would then indicate, it is claimed, that they were just as wicked as the rest of humanity. In response it can be said that even though it can be established, by a clever manipulation of certain numbers, that Methuselah, Lamech, and Jared all died during the year of the Flood, this does not preclude the fact that they may have died natural deaths. And even if they did die in the Flood, this does not establish that they were notably wicked men. Noah was spared because God chose him to save the race because of his exceptional righteousness. If some of the Sethites died by drowning in the flood, this would establish only that they were not chosen by God for this special calling and probably had not reached the level of godliness Noah had attained. Thus, there is no evidence that would call into question the relative virtue of the Sethites which distinguished them from the Cainites.

We now turn to a consideration of a theory that has been based on Babylonian history. About 300 B.C. a Babylonian priest by the name of Berosus wrote a history of his fatherland in Greek which carried the title *Babyloniaca.* This book includes a list of ten Babylonian kings who supposedly lived before the great Flood. (The Babylonians also have preserved a tradition about a flood.) There is a rather widely accepted theory that the biblical genealogies had their origin in Babylon. At the least, it is claimed, the genealogies in Genesis are closely related to that Babylonian list of antideluvian kings. This claim is based, first of all, on the mere fact that another such list of names of persons who lived before the Flood exists.

Further, it is claimed that both lists include only ten names. (This is not correct unless the names of Shem, Ham, and Japheth are omitted.) It is also claimed that there are definite analogies between the two lists which can be pointed out.

To evaluate the legitimacy of this latter claim, let us consider a few of these supposed analogies. The name of the third king in Berosus' list is Amelon. This is similar to the Babylonian and Assyrian word *amelu* which means "person." This is then related to the biblical name "Enosh" and the Hebrew word *enôš*, which also means "person." The name of the fourth king was Ammemnon. This is similar to the Babylonian word *ummanu* which means "skilled workman." This would then be equivalent to the name Kenan and the Hebrew word which is similar and means "smith." The seventh king is Euedorachos. He is identified with Enmedoeranki, who is listed as king of the city of Sippar in Assyrian-Babylonian history. He was considered to be the patron of fortunetellers. He supposedly was endowed by the gods with all the secrets of fortunetelling. So this name is made equivalent with Enoch, the seventh from Adam who, according to an ancient Jewish tradition presented in the Book of Jubilees and the Book of Enoch (see our treatment of 5:21–24), also was endowed with this secret wisdom. It is difficult to see in all of this more than an ingenious manipulation of ancient historical records. Substantial evidence for relating the list of kings compiled by Berosus to the biblical genealogy is nonexistent.

Another venture into the area of wild conjecture is the attempt to relate the time sequences of Berosus and the Genesis account. Berosus ascribed extremely long periods of rule to the kings he lists. It is then assumed that this is analogous to the long lives of the men listed in the Genesis genealogy. Berosus counted the length of a reign in *saren,* which were periods of 3600 years. The reigns of the kings he listed varied in length from 3 to 18 of these *saren,* and this adds up to from 10,800 to 64,800 years. These are enormous periods of time. By comparison the life spans of the biblical figures are insignificant. But the critics hit upon an ingenious solution to this dilemma by making 1 week in Genesis 5 equivalent to 5 years in Berosus' record. If this formula is used the numbers seem to coincide. When we examine this more closely, however, it soon becomes evident that this does not work out in every instance. Adam lived 930 years and Seth 912 years, according to the Genesis record. In Berosus the first king reigned 10 *saren* and the second only 3. This is rather a formidable discrepancy. Even if we limit our consideration to the overall span of the entire period, Berosus comes up with the figure of 430,000 years while the Genesis record covers 1656 years. Using the formula of the critics, 1656 years is 86,112 weeks and if we multiply this by 5, we come up with 430,560 years. Isn't this remarkable? Even if these figures coincided perfectly, which they do not, just what basis is there for this ingenious formula of 1 week = 5 years? Why not 6 years, or 7 years, or 100 years? The whole structure is completely arbitrary and certainly provides no substantial proof that the biblical record was based on Babylonian writings.

A question of a different nature is whether the list of kings in Berosus does not provide confirmation regarding the history of the human race before the Deluge. The historicity of Genesis 5 has been widely denied by the critics, partly on the basis of the long life spans that are ascribed to the people. It is argued that life spans of 900 years and more are impossible. It would seem, however, that a history such as that of Berosus indicates that there was a strong tradition among other peoples also regarding a time when men lived to be very old. This rings even more true when we note that the Babylonian tradition also ascribed long lives to people immediately after the Flood. Even though these were much shorter than those before the Flood, they were still longer than was common in later history. This accords with the biblical record in Genesis 11:10–32.

This same phenomenon of extremely long lives during this ancient period is also found in the traditions of other peoples. Thus, Egypt has a document about ten ancient kings who lived unusually long lives. India has traditions about four periods in history during which the lives of people were shortened by 100 years during each of those periods. The Greeks also refer to a golden period during which people did not age until they had lived many years. There are similar traditions among the Phoenicians, the Persians, and the Chinese. We certainly do not intend to validate the truth of Genesis 5 by pointing to these records among other peoples. The truth of the Bible stands on the basis of the testimony of God Himself. Even so, accepting the record of Genesis as true, we can certainly point with interest to the fact that humanity has preserved a tradition which confirms this unique phenomenon among the people of the prediluvian period.

We want to refer briefly to another peculiar circumstance in connection with these numbers in Genesis 5. There are other sources that give these numbers but there are some significant differences. The Samaritan Pentateuch gives identically the same numbers for the first five names of the genealogy, and also for Enoch and for Noah. In the case of Jared, his age at the birth of his son is given as 62 instead of 162. The remainder of his years is given as 785 instead of 800. His total life span is thus given as 847 instead of 962 years. The respective numbers in the case of Methuselah are 67, 653, and 720, instead of 187, 782, and 969. For Lamech the numbers are 53, 600, and 653, instead of 182, 597, and 777. As a result of these differences the total number of years from Adam to the Deluge is reduced from 1656 to 1307.

The differences between the Hebrew text and the Septuagint are even larger. For the first five names in the genealogy and for Enoch, the Septuagint gives the age of each man at the time of the birth of his son as 100 years less than that given in the Hebrew text, and the remaining years of his life as 100 years more. Thus the total life span remains the same in each case. With respect to Jared and Noah it agrees with the Hebrew text. In the case of Methuselah there are two different readings. One has his son born when Methuselah was 167 and then his remaining years as 802 for a total of 969 years. The other reading agrees with the Hebrew text. In the case of Lamech, it gives his age at the birth of his son as 188 instead of 182, and his remaining years as 565 instead of 595 for a total life span of 753 instead of 777 years. The total period according to the Septuagint is either 2242 or 2262 years.

Now which of these combinations of numbers must be considered to be correct? Although some have expressed a strong preference for the presentation of the Samaritan Pentateuch, the reasoning that supports this preference is not convincing. We will have to admit that no conclusive evidence has been adduced to enable us to determine with certainty which of the three records is correct. It is only proper, therefore, that we withhold final judgment on this matter.

That the genealogy of Genesis 5 must be seen as a complete list is open to serious question. If we take into account the conclusions we reach on the basis of our study of Genesis 11:10–26, this becomes all the more questionable. Although we have no positive evidence to indicate that the record of Genesis 5 is not complete, there is evidence that this is definitely the case in Genesis 11:10–26. We will discuss this in detail when we treat the passage in Genesis 11. We must, however, allow for the strong possibility that the record of Genesis 5 must also be considered incomplete, with some of the links in the chain being omitted.

5. *The Deluge* (6:1–9:17)

Chapters 4 and 5 portray the development of the human race along two distinct lines. The one line reveals a tendency to increase in godlessness. The other line generally maintains a fear of God and trust in His gracious promises. Now, in chapter 6, we come to a mixing of these two lines. This eventually leads to the judgment of God on all mankind in the Deluge that brings this period of history to a close.

Those who hold to a division of sources see the biblical narrative at this point as a blending of at least two different traditions. The one belongs to the "J" source, and the other to the "P" source. According to some there is also a third source and this is considered to be a combination of "J" and "P."

These two supposed sources are to be identified, it is claimed, by the names they give to God, "Jahweh" or "Elohim." Certain differences in language are also pointed out. These scholars have also insisted that there are a number of repetitions and these supposedly indicate more than one source. Thus, there are two statements that God saw the wickedness of mankind—6:5 and 6:12. Also, there are two announcements to Noah that God would destroy all mankind—6:17 and 7:4. Further, twice God commanded Noah to enter the ark—6:18-20 and 7:1-3. And twice we read that Noah entered the ark—7:7-9 and 7:13-16. Also, the coming of the Flood is mentioned twice—7:10 and 7:11. We are told twice, it is claimed, that the waters increased and lifted the ark—7:17 and 7:18. Twice it is mentioned that every living thing on the earth perished—7:21 and 7:22. Noah's decision that the time had come to leave the ark is mentioned twice—8:13 and 8:15-17. And, finally, twice it is mentioned that there would never again be a flood—8:21-22 and 9:8-17.

According to the critics, there are also presentations which conflict with each other. In "J" seven pairs of clean animals are preserved, while in "P" only one pair of all the animals is kept alive. In "J" the Flood lasted forty plus twenty-one days, while in "P" it lasted one year. In "J" the cause of the Flood is described as a great rain, while in "P" it is ascribed to the opening of the fountains under the earth as well as the descent of the waters from above. In "J" Noah himself investigated whether they could leave the ark, while in "P" God revealed this to him directly. It would be well for us to examine these charges by the critics carefully.

Of the arguments they have adduced to defend their theory, the claim that there are repetitions in the narrative is certainly the least cogent. Repeating a statement in slightly different words is, in many instances, a characteristic Hebrew style of writing. A good example of this would be 1 Kings 11:1-8. Such repetition may seem superfluous to us, but for the Israelites it was perfectly in order. Thus the presence of repetitions in the narrative, in itself, does not establish the use of more than one source.

In some instances the use of repetition even makes good sense to us today. Thus, in 7:7 we are told that Noah entered the ark. Then, in 7:13 we are given details about the exact time, etc., that this took place. So also, in verse 21 we have a listing of the creatures that perished in the Flood. Then, in verse 22 we have an inclusive confirmation of this fact. Such usage, we insist, must be seen as good and effective Hebrew style.

In addition to this, several of the supposed repetitions that have been pointed out are such in appearance only. Thus, in 6:7 the intended destruction of all mankind is offered as the motive for building the ark. But in 7:4, after the ark is completed, we are told that now the time had come for carrying out the judgment that had been previously announced. In 7:10 we read only that the Flood came. But in 7:11 the manner in which the Flood came is added. In 7:17 and 18 there really is no repetition at all. The gradual increase of the water is graphically described. First the ark was lifted from the ground where it had rested. Then as the waters rose and everything on the ground disappeared from view, the ark floated about freely on the waters. Further, it is not correct to say that Noah was told on two occasions that he could leave the ark. In 8:6-13 we read how he learned about the progress of conditions on the earth. Then, in 8:15-17 we are told that he decided that the time had come to leave the ark. Nor should 9:8-17 be considered to be a repetition of 8:21-22. In the earlier reference God communes with Himself. In the latter passage He communicates His intention to Noah. It becomes increasingly clear that if the case of the critics for two sources depended only on the matter of repetitions they would not have a case at all.

With respect to the use of the names "Jahweh" and "Elohim," it is indeed true that in the narrative of the Deluge we encounter alternating sections in which one of these names seems to be used exclusively. In 6:5-8 it is Jahweh; in 6:9-22, Elohim; in 7:1-5, Jahweh; in 7:9-16, Elohim; in 8:1-19, Elohim; in 8:20-22, Jahweh; in 9:1-17, Elohim. At the same time we must point out that in 7:16 both names appear side by side. In order to maintain their theory, the source splitters suggest that the redactor cut the material that he borrowed from "J" into small pieces and then worked these fragments into his "P" material in a piecemeal fashion. The result, then, would be that the final product is some kind of a mixture of these two sources. Such irresponsible theorizing hardly needs refutation. We would refer our readers, however, to our material in the Introduction and to our treatment of Genesis 5.

With respect to the references to "male" and "female" of each type of animals, which are supposed to be an identifying characteristic of "P," it should be noted that this usage also appears in 7:3, which, however, has strong "J" characteristics. The critics seek to escape this difficulty by ascribing the first part of the verse to a later hand as a gloss that was added at a later time.

Finally we come to the most significant argument for multiple sources, the conflicting presentations. The first to be considered deals with the animals that were taken into the ark. Was it seven pairs of clean animals and one pair of unclean animals, or one pair of all the animals? This is favorite ground for those who are eager to point out "contradictions" in the Bible. But there is no actual conflict here. First, in 6:19, Noah was told that two of all living creatures, a male and a female, were to be brought into the ark. Then, in 7:2–3, he was given more detailed instructions and a special provision was made for the "clean animals." In this case, seven of each kind were to be taken into the ark. For all of the rest it was to remain two. Then, in 7:8–9 we again have a general report of the actual happening and we are told that all kinds of animals came into the ark, as our translation has it, "in pairs." Now, there is nothing contradictory in these references. If there are seven pairs there certainly is one pair. The sole intent is to reveal that all animal life was to be preserved while a special provision was made for clean animals.

Regarding the alleged conflict concerning the duration of the Flood, we point out that 7:12 and 8:6–12 do not deal with the total duration of the Flood at all. They describe only certain phases of the great catastrophe that came on the earth. The only passage that deals with the total time span of the Flood or the time that Noah and his family spent in the ark is 8:13 and 14, when it is compared with 7:11. To describe this as a contradiction is being somewhat less than honest.

In the same way, the claim that there are two different presentations regarding the cause of the Flood is also unfounded. The fact that 7:11 and 12 use two terms for the same phenomenon, "rain" and "the floodgates of the heavens were opened," certainly provides no evidence for two conflicting narratives. The same figures are used again in 8:2 where we are told that the rain stopped when the floodgates of the heavens were closed. The conclusion that this indicates the use of two completely divergent sources is, at best, arbitrary.

Finally, there is the matter of how Noah was informed that the time had come to leave the ark. The verses 8:6–13 and 8:15–16 certainly do not present conflicting reports in this regard. The former, in narrative style, tells of Noah's own investigation of the progress of things. The latter reveals God's official pronouncement that the time had come to leave the ark. Once again, to interpret this as a conflict that necessitates elaborate theories of multiple sources is rather facetious.

The evidence for two or more sources for the narrative of the Flood is wholly unconvincing. Even some of the advocates of this theory will admit that these two sources are difficult to distinguish. Working out a plan for distinguishing these sources has required the efforts of several generations of scholars. It has been described as a "masterpiece of scholarship." There can be no doubt that the scheme that has been worked out is an ingenious one. But no matter how ingenious it may be, it does not establish the theory with substantial, factual evidence and thus it remains a very tenuous undertaking.

The opening section of the narrative (6:1-4) has often been considered to be an independent document that was later added to the narrative as a whole. This conclusion is the result of a specific theory of interpretation with which the entire passage is approached. Our interpretation of this passage neither needs nor allows such a designation of the opening section as being independent from the whole. This will be clarified when we proceed with the interpretation of the passage.

6:1, 2 *When men began to increase in number on the earth and daughters were born to them, the sons of God saw that the daughters of men were beautiful, and they married any of them they chose.*

In order to arrive at the meaning of this passage it is imperative that we have a clear understanding regarding the designation, ''the sons of God.'' Many of the ancient Jewish scholars, the early church fathers, and even present-day exegetes interpret this statement as being a reference to angels. They appeal to references in the Book of Job (1:6; 2:1; 38:7) where the term ''sons of God'' definitely refers to angels. If we accept this interpretation, we then have here in Genesis 6 a record of unnatural relationships between women and angels. This view is, in our judgment, untenable. In verse 2 it is clear that the entire episode is presented as a transgression on the part of the ''sons of God.'' They saw that the daughters of men were beautiful and they chose wives from among them. If these ''sons of God'' were indeed angels, the consequence should have been that God would have judged and punished the angels for their transgression (see v. 3ff.). Although verse 3 is difficult to interpret, no matter how it is interpreted it is unmistakably clear that it refers exclusively to the world of human beings.

In view of this, it is obvious that the term ''sons of God'' must be seen as a reference to human beings. There are, moreover, other places in the Old Testament where people are referred to as ''sons of God.'' In Deuteronomy 32:5 and Hosea 1:10 the Israelites are so designated. In Psalm 73:15 the righteous are so described.

There is another view which holds that the ''sons of God'' were members of the nobility and ruling class. This view is based on the fact that rulers and judges are sometimes referred to as ''gods'' (Exod. 2:6; 22:8; 1 Sam. 2:25; Ps. 82:1). This view is also found in some Jewish circles. However, it is open to the objection that, although rulers are sometimes called ''gods,'' at no time are children of the upper classes called ''children of the gods'' or ''sons of God.'' It should be observed also that if this term referred to the noble or ruling class, marriage between their sons and daughters and those of the common people would not have been such a serious sin that it would bring the judgment of God down on the whole human race. It is doubtful, moreover, that sharp distinctions between the classes were in effect in these early times.

In view of this, it would be better to accept the interpretation that has been held by orthodox scholars of Jewish, Catholic, and Protestant persuasion, that the "sons of God" were the god-fearing people in distinction from the godless. In light of chapters 4 and 5 we can then think of the distinction between the line of Seth and the line of Cain. What is revealed, then, is that these two lines did not maintain their distinctiveness. The "seed of the woman" and the "seed of the serpent" became mixed by way of intermarriage. The first step in this direction was taken by the god-fearing line. They were attracted by the beautiful daughters of their godless neighbors who undoubtedly were consciously seducing them. Thus they were lured into mixed marriages with all the devastating consequences of such unions.

6:3 *Then the LORD said, "My Spirit will not contend with man forever, for he is mortal; his days will be a hundred and twenty years."*

The destructive consequences of these mixed marriages are, however, not immediately described. But in the words of God which follow there is an expression of the judgment of God on this development. From this expression it can be deduced that the damaging effects of these marriages had already become evident.

Verse 3 presents some real difficulties both in translation and in interpretation. There are widely divergent views that have been presented in this regard.

The first difficulty lies in the word rendered "contend." This translation is based on an old Greek version, and it is grammatically possible. It is then translated, "My spirit shall no longer contend with these stiff-necked people by means of the testimony of the righteous and, specifically, of Noah." The intent would be that God would no longer warn the wicked by means of the righteous. This interpretation is not without difficulties. There is no previous mention of a warning being given to the wicked and, therefore, the term "no longer" makes little sense.

Others have translated the term "rule over" in the sense that "my Spirit shall no longer rule over man." The meaning then would be that God will withdraw the "spirit of life" from man, that is, take away his life. This presentation is linguistically rather forced.

We express a strong preference for translating the word "remain in."

This is also given as a marginal reading by our translators. Moreover, this is the translation used in the Septuagint, the Targum of Onquelos, the Vulgate, and the Syrian Peshito. What we read then is, "I will not let my Spirit (which is the Spirit of life for man as well as animals) remain in them." This would imply that God would take His Spirit away from them and would thus bring an end to their life on earth. This, then, would be the judgment that God would bring on mankind as a punishment for mixing the two lines through intermarriage and for compromising the godliness in the line which had carried this forward for many years. We believe that this interpretation does justice to the text and still makes good sense.

The second difficulty in this verse lies in the Hebrew word rendered "for," connecting the phrase "he is mortal" with the preceding in a causal relationship. We are not happy with this reading, even though it is used in the Septuagint, the Targum of Onquelos, the Vulgate, and the Peshito. We prefer the reading which apparently was intended by the Masoretes when they used the vowel points of the word which means "to err." We would then read this line, "My Spirit will not remain in man forever, now that he has erred." The phrase, "he is flesh," is then set apart as a separate statement. In other words, these men who have departed from God will be destroyed by Him.

But the judgment of God would not fall immediately. It was to be delayed 120 years. "His days shall be one hundred and twenty years." Some have applied these words to the life span of the people. This would then indicate that the long lives that were recorded in Genesis 5 would no longer be experienced. It would be difficult to defend this reading because the pronoun translated "his," in its Hebrew form, must refer to the generation living at that time. Many reached ages hundreds of years beyond this 120 years supposedly stipulated by God. Even if we were to apply this limit of 120 years to the generation that lived after the Deluge, it still would not harmonize with the facts recorded in Genesis 11. Several of that generation lived far longer than that. Note that Shem lived to be 600; Arphaxad, 438; Shelah, 433; Eber, 464; Peleg, 239; Reu, 239; Serug, 230; Nahor, 148. Even in later generations, Abraham reached the age of 175; Ishmael, 137; Isaac, 180; and Jacob, 147. The only acceptable interpretation of this limit of 120 years, mentioned in verse 3, is that it indicated the period of grace during which the judgment of God upon that generation would be postponed.

6:4 *The Nephilim were on the earth in those days—and also afterward—when the sons of God went to the daughters of men and had children by them. They were the heroes of old, men of renown.*

In this verse we are introduced to the Nephilim or giants in the earth. Those who interpret verses 1 and 2 as indicating that angels cohabited with women are naturally quick to conclude that these giants were the progeny of those unions. Others, who proceed more cautiously, recognize that the text indicates only that the giants were present at the same time as the marriages between the "sons of God" and the "daughters of men." They insist, however, that even though this is not specifically stated, we can readily assume that these giants must have been the fruit of those unholy unions.

It has been correctly pointed out that the text establishes no causal connection between these two historical phenomena. In fact, the text specifically states that the giants were already present when the "sons of God" produced children by the "daughters of men." The reference to the presence of the giants is, thus, no more than a designation of time. This is indicated by the word "then" or "at that time."

Obviously the writer of this record, describing the conditions in the world at the time of the Deluge, wanted to include a reference to one of the characteristics of that particular period in history, the interesting phenomenon that there were people who grew to much larger physical proportions than people of later times. The writer speaks of *the* giants. The use of the definite article suggests that he was pointing to a historical phenomenon that was familiar to his readers. Thus it was a meaningful designation of a specific period in history. Although this is not specifically stated, it can be assumed that this unusual physical development was related to the extreme longevity of the people of that period of time.

In later times there are also references to giants. But then they are introduced as exceptions to the normal stature of people. Thus the Israelites encountered giants when they first came to Canaan. These huge men struck fear in the hearts of the smaller Israelites, because they felt like grasshoppers before them (Num. 13:33; Deut. 1:28). Og, king of Bashan, is described as a giant in Deuteronomy 3:11. Still later, we encounter Goliath whose height is given as six cubits and a span (more than nine feet) in 1 Samuel 17:4. We read of other Philistine giants in 2 Samuel 21:16–22 and 1 Chronicles 20:4–8. In 1 Chronicles 11:23 we read of an Egyptian who was seven and a half feet tall. We can therefore safely assume that the writer of the Pentateuch was well aware of these later references to giants and inserted the phrase, "and also afterward." Many scholars hold that this term is an insertion of much later date, but this is by no means a necessary conclusion. It could be a natural and reasonable parenthetical statement on the part of the author of the entire Pentateuch.

We are also told that these giants were "heroes," as our translators have rendered the word. We prefer the reading "violent men," although a combination of these two ideas probably would be in order. It is obvious that these men were not only of enormous size, but that they also possessed great physical strength. Moreover, they were proud of their prowess and exploited it on the field of battle and elsewhere. Thus they may well be considered to have been men of extreme violence as well as renowned popular heroes.

In this same vein we are told that they were men of renown. Some of these warriors gained considerable historical fame, and thus their role in history was probably known to the readers of the Pentateuch. For them this was then a meaningful designation of a specific period in history.

Before leaving the subject of the giants, mentioned in Genesis 6, we should acknowledge the fact that other nations also had traditions about an ancient age when there were giants in the earth. We find such traditions among the Phoenicians, the Arabians, and especially among the Greeks and the Germanic tribes. In Greek mythology we have tales about gods and people cohabiting and producing children who were half-god. Because of these traditions among other nations, many scholars claim that Genesis 6:1–4 has a mythological origin and as such has no actual connection with the history recorded in the rest of the chapter. The passage is described as a foreign element that somehow slipped into this part of the Genesis account even though it has no relevance to the historical narrative as a whole.

From what has been said above it is apparent that we do not accept this theory of a mythological fragment that drifted into this passage. We have already established the fact that there is not one shred of evidence in the text for an actual cohabitation between human women and heavenly beings. The reference to giants, moreover, is no more mythological than the long life spans of people in that period. Once again, the real issue is whether we consider the biblical record to be trustworthy. We take the position that what God's Word says in this passage is historically accurate. The references to giants in some pagan mythologies can be easily explained as a recollection that has been carried forward by word-of-mouth tradition that there was a time when there were people of enormous physical stature. It should be noted that the giants in pagan mythology are not human beings at all and there is no indication that they were of human origin.

Genesis 6:1–4 should be approached as a straightforward description of the conditions that prevailed among the human race before the Deluge. All suggestions regarding the mythological character of this passage should be rejected. When we do this, moreover, there is no longer any reason for thinking of this passage as an unrelated fragment that has been inserted here. On the contrary, these verses form a significant introduction to the

157

narrative of the Deluge. They inform us of God's motivation in bringing His mighty act of judgment upon the world.

6:5, 6 *The LORD saw how great man's wickedness on the earth had become, and that every inclination of the thoughts of his heart was only evil all the time. The LORD was grieved that he had made man on the earth, and his heart was filled with pain.*

In these verses we are placed at the time when the 120 years of grace, mentioned in verse 3, were fast running out. Human conduct had made no change for the better as the day of destruction drew nearer. Mankind had not come to repentance. "The LORD saw how great man's wickedness on the earth had become, and that every inclination of the thoughts of his heart was only evil all the time." The time for judgment was fast approaching.

When we read in verse 6 that "The LORD was grieved that he had made man" and that "his heart was filled with pain," we are dealing with clear-cut anthropomorphic figures of speech. We certainly cannot conceive of God actually being grieved about something He Himself had done. Nor can we speak of God having regrets, as human beings have, about His own actions. "God is not a man, that he should lie, or the son of man, that he should change his mind" (Num. 23:19). But Scripture frequently uses expressions that are human in their scope and concept and then ascribes these to God. This is done only in order that the intent may become clear to our limited human understanding. Here we have a clear instance of the use of such an anthropomorphism. The intent is to express the serious breach that had taken place in the relationship of God to man as the devastating consequence of man's sin and rebellion.

6:7 *So the LORD said, "I will wipe mankind, whom I have created, from the face of the earth—men and animals, and creatures that move along the ground, and birds of the air—for I am grieved that I have made them."*

We now read that God decided to proceed to carry out the judgment He had announced to Noah (v. 3). He determined to destroy the humanity He had created. The verb used here is correctly rendered by our translators as "wipe out." The same word is used in 7:4 and 7:23. It is taken from the figure of washing a dish, wiping it clean, and turning it over. (See 2 Kings 21:13.) In the same way, God would wipe the earth clean of people, like a dish wiped clean of the residue of food it had contained.

Not only the people but also the animals would be destroyed. This is not because the animals were guilty of sin, but the judgment of God that would blot out human life from the earth would at the same time destroy all animal life.

6:8–10 *But Noah found favor in the eyes of the LORD.*
This is the account of Noah.
Noah was a righteous man, blameless among the people of his time, and he walked with God. Noah had three sons: Shem, Ham and Japheth.

God's decision to destroy human life from the earth was, however, not absolute. Noah, who was previously mentioned in 5:32, was to be an exception. He "found favor in the eyes of the LORD."

And so the inspired writer comes to the history of Noah. The history of heaven and earth, which commenced in 2:4, now turns its focus on the history of Noah. During Noah's life humanity would be destroyed and only he and his family would be spared. He, in turn, would become the starting point for an entirely new development of the human race.

The first thing we are told about Noah is that he was "righteous." This means that he conformed to the moral standard. He recognized and observed his responsibilities to God and to his fellowmen. Certainly, we cannot claim that Noah was without sin. The deeper question as to whether Noah was righteous *in himself* is not considered here. Genesis 9 makes it clear that Noah had no righteousness in himself, that before God he was sinful like everyone else. We are told here that he lived an exemplary life.

We are told, further, that he was blameless. This indicates that his conduct was above repute. The same word is used of a sacrificial animal that was "without blemish." Thus, Noah was a man whom no one could justly criticize. He lived an irreproachable life.

Added to this is the phrase, "among the people of his time." This literally reads, "in his generation." This informs us that Noah's exemplary life of righteousness was an exception among his contemporaries. This also casts further meaning on the statement that he was "righteous." We are not dealing, first of all, with Noah's position before God, but rather how he manifested himself in the midst of his fellowmen.

We also read that Noah "walked with God." This is the same expression that was used of Enoch in 5:22, 24. As we observed in that connection, this must be seen as living a life in close spiritual communion with God. The terms "righteous" and "blameless" refer more to his public conduct. His "walk with God" focuses more on his personal relationship to the Almighty.

Finally, we have a repetition of what was recorded in 5:32. Noah bore three sons, Shem, Ham, and Japheth.

6:11, 12 *Now the earth was corrupt in God's sight and was full of violence. God saw how corrupt the earth had become, for all the people on earth had corrupted their ways.*

In sharp contrast to the righteous and blameless Noah, the earth, that is the rest of humanity, was "corrupt in God's sight" and, even stronger, "full of violence." This latter statement seems to refer back to verse 4 and its reference to the heroes or warriors. It was an age in which brute strength was glorified. This in turn led to all kinds of acts of violence. God saw this from heaven and ascertained that the people of the earth had totally corrupted their ways. Their conduct and their way of life had become wicked and perverse. Unrighteousness had triumphed. This characterization of the moral condition of humanity is repeated as the transition is made to God's announcement of the coming judgment.

6:13 *So God said to Noah, "I am going to put an end to all people, for the earth is filled with violence because of them. I am surely going to destroy both them and the earth.*

This declaration of judgment is made to Noah. The time had come. God had determined to proceed with His intent to bring an end to the human race. God also would destroy the earth. Precisely how this judgment was going to be effected is not mentioned at this point. This becomes evident when God tells Noah how he and his family will be delivered from the pending doom. Later, in verse 17, it is specifically stated.

The verb translated "destroy" is used with two objects, the people and the earth. Understandably the meaning is a bit different in each case. The figure of speech is known as "zeugma." The people would be wiped out of existence, but the earth would remain, although it would be reduced to a state of destitution and desolation.

6:14 *So make yourself an ark of cypress wood; make rooms in it and coat it with pitch inside and out.*

Now God proceeds to instruct Noah regarding the means by which he would be delivered, namely, an "ark" or ship. The word used here is of Egyptian origin and in Egyptian it refers to a specific kind of vessel. It was a ship that was square-cornered and chest-like in shape. It was primarily used for transporting grain. Similar craft were used during the ancient feasts when the golden images, used in the processions, were brought across the Nile on them.

It is not without interest that the basket, made of bullrushes, in which the baby Moses was placed on the river, is described by the same word in Exodus 2. This would suggest that Moses' mother intentionally chose this shape for the watertight container in which she placed her child, knowing that it would be sure to attract the attention of the Egyptian princess. This princess might well have thought that it would contain one of their golden images. (See the interpretation of Exod. 2 in this series of Commentaries.)

It is worthy of note that Noah's ship was similar to the type of vessels used by the Egyptians when they planned long voyages over rough seas. They could be built to be very sturdy and stable. Certainly Noah's vessel would have to be unusually seaworthy, and at the same time have a capacity for an enormous cargo. It had to accommodate all the animals and their food supply. Thus, it is not surprising that this descriptive Egyptian word is used for the ark which Noah was to build.

The material from which the vessel was to be built was "gopher wood." This is the only place where this Hebrew word is used and it is difficult to determine exactly what kind of wood is intended. Our translators have rendered it "cypress wood" with a marginal note indicating that the meaning is uncertain. We are of the same mind.

Furthermore, the ark was to be divided into compartments or "rooms." The Hebrew word that is used is generally considered to be the plural form of the word for "nest." It is thought that numerous stalls or cages were to be installed to accommodate the many varieties of animals that would be brought aboard. It was especially urgent that the animals be confined within this vast ship. If, in a moment of panic, all of them should rush to one side of the craft it would certainly capsize. Some, however, read the word differently. They see it as an expression taken from Egyptian ship-building techniques. They believe that it refers to papyrus fibers that were used to close the seams of the ship. Which translation is correct remains an open question.

In order to insure that the vessel would be watertight it was painted with pitch, both inside and outside. Literally it reads, "pitched with pitch." Some translators also render it that way.

6:15 *This is how you are to build it: The ark is to be 450 feet long, 75 feet wide and 45 feet high.*

In this verse we are given the measurements of the ark. It was to be 300 cubits long, 50 cubits wide, and 30 cubits high. In our measurements this would be 450 ft. (150 m.) x 75 ft. (25 m.) x 45 ft. (15 m.) Thus it was a huge ship, containing some one and a half million cubic ft. of space. It was capable of carrying a large, heavy cargo. Various studies have been made concerning the seaworthiness of a vessel of these proportions. Models of the ark have been built and one man even put together a full-scale model. Most authorities are agreed that a ship with these dimensions would serve its purpose adequately.

6:16 *Make a roof for it and finish the ark to within 18 inches of the top. Put a door in the side of the ark and make lower, middle and upper decks.*

We are also given some additional details about the equipment and fittings of the ark. Some of these are difficult to determine and we cannot be sure of correct translation of terms in every instance.

The first detail that demands our attention is what our translators have termed the "roof." The Hebrew word used here appears nowhere else in the Old Testament. Its meaning is therefore obscure. There is a word similar to this in other Semitic languages which means "back." This word appears several times in the Amarna Tablets, for instance, and there it is translated "back." Some scholars feel that the word has a Canaanitish origin and that this term "back" refers to the roof of the ark.

Others, however, see the word as a singular form of the word which means "noon" or "midday." They then translate it as "an opening to admit light" or a "window." Our translators offer this as a marginal reading. Egyptian houses and temples often had typical rectangular or semicircular openings that were placed above the regular doors or windows. These openings would then admit light when the doors and shutters were closed. It is argued, then, that the ark was fitted with such an opening to admit light.

To support this theory an appeal is made to what follows. There we read, "and finish [it] to within one cubit [18 inches] of the top." This phrase also is variously read. Those who hold to the "opening for light" reading claim that this "window" or opening was placed within one cubit of the top. Others claim that the opening itself was one cubit in height. They insist that either of these readings would bring this in complete concurrence with the Egyptian practice of placing such openings in their buildings.

Many scholars, including our translators, have tied the pronoun in the phrase, "and finish *it*," to the ark itself. In other words, "finish the ark to within one cubit of the top." We defend this reading. We should then picture it as follows. The walls were finished to within one cubit of the flat roof. There were beams which extended all the way to the roof but the space between these beams was left open. With the roof overhanging the walls, rain would not be able to come in through this opening. Meanwhile this open space would provide ventilation and light for the ark.

Just for curiosity's sake, we might mention that in the Targum of Jonathan the word we have translated "roof" is rendered "precious stone." This jewel, according to this tradition, was brought from the Pishon River by Noah at God's direction. It was so brilliant that it spread light throughout the ark.

We are also told that the ark was to have a door, and that this door was to be in the side of the ark. The Hebrew word "side" is also used with respect to the Altar of Incense and the tabernacle (Exod. 30:4; 26:13). From these references it appears that the term designates the long side of a rectangular structure. This would then also be the case with the ark. There is an Egyptian analogy in which a similar vessel had the door placed in a corner. There is, however, no evidence of this in the biblical text. Undoubtedly, the door was placed above the waterline and thus would have been rather high on the side of the ship.

Finally we are told that the ark would have three "floors" or "decks." The word for "floors" is not provided, and all we have in the text is "lower," "second," and "third." These words are masculine in form and probably would have to be related to the word in verse 14 which we have translated "rooms" or "compartments." Thus we would get a picture of three levels or tiers of rooms. There has been much conjecture as to precisely how all of this was arranged in the ark, allowing for storage space and living quarters for Noah and his family as well as all the other cargo. Since the text gives no detailed information in this regard, all of this is guesswork and quite inconsequential.

6:17 *I am going to bring floodwaters on the earth to destroy all life under the heavens, every creature that has the breath of life in it. Everything on earth will perish.*

It is not until this point in the narrative that the exact nature of the judgment that was to come was clearly revealed. God now declares that He would bring a flood upon the earth that would destroy all living creatures. The word translated "flood" actually means "devastation." The word "water" is added so we get a picture of devastation by means of water. Later in the Old Testament it is frequently used without the word "water" even though it refers directly to this event (Gen. 7:6; 7:17; 9:28; 10:1; 11:10; and Ps. 29:10). Efforts have been made to relate the word to certain Babylonian and Syrian terms but the correctness of this is doubtful. In Hebrew the definite article usually precedes it and thus it designates a specific and severe devastation. Probably the best English rendering is "the

Deluge," designating it as the one, incomparable devastation which God brought upon the earth at this point in history.

This violent flood would not only destroy all mankind but also the animals. In verse 13 it seems to refer especially to humanity, because it was a punishment for man's sins. Now the term "every creature that has the breath of life in it" is used, and also "all life under the heavens," and these expressions definitely include animals. This, then, also concurs with God's pronouncement in verse 7.

6:18 *But I will establish my covenant with you, and you will enter the ark—you and your sons and your wife and your sons' wives with you.*

"But I will establish my covenant with you." This is the first time the word "covenant" appears in the Bible. The concept had been introduced in what is usually called "The Covenant of Works," revealed in Genesis 2:16–17. Also, we usually think of the "Protevangelium" in Genesis 3:15 as being the first announcement of the "covenant of grace." But here, in 6:18, we encounter the word "covenant" for the first time. It expresses a relationship or agreement between two parties, in which both accept certain specified responsibilities. Since there is no mention here of a reciprocal responsibility on Noah's part, some have hesitated to use the word "covenant" in this reference, substituting a word such as "arrangement." This, however, is not justified. It should be noted that in every instance in which God enters into covenant with man, He plays a one-sided role. He always establishes all of the conditions and all of the provisions of the covenant. Thus we describe God's covenants as being "monopluric." It must always be remembered that man never stands as an equal party when the other party is God. In a sense, then, the word "covenant" when used of a relationship with God is somewhat of an anthropomorphism. It lends a degree of intimacy and affection but still maintains an atmosphere of being unbreakable.

The question has been asked, "Which covenant is intended here?" Most expositors relate the "covenant," as it is mentioned here, to the covenant in chapter 9. The promise given here would then be fulfilled after the Flood. We do not agree with this presentation. It should be noted that, immediately after mention is made of the covenant that God would establish with Noah, God says, "You will enter the ark—you and your sons and your wife and your sons' wives with you." This can be seen only as part of the terms of this covenant. If we were to follow the theory mentioned above we would have to read this somewhat as follows: "I will establish my covenant with you at a later time, but for the present, you must go into the ark. Then later, after you have left the ark, we will get back to the terms of the covenant I am making with you.'' This is certainly a forced and unnatural reading of this most significant statement by God. It can be arrived at only if the entire passage is approached with a preconceived notion. Since mention is made of a ''lasting covenant'' after the flood is over, it is argued that these two references must refer to the same covenant. Of course, this argument is then supported by the theory that this concept of a lasting covenant is characteristic of the Priestly Codex, and since 6:18 is ascribed to that source, the reference here must surely be to the same lasting covenant mentioned in chapter 9. Such argument needs no response.

The real issue here is, What does verse 18 itself tell us? This verse clearly indicates that this covenant consisted of God's declaration that He would spare Noah and his family when He destroyed the rest of mankind. Noah and his family would become the special objects of God's care and would be saved from the terrible devastation that God was about to bring on the earth. No matter how horrible the Deluge would be, Noah need not be afraid. God's covenant faithfulness was his assurance that he would survive this judgment. And as Noah's part of the covenant, he was required to believe and obey God's word, build the ark according to God's instructions, and then enter it with his family. In that way only would he be saved.

It should also be noted that this covenant affected not only Noah but also his family. Thus we see that God's covenant with man is not individual but includes the family. This is one of the most significant aspects of the biblical covenant concept. It is revealed even more clearly in Genesis 17:1-7. The ark would serve as the means of deliverance, not only for Noah, but also for his wife, his sons, and his sons' wives. Thus this covenant is in complete accord with the promise of Genesis 3:15, which, as we have observed, was the first announcement of God's covenant of grace with His people. Now God establishes this covenant with Noah and his family. They are to be the ones who will preserve the ''seed'' when the rest of the human race is annihilated.

6:19, 20 *You are to bring into the ark two of all living creatures, male and female, to keep them alive with you. Two of every kind of bird, of every kind of animal and of every kind of creature that moves along the ground will come to you to be kept alive.*

In addition to preserving a ''seed'' to save humanity, God also made provision for the preservation of animal life on earth. Noah was to bring into the ark one pair, a male and a female, of all other living creatures.

Mention is made of animals, birds, and creatures that crawl. Just as was the case in Genesis 1:24, it is apparent that we are not dealing here with scientifically accurate classifications. The intent was that this program of preservation would be as complete as possible. In 7:14, where the carrying out of this mandate is recorded, still another group of creatures is mentioned. It is obvious, of course, why water creatures are not included since they are not threatened by a flood. The added statement, "of every kind," requires no further discussion here. Comparing this passage with Genesis 1:11, we can observe the enormous variety that God established in the animal world at the time of creation and which now is to be preserved by taking all kinds of animals into the ark.

6:21 *You are to take every kind of food that is to be eaten and store it away as food for you and for them."*

An adequate food supply also had to be placed in the ark to sustain both the people and the animals who would make this ship their home during the coming period of devastation. Noah was instructed to make provision for this as well. Some interpreters insist that this must have consisted only of vegetation, since no meat could be eaten in the ark. The text, however, does not suggest such a limitation. There is no reason to believe that carnivorous animals would not eat their usual diet. Most likely this point has been made to defend the theory that the Priestly Codex portion of the narrative mentioned only one pair of each kind of animal. The Jahwist source supposedly was the origin of the reference to seven pairs of clean animals. One scholar even admits this when he observes that, if meat was to be used for food, Noah would have been compelled to include more animals in the ark, as is acknowledged in 7:2ff. What an interesting admission for a scholar from this school which approaches the text of Scripture with a preconceived theory which must then, of course, be supported.

6:22 *Noah did everything just as God commanded him.*

We are now told that Noah meticulously carried out the instructions God had given him. At this point this includes only the construction of the ark and the other necessary preparations that had to be made. In 7:1 we are told about the actual entering of the ark. In the early church it was thought that the entire 120 years, mentioned in verse 3, was spent in this huge construction project. This view is still held by a few Roman Catholic and Protestant scholars, but there is no basis for this contention in the text. We do not even know when the mandate to build the ark was given to Noah. As was mentioned in connection with verse 5, the transition from verses 1–4 to 5ff. suggests that a major part of the 120 years that are mentioned may have been past when God actually announced the coming devastation to Noah.

It is also possible that Noah did not work alone in building this huge ship. Some of his contemporaries may have assisted him, even though they did not believe his preaching (Matt. 24:37–39; Luke 17:27; 1 Peter 3:20). If they did get involved in the project there can be little doubt that Noah was subjected to much ridicule with respect to his venture of faith.

7:1 *The LORD then said to Noah, "Go into the ark, you and your whole family, because I have found you righteous in this generation.*

When the ark was completed, the time for judgment to fall was fast approaching, so God commanded Noah to take his entire family into the ark. At this time he was again reminded that the reason for his being spared was that, of all the people in the earth, he alone was considered righteous before God (6:9).

7:2–3 *Take with you seven of every kind of clean animal, a male and its mate, and two of every kind of unclean animal, a male and its mate, and also seven of every kind of bird, male and female, to keep their various kinds alive throughout the earth.*

Now Noah was instructed to bring the animals aboard the ark. In distinction from 6:19–20, he is now told to bring seven pairs of clean animals and birds while taking only one pair of all the other animals. As was discussed in the introduction to this section, this has been seized by the proponents of multiple sources as a basic conflict in the record. In our treatment of 6:19–20 we pointed out that there is no real conflict between these two references. Here in 7:2–3 we have an added detail that is simply not mentioned in the earlier passage. We are not told why this exception is made with respect to the clean animals. It is possible, however, that this was done because only clean animals could be used for sacrifices. That animal sacrifices were already being made in this early period is evident from the incident of Cain and Abel (4:4). In the present situation, then, clean animals could be sacrificed during the stay in the ark without endangering any particular species.

There has been some doubt expressed about this early reference to clean and unclean animals. It is argued that this distinction was first introduced by the Mosaic Law. In reply, it should be observed that this distinction was recognized long before the Mosaic Law was given. When it was spelled out in the Law (Lev. 11 and Deut. 14) it was not presented as something new, as though it was now introduced for the first time. On the contrary, it was no more than the legal confirmation of a distinction that was already familiar. Thus, the contention that this distinction between clean and unclean animals could not have been made before the Deluge is without foundation.

The distinction probably was not as clearly defined earlier, and it may have had some different applications, but the distinction between clean and unclean certainly could have been familiar at the time of Noah. It is possible that these exact terms, "clean and unclean," were not being used during this early time. Even if these precise terms were not introduced until the time of Moses, it is wholly understandable that the writer of the Pentateuch, under the guidance of the Holy Spirit, recorded the words of God to Noah in terms that were familiar both to him and to his readers.

The fact that Abel offered animal sacrifices that were acceptable to God certainly provides indirect evidence that a distinction of some kind was already known before the Deluge. The practice of sacrificing animals certainly involved a careful selection of suitable animals and a rejection of those which were not. Some of the critics are so eager to defend their own positions in this regard that they go as far as to deny that there were any animal sacrifices prior to the Deluge. This obviously does violence to the record of Scripture.

Another issue that is raised relates to the above. There are those who insist that since the distinction between clean and unclean animals for sacrificial purposes was familiar before the Deluge, it would be implied that people also ate meat before this time. "Clean animals" were not only suitable for sacrifices but they were also acceptable for human food. In the Mosaic Law, in fact, it is this matter of suitability for food that is emphasized. Even so, in 9:3 we are told that people were not permitted to eat meat until after the flood.

It must be remembered that the distinction between clean and unclean animals at this time certainly did not include all the details and applications which later were expressed in the Mosaic laws. It is certainly possible, and even probable, that, prior to the Deluge, the distinction was applied only to the matter of animals suitable for sacrifices. It should also be observed that the application of this distinction to the matter of human food is treated as a separate issue in the Mosaic laws (Deut. 12:15, 22; 15:22).

One other issue that has been raised relating to these verses is the use of the number "seven." The Hebrew says, "seven sevens, the male and the female." Some claim that this means seven pairs of each kind, while others say that it means a total of seven of each kind. It is difficult to determine what the text actually means. Our translators have used the latter in the text and included the former as a marginal reading. The addition of the words "a male and a female" suggests that they came in pairs. On the other hand, the unclean animals came in single pairs and they are designated as "two" of each kind, "a male and a female." Some have concluded then that the clean animals included three pairs of each kind, with one left over without a mate. This single animal would then, it is suggested, be designated for sacrifice. This is an interesting theory but impossible to substantiate. No solid conclusion can be made in this matter.

We are also told that seven birds of each kind (the clean ones) had to be taken aboard. This is branded as a later insertion by some scholars, but it is without firm justification.

7:4 *Seven days from now I will send rain on the earth for forty days and forty nights, and I will wipe from the face of the earth every living creature I have made.''*

The exact point in time at which the judgment would begin is now announced. In seven days the rain would begin to fall, and this would initiate the mighty Deluge. The rain would continue to pour down for forty days and forty nights. As a consequence the entire earth would be inundated and all living creatures on the face of the earth would perish. It goes without saying that this would not be a usual, gentle rain. It was to be an unusual, violent downpour. This is stated in 7:12. It probably should be looked upon as a cloudburst which continued without letup for many days.

7:5 *And Noah did all that the LORD commanded him.*

Once again we are told, as in 6:22, that Noah carried out God's instructions with great care. This now refers to the process of entering the ark, as described in the following verses.

7:6 *Noah was six hundred years old when the floodwaters came on the earth.*

At this point we are informed about Noah's age at the beginning of the Flood. He was now 600 years old, and this would mean that his sons were approximately 100 years old (Gen. 5:32).

7:7–9 *And Noah and his sons and his wife and his sons' wives entered the ark to escape the waters of the flood. Pairs of clean and unclean animals, of birds and of all creatures that move along the ground, male and female, came to Noah and entered the ark, as God had commanded Noah.*

Thereupon we see Noah and his family (cf. 6:17) taking refuge in the ark in order to be saved from the coming catastrophe. Also, as God had instructed, all the various kinds of animals were taken into the ark. It should be pointed out that the clean and unclean animals are mentioned here together, but there is no indication of a difference in the number of each, as was the case in 7:2–3. This places those who insist on dividing sources and two separate records of the Flood, ''J'' and ''P,'' before a real difficulty. We refer our readers to what has been said in this regard in our Introduction. Here we have another confirmation of the view we have presented, that the rule was two of every kind. In the case of the clean animals, however, there was an exception to this general rule for specific reasons. Thus we have here a simple repetition of that rule, namely, two of each kind of animals, clean and unclean.

7:10–12 *And after the seven days the floodwaters came on the earth.*
In the six hundredth year of Noah's life, on the seventeenth day of the second month—on that day all the springs of the great deep burst forth, and the floodgates of the heavens were opened. And rain fell on the earth forty days and forty nights.

Seven days later the rain began to pour down, precisely as God had predicted (7:4). The exact day on which this occurred is designated. It was the 17th day of the 2nd month of the 600th year of Noah's life. We probably should understand this as the year following Noah's 600th birthday (see 7:6). This would be in accord with the Hebrew way of counting time, which is different from our usual way of doing so today. Just what month is intended by the 2nd month is uncertain. Those who ascribe this material to ''P'' claim that the first month of the year, according to the Babylonian and Persian practice, was in the spring of the year. The Flood would then have started in April or May. Others believe that the Hebrew year started in the fall of the year and that, consequently, the Flood came in October or November. We simply must declare that there is no way of knowing with certainty when the 2nd month fell.

As far as the sources of the flood waters are concerned, we are given more information here than we received in the announcement in 7:4. As we observed in our Introduction, those who divide the sources indulge in some rather fanciful interpretations in this regard. They refer to two independent directions from which the waters came. This, of course, must also support their theory of two independent sources for the narrative. In the one case the water supposedly came from a miraculous opening up of the vault of the sky where there was some kind of mythological ocean that was emptied out upon the earth. In the other instance, a subterranean ocean was mi-

raculously forced to the surface of the earth and thus the state of chaos
which prevailed during the first stage of creation temporarily returned.

We have already pointed out in our Introduction that there is no textual
basis for these theories regarding two independent sources for the narrative
of the Flood. Both here and in 8:2 there is a reference to water coming from
above and from below. It has been charged that the text lacks unity in this
regard and that the redactor rather ingeniously brought these divergent
elements together. This charge cannot be supported by the facts as they are
given in the text. It is no more than an attempt to defend a preconceived
theory. The ''floodgates of heaven'' is certainly a symbolic term. It describes what had been mentioned in verse 12, namely, that there was a
violent, pouring rainfall. The word used for ''rain'' is a stronger word than
the word used in 7:4. It actually means a ''deluge.''

This same symbolic meaning can be given to the breaking forth of the
''springs of the great deep.'' What this actually says is that there were
forces beneath the earth's surface that contributed to the great mass of
water which covered the earth. This can be understood if we consider the
effects of a great earthquake, when water beneath the earth's crust has
actually been known to burst forth in rivers. It is not our intention to
declare that this is what happened at the time of the Flood. The Deluge was
a totally unique event in the history of the earth. No other phenomenon has
ever been equivalent or similar to it. Even so, the Deluge can be accepted
as taking place in history without resorting to all kinds of fantasy or
mythological figures. This author has treated these matters in some depth in
his book, *De Goddelijke Openbaring*.

7:13–16 *On that very day Noah and his sons, Shem, Ham and Japheth, together
with his wife and the wives of his three sons, entered the ark. They had with them
every wild animal according to its kind, all livestock according to their kinds, every
creature that moves along the ground according to its kind and every bird according to its kind, everything with wings. Pairs of all creatures that have the breath of
life in them came to Noah and entered the ark. The animals going in were male and
female of every living thing, as God had commanded Noah. Then the LORD shut him
in.*

On that designated day, the 17th day of the 2nd month of Noah's 600th
year, Noah and his family entered the ark. The animals that were destined to
be preserved from annihilation joined them in the ark. It should be noted that
in addition to the three groups of animals mentioned in 6:20, a fourth group is
included here, namely, the wild animals. (With respect to this classification,
see our treatment of 1:24.) Once again, it should be remembered that this is
not intended to be an exhaustive list of all the animal species.

There are those who insist that at this point the narrative becomes very unrealistic. They argue that all the animals could not possibly have entered the ark in one day. We would reply that we should not have too limited a view of what can happen in one day in an emergency situation. At the same time, it should be observed that the text does not require that all of this happened in one day. The statement can be read to mean that this was the day on which the entrance into the ark was completed.

Then we read, "Then the LORD shut him in." This is the usual reading and also the one adopted by our translators. We feel that a closer or more correct reading would be, "Then the LORD closed the entrance to it," that is, the entrance to the ark. What it says then is that after Noah and his family and all the animals had entered the ark, God barred the entrance to anyone else who might try to enter.

7:17–20 *For forty days the flood kept coming on the earth, and as the waters increased they lifted the ark high above the earth. The waters rose and increased greatly on the earth, and the ark floated on the surface of the water. They rose greatly on the earth, and all the high mountains under the entire heavens were covered. The waters rose and covered the mountains to a depth of more than twenty feet.*

We are now given a description of the actual Flood, and this again relates to the designated period of 40 days and 40 nights, mentioned in verse 12. When we read that the Flood was on the earth 40 days and 40 nights, this is not a designation of the length of time that the water covered the earth. This was, rather, the amount of time required for the water to reach its maximum height. Graphically the steadily rising water with its increasing power is described. First the water covered the ground where the ark rested. Gradually it continued to rise until the large vessel with its life-preserving cargo began to float. Soon it was driven about by waves and currents. And then all was water. The entire earth became one vast sea, with only a few mountain peaks reaching above the surface. Then those mountain peaks also disappeared beneath the surface of the water. The water continued to rise until the highest peak was submerged to a depth of 15 cubits. (7½ m., 22½ ft.). No land creature could survive on the earth.

7:21–23 *Every living thing that moved on the earth perished–birds, livestock, wild animals, all the creatures that swarm over the earth, and all mankind. Everything on the dry land that had the breath of life in its nostrils died. Every living thing on the face of the earth was wiped out; men and animals and the creatures that move along the ground and the birds of the air were wiped from the earth. Only Noah was left, and those with him in the ark.*

As a result, every living creature on the earth perished, both human beings and animal life. Once again, the list of animals given at this point is different from those in 6:7 and 7:14. Here mention is made of birds, cattle, and wild animals, as well as "all the creatures that swarm over the earth." In 1:20 this expression is used to describe water creatures. Here, however, it designates all the countless kinds of land creatures that are not specifically included in the other categories. Verse 22 limits the creatures that were destroyed by the Deluge to those that normally lived on dry land, in distinction from those that normally lived in the water. Although this is an obvious fact, it is repeated here for the sake of clarity.

7:24 *The waters flooded the earth for a hundred and fifty days.*

After the water reached its maximum height (depth) it remained at that level for a time. The text says that the water flooded the earth for 150 days. Those who divide sources go to some effort to read this differently. They insist that this reference came from "P" and that it says that the waters rose for 150 days, and thus it is in conflict with "J" which allows only 40 days for this process. But the text does not require this kind of manipulation. The Hebrew verb translated "flooded" has also been translated "prevailed." There is nothing in the word which implies that it must indicate an increase of the water. Once again, there is no conflict here unless it is forced upon the text by a preconceived notion.

There may be some question regarding the starting point of the 150 days. Does this time span include the 40 days of 7:4 and 7:12, or does it follow on those 40 days? When we turn to 8:4, it becomes clear that the former is the case. There we read that the ark rested on Mt. Ararat and the exact date is recorded. It was the 17th day of the 7th month. Thus it was exactly 5 months after the beginning of the Flood. If the 150 days are added to the 40 days it would come to more than 6 months, while 5 months is, in round numbers, equivalent to 150 days. Thus the 150-day period begins with the commencing of the Flood and covers the entire time that the water covered the earth until that point when the water began to recede.

8:1–3 *But God remembered Noah and all the wild animals and the livestock that were with him in the ark, and he sent a wind over the earth and the waters receded. Now the springs of the deep and the floodgates of the heavens had been closed, and the rain had stopped falling from the sky. The water receded steadily from the earth. At the end of the hundred and fifty days the water had gone down.*

After 150 days, then, the water began to recede. We are told that God remembered Noah and all the animals that were with him in the ark. This, of course, does not imply that God had forgotten them prior to this point. It declares, rather, that God took care of them throughout the great Flood and thus fulfilled His covenant promise to Noah (6:18). And now God would complete His work of deliverance by causing the waters to recede.

The means God used to bring down the level of the water were (1) a wind and (2) the cessation of the rain. Regarding the latter, we must consider that for 40 days the rain poured down in violent torrents to build the water up to its highest level. For the balance of the 150 days there were continued rain storms, but of less severity. These would serve to keep the water at its height. Thus there was a difference between the intensity of the rain in the first 40 days and the intensity of the rain in the next 110 days. After a total of 150 days, the rain ceased and the waters began to recede.

With respect to the "wind" that is mentioned, there has been much conjecture. Some have interpreted this as the hot south wind known as the Sirocco. Others have attacked this as unrealistic, and some have even charged that the text is misleading on this score. In defense of the text, let it be noted that the word does not indicate any special kind of wind. It is rather apparent that it could not have been the Sirocco wind since this is a hot wind sweeping off the desert, and this would have been quite unlikely while the earth was covered with water.

Others have charged that there would have been no place for the wind to drive the water if the whole earth was covered with water, and hence, they claim, the statement is dubious. All of this discussion is actually meaningless. The text simply says that God sent a wind. It certainly should be obvious that wind causes evaporation and this would then be a contributing factor in the process of lowering the level of the water. Just as in 7:17–20 the gradual increase and rise of the water was described, so here the gradual decline and lowering of the water is graphically described.

8:4 *And on the seventeenth day of the seventh month the ark came to rest on the mountains of Ararat.*

Finally the ark rested on firm ground, and that on one of the mountains of Ararat. The date that is given indicates that the ark lodged on this mountain peak almost immediately after the water began to recede. With its height and its heavy cargo the ship must have had considerable draft below the surface of the water. Since the water reached the level of 7½ m. (22½ ft.) above the highest mountains, even a slight decline in the level of the water could cause it to run aground on one of the higher peaks. Once again, the period of 150 days as being equivalent to 5 months need cause us no concern. It would be understandable if the author simply used round numbers, even though the actual time period may have varied a few days one way or another. It is also possible that he used the Babylonian calendar, which had months of an even 30 days. To enter into a lengthy discussion concerning whether these were lunar months or solar months is really quite pointless.

The land of Ararat is mentioned in other places in the Old Testament (2 Kings 19:37; Isa. 37:38; Jer. 51:27). Undoubtedly, we must think of this as the area that conforms to the modern country of Armenia, as it is referred to in the early tablets of Urartu. The highest peak in the Armenian mountains is called "Massis." It is about 17,000 ft. (5,150 m.) high. Whether this is the exact peak on which the ark came to rest is not known. It could well have been one of the other peaks in the same mountain range.

8:5 *The waters continued to recede until the tenth month, and on the first day of the tenth month the tops of the mountains became visible.*

The water evidently continued to recede with each passing day. As a result, 2½ months after it began to lower, the tops of the mountains came into view. If we assume that the ark had run aground on one of the higher peaks, and bear in mind the fact that the height of the surrounding peaks varied considerably, being able to see the mountains round about could indicate that the level of the water had declined thousands of feet by this time.

8:6, 7 *After forty days Noah opened the window he had made in the ark and sent out a raven, and it kept flying back and forth until the water had dried up from the earth.*

Now we have another reference to 40 days. This has been variously interpreted by those who divide the sources of the narrative. Many hold that this 40-day period is the same as the 40 days mentioned in 7:4, 12, and 17. That was the period during which the rain fell. According to these scholars, the duration of the entire Flood was 40 days plus 21 days (cf. 8:8–12), and this is the feeling of "J." Others are of the opinion that this 40-day period must be counted from the point when the rain ceased. They then consider the duration of the Flood to have been 40 plus 40 plus 21 days. If we adhere to the text as it is, however, without indulging in the exercise of splitting it up into various sources, it is obvious that this 40-day period follows on what is recorded in verse 5. It should be remembered that the ark lodged on a mountain peak which was part of a vast and rugged mountain range. From this vantage point Noah probably was not able to see what conditions were out on the lower plains. He was literally surrounded by mountains. It was for this reason that he sent out the raven, to see how this hardy bird would fare with conditions as they were at this time. The "window" mentioned here was not specifically mentioned at the time of the construction of the ark. Some have claimed that this window Noah had built into the ark must have been on the roof. Their argument is that, if it had been in a wall, Noah would have been able to see out and consequently there would have been no need for sending out the bird to explore conditions on the earth. Such arguments reveal a total ignorance of the terrain in which the ark came to rest. Even if the ark had windows on all sides, it still would have been most unlikely that there would have been a view of the lower plains from this vantage point in the remote mountains of Ararat.

The raven did not return. We read that it flew back and forth until it found enough dry ground on which to survive. Another factor is that the raven feeds on carrion and there probably were many dead bodies floating around on which this bird could feed.

8:8–12 *Then he sent out a dove to see if the water had receded from the surface of the ground. But the dove could find no place to set its feet because there was water over all the surface of the earth; so it returned to Noah in the ark. He reached out his hand and took the dove and brought it back to himself in the ark. He waited seven more days and again sent out the dove from the ark. When the dove returned to him in the evening, there in its beak was a freshly plucked olive leaf! Then Noah knew that the water had receded from the earth. He waited seven more days and sent the dove out again, but this time it did not return to him.*

Thereupon Noah released a dove, which was a more sensitive bird. He probably decided that the experiment with the raven had not provided him with the information he sought. Although the lapse of time between the sending forth of these two birds is not mentioned, it can be assumed from verse 10. There we read that he waited "seven more days." This would suggest that the first delay also had been seven days. Thus, we get the picture that Noah carried on these experiments for three periods of seven days. The dove, sent out seven days after the raven, returned to the ark because it could not find suitable food or nesting areas.

After another seven days Noah sent the dove out once again. This time the bird stayed away all day and in the evening it returned with a freshly plucked leaf from an olive tree. Thus it was not something the bird had found among the flotsam. This indicated that the trees on the lower plains were again sprouting leaves. It should be observed that olive trees are capable of sprouting shoots under water and thus they could have survived the Flood.

The third time he sent forth the dove it did not return. This revealed that the dove found it possible to return to its normal life pattern. The waters had dried up.

8:13 *By the first day of the first month of Noah's six hundred and first year, the water had dried up from the earth. Noah then removed the covering from the ark and saw that the surface of the ground was dry.*

We now find another designation of time. It was the 601st year of Noah's life, the 1st day of the 1st month. This would seem to indicate that, after the last sending out of the dove, Noah still waited for another period of time. If we count the 40 days of 8:6 from the 1st day of the 10th month of verse 5, and then allow 7 days between the sending of the raven and that of the dove, there would have been 61 days between the point of 8:5 and the last sending out of the dove. This is about 2 months. But from the 1st day of the 10th month to the 1st day of the 1st month is actually three months. Thus it would appear that Noah waited approximately another month after the dove was sent out the last time.

At this point the text says, ''the water had dried up from the earth.'' This must be understood as Noah's own conclusion. He now took the first step toward terminating their stay in the ark, and we read that Noah removed the covering from the ark. Just what was this covering? Many hold that this was the roof of the ark. We consider this to be doubtful, however. The Hebrew word is used various times in the Old Testament and it always refers to a cloth cover of some kind: the covering of the tabernacle (Exod. 26:14; 35:11; 36:19; 39:34; 40:19; Num. 3:25; 4:25), the covering of the ark of the covenant (Num. 4:8) and of the golden candelabra (Num. 4:10), of the altar of incense (Num. 4:11), and of the vessels for the sacrifices (Num. 4:12). All of these covers were used when these items were carried. It would seem to be consistent, then, to think of the covering of Noah's ark as a deck cloth, probably made of the skins of animals. This would have been fastened over the roof of the ark to make it more waterproof.

Those who understand this covering to have been the roof itself come up with two possible explanations for this ''removal.'' Some suggest that Noah removed it in order to get a better view of the surrounding country, but this would certainly be a radical step to take merely to get a better view, especially when we consider the earlier reference to the window in the ark (8:6). Others suggest that this was Noah's first step in dismantling the ark that he would no longer need. This also seems difficult to accept. Why would Noah start tearing the ark apart when he would still be living in it for another two months (vv. 14–19)?

177

If, on the other hand, we consider this covering to have been a deck cloth, its removal would seem to be reasonable. Noah knew that the Flood had ended and that there was no longer any need for this added covering for the ark. Its removal, moreover, would help to dry out the atmosphere inside the ark. The removal of this covering was undoubtedly done on the roof of the giant vessel and this would give Noah and his sons a good opportunity to look around to see that the earth was free of water as far as their view extended.

8:14 *By the twenty-seventh day of the second month the earth was completely dry.*

That the earth was free of water did not mean, however, that the ground was dry enough to permit them to move about freely. After such a long period of inundation, it certainly would be soft and muddy for some time. Thus, it was not until the 27th day of the 2nd month that the ground was sufficiently dry to allow men and animals to move around freely on the earth. It should be noted that the word used in verse 13 means "free of water," while the word used here means "dry and firm."

8:15–17 *Then God said to Noah, "Come out of the ark, you and your wife and your sons and their wives. Bring out every kind of living creature that is with you—the birds, the animals, and all the creatures that move along the ground—so they can multiply on the earth and be fruitful and increase in number upon it."*

Finally, the time had come for Noah and his family to leave the ark. Just as God had commanded them to enter the ark before the Flood started, so now He commanded them to leave the ark. The emphasis falls strongly on the fact that the saving of this one family out of the whole human race was not a matter of human ingenuity, but that it was exclusively an act of God. Once again, as in 6:18, the various members of Noah's family are listed. Also, the various kinds of animals are recorded as they leave the ark. It probably should be pointed out that the word translated "living creatures" is the same word that is used in 1:24 and 7:14, 21 as referring to wild animals. Here it obviously has a broader meaning. In our treatment of 1:24 we observed that its basic meaning is "that which lives." That is how it is used here. We are also told that the creation blessing on the animal world again becomes effective. Once again they were to become fruitful and multiply and replenish the earth, each after its kind (see 1:22).

8:18, 19 *So Noah came out, together with his sons and his wife and his sons' wives. All the animals and all the creatures that move along the ground and all the* *birds—everything that moves on the earth—came out of the ark, one kind after another.*

God's command was obeyed. Noah and his family, referred to in verse 16, now left the ark. All of the various animals also went forth upon the earth. The addition of ''one kind after another'' has caused some to interpret this as though the animals left the ark in a definite order, kind by kind. This is, however, not what the text says. The term used has nothing to do with the order in which they left the ark. It indicates, rather, that all the various kinds of animals again returned to their natural habitat in the earth.

8:20 *Then Noah built an altar to the LORD and, taking some of all the clean animals and clean birds, he sacrificed burnt offerings on it.*

The first act Noah performed after leaving the ark was to build an altar and offer a sacrifice to the Lord. This sacrifice must be understood as an expression of thanksgiving for the deliverance experienced. But it also constituted a prayer for further preservation as they went forth to make their new life on the earth. This is the first time we have a reference to an altar, for the sacrifices of Cain and Abel make no mention of an altar. Noah's offering consisted of clean animals and birds.

It should be noted that the word for sacrifice used here is different than the word used in 4:3–5. The word used there later, when the laws of Moses were given, designated a grain offering. The word originally meant ''gift'' or ''present.'' The word used here later designated burnt offerings. It is derived from the Hebrew word which means ''to ascend.'' The significance lay in the fact that the offering went up in fire and smoke. The symbolism is readily understandable. It suggests that what is offered ascends up to God.

8:21 *The LORD smelled the pleasing aroma and said in his heart: ''Never again will I curse the ground because of man, even though every inclination of his heart is evil from childhood. And never again will I destroy all living creatures, as I have done.*

''The LORD smelled the pleasing aroma.'' This is an obvious anthropomorphism which says that the sacrifice was well-pleasing to God. Thereupon, God determined (said in His heart) never again to bring a judgment on the earth that would destroy all life. This decision, mentioned here, is announced by God in 9:8–17.

Here we face a serious difficulty in translating the clause that is attached, ''even though every inclination of his heart is evil from childhood.'' This is the reading our translators have adopted. A marginal reading suggests that the word "for" can be used instead of "even though." The usual translation would make the content of this statement the basis for God's decision never again to bring an all-destructive judgment on the earth. But this, obviously, makes no sense. In 6:5–7 we are told that God decided to destroy the world for this reason. How can He now decide not to destroy the world for the same reason? Few interpreters have succeeded in resolving this difficulty. Many scholars, both Roman Catholic and Protestant, try to find an expression of God's mercy and longsuffering in this statement, thus they translate it "even though." But this is linguistically not permissible.

The difficulty stems from establishing the wrong connection within the verse. The evil inclinations of men's hearts should not be related to God's decision not to bring an all-destructive judgment upon the earth. It must, rather, be seen as the basis for that judgment itself. The passage then would read as follows: "I will not again judge the evil inclinations of men's hearts by means of bringing an all-destructive judgment upon the earth." When it is read this way, there is no conflict between 6:5–7 and 8:21. All we have here is a referral back to 6:5–7. God in essence says, "I have now brought judgment upon the evil inclinations of men's hearts by sending this great deluge. I will not again bring such a judgment upon the earth for this cause."

The expression itself, "every inclination of [man's] heart is evil from childhood," testifies to the original corruption of human nature. Thus we have a significant proof here for the doctrine of original sin, especially as it refers to original corruption.

There are some scholars who think that the statement, "Never again will I curse the ground because of man," indicates that the curse that is revealed in 3:17–19 is now nullified, either in part or in its entirety. But this is in conflict with what the text clearly states. The issue here is not the removal of a curse or the nullifying of it to some degree. It is solely that the curse will not again be applied in the same way it was in the case of the Deluge. The parallel statement, "never again will I destroy all living creatures," makes this clear. This is especially true of the last part of the statement, "as I have done." But this is something completely different from the actual curse pronounced in 3:17–19.

The motive God had for not bringing another all-destructive judgment on the earth is not specifically stated here. The close connection between God's decision and "the pleasing aroma" of Noah's sacrifice suggests that this is where the motive is to be found. The sacrifice was not only an expression of gratitude but it was also a prayer for God's continued preservation. God's decision not to again destroy the world is the answer to this prayer. Of course, God's decision goes much deeper than Noah's prayer. We can envision that Noah's earnest longing was that he and his family might be spared in the future. But God's provision went much farther. In His sovereign grace and good pleasure, God decided never again to bring an all-destructive judgment on the earth.

The question could still be asked whether this decision was made by God at this moment. Our answer would be that, from a human perspective, this can be looked on as an answer to prayer. But a definite answer to prayer in no way diminishes the eternity of God's counsel. Here we can apply the concept that what God does is known by Him from eternity (Acts 15:18).

8:22 *"As long as the earth endures, seedtime and harvest, cold and heat, summer and winter, day and night will never cease."*

Besides the negative decision that no all-destructive divine judgment would again be brought upon the earth, there is also a positive provision. The ordinary course of the world would continue henceforth without interruption by a catastrophe similar to the Deluge. There have been efforts to group the statements "seedtime and harvest," "cold and heat," "summer and winter," in such a way that they would designate different times of the year. According to the Talmud, these would indicate six periods of two months each. Thus this would make an orderly division of the year. According to Yahuda, these terms would indicate just two periods of the year which would then be described by three parallel terms. According to this presentation, the three expressions would also describe three different geographical areas. "Cold and heat" would describe those areas that have a climate like Egypt. Such schemes, however, run into serious difficulties and are, at best, rather arbitrary. There is, moreover, the obvious objection that the term "day and night" would not fit into any of these schemes. Thus we can conclude that such a division of the year is not intended here. What we have is a simple list of phenomena which indicate that the normal order of nature would continue without interruption.

The added words, "as long as the earth endures," are significant. The divine decision mentioned here does not imply that the earth itself will continue in its present form forever. Thus this decision of God is not in conflict with the prediction of a final judgment which the Scripture announces in connection with the return of Christ. Here we are dealing only with a divine judgment that will occur in the course of the history of this present world, similar to the Deluge. The final judgment will be something entirely different. It will bring this world and its history to an end. Time will be no more and eternity will be ushered in.

9:1 *Then God blessed Noah and his sons, saying to them, "Be fruitful and increase in number and fill the earth.*

God now directs a message to Noah and his sons. It is interesting that He does not at this time announce the decision mentioned in 8:21–22. Instead, He pronounces a blessing on them. Here we have, in essence, the renewal of the creation blessing of Genesis 1:28. It is similar to what is expressed with regard to the animal world in 8:17.

9:2 *The fear and dread of you will fall upon all the beasts of the earth and all the birds of the air, upon every creature that moves along the ground, and upon all the fish of the sea; they are given into your hands.*

In this connection the supremacy of human beings over the animals is again emphasized (cf. 1:26, 28). This supremacy is indicated by the fear animals would develop for human beings. This fear was part of the curse that came upon the earth as a consequence of the Fall. The Scripture does not offer concise statements describing the forms in which this curse would be manifested. In Genesis 3:17–19 there is a reference to a curse upon the ground, from which man's food was to grow. Specific mention is made of "thorns and thistles" that the ground would produce. But it is obvious that the dislocation that the Fall into sin would bring had not been described in detail prior to this scene after the Deluge. When we compare what is said about the relationship between animals and humans in the creation account with what we are told here, it is evident that we are here given a specific detail about the dislocation that would take place. It is unmistakable that a change in the relationship took place. Animals were now considered to be dangerous to humans. To limit this threat to mankind, God instilled in animals a certain fear of people. Thus the extermination of mankind by the animals is prevented. This obviously constitutes a definite change in the relationship between human beings and animals.

9:3 *Everything that lives and moves will be food for you. Just as I gave you the green plants, I now give you everything.*

Furthermore, an entirely new element is added to this supremacy of human beings over animals. For the first time people are permitted to use the flesh of animals for food. In the original order of things this was not permitted (Gen. 1:29) since man had an exclusively vegetarian diet. It should be noted that there is a reference here to the creation narrative in the words, "as I gave you the green plants." Thus a definite change takes place as man is now permitted to eat meat.

Some have claimed that this implies that man did not kill animals prior to the Deluge. This is not what is stated here, however. Moreover, Genesis 3:21 and 4:4 definitely deny this claim. It should be noted that Scripture gives no data as to whether man was permitted to eat meat prior to the Deluge. All we can say with certainty is that God now specifically authorized man to kill animals for food. Prior to this he was authorized to slaughter animals for sacrifices and for making clothes from the hides. It is interesting that there is no mention made at this point regarding the distinction between clean and unclean animals. We refer our readers to what we have said regarding this distinction in our treatment of 7:2–3.

9:4 *"But you must not eat meat that has its lifeblood still in it.*

The divine authorization to eat meat was, however, immediately restricted by a definite exclusion. Eating flesh with its "lifeblood" still in it was forbidden. Thus it was not permissible to eat the flesh of freshly killed animals before the blood had been drained out. The reason for this prohibition can probably be found in the intent to avoid becoming wild, and devouring raw, bloody, unprepared meat.

The word translated "life" is the same Hebrew word that is elsewhere translated "soul." Here the meaning of the word is determined by its being joined with the word "blood." Compare Leviticus 17:11, 14; Deuteronomy 12:23. There we read that "the blood is the *life*." Certainly it would be wholly unacceptable to read "the blood is the *soul*," as we understand the word soul today. It makes sense to understand it specifically as physical life, because when the blood is drained from an animal it dies.

9:5 *And for your lifeblood I will surely demand an accounting. I will demand an accounting from every animal. And from each man, too, I will demand an accounting for the life of his fellow man.*

After the instruction with respect to the blood of animals, God moves on to include the blood of fellow human beings. He would demand an accounting from animals for the blood of human beings, but He would also demand an accounting from mankind with respect to the blood of his fellowmen. God is thus making provision for the protection of human life over against the threat posed by wild animals and by other human beings as well. It is somewhat surprising that animals are mentioned first, but that is explained by the context. In this entire pericope we are dealing with the relationship between people and animals. Human beings are given freedom to dispose of animals and to use their meat for food. Animals are not given the same freedom with respect to human beings. God protects human beings over against animals (cf. v. 2), and speaking of protecting human beings, they are given protection not only against animals but also against other human beings.

9:6 *"Whoever sheds the blood of man, by man shall his blood be shed; for in the image of God has God made man.*

How God provided this protection of human life against threats by other human beings is set forth in verse 6 in the well-known words, "whoever sheds the blood of man, by man shall his blood be shed." God demands the blood of the murdered person from the murderer. This implies that the murderer must be killed by others. The words do not give a bare statement of fact, but this is in the nature of a prescription. To be sure, the statement can be read either way. But taken in the light of the intent of verse 5, where God provides for the protection of human life, and He appears as the avenger of human blood that is shed, this statement in verse 6 can be seen only as an expression of the will of God. God willed that persons should shed the blood of a murderer of another person, in order to exact a pentaly for the shed blood. This is the understanding of most interpreters, both those who hold to the Christian faith and those who do not.

Although we are dealing here with a divine prescription, there is no indication here as to how this prescription is to be carried out. We have the *what* of the matter, but not the *how*. It is not stated, for instance, that the execution of a murderer can be carried out only after a proper judicial sentencing. We may be convinced that the only legitimate execution of a murderer is that which is carried out by a recognized governmental authority. But this is not stated in the text, at least not at this point. We can say that this speaks for itself, but the Old Testament does suggest in other places that there are other ways in which this sentence can be carried out. The Mosaic laws do not deny the right of blood vengeance, but they do restrict it somewhat. Thus Numbers 35:19–21 and Deuteronomy 19:12 indicate that blood vengeance, even though somewhat restricted, is a permissible way of avenging a murder that has been committed. It is then possible that reference to the manner in which the murderer should be punished is omitted here with intent. The circumstances that prevailed immediately after the Deluge were most unusual. An entirely new human race was to develop, but various possibilities were left open at this point. Justice could be administered, for instance, by the family as well as by the government. In the New Testament we have a designation in this regard in Romans 13:4, namely, that the administration of the death penalty was in the hands of the government. But in Noah's day there was no established government, as we usually understand this. Therefore, Genesis 9:6 simply sets forth the principle that murder demands the death of the murderer. How this principle was to be carried out is not specified in this passage.

The question could be asked why God now gives the command about the death penalty when earlier He spared the life of Cain who had murdered his brother. This is the more surprising since Cain himself seemed to sense that he deserved the death sentence and that anyone who would find him would kill him (4:14-15). Some have answered this by suggesting that in the case of Cain the issue was indeed blood vengeance, while in our passage we are dealing with the death sentence as it would be administered by government. This cannot be supported by the text, however. The answer lies, rather, in that prior to the Deluge there was so much violence and bloodshed that there was a special need for a provision to prevent the return of such conditions. Therefore, murder was now to be restrained by the death penalty.

There is still another question. If it is a God-given principle of justice that the death penalty must be administered to anyone who sheds man's blood, does this mean that everyone who has killed another person, even accidentally, must be put to death? This could be concluded from a literal application of the divine prescription. That this is not the case, however, is evident from the provisions God made later in the Mosaic Law, for protecting the life of anyone who killed another person accidentally (Exod. 21:13; Num. 35:6-34; Deut. 19:1-13). It can even be pointed out that the intentional murderer need not in every case and under all circumstances be put to death. Deuteronomy 19:15 appears immediately after the distinction is made between intentional and unintentional murder, and just before legal provisions regarding false witnesses. It is in this context that the stipulation is made that a person may never be convicted on the testimony of only one witness. Additional witnesses are required in all criminal proceedings, but especially and primarily in a murder trial. Exodus 22:2 also presents another restriction on the application of the death penalty. It stipulates that anyone who kills a thief caught in the act of stealing should not be penalized.

Now it is generally accepted that the laws of Israel, in their original form, do not literally apply to us today. Even so, the principles that are laid down in these laws certainly have something to say to people of all times. Although these principles are not always easy to ferret out, in this case we can safely say that the administration of the death penalty for murder

185

demands that careful consideration must be given to all the circumstances involved in the incident. We cannot make a blanket statement that the Old Testament requires that all murder must be punished by death. The government also must exercise great discretion in the application of the death sentence. This reveals the great benefit that flows from the authority vested in government. The government becomes the responsible agent, before God, to carefully investigate time, place, and circumstances under which a crime has been committed before proceeding with execution of the sentence. This the blood avenger does not do. He does not ask for the testimony of witnesses. He does not take into account any extenuating circumstances. For the avenger, the mere fact that blood has been shed is all that is taken into account.

Thus we may assume that Genesis 9:6 includes the germ of the concept of civil government, which would later develop. The divine stipulation that the death penalty was applicable to murderers leads inescapably to the rise of government. That is the normal order of life for the human race as God ordained it. But at this time government had not yet been established, and that is why only the basic principle, with nothing added, is given immediately after the Deluge. The manner in which this principle was to be applied in actual practice would be revealed when the need arose, as the human race developed. There were various possibilities for the manner in which the principle could be put into practice. Certainly, the rise of government was the most logical of these possibilities. When civil government did develop later among the growing population, the application of this principle became one of its required functions. Government was to have discretionary power in this regard but this authority might not be misused. Eliminating the death sentence altogether, or making it only a nominal thing by undue clemency, would seem to violate the principle. The authority of government included the *how* but not the *what* of the principle God laid down.

This leads us to a treatment of the closing statement in this verse, "for in the image of God has God made man." Usually these words are interpreted as giving the rationale for the principle of the death sentence for murder. But is this really correct? If this is the meaning, the motivation does not relate too well to that which it supposedly motivates. If the creation of man in the image of God is the motivation for applying the death penalty to murderers, we have opened a line of reasoning that could have far-reaching consequences. It would imply that every attack on the human person would be a violation of the image of God, and therefore would warrant the death sentence. It may well be questioned whether the structure of this sentence warrants such a close causal connection between the two halves of verse 6.

It should be observed that the causal conjunction ''for'' need not refer only to that which immediately precedes it. Grammatically it can also apply to that which is further removed from it. Thus it would be permissible to assume that the rationale that is included in ''for in the image of God has God made man,'' refers to everything that precedes it in this pericope. We may well ask why God's special care is extended to the human race which has been spared through Noah. Why does God here renew the creation blessing? Why is humanity offered protection from the destructive attacks of wild animals and from his fellowmen? Because man was created in the image of God. If we interpret it thus, we avoid some rather untenable consequences.

This interpretation, moreover, is supported by two other considerations, one material and the other more formal. The material consideration is this. In Genesis 1:26–28 a close connection is established between man being created in the image of God and the blessing of fruitfulness and man's dominion over the animals. Here in our passage the creation blessing is repeated. Verse 2 repeats man's dominion over the animals and this is further developed in 3 and 4. Then, finally, the promise that man's life would be protected is also added. Thus it is reasonable to accept the fact that the motivation that man was created in the image of God refers to the entire preceding pericope. Why did God spare the human race from the destruction of the Deluge? Why did God bless humanity with fruitfulness? Why did He protect people from the threats of wild animals and other human beings? Because God created man in His own image. If this were not the case, He could very well have wiped out humanity in the Deluge and then have created a new humanity, a new race.

The second consideration is more formal. As many interpreters have pointed out, the first part of verse 6 has a unique form which distinguishes it from the rest of the entire passage. This statement divides into two parts, each of which contains the same words exactly. In the second part, however, the words are arranged in reverse order from the first part. This is a striking figure of speech which makes verse 6 stand out by itself. This would then confirm the view, stated above, that the close of verse 6 gives the motivation for what precedes in this entire pericope, while the first part of verse 6 must be seen as intervening comment in which we are told how God would protect human life from the lust to kill on the part of his fellowmen.

We must still make a few observations about the rather surprising change from first person to third person in speaking about God, in the closing part of verse 6. In verses 1–5 God was speaking in the first person. This can be explained by a unique linguistic usage which, although strange to us, is not uncommon in Hebrew. There is, however, another explanation that would be consistent with our interpretation of verses 1–6 above. That is that 6b actually is not part of the words which God spoke to Noah and his family. These words are, rather, an addition on the part of the inspired writer by which he, under the guidance of the Holy Spirit, points out the motivation for the words of God that precede.

The Jewish rabbis based a list of seven commandments on Genesis 9:4–6. These commandments were distinguished from the Mosaic Law, which all Israelites had to observe unconditionally. The seven commandments, it was claimed, were binding *for all people,* thus they formed a kind of natural law or religion. The rabbis arrived at this conclusion by insisting that these commandments were given by God as universal law for all of Noah's descendants up to the time of Abraham. Consequently, the Jews demanded that all the heathen who lived in their land, even those who were considered to be ''proselytes'' or ''god-fearing,'' must observe these laws. The seven commandments considered binding for all non-Jews were: (1) recognizing the government and the system of justice; (2) forbidding blasphemy of God's name; (3) forbidding idolatry; (4) forbidding consanguinity; (5) forbidding murder; (6) forbidding stealing and robbery; (7) forbidding the eating of flesh taken from a living animal. Obviously it would be difficult to find support for all of these commandments in Genesis 9:4–6. In later times the Jews went even farther and compiled a list of as many as 30 laws which, presumably, were based on this passage.

9:7 *As for you, be fruitful and increase in number; multiply on the earth and increase upon it.''*

We now return to the blessing that God pronounced upon Noah and his family. It begins with a repetition of the blessing of fruitfulness and increase upon the earth. Some have related this specifically to the forbidding of bloodshed, and this would then indicate why God held this in such abhorrence. God wanted life on earth to multiply and increase and this should not be hindered by murder and bloodhsed. The Talmud used this verse to place a strong judgment upon anyone who did not try to produce a family. The main consideration, however, was that God wanted to see a new human race develop on the earth, after it had been emptied by the Deluge.

9:8–11 *Then God said tó Noah and to his sons with him: ''I now establish my covenant with you and with your descendants after you and with every living creature that was with you–the birds, the livestock and all the wild animals, all*

188

*those that came out of the ark with you–every living creature on earth. I establish
my covenant with you: Never again will all life be cut off by the waters of a flood;
never again will there be a flood to destroy the earth.''*

Now we come to the announcement of God's decision to never again
destroy all living creatures (see 8:21–22), and this announcement came in
the form of a covenant. This covenant was described in the same language
as was used in 6:18. (See our discussion of that verse regarding the concept
of covenant-making.) In this case the covenant applied not only to Noah
and his family, but also to the animals. The content of the covenant was
that God would not send another deluge to destroy all living things upon
the earth. Thus this covenant had a much wider application than the one
mentioned in 6:18. It involved the natural life of humanity and of the
animals until the end of the world.

In verse 10 the Hebrew word *hayyâ* is used twice. It does not have the
same meaning in both cases, however. In the first instance it refers to one
of the groups of creatures that were in the ark with Noah, and we have
translated it "wild animals." The second usage refers to all the creatures
that left the ark with Noah. In this case we have translated it "every living
creature on earth."

9:12–17 *And God said, "This is the sign of the covenant I am making between me
and you and every living creature with you, a covenant for all generations to come:
I have set my rainbow in the clouds, and it will be the sign of the covenant between
me and the earth. Whenever I bring clouds over the earth and the rainbow appears
in the clouds, I will remember my covenant between me and you and all living
creatures of every kind. Never again will the waters become a flood to destroy all
life. Whenever the rainbow appears in the clouds, I will see it and remember the
everlasting covenant between God and all living creatures of every kind on the
earth.''*

*So God said to Noah, "This is the sign of the covenant I have established
between me and all life on the earth.''*

This covenant also included a sign. Such a sign was an ongoing reminder
of the covenant and a guarantee of the promise that had been given. This
sign was given by God, and it consisted of the "bow in the clouds," the
rainbow. The rainbow thus assures all who descended from Noah that
never again will God send an all-destructive deluge upon the earth.

It is now well-known that the rainbow consists of the refraction, reflec-
tion, and dispersion of the sun's rays against drops of water or mist. It
contains all the colors of the spectrum. It is seen when the sun is behind us
and a gathering of moisture is in the air in front of us.

189

Are we to conclude from this passage that the rainbow had not appeared to mankind prior to the Deluge? Those exegetes who do not accept the divine authority of Scripture have no difficulty with this question. They simply declare that of course the rainbow had always appeared but the writer of this passage was ignorant of this phenomenon. Therefore, he now presents it as something new and pours some religious significance into it. Those who hold to the authority of Scripture give this matter more serious consideration, however. Many different answers have been given.

Some feel that the rainbow was seen prior to the Flood, while others are convinced that it appeared for the first time after Noah's deliverance. A careful examination of the text reveals that this question is in no way treated in the passage before us.

Some scholars have pointed to the pronoun "my" in God's designation of the rainbow. They argue that since God refers to it as *"my* bow" it must have already existed. The same expression could have been used, however, if the rainbow was a new creation of God at this time. Others claim that since God said, "I *set* . . ." this indicates that now God initiated this phenomenon for the first time. But, once again, the verb used here can, with equal justification, be translated "I have set," as our translators have done, and thus indicate something established in the past. But we are concerned only with what Holy Scripture tells us, and all we can say with certainty is that, whenever the rainbow appears, it must be seen as a reminder and guarantee of God's covenant.

Some have concluded, on the basis of Genesis 2:5, that it did not rain before the Flood. That verse, however, says nothing about the condition of the natural world between the time of Creation and the Flood (see our interpretation of 2:5). Others have suggested that radical changes took place in the earth's climatology at the time of the Deluge. But this is pure supposition, from which no firm conclusions can be drawn. Still others insist that the sign would have been less impressive if the rainbow had been a familiar phenomenon all along. But this is merely a matter of opinion and proves nothing regarding this phenomenon as such. When God chose to designate a sign for His covenant, He could just as well have selected something He had created earlier, rather than creating something entirely new for this purpose. What He chose to do certainly does not depend on our judgment regarding the effectiveness of His sign. Our judgment has no bearing whatsoever on what actually happened in history.

To sum it all up, we must simply accept the fact that God designated the rainbow as a sign of His covenant with Noah. Beyond this we acknowledge only that Scripture reveals nothing about the nature and origin of this sign.

We have now reached the end of our exposition of this passage. There are, however, a few general matters relating to the Deluge that should be brought into consideration and discussion.

The first of these is the whole question of the duration of the Flood. Although we have given some consideration to this in our commentary above, it might be well to review this material more systematically.

The total duration of the Flood would appear to be easily determined. According to 7:11, the Flood began on the 17th day of the 2nd month of Noah's 600th year. According to 8:14, Noah and his family left the ark on the 27th day of the 2nd month of the following year. Thus we have one year and ten days. But we are not able to give a conclusive answer regarding the total number of days included in this period. We do not know whether the inspired writer used the solar year of 365 days or the lunar year of 354 days. Presumably, we could come up with an answer by adding up the number of days in all of the subordinate periods mentioned in the narrative, but there is some uncertainty in this regard also. For instance, we do not know how many days must be ascribed to a month. Thus we cannot determine the precise time span between the 17th day of the 7th month, when the ark ran aground (8:4), and the 1st day of the 10th month, when the tops of the mountains came into view.

It has been suggested that the number of days included in a month by the biblical author can be determined by comparing 7:24 and 8:3 with 7:11 and 8:4. There we have a reference to 150 days coinciding with 5 months. Thus we come up with a month of 30 days. But this is by no means conclusive. We pointed out in our treatment of 8:4 that there are three possible interpretations of this reference, none of which can be established with dogmatic certainty.

Another element of uncertainty is the time span to be allowed between 8:5 and 8:13 which was designated as exactly three months. But we cannot determine the number of days in a month with certainty.

In view of these uncertainties, it is not possible to determine with mathematical precision how many days the Deluge lasted. In the final analysis, this is not a serious matter. Insofar as is possible we certainly should put forth a sincere effort to fix such details. But when there is not sufficient data to reach absolute certainty, no serious harm results to the text or to our faith.

A second major question deals with the extent of the area covered by the Deluge. The text repeatedly emphasizes the fact that the catastrophe annihilated all human and animal life on earth. Thus, in 6:17 God announced that He would destroy ''all life under the heavens, every creature that has the breath of life in it. Everything on earth will perish.'' In 7:4 we read, "I will wipe from the face of the earth every living creature I have made." When the divine decision became a reality, we read in 7:19, 21–23, "The waters rose greatly on the earth, and all the high mountains under the entire heavens were covered. . . . Every living thing that moved on the earth perished—birds, livestock, wild animals, all the creatures that swarm over the earth, and all mankind. Everything on dry land that had the breath of life in its nostrils died. Every living thing on the face of the earth was wiped out; men and animals and the creatures that move along the ground and the birds of the air were wiped from the earth." It has generally been understood that these passages indicate that the Deluge covered the entire surface of the earth.

But there have also been other voices that have insisted that only that part of the earth which was populated at that time was involved. The question is whether this view is exegetically acceptable.

It cannot be denied that the annihilation of all people and animals did not necessarily require the inundation of the entire surface of the earth. From the nature of the facts, that part of the earth that was populated at that time could not have been very extensive. Moreover, we do not know with any degree of certainty how widely the animals had scattered over the face of the earth. It is possible that only a small part of the total surface of the earth was occupied by "living creatures" at that early point in history. Even the reference to the mountains being covered with water does not compel us to accept the position that the entire earth was inundated. This might well be a mode of expression, not uncommon in Scripture, which indicated that the then-known world and the then-populated part of the earth were thus covered.

We find similar expressions in other places in the Old Testament. In Joshua 4:24 we are told that God made the riverbed of the Jordan dry "so that all the peoples of the earth might know that the hand of the Lord is powerful." So also in 1 Kings 4:34, "Men of all nations came to listen to Solomon's wisdom." Jeremiah called Nebuchadnezzar the ruler of "all the kingoms . . . in the empire" (Jer. 34:1). Daniel spoke of the Persian Empire as ruling "over the whole earth" (Dan. 2:39). First Samuel 17:46 offers a clear example of this usage. There David declared regarding his conquest of Goliath, "and the whole world will know that there is a God in Israel." To offer just one example from the New Testament, Paul says of the messengers of the gospel (Rom. 10:18) that "their voice has gone out into all the earth, their words to the ends of the world." These examples, to which many others could be added, clearly indicate that it would be in keeping with the usage of Scripture to limit the extent of the Deluge to the then-known world. There certainly is no demand for us to prove that the waters of the Flood rose 15 feet above Mt. Everest or Mt. McKinley.

At the same time it should be pointed out that there is no exegetical basis either for the position that the Flood covered only the then-known world. The biblical text simply does not establish either position with any degree of certainty. On the basis of the biblical text it is conclusive, however, that the Deluge was extensive enough to annihilate all human and animal life existing at that time, with the natural exception of water creatures (7:22).

The third question that must be faced deals with the date of the Deluge. In this connection we can ask, first of all, how long after the creation of man the Flood occurred. This question could conceivably be answered by counting up the life span of each of Noah's ancestors, going back to Adam, as given in Genesis 5. Since we know that the Flood came in Noah's 600th year (7:6), we should be able to come up with an accurate date. But, as we have observed in our treatment of Genesis 5, the numbers given there leave some room for question as to their accuracy. This is especially true when they are compared with those given in the Samaritan Pentateuch and the Septuagint. Moreover, we also observed that the genealogy of Genesis 5 probably is not complete (see our conclusion of ch. 5).

A second aspect of this question deals with the length of the period between the Deluge and the advent of our present calendar. Formerly this was accepted as being approximately 2350 years. This figure was arrived at by adding up various chronological data given in Scripture. On the basis of the genealogy given in Genesis 11:10–26, it was decided that Abraham was born 292 years after the Flood. Abraham supposedly was born about 2050 years before Christ and thus the date of the Flood was set at 2350 B.C.

Further research has revealed, however, that this figure cannot be accurate. Although dating Abraham at approximately 2000 B.C. is not too far from correct, allotting only 292 years from the Flood to Abraham is now considered to be obviously incorrect. The narrative of Abraham indicates that when he was called from Ur of the Chaldees there was already a highly developed civilization there. When he moved to the land of Canaan, he found a well-developed civilization there also. And then, when he went to Egypt, there was an advanced culture there as well. All of this cultural development could not possibly have emerged in the space of 300 years. But, as we will see in our consideration of the genealogy in Genesis 11, there are good reasons for believing that this genealogy is not complete, just as in the case of other scriptural genealogies. In short, simply adding up numbers given in genealogies is not a reliable method for determining historical time spans.

Unquestionably the Deluge must be dated earlier, probably much earlier, than was formerly accepted. How much earlier is difficult to determine with any degree of certainty. The recorded history of Babylon and Egypt goes back to well before 3000 B.C. It is interesting to note that excavations done in the area of ancient Ur have revealed traces of a violent flood, which many geologists considered to be the Deluge described in Genesis. This could not have been the same "flood," however, because the same excavations indicate that life went on as usual in spite of the Flood. The water rose up against the walls of the city, but it did not enter the city. Thus, this could not have been the Deluge described in Genesis, which annihilated all human beings. This was, of course, no problem for the scholars who did the excavating because they did not accept the historicity of the Genesis account anyway. But for those who accept the trustworthiness of the Bible, the flood at Ur could not have been the Genesis Deluge.

As a consequence of these studies, the Flood described in Genesis must be placed at an earlier date than the flood in ancient Ur. The latter has been rather accurately dated at 3700 B.C. This then leads us to the conclusion that the Deluge must be dated before 4000 B.C. This is, however, as far as we can go with the limited data available to us at this time. All we can say with any degree of certainty, naturally, depends on such given data.

The fourth and last question we must consider deals with the historicity of the Deluge. That the Bible intends to present the Deluge as a historical event cannot be questioned. Questions regarding the historicity of the Deluge cannot be based on an exegesis of Scripture. Every honest exegete must acknowledge that the narrative is presented as history. The issue, then, is determined by one's view of Scripture. Is the testimony of Scripture trustworthy beyond question, or, do we have the freedom to critically evaluate the biblical record? In this connection it should be observed that other references in Scripture also consistently treat the Deluge as an actual event in history. We can point to passages such as Isaiah 54:9; Matthew 24:37–39; Luke 17:26–27; Hebrews 11:7; 2 Peter 2:5; 3:6; and probably also Job 22:15–18.

Those who question the historicity of the biblical narrative point out that similar narratives appear among other peoples also. Special mention is usually made of the Babylonian narrative of the flood. It is claimed that this bears such a striking resemblance to the biblical account that the latter is no more than a slightly altered repetition of the former. The biblical narrative, then, would be nothing more than ancient Babylonian tradition, for which there may have been some historical basis (note the reference to the flood in Ur that we mentioned above). The form in which the narrative is given in the Bible has, however, according to this view, no historical justification.

It cannot be denied that there is a strong resemblance between the biblical narrative and the Babylonian account. In fact, there is no section of the

Bible that has been compared with Babylonian writings in which this similarity is so striking. Many points of similarity can be listed. Both accounts speak of a violent flood which wiped out all human life. Both include one man who is saved, with his family and other creatures, by means of a large ship. In both accounts he was informed in advance by divine revelation of the coming disaster, and was instructed regarding the means by which they were to be delivered. In both cases the ship that was built had various levels and came to rest on a mountaintop when the waters receded. In both accounts the ship had a window, and before the occupants left the ship, birds were released in order to determine whether the waters had dried up, and these birds included a raven and a dove. In both narratives those delivered offered sacrifices when they left their respective ships.

The question is, do these similarities, striking as they may be, warrant the conclusion that the biblical narrative was copied from the Babylonian account? It should be observed, first of all, that although there are striking similarities, there are also basic differences between the two narratives. One primary difference is that the Babylonian account is thoroughly permeated with polytheism. In several places this worship of many deities comes through in a very crude way. For instance, the gods consult together in the process of deciding to initiate the flood. But one of the gods betrays the others and secretly informs the one who is to be saved from the coming disaster. Furthermore, when the flood actually came, the gods themselves were terrified with fear and, according to the primary Babylonian text, they huddled together like dogs and crawled against the outside wall of the palace of heaven. Especially significant is the record that, when the flood actually came, the gods regretted their decision to bring it upon the earth. Moreover, when the one who was delivered brought a sacrifice at the conclusion of the disaster, the gods, who had for so long been deprived of sacrifices, descended upon the offering like so many savage wolves.

Another significant difference between the two accounts lies in the cause that is ascribed to the flood. The biblical narrative stresses the fact that the Flood was sent as punishment for man's sin. In the Babylonian account it comes as an arbitrary decision on the part of the gods. The primary Babylonian text, in fact, implies that the god who was the primary initiator of the flood, later had deep regrets for his lack of consideration. He felt that if there were people who had sinned these should be punished, but to send a disaster which would wipe out all the people was unreasonable. Nowhere in the Babylonian text is there the slightest hint that the flood was sent as a punishment for general moral unrighteousness, and this is the cornerstone of the biblical account.

In this connection, it should also be pointed out that in the Babylonian accounts, at least the more recent texts which have been discovered, there is no indication that the one who is saved was righteous and blameless among his evil contemporaries. The biblical narrative, moreover, stresses the fact that God decided from the outset that Noah would be saved, while the Babylonian texts present the saving of one man as wholly unplanned and as the rather facetious afterthought of one of the gods.

Besides these basic differences, we can also observe many minor distinctions between the two accounts. Noah's ark had three levels while the Babylonian ship had six floors. The Babylonian ark was a cube with a dimension of 120 cubits (180 ft.—60 m.). It provided refuge for more people since it not only included the immdeiate family of the one who was saved but also his other relatives and possibly even those who had worked in the construction of the ship. The duration of the flood was much briefer in the Babylonian account, with most accounts limiting the flood to six or seven 24-hour days. In the biblical account the raven is first sent forth from the ark. In the Babylonian narrative it was first a dove, then a swallow, and then a raven. In the Babylonian account, the one who was delivered, and his wife, became immortal and thus were elevated to the position of gods. Finally, the Bible indicates that God designated the rainbow as a sign of His promise that He would never again destroy the world by a flood, and the Babylonian account offers no trace of such a promise.

Another matter of some significance is that there are weighty etymological differences between the two narratives. It is striking that there is no similarity between the names given to the individual who is saved from the flood. The same is true of the names given to the mountains on which the ships came to rest. In fact, the word used to describe the biblical Deluge itself has a radically different connotation than the word used to describe the Babylonian event. Efforts made to establish some etymological connection between the Hebrew word and certain Babylonian and Assyrian words have met with complete failure. Moreover, it is significant that the word used for the ark in Scripture is not of Babylonian origin at all. It is more likely that it is of Egyptian origin. Certainly, if the biblical account of the Flood was simply an altered copy of the Babylonian record, as is claimed by the critics, it could be expected that there would be strong Babylonian ties in these key concepts of the story. The fact that there is no evidence of such ties strongly suggests that the whole assumption of the Babylonian origin of the biblical narrative is without foundation.

It should be observed, moreover, that Babylon is not the only country that has a tradition about a great flood. Such a record was also preserved in

Egypt. There the god Aton decided to destroy all living things by a flood. In the Greek flood narrative it was Deucalion and Pyrrha who were the only ones who survived, and that by means of a large ship. Similar traditions are found among the Persians, the Indians, the Chinese, the Japanese, and the American Indians. Flood traditions are found among peoples as far apart as the Australians and the Islands of the Atlantic Ocean. In fact, no tradition is so universal and so ancient as that of a violent, all-destructive flood which took place some time in the distant past.

Various scholars have attempted to gather these flood narratives, and some have assembled extensive collections of such accounts. Even though these collections are by no means complete and exhaustive, more than 300 such narratives have been discovered. Among all of these there are certain general similarities to the biblical account. In many of them the rescue of an elected remnant is effected by means of a ship of some kind. In several instances, however, escape was made by climbing high mountains. Among several there is some reference to the rainbow, although, as we mentioned above, this was not included in the Babylonian account. In many cases the flood was ascribed to the wickedness of people on earth. In several cases there are references to birds being used to determine the condition of the earth. Besides the birds that are identified in the biblical and Babylonian accounts, we find references to a vulture, a crow, and a hummingbird. The duration of the flood is described with many variations, all the way from a few days to an extended period of 52 years. It is worthy of our attention that a few of the narratives go counter to the biblical account by suggesting that the flood will definitely be repeated.

How are we to understand this almost universal appearance of flood traditions and the strong similarities to the biblical account in these traditions? It should be obvious that this cannot be explained by making the Babylonian account the original narrative, as many scholars are ready to do. In spite of all the explanations that have been advanced to account for this phenomenon, the most natural and obvious explanation is that we are dealing with the lingering traditions, among many peoples, of an event which actually took place in ancient times. The number of these presentations regarding a great flood which have been discovered among such a wide range of peoples unquestionably points to an actual event. Rather than being an objection to the historicity of the flood narrative in Scripture, these many and varied accounts actually confirm its historicity.

We probably should add one word here about the assertion, made by some scholars, that the flood narrative is of Egyptian origin. Arguments that have been advanced in favor of this position are the use of the name "ark," the idea of rooms or partitions of papyrus fibers (6:14), and the "roof" of 6:16 as a "light opening," all of Egyptian origin. So also, the location of the door has been suggested as a consideration, as we have observed above. The primary connection with Egypt, however, has been made by those who see the time spans given for the flood in the biblical narrative as being nothing more than the usual time factors involved in the annual overflowing of the Nile River.

This argument goes something like this. The flood lasted a year and ten days. The rise and fall of the Nile also requires a year. The waters of the flood receded after 150 days. That is precisely the length of time required for the Nile to reach its crest and begin to recede. The receding of the waters of the flood went through various stages and so also does the receding of the overflow of the Nile. The water first returns to the normal riverbed, making the land visible again. Then follows the period during which the mud and slime dry up to again form tillable soil.

Our reply to these theories is that there is an inevitable similarity between certain aspects of the Deluge and the annual overflow of the Nile, just as there would be to any instance of annual flooding anywhere in the world. Thus, that the receding of the waters went through various stages is of course true of every instance of flooding. Concerning the specific time spans that have been indicated, these scholars seem to have lost sight of the fact that for a considerable part of each year the Nile flows normally between its banks and the countryside is completely dry. Comparing the 150 days of the Flood to the five months during which the Nile rises to reach its crest, also is open to question since the Deluge came about in 40 days of rising water. It is also significant that the Deluge lasted 10 days more than a year and this makes the comparison with the annual cycle of the Nile, or any other river, questionable at best. No matter how the year is figured, the solar year, the lunar year, or what have you, the fact remains that the biblical account presents the duration of the Deluge as ten days more than a year and an annual happening can in no way be reconciled to that.

Finally, it has been pointed out that just as the Deluge brought the level of the water 15 cubits (about 300 inches) above the highest mountain, so also the Nile rises 15 cubits, plus a fraction, each year. The excavation of ancient gauges, used to measure the level of the Nile, has established the fact that the Nile never rose as high as 16 cubits. Even today the normal, annual rise of the Nile is 15⅔ cubits. It should be obvious that the parallel sought here is completely irrelevant. It certainly is a radically different matter for water to rise 15 cubits above the highest mountain than to rise approximately 15 cubits above its normal level.

Our conclusion, therefore, must be that the attempts to base the biblical narrative of the Deluge on the Egyptian accounts of the annual overflow of the Nile have been complete failures.

An entirely different objection to the historicity of the Deluge comes from the direction of natural science, especially from the field of geology. According to many geologists, research devoted to the crust of the earth finds no evidence for an event such as the Deluge. We can safely say, however, that this conclusion, at best, is premature. The issue is how we are to explain the changes that evidently have taken place in the course of history in the crust of the earth. Countless layers have been discovered. In some of these layers remains of ancient animals and plants (fossils) have been found. Can all of these phenomena be explained only by an endless, slow process of change and evolvement, or can they also be explained, at least in part, by sudden catastrophes of exceptional power?

In former years the catastrophe theory was rather generally accepted. At that time the Deluge was given a significant place in the development of the earth's crust as we now know it. In more recent years the effects of a catastrophe of great magnitude on the earth's crust have been largely ignored. Scientists do recognize, however, that the increasing discovery of vast deposits of fossils may well offer evidence for a major catastrophe in the development of the earth. The formation of fossils actually does require a sudden change of conditions by which animal and plant life were suddenly cut off from the atmosphere by a layer of some kind. Such a change of conditions could conceivably be explained by natural evolvement, but a great catastrophe would offer a far more logical explanation.

It should also be noted that in the process of excavating the layers of the earth's crust, sea creatures, which normally live at great depths, are found in the same layer with creatures who lived in the shallow waters near the coast. Such phenomena can be explained only by some massive upheaval which disturbed the whole order and arrangement of the earth's surface. In the layers of coal, which were formed by land plants, fossils of fish have been discovered. It is not unusual, moreover, to find fossils heaped together in great numbers. An example of this would be the discovery in Alabama of the vertebrae of an extinct species of whales in such quantity that the bones were used to build fences or burned to dispose of them. Likewise, in Siberia the remains of mammoths were found in such abundance that a thriving business in marketing ivory from mammoth tusks was carried on for generations. These facts argue strongly for the concept of catastrophe playing an important role in the history of the earth.

In various places fossils have been found which clearly indicate that the animals from which they came were wiped out suddenly and with great violence. Examples of this were discovered, among others, in Scotland, where whole schools of fish were uncovered. Moreover, the mysterious, sudden disappearance of specific groups of plants and animals from the earth can be explained by catastrophic changes in the earth's surface. This is true of the giant lizards and other monsters which at one time roamed about on our planet.

If we, then, accept the theory of great catastrophic changes in the constitution of the earth's crust, the historical reality of the Deluge also becomes altogether credible. It is worthy of note, therefore, that there are an increasing number of geologists who accept the historicity of the Deluge or some similar catastrophe. Of special interest is a theory, advanced by some scientists, that a large mass of ice, which drifted about in space, encountered the earth's atmosphere and poured out an enormous volume of water upon the earth in a short space of time. Naturally, it is not our purpose here to defend this theory or any other theory. We mention it here only to indicate that the historicity of the Deluge is not outside the realm of possibility, even in the minds of scientists who are not Bible-believing Christians. Such theories and scientific discoveries should never become the basis for our faith in the historicity of Scripture narratives. This should rest on the testimony of Scripture only. The facts as such, however, do not call the historicity of the Deluge into serious question. If they did, obviously no reputable scientist or geologist would accept the reality of the Deluge.

6. *After the Flood* (9:18–29)

Aside from a few comments about the development of the new humanity after the Deluge, and a reference to the life span of Noah, this section deals with only one episode in the life of Noah and his family after they left the ark. Those who split sources usually ascribe the section to "J," except for the closing verses (28–29), which are assigned to "P."

The material dealing with Noah's drunkenness and the curse of Canaan (vv. 20–27), is considered by many to have come from another source and then to have been inserted into "J" by the redactor of Genesis. Noah, the farmer and the keeper of a vineyard, would appear to be, to these scholars, an entirely different person from the righteous and blameless man to whom we are introduced before the Deluge. His sons, moreover, here appear as young boys, it is claimed, rather than married men with their own families. The action of Ham would seem to be more of a prank on the part of a naughty little boy, rather than the conduct of a mature man. One indication that this is an interpolation, it is claimed, is that Canaan is cursed for an evil deed which was actually performed by Ham. It is suggested, then, that in this source the three sons of Noah are Shem, Japheth, and Canaan, and that the name of Ham is inserted here by the redactor in a rather clumsy effort to make it conform with what precedes.

Opposing this theory, it must be observed that there is no reason to make this Noah a different figure from the hero of the Deluge. The fact that he became drunk certainly is no evidence that this was not the righteous man who lived before the Flood. This is not the only place in Scripture where God's heroes of faith fell into nasty sins in some part of their lives.

The claim that Noah is presented here as the first "tiller of the soil," overlooking the reference to Adam and Cain in Genesis 3 and 4, cannot be established by the text. The text simply says that Noah was a man of the soil and that he began to plant a vineyard. The only aspect which appears to be new was the development of the cultivation of a vineyard. This, however, in no way conflicts with the earlier Genesis records.

The suggestion that his sons are presented here as young, unmarried lads is also without basis. The text does not say that they lived in the same tent with their father. That they had an easy access to Noah's tent would suggest only that they lived nearby and, considering the circumstances under which they lived, this would have been likely. The small family group that left the ark would have been inclined to stay close together as they resumed their normal course of life.

As far as Ham's disrespect for his father was concerned, such attitudes are by no means limited to naughty little boys. In fact, such behavior is altogether too common among adults as well.

The theory that an intermediate redactor changed the record is certainly less than plausible. Had there been such a redactor, he certainly would have made the changes in such a way that the resulting document would have been free from confusion. This was, after all, the very reason for introducing such a redactor. But since obvious changes, such as making Canaan the perpetrator of the deed as well as the recipient of the punishment, are not made, there is no case left for the presence of such a redactor. In short, when all the evidence is considered, there is no reason to consider this episode to be an interpolation from another source.

Verses 28 and 29 are ascribed by the critics to "P" because there is a formulation there that is similar to a passage in chapter 5, which is also ascribed to "P." After what we have already mentioned in our treatment of chapter 5, we can limit our comment here to one observation. The inspired writer described the life span of Noah in the same terminology that was used in the genealogy recorded in chapter 5. It has been suggested that the record about Noah originally appeared at the close of the earlier genealogy and was transposed to this passage. There is no convincing support for this suggestion, however.

9:18, 19 *The sons of Noah who came out of the ark were Shem, Ham and Japheth. (Ham was the father of Canaan.) These were the three sons of Noah, and from them came the people who were scattered over the earth.*

The three sons of Noah have already been mentioned in 5:32; 6:10; and 7:13. A study of their names was provided in our commentary on 5:32. Here we are given the added information that Ham was the father of Canaan. The reason for this addition is found in what follows in verses 25–27. The latter material would have little meaning unless this information had been provided.

It should be observed that the entire human race after the Deluge originated from these three sons of Noah. The original says that "the whole earth was scattered from them," but it is obvious that what is intended is the *people* of the whole earth.

9:20 *Noah, a man of the soil, proceeded to plant a vineyard.*

Verse 20 has been translated in many different ways. Our translation (NIV) reads, "Noah, a man of the soil, proceeded to plant a vineyard." Literally the verse reads, "Noah began as tiller of the soil and planted a vineyard." We find a similar construction in Ezra 3:8, "Zerubbabel . . . began . . . appointing Levites. . . ." The natural translation of this would appear to be that Zerubbabel began to appoint the Levites. Thus, the NIV translation of our present passage is the most natural. Noah began his activity as a tiller of the soil by planting a vineyard. This was, in fact, a significant cultural development.

9:21 *When he drank some of its wine, he became drunk and lay uncovered inside his tent.*

We are further told that Noah drank of the wine and became drunk. This implies that he had become acquainted with the process of making wine from grapes by pressing out the juice and then letting it ferment and become wine. Thus the purpose of planting the vineyard was obvious. It was not intended to provide grapes for edible fruit but, rather, to produce wine. So Noah was the father of the "wine makers."

There are various opinions as to whether Noah knew, before this incident, that fermented grape juice could cause drunkenness. In our judgment, there is no basis for excusing Noah from responsibility for his actions. At the same time, there is no substance to the charge that Noah was a secret drunkard. In any case, he must have found the wine to be tasty and this led him to drink too much of it. Certainly a moderate partaking of this wine would not have caused him to fall into a drunken stupor. Thus, he cannot be presented as a helpless victim of the fruit of his production. At the same time we can grant that he probably was not fully aware of the devastation that overindulgence of this delicious drink could cause.

In his state of drunkenness, Noah exposed himself and thus his overindulgence led him into a shameful act. The fact that this did not occur in public, since he remained in the shelter of his tent, must be considered as an ameliorating factor. There are those who insist that the reference to a "tent" is not in keeping with Noah's life style as a tiller of the soil. They argue that since his place of abode was now fixed, he would no longer be living in nomadic tents but would have a permanent house of some kind. In reply it can be observed that it is possible and even probable that, during the period immediately following the Deluge, Noah and his family continued to live in tents. It should be noted that later Abraham and Isaac and even Jacob lived in tents, even though they had a fixed abode in a specific location.

This incident certainly implies a strong warning against the excessive use of wine. Wine must certainly be considered to be a gift of God, for God provided wine for His people as well as bread (Ps. 104:14–15). But Noah's example sounds a clear note of warning against the excessive use of wine and the problems this can cause in people's lives.

9:22 *Ham, the father of Canaan, saw his father's nakedness and told his two brothers outside.*

While Noah was lying naked in a drunken stupor, his son Ham walked into his tent. He was amused by what he discovered, and later mockingly shared his amusement with his brothers. Ham, by his very attitude, displayed a tendency toward uncouthness and lack of respect for his father.

There are those who are not satisfied with this interpretation but are convinced that Ham's offense against his father was far more serious. They argue that mere amusement at his father's nakedness certainly was not serious enough to warrant the terrible curse that is later placed on Ham (v. 25). Moreover, they find a reference in verse 24 that gives further light on the nature of Ham's sin against his father. From this verse they have deduced that Ham actually physically abused his father while he was in his drunken stupor. But there is no basis in the text for these radical conclusions. The disdain and disrespect that Ham showed toward his father was serious enough to warrant his condemnation.

9:23 *But Shem and Japheth took a garment and laid it across their shoulders; then they walked in backward and covered their father's nakedness. Their faces were turned the other way so that they would not see their father's nakedness.*

How different was the attitude and conduct of Shem and Japheth. It is evident that Ham thought that his brothers would respond in the same way he had. But he was altogether mistaken in this regard. His brothers took a mantle and covered their father's nakedness, thus displaying utmost consideration and respect for their father.

9:24 *When Noah awoke from his wine and found out what his youngest son had done to him,*

When Noah awoke from his stupor, he learned what his son Ham had done. Just how this knowledge was conveyed to him is not indicated. Some have suggested that he received a divine revelation of some kind. It is also possible that his other sons felt constrained to inform their father of what had taken place.

Ham is here called the *youngest* son. The Septuagint and the Vulgate translate this "younger" son. The original Hebrew simply says, "his small son." The Hebrew language does not have comparative and superlative degrees of comparison, so in cases like this it simply uses the positive degree form of the adjective. Then it can be read as positive, comparative, or superlative, depending on the context. Thus we can read the word used here as "small," "smaller," or "smallest," according to the demands of the context. Since Genesis 10:21 indicates that Shem was the big brother of Japheth, we can avoid a conflict with our present verse by making Japheth the middle son and then making Ham the youngest. This, however, seems to be in conflict with the usual order in which the three sons are listed— Shem, Ham, and Japheth. Although this order is generally considered to indicate the order of their birth, it can also be explained by other factors. It could be, for instance, that the Hamites maintained a closer affinity with the Shemites and for that reason the name of Ham is placed beside that of Shem. It has also been suggested that the usual order may be explained simply on the basis of euphony when the three names are sounded together. In any case, we hold that the designation of Ham as "the youngest son" is the most acceptable.

9:25 *He said, "Cursed be Canaan! The lowest of slaves will he be to his brothers."*

When Noah learned what Ham had done, he pronounced a severe curse on Ham's son Canaan. This should not be seen as the mere venting of a father's anger upon a disrespectful son. The pronouncement is in the form of a prophetic announcement with respect to the future. Pronouncements of blessing and curse have this prophetic quality in other instances as well. To confirm this we can consult Genesis 27:27-29, 39ff.; 48:15-20; 49:2-28. All of these passages offer much more than expressions of good or bad wishes. They offer, rather, revelations about future happenings and conditions. Thus such blessings and curses include a certain effectiveness, just as the words of a prophet of the Lord include the certainty of the event that is prophesied. (See passages such as 1 Kings 17:1; Hos. 6:5; Jer. 28:15ff.) Thus, the pronounced blessing or curse included the actual events by which the bliss or woe of the recipient would be realized in the future. These pronouncements, then, were a form of divine revelation which became effective by divine power. In a sense, the spoken word can be seen as the effective cause of the ensuing events and the later events can be seen as the fulfillment of those words.

Obviously, the immediate question that confronts us here is why the curse was pronounced on Canaan instead of Ham. It is suggested by some scholars that it actually was Canaan who had committed the disreputable deed and that Ham simply took his son's place. That this is unacceptable has been pointed out in our introduction to this section; but we cannot avoid the dilemma that is presented here.

It is possible that Canaan had given indications of having character faults similar to those of his father. A strong argument in favor of this assumption is found in the statement in the curse, "the lowest of slaves will he be to his brothers." The term brothers is generally accepted in a broad sense as "relatives." This then would include, first of all, his uncles, Shem and Japheth. But does it not seem more likely that the term, brothers, must be taken in the literal sense as referring to the other sons of Ham? Could we then not also conclude that Canaan differed in character from his brothers? This approach is supported by verses 26 and 27, in which the blessing pronounced on Shem and Japheth again speaks of Canaan's slavery. There, however, a more moderate word is used. In the case of Ham's uncles, Shem and Japheth, it is predicted that Canaan would be "a slave" to them. With respect to his brothers his position is presented as "the lowest of slaves," in both instances. Thus, there is a difference in the description of Canaan's relationship to his brothers and his position with respect to his uncles.

There is an interesting Jewish tradition that translates "his small son" as "his grandson." This would imply that Canaan indeed was involved in the despicable act which called forth the curse.

Although the curse of Canaan can be explained by the fact that he demonstrated the same weaknesses of character as his father, Ham himself is also affected by this curse upon his son. Just as Noah is grieved by his son Ham, so Ham, in turn, is punished in his son.

Now we come to the actual meaning of the curse. The focal point of the curse lies in that Ham would become the "lowest of slaves" or a "servant of servants." This is one way in which the Hebrew language expresses the superlative degree. Clear examples of this usage are found in statements such as "God of gods"; "Holy of holies"; and "Song of songs." In each case the terms express the highest possible level, the superlative degree. Thus a slave of slaves would be someone who was subjected to the most humiliating type of slavery. The intent would be to indicate that Canaan would be oppressed by and subjected to his brothers. This is even suggested by Canaan's name, which, according to some scholars, means "subjected" or "humiliated." It should not be forgotten, however, that we are still in the period before the confusion of languages and, as such, the Hebrew language did not yet exist. Thus it is generally conceded that there is no etymological significance in the name "Canaan."

Meanwhile, the actual curse that is pronounced can hardly be applied to Canaan as a person. To be sure, one individual could be relegated to a position of total subjection to his brothers, but the sentence can more fittingly be applied to a wider group of people or a tribe or nation. Thus we could apply the curse to Canaan's descendants. That this is the case is confirmed by comparing this curse with the blessings pronounced on Shem and Japheth (vv. 26–27). There we note a reference to dwelling "in the tents (plural) of Shem." This would be descriptive of the tribal group that descended from Shem. Thus, also in the case of the curse of Canaan, we should think of the tribe that descended from him.

How are we then to think of the fulfillment of this curse? Let it be emphatically stated that this does not refer to the slavery of the black person. There was a time when the practice of slavery was readily defended by an appeal to the curse of Ham, but there is not one shred of biblical evidence to support this theory.

Many modern exegetes have attempted to find historical situations with which the curse and blessing here recorded can be fitted. They work back from some historical situation and then seek to explain that situation by declaring that it took place because of a certain blessing or curse that had been previously pronounced. For some interpreters the curse of Ham and the blessing of Shem and Japheth did not apply to real people who lived in history, but must be seen as personifications of nations or national groups. It is obvious that such interpretations do not consider the curse or the blessing to be in the nature of a prophecy that would be specifically fulfilled. Those who do look upon these pronouncements as being prophetic in character cannot accept these rather symbolic interpretations. We need not, therefore, dwell on the many different efforts that have been made to point out specific historical situations which can be explained by this curse or that blessing. We might add that the mere fact that this kind of interpretation leads to such numerous and very different conclusions does not recommend the method as a legitimate use of Scripture.

But even if we accept the curse of Canaan as a genuine prophecy, we still must face the question of how this prophecy was fulfilled. To be sure, we need not limit this to one historical event. The prophecy regarding the subject position of the Canaanites among closely related peoples, which is how we would interpret "brothers," could be fulfilled in the course of time in various events and different situations.

We want to point out then, that in Genesis 10:6 Canaan's brothers are designated as Cush, Mizraim, and Put. Mizraim is the Hebrew name for Egypt, but it is more difficult to identify the descendants of Cush. Usually the Old Testament refers to Ethiopia by this name, but it is obvious that the name Cush must be applied to a broader group of peoples. In 10:7 (see our discussion of that verse) a number of Arabian tribes are included among the descendants of Cush, and in 10:8–10 various kingdoms from the area of Babylonia are also included. We are not absolutely sure about the location of Put. Many are of the opinion that we must understand this as the kingdom of Punt, which is referred to in ancient Egyptian records. This can probably be located in the costal area of Abyssinia, on the Red Sea, opposite the southwestern tip of Arabia.

When we put all this data together, our interpretation of "the lowest of slaves" as a designation of a position of subjection under the control of other larger and more powerful nations becomes plausible. The Canaanitish tribes always were in a place of subjection and inferiority to the great powers such as Egypt and the Mesopotamian Empires. We know, in fact, that before Israel occupied the land of Canaan, the area was in complete subjection to Egypt. This, to our minds, would suffice as a fulfillment of Noah's curse on the descendants of Canaan.

9:26 *He also said, "Blessed be the Lord, the God of Shem! May Canaan be the slave of Shem.*

Noah, however, did not stop with a curse on Canaan, in which the guilt of Ham was to be punished. He also pronounced blessings on Shem and Japheth; their concern and respect for their father was to be rewarded.

Genesis 9:26

The wording of the blessing on Shem is a bit strange. The blessing was not bestowed on Shem himself but on the God of Shem. Some interpreters have tried to alter the text so that it would read, "the Lord bless the tents of Shem." But there is no justification for such tampering with the text. The statement, "Blessed be the LORD, the God of Shem," implies that Shem would indeed be blessed, but this blessing would come only from the Lord. Noah, as an old man, looking into the future with prophetic vision, saw the rich blessings that would be experienced by Shem and his descendants. He was so overwhelmed by what he saw that he burst forth in a doxology of praise to the Lord, the God of Shem. This expression of praise actually announced, then, the blessings that would be Shem's portion.

A question has been raised about the use of the name "Lord" at this point. This question is the more pertinent since in verse 27, in the blessing of Japheth, only the name "God" is used. When we compare the two pronouncements of blessing, however, the answer to the question seems apparent. The intent obviously was to indicate that Shem would stand in a relationship to God which would be somewhat beyond that of his brother Japheth. This special relationship is expressed by the use of the name "Lord."

Admittedly, we must be on guard against reading something into this use of the name "Lord" that actually belongs to a later period of revelation. Thus, we cannot pour into the name "Lord" when it is used here, immediately after the Deluge, a meaning that is not revealed until the time of Moses. We must also again remind ourselves that we are still dealing with the period before the confusion of languages and, as such, the Hebrew language did not yet exist. At the same time, it must be granted that the Hebrew name "Lord," which later was designated as God's personal name "Jahweh," placed in the mouth of Noah, must have a special significance. We can safely say that this indicates that Shem's special relationship to God is indicated by the use of this name. God would be Shem's personal Lord. When we recognize this, we catch a glimpse of the essence of the blessing that was pronounced on Shem. To stand in a special, personal relationship to God is certainly the highest and greatest blessing anyone can experience.

At this point we should repeat what was said earlier regarding the curse of Canaan. These words of blessing do not apply exclusively to the person named but also to his descendants. The special relationship with God, which was promised to Shem, would also be the portion of Shem's descendants. In this connection, it has been objected that not all of Shem's descendants worshiped Jahweh, the only true God. Although we must grant this, it does not, as such, militate against the fulfillment of this blessing in Shem's descendants. Certainly the prediction is not that every individual descendant of Shem, without exception, would be included in this blessing. In the case of Canaan, certainly not all of his descendants, without exception, would be included in his curse. In this connection, we must keep in mind the conditional nature of prophecy (see Jer. 18:7–10). The very nature of prophecy precludes such rigid generalizations. If a descendant of Shem departed from God, he would most certainly not share in the blessings of Shem. Likewise, if a descendant of Canaan was converted to the service of Jahweh, he would share in the blessings of Shem. Examples such as Rahab (Josh. 6:22–25; Heb. 11:31) certainly make this unmistakably clear.

We should, moreover, compare the blessing pronounced on Shem with the divine promise to Abraham and his seed. There certainly were groups of Abraham's descendants who were excluded from the fulfillment of the Covenant promises. We need only mention Ishmael and his family. Mention also could be made of the tribes that stemmed from Abraham's later marriage to Keturah (Gen. 25:1–4), and, of course, Esau and his descendants. In the same way, we must accept the reality that not every group of Shemites from that day forward would stand in that special relationship to God which was included in the blessing of Shem. The blessing was bestowed first of all on Shem and his family. The holy line that ran from Seth to Enoch to Noah, before the Deluge, would now be continued in Shem. Just how this line would run in later generations is not revealed at this time. This would, however, be revealed in the unfolding of God's program of grace in the future.

The designation of a "holy seed" must also be related to the promise of the victorious "seed of the woman" in Genesis 3:15. Although the "seed of the woman" is not specifically mentioned here, it is obvious that this victorious "seed" was to be carried forward in the line of Shem. When we bear in mind the fact that a dividing line is drawn between the "seed of the woman" and the "seed of the serpent," it is clear that the "holy seed" that is promised to Shem is predicated on the fulfillment of the maternal promise in Genesis 3:15. Thus we have here the second stage in the unfolding of the Messianic promise. We are informed that the messianic line would be carried forward in the descendants of Shem.

The blessing on Shem also included a repetition of part of the curse of Canaan. Canaan's servitude to his brothers was also announced to Shem. With respect to the development of the relationships between nations and peoples, this meant that those who descended from Canaan would be on a lower level than those who came from Shem. And since the blessing involved spiritual position before God, it implied that in the future the

Canaanitish people would be subject to the Semitic nations. It is only natural that we should think, in this connection, of the subjection of the Canaanites to Israel.

9:27 *May God extend the territory of Japheth; may Japheth live in the tents of Shem, and may Canaan be his slave."*

The blessing pronounced on Japheth consisted of two parts. In the first place, it declared that God would grant "increase" to Japheth. The meaning is obvious. This did not refer to personal gain for Japheth, but rather, an abundant increase in the case of Japheth's descendants. The use of the name "God" here has already been discussed in our treatment of verse 26. God would also bless Japheth's descendants with material blessings, especially in the extension of their territory. But a special relationship to God is not mentioned. The Hebrew, at this point, indulges in an interesting play on words. The Hebrew form that we have translated, "extend the territory," has the same sound as the name "Japheth." What we have here, then, is "*japt*—Japheth."

The second part of the blessing declares that Japheth would "live in the tents of Shem." This has been interpreted in various ways. Some have suggested that the subject of the verb "live" is not Japheth but God. The more natural meaning, however, is that Japheth, the one upon whom the blessing is pronounced, is intended as the subject. The other translation would actually ascribe the blessing to Shem, rather than to Japheth, and that would violate the intent of the passage.

But what is meant by the statement that Japheth would live in the tents of Shem? A few modern scholars have suggested that it implies that Japheth would drive Shem out of his territory and occupy it in his place. They appeal to passages such as 1 Chronicles 5:10 and Psalm 78:55. There living in another's tents actually has that meaning. But such an interpretation would be most unlikely in this context. After the blessing pronounced on Shem in verse 26, it would be most unlikely that this would be followed by what is tantamount to a curse.

Another interpretation limits the statement to a national-political significance. It suggests that the figure means no more than that they would be good neighbors. Friendly relationships would be maintained between the descendants of Japheth and those of Shem. To support this theory an appeal has been made to Psalm 84:10 and Psalm 120:5. These passages, however, refer to someone being a guest in another person's home. They make no reference to good relationships between the parties involved. The entire context is different from the statement here in Genesis 9:27. A unique interpretation holds that the word "Shem" as used here is not the name of a person at all. The word, it is claimed, means "name," and the statement would then read, "he will dwell in tents of name (or renown)." This interpretation would never have occurred to anyone if the passage did not offer some difficulty. But it does not succeed in removing the difficulty.

A proper understanding of the statement can be arrived at if it is kept in close context with the blessing on Shem that immediately precedes it. The renewed reference to Shem here certainly points back to what was said concerning him earlier and it must be seen in that light. To live in anyone's tent involves sharing in that person's lot. In other words, what we have here is an announcement that Japheth would share in the blessing of Shem.

It is certainly significant that this statement about dwelling "in the tents of Shem" follows the declaration that Japheth would "extend." Thus it is evident that this sharing in the blessing of Shem would not occur immediately. It would be realized only after the promise of increase had been fulfilled. Thus, after the spiritual blessing that was promised to Shem would be realized, there would come a time when that same spiritual blessing would be shared by the descendants of Japheth. God would also enter into a special relationship with them. The Japhethites would also be included in the religion of Shem and would share in the promise of the "seed of the woman." When and how this would take place is not revealed at this time. In the light of ensuing history, we would be inclined to think of the conversion of the Gentiles in the New Testament church.

Here also, the blessing is followed by a reference to the curse of Canaan. Canaan would be the servant of Japheth. Thus the Canaanites would be subservient not only to the Shemites but also to the Japhethites. It should be pointed out that the descendants of Japheth include the Medes and the Greeks. Both of these kingdoms played a significant role in the culture of the ancient world (see our interpretation of Gen. 10:2). Thus the fulfillment of this prophecy becomes obvious.

Now that we have come to the end of Noah's curse and blessings of his sons, it should be noted that Ham is not even mentioned in these declarations. Ham is not cursed, and consequently is not included in the judgments that came upon his descendants. But he is not blessed either. Thus, he is not included in the blessings that are pronounced on Shem and Japheth. Verse 25 speaks about the distinction between the Canaanites and the rest of the Hamites. From this we can conclude that the rest of the Hamites are neither blessed nor cursed. We should repeat here what we said in our consideration of verse 26. The conditional nature of prophecy would always leave the door open for the Hamites to be converted and then to share in Shem's blessing. Although it is said only of Japheth that he would live in Shem's tents, this certainly does not imply that all of Ham's descendants would forever be barred from this privilege. There is room at the cross of Jesus also for the Hamites. The gospel should never be withheld from them, nor from any other people, because we may think that God has closed the door to them. We need only take note of the promises made to the Hamitic Egyptians in passages such as Isaiah 19:18–25 and Zechariah 14:18.

9:28, 29 *After the flood Noah lived 350 years. Altogether, Noah lived 950 years, and then he died.*

Finally we read that Noah lived after the Flood (here reckoned from the beginning of the Flood) 350 years. Thus his entire life span was 950 years. When we compare this with the numbers given in Genesis 11:10–26, it becomes evident that Noah would have lived to be a contemporary of Abraham. The latter was born 292 years after the Flood.

It cannot be proved with definite data from Scripture that Noah was no longer alive when Abraham was on the scene. Even so, the entire history of the patriarch in Genesis 12ff. gives the strong impression that considerable time had elapsed since Noah's days. This further confirms the position we set forth in our interpretation of Genesis 5 and 6, that a considerable period of time separated Abraham from the Deluge. This period undoubtedly was far longer than a simple addition of the numbers given in the genealogies would suggest.

7. *The New Humanity* (10:1–32)

This chapter describes the development of a new human race following the annihilation of the former humanity by the Deluge. The sons of Noah (Shem, Ham, and Japheth), who survived the Flood, now become the progenitors of a new humanity. This fact was briefly pointed out in 9:18–19. Now, in chapter 10, it is set forth in considerable detail.

Even a casual reading of the chapter leads to the obvious conclusion that we are dealing with a table of tribes and nations rather than a genealogy of individual persons. This becomes immediately evident when we come upon names of well-known nations. To mention only a few, we find a reference to Egypt in verse 6, the Medes (Madai) in verse 2, and Elam, Assur, and Syria in verse 22. In verse 15, moreover, we have a reference to the well-known city of Sidon. It is also of interest that there is a frequent use of plurals, such as the Kittim, and the Rodanim in verse 4, the Ludites, the Anamites, and the Lehabites in verses 13 and 14. Such plurals certainly have no place in the genealogy of individual persons.

There are, furthermore, names that are so formulated that they cannot possibly refer to individuals. These are similar to our English terms such as Englishmen or Frenchmen. Then, there are direct references to places of abode, in verses 19 and 30. In verse 21 we are told that Shem was the father of "all the sons of Eber [Hebrews]." Finally, in several instances we are specifically told that the reference is to a nation or tribe rather than an individual (see vv. 5, 18, 20, 31, 32). Thus it is abundantly clear that we are dealing here with a table of nations rather than a personal genealogy.

It is also evident that this chapter does not pretend to present a complete catalog of all possible nations and tribes that appeared on the earth from the Deluge to the present time, plus those that will still appear before the Lord's return. All efforts to fit all known nations and tribes into this "tree of nations" are therefore doomed to failure. This simply was not the purpose of this record.

We cannot even justify the assertion that the Table of Nations gives a complete overview of the various nations that made up the ancient Eastern world. All we can say with certainty is that we are given a list of many of the nations and tribes that were represented in the ancient East and neighboring areas, and that these are related to the three sons of Noah. The specific tribes and peoples that are included can be explained by the point in time at which the list was compiled. The choice was no doubt determined by the available knowledge of the facts at that time, and the historical perspective from which these facts were viewed.

This interpretation of the Table of Nations in Genesis 10 in no way curtails the revelatory significance of the chapter. It certainly was not the intent of this revelation to dispense geographical and ethnological data which was beyond the horizon of the instrument of revelation itself, and of those to whom this revelation was first directed. It would be foolish to assert that God, by means of Genesis 10, intended to inform His Old Testament people about nations and peoples which were wholly unknown to them, or which could not be known because they were not yet in existence. The intent, rather, was to present the original readers of this revelation with a clear understanding that the nations and peoples of the earth, as they knew them, had stemmed from the three sons of Noah.

For later generations this limited analysis would convey the concept that, in this same way, the entire population of the earth as they knew it in their time, also stemmed from the sons of Noah.

Precisely how each given national or tribal group is related to each specific son of Noah is not indicated. This determination is the task of the science of ethnology. Many have denied that all races and tribes which are known to exist, or to have existed in the past, can be traced back to Noah.

This, in turn, has led some who still hold to the historicity of the Deluge to insist that the Flood was not universal. They reason that there must have been people in other parts of the world who survived the Deluge, and this would then explain the enormous variety of races and tribes that are known to have existed. But this position is in conflict with the Genesis record which declares that all people on the earth were wiped out by the Flood, with the single exception of Noah and his family. The Scripture thus locks us into a view that, no matter how numerous and divergent the peoples of the earth may be, all of them must ultimately have stemmed from Noah's family. The sciences of anthropology and ethnology have generally acknowledged the unity of the whole of humanity. The essential physical similarity and the unrestricted capability of cross-generation of all races, point incontestably to this unity of the human race. (See also our *De Goddelijke Openbaring in de Eerste Drie Hoofdstukken van Genesis,* p. 319.)

Those who hold to the source-splitting theory claim to be able to distinguish both "J" and "P" in the Table of Nations in chapter 10. "J" is supposedly represented in 1b, 8–19, 21, and 25–30. "P" is then to be found in 1a, 2–7, 20, 22–23, 31–32. Verse 24 is ascribed to the redactor who combined these sources into the present list.

The following factors are adduced as bases for splitting the sources in this way. (1) There is an apparent conflict between verse 7, in which Sheba and Havilah are presented as sons of Cush and thus of Ham, and verses 28 and 29, in which the same names are listed as sons of Joktan and thus of Shem. (2) The family tree of Shem begins at two different places—in verse 21 and in verse 22. (3) The same is true of the entire Table of Nations, with beginnings in 10:1 and also in 9:18 and 19. (4) Genesis 10 consists in part of mere names, while it also contains broader historical details as in verses 8–11.

A careful examination of these alleged bases for multiple sources indicates that the last three give no substantial evidence for more than one source. To begin with (4), it should be noted that Genesis 5 also consists of a list of names, while at the same time it includes broader historical data, as in verses 22–24. Yet this chapter is ascribed to one source, "P," and none of the source splitters have questioned this. Obviously, making this factor a basis for multiple sources is not a consistent principle with these scholars. Consequently it carries no weight here either. With respect to the alleged double beginnings for the family tree of Shem and for the entire Table of Nations, we would observe the following. In order to defend this charge, 9:18–19 must be torn from its actual context. Moreover, 10:21–22 can readily be fit logically into its context. There is no evidence here of a definite hiatus which implies a double beginning for the same record. It is true that the term "the sons of Shem" is used in a broader sense in verse 21 than in verse 22. But, as we will point out later, this can be explained without resorting to a radical two-source theory.

We now come to the first, and also the most cogent, of the arguments for two distinct sources, the alleged conflict between verse 7 and verses 28, 29. In this connection, the first question we should ask is whether ascribing these verses to two different sources actually resolves the alleged conflict. The redactor who combined these two supposedly distinct sources into one record must also have been responsible for selecting the materials he included. Unless he made his selection arbitrarily and haphazardly, he certainly would have been aware of this seeming conflict in the case of the names of Sheba and Havilah. And if he was aware of this, he most certainly would have covered this over in some way in preparing this significant record. The critics themselves insist that verse 24 is the work of the redactor because there, they claim, he tries to reconcile verse 21 with 11:1-14. Applying this same theory then, to the issue of verse 7 and verses 28-29, there remains no basis for the two-source theory. Ascribing this material to two sources certainly does not resolve the alleged conflict.

How can we then interpret what appear to be conflicts in the record? Some have suggested that the naming of some of the tribes under different national groups resulted from an intermingling of some of these groups in such a way that the same tribe actually was present in more than one place. Even more plausible is the interpretation that the use of the same name for different tribes need not indicate that the same tribe is actually intended. The same name could be used to refer to two tribes, in different areas, that happened to carry the same name. This could certainly have been the case with "Havilah," which probably was not even the name of a person in the original Hebrew. It is likely that it was the Hebrew word which means "sand." It could then refer to any people who lived in a sandy area, and there certainly were several such areas in that part of the world. It should be noted that the word is used without the definite article in verses 7 and 28, while it has the definite article in 2:11. This strongly suggests that in our present passage it does not refer to a definite tribe or territory, while in 2:11 it refers to a specific territory called "Havilah, where there is gold." In this connection we would also refer our readers to *De Goddelijke Openbaring,* page 444.

The name Sheba is more likely to be a reference to a particular person or people. But, even so, it is altogether possible that the name could be applied to different people in different areas. There are other examples of such usage in the Old Testament, and we will mention just a few of them.

Goshen was a section of Egypt, but in Joshua 15:51 it refers to a city in the land of Judah. (See also 10:41.) Cush, which appears in this chapter, generally referred to Ethiopia, but in 2 Chronicles 14:9ff. it obviously refers to another area. It is also possible that in our present passage it refers to some other people besides Ethiopia. (See above.)

Once again, it should be abundantly obvious that basing a two-source theory for interpreting this passage on this evidence is nothing short of facetious.

10:1a *This is the account of Shem, Ham and Japheth, Noah's sons,*

The first half of verse 1 gives us a heading for the chapter that presents the general content of what follows. The word "generations," as it is used in the Old Testament, refers to that which is generated or born. Sometimes the word also indicates the history of a family or people (Gen. 2:4; 6:9; 25:19; 37:2; Num. 3:1). Here it apparently has the meaning of descendants and it intends to describe the way in which the new humanity descended from Noah's sons.

10:1b *Who themselves had sons after the flood.*

The actual description of the new humanity begins with the declaration that after the Flood Shem, Ham, and Japheth brought forth sons. This sentence begins with a conjunction that indicates that it explicates what went before, much like our English, "that is. . . ." The term "after the flood" indicates that Noah's sons had no children before the Flood. The development of the new humanity commenced with Noah's sons after the Flood.

10:2 *The sons of Japheth: Gomer, Magog, Madai, Javan, Tubal, Meshech and Tiras.*

It is striking that the description of these descendants begins with Japheth, while his name usually appears last in the listing of Noah's sons. As we have already observed, the usual order is probably not chronological because Shem was the oldest and Ham, most likely, was the youngest. (See our conclusion to the section on the Flood.) It is difficult to say why Japheth is mentioned first in the Table of Nations. It has been suggested that the order used here is determined by the relationship which the various national groups had with Israel, the chosen people of God. Israel had the least contact with the descendants of Japheth, and therefore they are mentioned first. Israel had considerably more contact with the Hamites, even though these were often hostile contacts, and therefore they were placed next to the Shemites, from whom Israel descended. Thus the order represents a building up to the chosen people, Israel.

Others have suggested that the order has a geographic orientation. They feel that the descendants of Japheth are mentioned first because they lived farthest away. Several scholars agree that Shem is listed last because in the rest of the Genesis account the focus is on the Shemite peoples. Although there may be a measure of truth in all these suggestions, the fact remains that we cannot point to a conclusive reason for the rather unusual order of the material before us.

The first group that is mentioned under the sons of Japheth is "Gomer." This tribal name appears in the parallel passage (1 Chron. 1:5, 6), and also in Ezekiel 38:6. This is probably the same name that was discovered in the clay tablets that were excavated at Gimirrai. The Greek writer, Homer, calls them the Cimmerians. These people were originally found on the north coast of the Black Sea. Later, during the 8th century B.C., they attacked Armenia and established themselves at Lake Van. About 700 B.C. they moved farther west and conquered the kingdom of the Lydians under Gyges.

The second group is called "Magog." Besides here and in the parallel passage in 1 Chronicles 1:5, the name appears in Ezekiel 38:2 and 39:6. There is a great divergence of opinion among scholars regarding these people. We will not burden our readers with a detailed treatment of all of these views, but one view, held by many scholars, is that the term refers to the Scythians. The only substantiation for this interpretation is that this was the view of the ancient Jewish historian, Flavius Josephus. Another possible interpreation finds its basis in a reference discovered in the Amarna Tablets. There, in a letter to the Egyptian Pharaoh Amenophis III, we find a reference to "the land of Gagaia." If this is the same as Magog, this tribe would be found in the area of Carchemish in northern Syria. One of the outstanding scholars researching the Amarna Tablets, however, has concluded that "Gagaia" is nothing more than an archaic form of "Carchemish." It is clear that there is no certainty about the people who carried this name.

The third group is "Media" (Hebrew–Madai). This name appears frequently in the Old Testament. In addition to our present reference and its parallel in 1 Chronicles 1:5, we find it in 2 Kings 17:6; 18:11; Ezra 6:2; Esther 1:3, 14, 18–19; 10:2; Isaiah 13:17; 21:2; Jeremiah 25:25; 51:11, 28; Daniel 5:28; 6:9, 12, 15; 8:20; 9:1. The territory of the Medes was to the east of Assyria, in the mountains that form the northwestern section of Iran, to the south of the Caspian Sea. In the Tablets we find the first

217

reference to these people in the 9th century B.C. They appear as a rising enemy to Assyria and in 612 B.C. they destroyed Nineveh. Approximately in the middle of the 6th century B.C. their kingdom was absorbed by Persia.

The fourth group is called "Javan." This name appears, besides here and in the parallel passage in 1 Chronicles 1:5, 7, in Isaiah 66:19; Ezekiel 27:13, 19; Daniel 8:21; 10:20; 11:2; Zecheriah 9:13. There can be no question that this refers to the Greeks. The name seems to be a Hebraistic form of the "Ionians," the most important tribe from which the Greeks stemmed. Thus, among the Hebrews, this became the usual name for the Greeks. Some claim that this name already appeared in the Egyptian Texts from the time of Pharaoh Rameses II.

The fifth group is called "Tubal." In addition to this verse and the parallel in 1 Chronicles 1:5, this name appears in Isaiah 66:19; Ezekiel 27:13; 32:26; 38:2, 3; 39:1. These people are generally identified as the Tabali mentioned in the ancient Tablets. Herodotus, the Greek historian, calls them Tibarenoi. It is generally accepted that they lived north of Mesopotamia. About 1100 B.C. they were at war with Tiglath-pileser I. Later they were pushed to the west.

The sixth group is "Meshech." Besides here and in 1 Chronicles 1:5, this name appears in Psalm 120:5; Ezekiel 27:13; 32:26; 38:2-3; 39:1. In 1 Chronicles 1:17 the Hebrew text also mentions Meshech among the sons of Shem. This, however, is generally accepted as a copyist's error and should read "Mash," just as in Genesis 10:23. This is probably the same as "Mushki" in the ancient Assyrian Tablets, dated about 1100 B.C. These people were to be found in Asia Minor, to the northwest of Assyria. Psalm 120:5 mentions them in one breath with Kedar, which is in Arabia. This offers no problem, however, since the poet uses these names as symbols of wild tribes, without any consideration as to their location.

The seventh and last group is "Tiras." In Egyptian texts of the time of Pharaoh Meren-Ptah (c. 1231 B.C.), this name is given to the Turusa people. At that time they were known as sea pirates who raided the west coast of Asia Minor and the Greek Islands off the coast, and probably were the same people known as the Etruscans by the Romans. At that time they were found in northern Italy. Most likely these were the people referred to by the Hebrew word *Tiras*.

It is obvious that the order of these names is not determined by geographic location. Although the list does end with the people who lived farthest to the west, the Medes would form the eastern terminus, and thus, if the order was intended to move from east to west, it should have started with the Medes. Just what determined the order in which the names appear is difficult to say. At the close of our discussion on this chapter we will make certain observations regarding the time when this list was given its present order, and this will cast some light on this matter.

10:3 *The sons of Gomer: Ashkenaz, Riphath and Togarmah.*

A few of the groups mentioned in verse 2 are not given further subdivisions. The first of these is "Gomer." Under this group we are given the name of "Ashkenaz." Besides here and in 1 Chronicles 1:6, this name appears in Jeremiah 51:27. It is not easy to determine exactly what people are intended by this name, but they may have had some connection with the Ashkuza, mentioned in early Tablets. In Jeremiah 51:27 they are mentioned in connection with the kingdoms of Ararat and Minni. Both of these were situated in the Armenian highlands and thus it can be assumed that this was also the area where the people of Ashkenaz lived. They have frequently been identified with the Scythians.

A second group mentioned as a subdivision of "Gomer" is called "Riphath." In 1 Chronicles 1:6 this name is spelled "Dipath," but this is probably an error of the copyists. The letters "d" and "r" are easily confused in Hebrew, so it is difficult to determine what people are intended by this name. Flavius Josephus identifies the Ripheans with the Paphlagonians, through whose country the Rhebus River flowed. Another view is that we must think of the city of Arispas, which is mentioned in the inscriptions that were found at Boghazkoy. This city supposedly was located in the area of modern Erzerum. It is not possible to arrive at any certainty about these people at this time.

The third group mentioned in verse 3 is "Togarmah." This name is mentioned in Ezekiel 27:14; 38:6, as well as in the parallel reference in 1 Chronicles 1:6. In Hittite writings, which date back to the 14th century B.C., there are references to Tegarama which probably is the same as this Togarmah. In those writings this name designated an area that lay on the borders of the Hittite kingdom in Asia Minor. The reference in Ezekiel 38:6 mentions Togarmah in conjunction with Gomer, which also was located to the north of Palestine. This would then confirm the location mentioned above.

10:4 *The sons of Javan: Elishah, Tarshish, the Kittim and the Rodanim.*

In this verse we get further subdivisions of the Javan group which is generally accepted to be the Greeks. The first name mentioned here is "Elishah." This name, besides here and in 1 Chronicles 1:7, is also mentioned in Ezekiel 27:7. Opinions vary as to this designation. Some hold that

219

it refers to Carthage. Others view it as the Greek Peloponnesus. Still others consider it to be Sicily in lower Italy. The most probable view is that it refers to Alsa, a kingdom mentioned in the Amarna Tablets and also in a few ancient Hittite inscriptions. This can probably be identified with the Island of Cyprus.

The next name mentioned is "Tarshish." Besides here and in the parallel passage in 1 Chronicles 1:7, this name appears in the Old Testament in Psalm 72:10; Isaiah 23:6, 10; 66:19; Jeremiah 10:9; Ezekiel 27:12; 38:13; Jonah 1:3; 4:2. It usually refers to a land that could be reached from Palestine only by going overseas by ship. Formerly it was held that it referred to an area in Spain, called Tartessus. According to the Greek historian Herodotus, this land lay beyond the Straits of Gibralter. The Greek geographer, Strabo, claims that the river which today is called Guadalquiver was called Tartessus in ancient times and that a city with the same name lay at the mouth of that river. But newer data strongly suggests that we must think of a North African location, probably in the area where modern Tunis is located.

The next reference is to "Kittim." The name must be derived from Kition, a former city on the Island of Cyprus. It was a significant center of commerce. Thus the Kittimites must be seen, in a limited sense, as those who lived in that city. In a broader sense, however, they probably would include all the people of the Island of Cyprus. It is possible that the name can have an even broader reference. According to Jeremiah 2:10 and Daniel 11:30, it may well refer to the Greeks as a whole. Even so, this broad usage is probably not intended here. The name also appears in 1 Chronicles 1:7; Numbers 24:24; Isaiah 23:1, 12; Ezekiel 27:6. The most reasonable conclusion is that it here refers to that portion of the Greek population that lived in the general area of Cyprus.

The final reference is to the "Dodanim." Most interpreters give preference to the reading in 1 Chronicles 1:7, where these people are called "Rodanim." We also favor this reading. It is generally thought that it refers to the people who lived on the Island of Rhodes. We are convinced, however, that the name should read "Dardanim," and that we should think of the residents of Asia Minor, along the coast of the Hellespont in the area of the ancient city of Troy. This city traced its origin to a certain Dardanus. Later there was a city by the name of Dardanus and the area was known as Dardany.

As was the case in the other lists of names, it is apparent that the order that is followed is not a geographic one because the locations leap from east to west and back to the east, with no semblance of a planned order.

10:5 *(From these the maritime peoples spread out into their territories by their clans within their nations, each with its own language.)*

Here we read, "From these the maritime peoples spread out into their territories." The question we must face is, To what does "from these" refer? Does it tie in with the last mentioned group only or to the entire conglomerate of the descendants of Japheth? If the latter was the case, we would expect some kind of summary statement such as we find in verses 20 and 31. The former seems more likely since in Old Testament times the "coastal areas" or "maritime provinces" usually referred to the Greek coasts of Asia Minor and the islands lying off that coast.

Others have tried to broaden this designation and have translated the verse somewhat as follows: "From these the coastal territories of the peoples were divided. These are the children of Japheth according to their generations as peoples." This rendering requires the insertion of certain words that are not in the original text and there is no justification for such insertions. The fact that the term "coastal areas" usually refers to the Greek coastal regions with the adjoining offshore islands actually removes any impediment to making the term refer to all the descendants of Japheth. In Ezekiel 39:6 the term "coastal areas" is used for the territory of Magog. There we are told that Gog ruled not only over the land of Magog, but also over the area which in verse 2 is ascribed to Meshech and Tubal (Ezek. 38:2; 39:1). This gives us every reason to include under the designation, "coastal areas," the entire territory surrounding the Caspian Sea and the Black Sea. (I have developed this material in my tractate, *Herstel van Israel volgens het O.T.*)

In the light of the above, we contend that the term "coastal areas," here in verse 5, should be given a far broader interpretation. It should include the entire area around the Caspian Sea, the Black Sea, and the Mediterranean Sea. The descendants of Japheth scattered over this entire area, and that according to their languages. It should be observed that the division of languages, although not recorded until chapter 11, is already assumed here. The family tree of humanity is given here up to the time long after the division of languages had become a reality. The statement, "by their clans within their nations," points out the fact that there were further divisions among the national groups as they broke into various tribal groups.

10:6 *The sons of Ham: Cush, Mizraim, Put and Canaan.*

We now move on to a consideration of the descendants of Ham. The first group mentioned here is "Cush." We have already observed under 9:25, that in the Old Testament this name usually refers to Ethiopia. Examples of this would be 2 Kings 19:9; Esther 1:1; 8:9; Psalm 68:31; Isaiah 11:11; 18:1; 20:3–5; 37:9; Jeremiah 46:9; Ezekiel 29:10; 30:4ff.; 38:5; Nahum 3:9. Some translators render it "the Moors." Cush is thus a Hebraized form of the Egyptian "Kos," and refers to the area to the south of Egypt. It starts at the first great waterfall, on the Nile, and corresponds to the present-day Nubian Desert.

We must observe, however, that in 2 Chronicles 14:9ff. "Cush" has another meaning. In our interpretation of Genesis 2:13 we also pointed out that the word can have another meaning. In Central Arabia there is an area that probably was called "Kosh." This could be referred to by the Hebrew word "Cush." Moreover, if we consider the data given in verses 7–12 regarding Cush, it becomes unlikely that we must think of Ethiopia in this reference. Among the descendants of Cush, mention is made of Sheba and Dedan. Both of these must probably be located in Arabia. Furthermore, when in verses 8–12 we are told that Nimrod was one of the descendants of Cush, and he is then presented as the founder of certain kingdoms in the region of Mesopotamia, it becomes obvious that Cush must be taken in a broader sense here also.

The second group is designated as "Mizraim." In the Old Testament this regularly refers to Egypt.

The third group is "Put." Besides in the parallel passage in 1 Chronicles 1:8, this name appears in Jeremiah 46:9; Ezekiel 27:10; 30:5; 38:5; Nahum 3:9. Many modern scholars are convinced that this refers to the kingdom of Punt, which is mentioned in Egyptian records. This would then supposedly be found in the coastal areas of Abyssinia on the Red Sea, opposite the southwest point of Arabia, extending as far as Somaliland. (See 9:25.)

The fourth group is "Canaan." The name appears in Egyptian texts of the so-called New Kingdom, which date approximately 1350 B.C. It was also found in the Amarna Tablets. It generally designates an area along the Mediterranean coast from Lebanon to the borders of Egypt. It is obvious that, as it is used here, it must be taken in this broader sense.

Here, also, there is no indication of a geographic order in the listing of the various national groups. From Egypt the location moves to Put to the far south, and then returns to the north with Canaan. Some have explained the order by suggesting that Canaan was the youngest son of Ham, but this has little basis (see our interpretation of 9:18, 20).

10:7 *The sons of Cush: Seba, Havilah, Sabtah, Raamah and Sabtecah. The sons of Raamah: Sheba and Dedan.*

Just as in the case of Japheth, we now also have a subdivision. In this case three of the four groups are subdivided, with Put being omitted.

We start with Cush. The first subgroup is named "Seba." This name appears in the parallel passage, 1 Chronicles 1:9, and also in Psalm 72:10 and Isaiah 43:3. It has generally been located in Africa, but the Greek geographer, Strabo, refers to a people called "Saba" on the coast of the Red Sea.

Then we have "Havilah," which we discussed in the introductory notes to this chapter. This is followed by "Sabtah," and this name appears only here and in 1 Chronicles 1:9. Strabo identifies this with the Arabian city of Sabbatha, which was probably located in what today is Yemen. We then have a reference to "Raamah." This appears, in addition to 1 Chronicles 1:9, in Ezekiel 27:22. In the Sabean inscriptions it appears in a similar form. According to Strabo, this refers to the Raamanites who are found in southeastern Arabia. Finally, "Sabtecah" is mentioned, and this is found only here and in 1 Chronicles 1:9. Some have held that this refers to the people of Samydake, on the Eastern shores of the Persian Gulf, while others have located it on the Red Sea. There is no certainty as to the exact location of these people.

The Raamah people are again subdivided into groups designated as Sheba and Dedan. Besides here and in the parallel passage in 1 Chronicles 1:9, Sheba is mentioned several times in the Old Testament. It appears in Genesis 25:3; 1 Chronicles 1:32; Job 1:15; 6:19; Psalm 72:10, 15; Isaiah 60:6; Jeremiah 6:20; Ezekiel 27:22, 23; 38:13. It received considerable renown form its queen who visited Solomon (1 Kings 10:1–13; 2 Chron. 9:1–12). Even so, we have little data as to the exact location of these people. It seems almost certain that they must be found somewhere in Arabia, probably in the area of Midian. In the time of Samuel and Saul we find a tribe called the "Sabaeans," and traces of the Sabaeans have been found in the area of Midian. Later they seem to be located in what is now Yemen, in the southernmost part of Arabia. Are we dealing with two different peoples or must we agree with those who hold that the Sabaeans relocated from north to south about 700 B.C.? The fact that there are two references to Sheba in the Table of Nations, and that the name Sheba appears again among the descendants of Abraham via Keturah (Gen. 25:1–3), and that Midian there appears in the same context, strongly suggests that we may be dealing with two different tribal groups.

Dedan, besides here and in 1 Chronicles 1:9, is mentioned in Genesis 25:3; 1 Chronicles 1:32; Jeremiah 25:23; 49:8; Ezekiel 25:13; 27:15, 20; 38:13. We know that this was an Arabian tribe which was located on the borders of Edom's territory, probably to the south of Tema in northwest Arabia.

10:8 *Cush was the father of Nimrod, who grew to be a mighty warrior on the earth.*

With this verse the rather dull listing of tribes and peoples is interrupted by the recording of a historical detail. This event deals with Nimrod, who undoubtedly must be considered as an individual person. Just who was Nimrod? It goes without saying that, since the names that are listed here nearly all represent tribes and national groups, we cannot specifically identify Nimrod as the great-grandson of Noah. Although Ham must be considered the tribal head of the Hamites, Cush is the name of a tribe or a nation. Thus, when Nimrod is introduced as a descendant or progeny of Cush, we cannot conclude that he was the direct son of Cush, but only that he was a member of the tribe or nation that went by the name of Cush.

A precise identification of Nimrod is difficult. This difficulty has led some interpreters to think of Nimrod as some kind of legendary deity or folk hero. Some have identified him with the Babylonian god, Marduk. Others believe that he was the Sumerian war god, Ninurta. Still others equate him with the hunter-king of Erech, Gilgamesh, to whom a Babylonian historic ode was dedicated—the so-called Gilgamesh Epic. There is, however, no substantial basis for such efforts to avoid accepting Nimrod as a historical person. Even though we may not be able to identify him with certainty, this gives no cause for denying his historicity.

Numerous attempts have been made to identify Nimrod with some other figure in history. Some hold that this was King Nazi-Maruttash of Babylon. He belonged to the so-called Cassite dynasty during the 14th century B.C. This dynasty supposedly came to power in Babylon as a result of an invasion by the Cassites, also called Cossiers, and these people were tied in with the name Cush. This dynasty was in power from 1746–1170 B.C. Others refer to a certain King Lugalanda from the second Babylonian dynasty after the Flood. His name has also been read, Nin-Maradda. Still others are convinced that this is a reference to the powerful King Naram-Sin of Akkad. He supposedly reigned about 2700 B.C. and belonged to the dynasty of Kish, which is then related to Cush. Even if none of these attempts to identify him with a specific historical figure who appears in other records can be established, and we would be compelled to admit that the identity of Nimrod remains an unresolved question, we should still insist that Nimrod was indeed a historical personality.

Moving now to what we are told about Nimrod, we learn that he became "a mighty warrior on the earth." Just what is denoted by this description has raised many questions also. The "might" Nimrod manifested must be related to verse 10 where mention is made of the kingdom he established. The Hebrew word which our translators have rendered "mighty warrior" really says no more than that he was a mighty man, a man of great power. His power, in turn, came into expression in his effectiveness in establishing a strong, extensive kingdom. As such, Nimrod is introduced not so much as the first great warrior as an individual person, but rather as the founder of the first "power state." The rise of these "power states" became the main line of history from that point on as one mighty kingdom succeeded the other as the predominant force in the world at that particular time. The history of humanity actually became the record of mighty kingdoms, and Nimrod was the one who "fathered" that basic characteristic of human history.

10:9 *He was a mighty hunter before the Lord; that is why it is said, "Like Nimrod, a mighty hunter before the Lord."*

Our author considers what we are told in verse 9 about Nimrod to be no more than a bit of added information about him. This mighty man was also a mighty hunter. Some interpreters have insisted that this implies that he not only hunted wild animals, but also that this was descriptive of his skill in pursuing and conquering people of other tribes and nations. However, this is not implied in the word "hunter" as such, and there really is no need for imposing this added meaning on the word here. Throughout history one of the marks of distinction for men of might and position has been that they were fearless and successful hunters, especially of dangerous wild animals. It is completely understandable that the new humanity, after the Deluge, also developed skills and techniques for the hunt. It is also logical, then, that it should be a matter of record that this man of distinction, in addition to his other claims to fame, was also legendary for his prowess as a hunter.

This leaves the question as to what is meant by the descriptive term that he was a mighty hunter "before the Lord." Some have claimed that this is used in an unfavorable sense, suggesting that the Lord did not approve of Nimrod's triumphs as a hunter. Others claim precisely the opposite, insisting that this is an expression of God's approval. Actually, neither of these positions can be established. All we have here is an acknowledgment that God was aware of Nimrod's skill. In Genesis 6:11 we are told that "the earth was corrupt in God's sight." This simply indicates that the all-knowing God was well aware of man's state of corruption. At this point there is no mention of God's judgment upon man. It is just a declaration that God knew what was going on. So too, with Nimrod, we are told that God was fully cognizant that this man of might was also a renowned hunter. In itself, this was not an expression of God's disfavor, and this is evident from Jonah 3:3 where Nineveh is described as an exceedingly large city in the words that it was "important before God." This characterization says nothing about whether the city was morally good or bad.

10:10 *The first centers of his kingdom were Babylon, Erech, Akkad and Calneh, in Shinar.*

The basis for (literally—"beginning of") Nimrod's mighty empire was composed of four cities gathered together under his rule—Babylon, Erech, Akkad, and Calneh. The first three cities mentioned are well-known in the history of the period. First to be mentioned is Babylon, which gained considerable fame as early as 2800 B.C. Under the renowned King Hammurabi, it became the capital of the entire Babylonian empire. Erech, which is mentioned next, is also called Uruk, and was a city in southern Babylonia. Its ruins are still in evidence, and it was known as Warka by the Babylonians. Finally, there was Akkad, or Acade, situated in northern Babylonia. This was the residence of the famous Akkadian Dynasty, established by Sargon I. It was from this line that the dynasty of Naram-Sin stemmed. Concerning the fourth city, Calneh, there is considerable uncertainty. It has been surmised that it was the same as the significant city in northern Babylonia known as Nippur.

We are told that these cities were located in Shinar. In the Old Testament this name is used to designate the entire territory of Babylonia, including both southern Babylonia (Sumer), and the northern area (Akkad). See Genesis 11:2; 14:1, 9; Joshua 7:21 (the robe mentioned is described as a "robe from Shinar" in Hebrew), Isaiah 11:11; Zechariah 5:11; Daniel 1:2. Just what was originally included under the name Shinar is not wholly certain. In early times it was identified with Sumer, which is southern Babylonia. Later discoveries have suggested that the name relates to "Sanhar," used in some of the tablets that have been discovered. Whether this also refers to Babylon is not sure. Some scholars believe that it refers to a territory in northwestern Mesopotamia. In any case, it would include all of Babylonia since both northern and southern sections of Babylonia are included.

10:11, 12 *From that land he went to Assyria, where he built Nineveh, Rehoboth Ir, Calah and Resen, which is between Nineveh and Calah; that is the great city.*

In verse 11 we face the problem of the proper relationship of words. Some translations read, "Asshur went out from that land." Newer transla-

tions such as NIV and others make Nimrod the subject of this sentence also
and then read, "Nimrod went out from that land to Assyria." This would
harmonize with what we read in Micah 5:6, where Assyria is called the
land of Nimrod. Thus it would appear that Nimrod migrated to Assyria and
built cities there to further expand his empire.

Once again, the first three cities are well-known. The first is Nineveh.
Later, about 1100 B.C., this became the capital of the kingdom of Assyria.
The next city is Rehoboth-Ir, a Hebrew name which literally means "city
squares." This probably refers to the suburb of Nineveh which the Assyrian inscriptions named "Rebit-Ninua." This was located where the
modern city of Mosul stands. Then there is Calah, which probably was
situated where the Greater Zab joins the Tigris. Shalmaneser I established
his residence there in 1300 B.C. The fourth city, Resen, which is here
located between Nineveh and Calah, is unknown to historians. It probably
formed a part of what is further described as "The Great City."

This term, "The Great City," certainly cannot refer to Resen alone. Nor
can it refer to Calah, mentioned just before it, since that can hardly be
described as the great city when compared with Nineveh. Thus, the only
conclusion we can reach is that "The Great City" refers to the whole
complex of four cities, located in close proximity to each other, forming
one huge metropolis.

10:13, 14 *Mizraim was the father of the Ludites, Anamites, Lehabites, Naphtuhites, Pathrusites, Casluhites (from whom the Philistines came) and Caphtorites.*

We are now given the subdivisions of Egypt. The "Ludites" are the first
to be mentioned. The Hebrew plural "Ludim" appears here, in the parallel
passage in 1 Chronicles 1:11, and in Jeremiah 46:9. The name also appears
a few times in its singular form as "Lud," in Isaiah 66:19; Ezekiel 27:10;
30:5; and this apparently refers to the same people. In Ezekiel 30:5 the
singular form is used in combination with Put. In Isaiah 66:19 we probably
are dealing with the same two names although the Received Text there
reads, "Pul and Lud." The former name is , however, an obvious copy
error for Put. (See Ridderbos: *Isaiah*.)

Just what nation is intended here is difficult to determine. Some have
tried to identify these people with the Lydians who lived in Asia Minor and
formed a strong kingdom there. The Persian King Cyrus defeated them in a
war in 546 B.C. This, however, offers some difficulty since it would be
logical to then locate them in Africa. Many believe that the name should be
"Lub" and that this is an early reference to what today is known as Libya,
which lies to the west of Egypt. To accept this interpretation involves the

difficulty of accepting the same copy error in several different places, and this is not likely. Thus we cannot say with any degree of certainty what people are referred to by this name.

The second group mentioned is the ''Anamites.'' This name appears only here and in the parallel passage in 1 Chronicles 1:11. The best we can do in this case is to surmise that this could refer to the Kenamites who occupied a large oasis to the west of Egypt. This would then be explained by substituting a Hebrew ''A'' for the Egyptian ''K.''

The third group is named the ''Lehabites,'' and this name also appears in 1 Chronicles 1:11. It is generally accepted that the Hebrew ''Lehabim'' is the same as ''Lubim'' which is found in 2 Chronicles 12:3; 16:8; Daniel 11:43; and Nahum 3:9. If this is correct, this would then be a reference to the Libyans. This would give an added reason, also, for ascribing the name ''Ludites'' to another people.

Fourthly, we have the ''Naphtuhites,'' mentioned only here and in 1 Chronicles 1:11. This was long considered to be a reference to a people who occupied North Egypt. A modern Egyptologist has pointed out the similarity of the name to the Egyptian ''Napatoech,'' which is a word often used to describe the people living in the Nile Delta.

Next we have the ''Pathrusites.'' These are generally accepted to be the people who occupied South Egypt, or Upper Egypt. The only other place this name appears in this form is in 1 Chronicles 1:12, but we do find the name ''Pathros,'' to designate Upper Egypt, in Isaiah 11:11; Jeremiah 44:1, 15; Ezekiel 29:14; 30:14. It is the same as the Egyptian ''Patoris,'' which means ''land of the midday.''

Then we have the ''Casluhites,'' which also are mentioned only here and in 1 Chronicles 1:12. These people are further described as ''from whom the Philistines came.'' According to Amos 9:7, the Philistines originated in ''Caphtor.'' Consequently, most commentators are agreed that this descriptive phrase has been misplaced and should appear after ''Caphtorites,'' but this is not necessarily true. It is possible to resolve this matter in such a way that the Received Text can be received as correct. If we consider these unknown ''Casluhites'' to be the dwellers of the area which borders on Mt. Cassius to the east of the Nile Delta, it would be possible that part of the Philistines sojourned there about 1200 B.C., and that they later migrated to what is actually Philistia. Meanwhile, another part of the Philistines could have come from ''Caphtor,'' thus explaining the Amos reference.

The last group of people to be classified as Egyptian are the ''Caphtorites.'' This name appears in 1 Chronicles 1:12 and also in Deuteronomy 2:23. The name of the territory of Caphtor also appears in Jeremiah 47:4

and, as mentioned above, in Amos 9:7. It is reasonably sure that this name relates to the Egyptian "Kephto," which is mentioned in texts which date between 1600 and 1200 B.C. Kephto seemed to include a rather extensive area, including coasts of Asia Minor and Greece and some of the islands to the west of Cyprus. But the area designated as Caphtor in the Old Testament usually was a smaller area. Jeremiah 47:4 refers to the "Island of Caphtor," which most likely was Crete. It is probable that the reference here must be seen in this light also, and then it would include the coastal areas mentioned above with a special focus on the people who occupied the Island of Crete.

Again it should be pointed out that it is obvious that this list of peoples is not given in a geographic order. In general, we can see a trend to move from West to East and from North to South. But this is by no means consistent, since the Caphtorites lived to the north and they are mentioned last.

10:15 *Canaan was the father of Sidon his firstborn, and of the Hittites,*

Now we come to the third primary group, the Canaanites. The first subgroup mentioned here is identified with "Sidon," the well-known city of the Phoenicians. It lies on the coast of the Mediterranean Sea, approximately halfway between the other famous Phoenician city of Tyre and the modern city of Beirut. When we are told that Sidon was Canaan's firstborn, this must be understood as indicating that, in the Table of Nations, Sidon was the first branch of the main group of "Canaanites" to establish an independent nation. Thus the name "Sidon" probably designates the entire Phoenician people. The fact that Sidon is mentioned and not Tyre, when later the two are usually mentioned together, can be explained by the development of Sidon as the leading city of Phoenicia in the early centuries. In the Amarna Tablets, approximately 1400 B.C., Sidon also is given considerable prominence while Tyre was of later origin. Tyre, however, flourished and surpassed Sidon during the 9th and 10th centuries B.C.

The second branch of the Canaanites to be mentioned is Heth, or the "Hittites." These are probably the people called "Cheta" by the Egyptian texts, and "Chatti" in the early clay tablets. This people settled in the northern part of Syria and formed a powerful kingdom between 1500 and 1200 B.C. They spread their control over Asia Minor and, in the other direction, far to the south and the southeast, where they came into conflict with Egypt. The capital city of this kingdom lay in the heart of Asia Minor near the location of the present town of Boghazkoy. This is the location where thousands of clay tablets have been discovered which give much information about this ancient period. In addition to the clay tablets, the Hittites also used a type of hieroglyphic writing, similar to that used by the Egyptians. Recently much effort has been put forth to decipher and translate these ancient Hittite writings.

10:16–18 *Jebusites, Amorites, Girgashites, Hivites, Arkites, Sinites, Arvadites, Zemarites and Hamathites.*
Later the Canaanite clans scattered

In these verses we are introduced to the several subdivisions of the Canaanitish people who lived in the area we now know as Palestine. The Jebusites lived in the area of Jerusalem (Josh. 15:8, 63; Judg. 1:21; 19:10–11; 1 Chron. 11:4). The Amorites were found in an area east of the Jordan and in the mountains of West Jordan, at the time when Israel entered the land of Canaan (Num. 13:29; Deut. 3:8; 4:47; 31:4; Josh. 2:10; 9:10). At an earlier time they formed a mighty kingdom to the west of Babylon, which ruled even over Babylon itself for a time. Hammurabi stemmed from this Amorite dynasty. The Girgashites are mentioned in 1 Chronicles 1:14, but also in Genesis 15:21; Deuteronomy 7:1; Joshua 3:10; 24:11; Nehemiah 9:8. Their exact location is not known. Finally the Hivites are mentioned and they also were among the inhabitants of Canaan when Israel occupied the land. They seemed to live in the vicinity of Shechem (Gen. 34:2) and Gibeon (Josh. 9:1, 3–7); thus, in central Palestine.

Next, we find the people who occupied several cities in the territory of Phoenicia. The Arkites, mentioned only here and in 1 Chronicles 1:15, lived in the city of Arka, which is known as Irkata in the Amarna Tablets. This was located about five hours to the north of Tripoli and in more recent times was known as Tell Arka. The Sinites, also mentioned only here and in 1 Chronicles 1:15, lived in the city of Sinna. This city is mentioned by the geographer, Strabo, and it is called Sianoe in the Tablets. This lay to the south of the Arka River and was near the city of Arka, mentioned above. The Arvadites, also mentioned only here and in 1 Chronicles 1:16, lived in the city of Arvad, which is mentioned in Ezekiel 27:8, 11. In the Amarna Tablets it is known as Arwada. It was located on an island by the same name, which was just off the coast of Tripoli and in modern times is known as Ruwad. The Zemarites, again mentioned only here and in 1 Chronicles 1:16, lived in a city called Samar in the Egyptian texts, Soemoer in the Amarna Tablets, and Simirra in the Assyrian Inscriptions. Today it is called Soemra, and it lies between Tripoli and Arvad.

Finally, mention is made of the Hamathites. This is a tribal name, which appears only here and in 1 Chronicles 1:16. It refers to the city of Hamath in Syria, and the city is mentioned various times in the Old Testament. It was situated on the Orontes River.

An explanatory note is added to this list of tribal names and this has given expositors some difficulty. Our translators have rendered the line, "Later the Canaanite clans scattered." This seems to imply that the division into the various tribal groups took place at a later time. We prefer the reading, "After this the descendants of the Canaanites were scattered." Our position is that the various tribal groups were already in existence at the time of this writing.

10:19 *And the borders of Canaan reached from Sidon toward Gerar as far as Gaza, and then toward Sodom, Gomorrah, Admah and Zeboiim, as far as Lasha.*

This verse gives the boundaries that encompassed the entire Canaanite territory, and the closing statement of verse 18 would then be seen as a transition statement. Then verse 19 gives the boundaries which broadly marked out the territory occupied by the Canaanitish tribes that are mentioned in verses 15–18. Along the coast the boundary lay from Sidon in the north, down to Gaza, the well-known city of the Philistines, in the south. Gerar is mentioned as a city near Gaza. Moving inland from west to east, the Canaanites spread as far as Sodom and Gomorrah, the cities which later became famous for their terrible destruction (Gen. 19:24–29). The farthest point to the east was Lasha, but this city has been difficult to locate. On the basis of ancient Jewish writings, quoted by the patristic writer Hieronymous, this can be accepted as a reference to the village of Kallinhoe, which is located on the east bank of the Dead Sea. Some, however, think of the city of Laash that is near Hamath. They then suggest that the second half of the verse indicates the entire length of the eastern border, running from the area of Sodom and Gomorrah in the south, up to Laash in the north. This is, however, most improbable. The reference to Sodom and Gomorrah does not designate a southern boundary, but rather the easterly direction from Gaza, which is mentioned before. Moreover, to identify Laash in the north with Lasha, mentioned here, would require a reversal of the two final consonants, and this is a dubious translation. It is obvious that the delineation of these boundaries is, at best, vague. Only two lines are established. One line runs along the coast from north to south. The other line runs inland toward a certain point, thus from west to east.

Because of this vague delineation, some of the critics have argued that part of this description must have come from a later hand. They claim that since Arka, Arvad, Simirra, and Hamath lie north of Sidon, they would then lie outside the boundaries that had been established. They argue that, since the southern boundary is clearly set, the northern boundary must also be definitely established at Sidon. But nothing could be farther from the truth. The southern boundary is given as "toward Gerar as far as Gaza." If we recognize that Gerar lies about 3½ hours to the south-southwest of Gaza, it is obvious that this is no more than an approximation as to where the southern boundary would fall. Likewise, the reference to "toward Sodom . . . as far as Lasha" gives no fixed boundary on the south. It rather points only to the general area inland from the coast to which the land of Canaan extended. This would be approximately from Gaza to Lasha, but it is obvious that this is a very loose delineation. In the same way, when Sidon is mentioned as the northern point on the coast, we must accept this as an approximate northern boundary. Sidon was chosen because it was a well-known city in Phoenicia. This certainly did not imply that a few of the cities which lay a bit farther north than Sidon were thereby declared to be outside these borders. Moreover, the mention of Hamath strongly suggests that here again we have only a general line running inland from the coast. Once again, the reason for selecting Hamath was that it was a well-known city, but since it lies considerably farther north than Sidon, this line is of necessity very vague and undefined. One interesting factor is that Hamath lies about the same distance from Sidon, in the north, as the distance from Lasha to the Mediterranean Sea, in the south. This would also support the authenticity of the use of Hamath in the original text.

10:20 *These are the descendants of Ham by their clans and languages, in their territories and nations.*

The list of the Hamitic peoples and tribes is concluded with a summary statement, similar to that which appears in verse 5, with respect to the descendants of Japheth. For the interpretation of the terms: "clans," "languages," "territories," and "nations," see our commentary on verse 5.

10:21 *Sons were also born to Shem, whose older brother was Japheth; Shem was the ancestor of all the sons of Eber.*

We now proceed to the third and last of the families of nations that descended from the sons of Noah, namely the Semites, the descendants of Shem.

It is striking that the author does not immediately plunge into listing the sons of Shem, as had been done in the cases of Japheth and Ham. Another fact about Shem is mentioned first, namely, that he was the "older brother of Japheth,'' or, ''whose older brother was Japheth.'' We have presented a discussion regarding the relative age of the sons of Noah under 9:24, but actually this is of no great importance.

Of considerable importance, however, is the statement that Shem was the father of all the sons of Eber, thus the Hebrews. Does this mean that all the descendants of Shem were Hebrews? Certainly not. In verses 22 and 23 certain tribal groups are mentioned as stemming from Shem who were definitely not Hebrews. Must we then agree with those critics who insist that there is a conflict between verse 21 and verses 22–23 which would support the theory of multiple sources? Again we reply in the negative. Shem could very well have been the father of all the Hebrews, as verse 21 suggests, and he could have been the ancestor of other tribal groups as well. Granted that all Hebrews are Semites, this does not imply that all Semites are Hebrews, and this is not stated here either.

But why is it specifically mentioned here that Shem was the father of all the Hebrews? Van Gelderen, in his article on the Semites in the *Christelijke Encyclopaedie,* suggests that this is the most important factor about Shem for the purpose of this record. It was from this line that the Israelites as the children of Abraham stemmed and this was of primary significance at this point. Although the children of Abraham are not mentioned here, the genealogy of Shem, given in 11:10–26, makes this tie clearly as the line is drawn from Shem to Abraham.

A second question that must be faced is, Who are meant by the term ''Hebrews,'' or ''the sons of Eber''? If we follow the line of descendants of Eber, in verses 24–30, it becomes evident that the name ''Hebrews,'' as it is used here, must be taken in a very broad sense. Sometimes we are inclined to use the terms ''Hebrews'' and ''Israelites'' interchangeably. We do this especially when we designate the Hebrew language as being exclusively the language of the Israelites. The name Hebrew taken by itself, however, has a broader connotation. This is also established by the use of the word in later Scriptures. When Abraham was still living the life of a Nomad, before the people of Israel existed, he was called a Hebrew in Genesis 14:13. So also, Joseph stated that he had been stolen ''off from the land of the Hebrews'' in Genesis 40:15. In fact, during Joseph's time there was a sharp distinction between Egyptians and Hebrews (see Gen. 43:32). Still later, during the time of Saul, when Israel already existed as a nation, a distinction was made between Israelites and Hebrews, in 1 Samuel 13:6–7 and 14:21. Some of the ancient secular texts probably refer to the Hebrews, using the name ''Chambiri'' or ''Chambiro,'' which linguistically can coincide with the word Hebrew. Dr. Koopmans, in an article in *Christelijke Encyclopaedie,* points out that these people lived in the middle of Palestine before Israel occupied the land, and that they formed a threat to the other nations that lived in the area. The point we must make here is that all of these people were descendants of Shem.

10:22 *The sons of Shem: Elam, Asshur, Arphaxad, Lud and Aram.*

As with Japheth and Ham, the passage now continues with a listing of the various tribal groups that stemmed from Shem.

The first is "Elam." This is a people or territory which, in addition to 1 Chronicles 1:17, is mentioned a number of times in the Old Testament (see Gen. 14:1, 9; Isa. 11:11; 21:2; 22:6; Jer. 25:25; 49:34–39; Ezek. 32:24; Dan. 8:2). Geographically they must be located on the Persian Gulf. Their territory must have been bounded on the east by the Tigris River, and on the west by Babylonia, on the north by Media, and on the east by Persia. Already in early times it was considered to be a powerful kingdom, a formidable enemy for Naram-Sin. Recently the language of the Elamites has been effectively decoded and we have gained considerable information about these amazing people. Prof. Van Gelderen was one of the scholars who devoted much research to this study.

The second group mentioned is "Asshur," one of the ancient peoples who are well-known to the readers of the Bible, for Asshur is repeatedly mentioned in the Old Testament. These were the people who lived on both sides of the upper Tigris River. As early as 2000 B.C. we find clear evidences of an independent Assyrian kingdom.

The third name is "Arphaxad." This name appears only here, in 1 Chronicles 1:17–18, and in Genesis 11:10–13 and 1 Chronicles 1:24. There is considerable difference of opinion about this name. It seems that we should think of the territory that the Greeks called "Arrapachitis" and this lay in the hills of the upper part of the great Zab River.

The fourth name is "Lud." It is obvious that we are not dealing here with the same people as the "Ludites," mentioned in verse 13. Most interpreters relate this present name to the country of Lydia in Asia Minor. But this is as unlikely here as it was with the Ludites, in verse 13. It is more likely that we have a reference here to a territory that was called Lubdo, or Lubdi, which is mentioned in some of the tablets that have been discovered. This would then be located in the far north of Mesopotamia, on the southern border of Armenia.

Finally, the fifth name is "Aram" (which is Hebrew) or "Syria." There are references to these people as early as 1500 B.C. Their primary location was on the steppes between Palestine and Mesopotamia. Throughout the Old Testament there are frequent references to the Arameans and the Syrians. Especially well-known was the Syrian kingdom, centered in Damascus, with which Israel had many contacts and wars.

It is worthy of note that this list of peoples is arranged in somewhat of a geographical order. These five nations form a large crescent, starting at the Persian Gulf, then swinging in a northerly direction up to the borders of Armenia, and then extending down in a southwesterly direction ending in Syria.

10:23 *The sons of Aram: Uz, Hul, Gether and Meshech.*

In this verse we are given subdivisions of the primary groups given in verse 22. We start with the Arameans, or Syrians. The first name mentioned in this group is "Uz." It is difficult to determine what people must be identified by this name. The name appears in the parallel passage in 1 Chronicles 1:17, but it is also used in Genesis 22:21 as the name of one of the sons of Nahor. Then in Genesis 36:28, and its parallel, 1 Chronicles 1:42, it designates one of the descendants of Dishan. The land of Uz is also mentioned in Jeremiah 25:20 and Lamentations 4:21. However, the best-known reference to this name is found in Job 1:1, where it is given as Job's homeland. In Lamentations 4:21 we are told that the daughter of Edom lived in the land of Uz. This would suggest that it should be located to the south of Canaan. Its use in Jeremiah 25:20 seems to concur with this location since there it is placed between Egypt and the land of the Philistines, and in verse 21 it is grouped with the Edomites, Moabites, and Amonites. This would also seem to be supported by Genesis 36:28 and 1 Chronicles 1:42.

But a people which would supposedly be descended from the Arameans would be difficult to locate in this designated area. It would seem more likely that they should be located in the area of Syria. This, in turn, would be supported by the fact that the name is also carried by one of the sons of Nahor. It is possible that we should think of two different peoples, one located near Syria, and the other to the south between Egypt and Arabia. The latter, then, would be referred to in Jeremiah 25:20 and Lamentations 4:21.

We then move on to "Hul" and "Gether," both of which are mentioned only here and in 1 Chronicles 1:17. We know nothing about these people or their territories. Some have tried to locate Hul at the sources of the Jordan River and to identify Gether with Gessor, between Bashan and Mt. Hermon. This, however, is pure guesswork.

This family is concluded with "Meshech," which name also appears only here and in 1 Chronicles 1:17. Although we have no solid information about this tribe, it is generally accepted that they were located near the mountain "Masius," which must be located on the borders of Mesopotamia and Armenia. Others have located it in the mountains of which Lebanon is a part, and this is also suggested by the Babylonian Gilgamesh Epic.

10:24 *Arphaxad was the father of Shelah, and Shelah the father of Eber.*

The second group to be subdivided is Arphaxad. This group is introduced by establishing the family tie between Arphaxad and Eber, through whom Shem became the father of all the Hebrews (see v. 21). As was observed in the introduction to this chapter, this verse has been ascribed to a "redactor" by the critics. They argue that the redactor tried to bring this passage into agreement with the Semitic family tree in Genesis 11:10ff., but why call in a redactor to explain this? It is certainly reasonable to assume that, in the case of Shem, this more personal genealogical touch is included in the "family of nations." We have a similar instance in the case of "Cush was the father of Nimrod," in verse 8.

This personal genealogy then moves from Arphaxad to Shelah to Eber. That Arphaxad appears as a personal name, the son of Shem and the grandson of Noah, is obvious. Whether Shelah and Eber also must be seen as personal names, rather than tribal names, is not definitely established. The Hebrew words can be used in a broader sense. We will give some further discussion to this at the close of our study of the genealogy of Shem in Genesis 11:10–26.

10:25 *Two sons were born to Eber: One was named Peleg, because in his time the earth was divided; his brother was named Joktan.*

This verse continues a personal genealogy by declaring that Eber had two sons, "Peleg" and "Joktan." Although these are personal names, they are given with the intent of indicating that there were two groups of nations that descended from Eber. Nothing is further mentioned about the line of Peleg, but this information is included in the genealogy recorded in Genesis 11:10ff. The other group of peoples that descended from Joktan is listed in verses 26–29.

The statement that demands our attention here is translated, "in his time the earth was divided." It can be assumed that this refers to the people on the earth. This division of the population of the earth can refer to nothing else than the confusion of speech, which is recorded in Genesis 11:1–9. The author, thus, reaches ahead to what will be recorded later. He does the same thing in verses 5 and 20, where he refers to multiple languages. In this connection, see also verse 31. In our present verse he establishes a connection between the name of Peleg and the division of the people, with the use of the word "because." It would seem that Peleg received his name from the incident of the confusion of speech. The word *peleg,* in Hebrew, indeed does mean to divide or to split. The word can also refer to a fissure caused by a stream of water, and it is sometimes used to designate a stream or a brook. Since the name must have been given after the division of the peoples took place, and since Peleg is the ancestor of a people who spoke the Hebrew language, there can be no objection to establishing this connection between his name and the event of the division of peoples.

10:26–29 *Joktan was the father of Almodad, Sheleph, Hazarmaveth, Jerah, Hadoram, Uzal, Diklah, Obal, Abimael, Sheba, Ophir, Havilah and Jobab. All these were sons of Joktan.*

We are told that Joktan, who is mentioned only here and in 1 Chronicles 1:19, 23, was the father of a number of tribal groups whose names appear only here and in the parallel passage in 1 Chronicles 1:20–23. The exceptions to this are "Uzal," who is mentioned in Ezekiel 27:19, Sheba and Havilah, who have already been discussed, and Ophir, the well-known land of gold which appears in 1 Kings 9:28; 10:11; 22:48; 1 Chronicles 29:4; 2 Chronicles 8:18; 9:10; Job 22:24; 28:16; Psalm 45:10; Isaiah 13:12.

In general, it is difficult to locate the various peoples who are mentioned here. It seems certain that they must be found in the general area of Arabia. Thus, "Hazarmaveth" can be identified with Hadramaut, mentioned in Sabean inscriptions. It was an Arabian territory on the coast of the Indian Ocean. It was known for its incense, myrrh, and aloes. Uzal has been equated with San'ā', the capital of what is today Yemen. Ezekiel 27:19 mentions that iron was produced in Uzal. Even today the steel of San'ā' is highly regarded. Diklah probably means "land of palms," and this also would point in the direction of Arabia. It should be observed that the Sheba and Havilah mentioned here are probably not the same as the identical names in verse 7.

Of special note is the fact that Ophir, the land of gold, cannot be located with any degree of certainty. In connection with what has been said above, it should probably be located in the general area of Arabia. Prof. Van Gelderen suggests that the name "Ophir" is a different pronunciation of Hapir or Apir. This would then tie in with the Elamites, who called themselves by this name in ancient times. The Elamites supposedly established a colony on the southeast coast of Arabia some three centuries before the time of Solomon, in the area which today is known as Oman. This latter name is probably taken from their chief god, who was called "Hoemban." Van Gelderen, in his commentary on the Books of Kings, suggests that this colony was eventually taken into the tribal descendants of Joktan so that "Phir" is then included in the family of Joktan in the table of Nations. In the Arabian tradition the name is "Quactan."

10:30 *The region where they lived stretched from Mesha toward Sephar, in the eastern hill country.*

This verse gives certain boundaries for the area where the descendants of Joktan settled. Neither of the two names can be definitely located, however. "Mesha," which appears only here in the Old Testament, is often identified with Mesene, at the mouths of the Tigris and Euphrates Rivers on the Persian Gulf. Another interpretation holds that the spelling has been altered and that it should read "Massa," which was the name of an Arabian tribe located halfway between the Gulf of Aqaba and the Persian Gulf. Several interpreters vacillate between the two locations. "Sephar" is sometimes located in southern Arabia. Most commonly, however, it is located in southeastern Arabia and then is identified with Sphar, which today is called Dophar. In favor of this interpretation is the added statement "in the eastern hill country." Near the present location of Dophar there is a high mountain. It should be noted, however, that it is difficult to determine whether the term "in the eastern hill country" refers to the entire group of tribes or only to the location of Sephar. Both are linguistically possible. What is not possible, however, is to try to read into this statement, as some do, an extension of the borders for this entire group. It would then be made to say, "from Mesha in the area of Sephar all the way to the eastern mountains." There is no grammatical justification for making this statement a third indication of the boundaries of this entire group of nations and tribes.

10:31 *These are the sons of Shem by their clans and languages, in their territories and nations.*

The list of the Semitic tribal groups concludes with a summary statement that is almost identical with that used of the Hamitic peoples in verse 20. The only difference is that here we read "by" their clans etc., and in some translations in verse 20 the term "in" is used. Our translators have not noted this inconsequential difference. For the meaning of the terms "clans," "languages," "territories," and "nations," we refer you to our interpretation of verse 5.

10:32 *These are the clans of Noah's sons, according to their lines of descent, within their nations. From these the nations spread out over the earth after the flood.*

At the conclusion of the entire Table of Nations there is a summary statement that applies to all three groups. The descendants of Noah's three sons developed families and these families formed nations and tribes. Thus from these three the nations and peoples that scattered all over the earth had their origin.

Now that we have come to the end of our interpretation of the Table of Nations, is is fitting that we give some consideration to the light which this material sheds on the time when this chapter was written.

In general, we would insist that this Table of Nations gives no substantial internal evidence for a late date for this material. For the most part, there is considerable evidence that these nations, territories, and cities existed before the time of Solomon. The name "Magog," in verse 2, probably appears in the Amarna Tablets and would fall during the time of the Egyptian Pharaohs Amenophis III and IV. This would place it at about 1411–1360 B.C. Javan would probably appear during the reign of Rameses II, 1292–1225 B.C. Tubal was at war with the Assyrian King Tiglath-pileser I, which places him at about 1100 B.C. Meshech is mentioned in some of the clay tablets that go back to 1170 B.C. Tiras appears in Egyptian texts from the time of Pharaoh Meren-Ptah, about 1231 B.C. Togarmah (v. 3) is mentioned in the Hittite Inscriptions which date back to the fourteenth century B.C. Elisha (v. 4) is probably the same as Alisa in the Amarna Tablets and is also mentioned in ancient Hittite writings. The name "Canaan" (v. 6) appears in Egyptian texts from about 1350 B.C., and also in the Amarna Tablets. Seba (v. 7) was already on the scene in an inscription that dates from the time of Samuel and Saul. Nimrod (v. 8), can be placed, at the very latest, in the 14th century B.C. The cities of Babylon, Akkad and Erech (v. 10), certainly existed before 2000 B.C. Nineveh (v. 11) has an even earlier date, although it did not become the capital of Assyria until about 1100 B.C. Calah was the residence of Shalmaneser I about 1300 B.C. Caphtor (v. 14), has been identified with the Egyptian Kefto and appears in ancient Egyptian writings from 1600–1200 B.C. The cities Arka, Arvad, and Zemar (vv. 17–18), appear in the Amarna Tablets. The "Hebrews" (v. 21) are mentioned before Israel entered Canaan. Elam and Asshur (v. 22) both existed long before Solomon. Asshur can actually be traced back as an independent city to 2000 B.C. There are references to the Aramean and

Syrian peoples going back to 1500 B.C. The only nation of which no mention is made before the 9th century B.C. is the Medes. They could well have existed before that time, however.

If we seek out references that point to a specific time when this material could have been written, we can point to verse 14 where the Philistines are mentioned. There we are told that they stemmed from the Casluhites. We observed, in our commentary on verse 14, that part of the Philistines originally occupied an area to the east of the Nile Delta, and then later moved to the territory to the southwest of Israel in what was then known as Philistia. It goes without saying that this could have been described only after the event took place. The location of the Philistines in Cassius on the Nile must have occurred about 1200 B.C. Thus the Table of Nations must have been written after that date. But how much later?

An answer to this question can be found by comparing Genesis 10:14 with Amos 9:7. In the latter passage mention is made of a second departure of the Philistines which must have been their departure from Caphtor. It is clear that Genesis 10:14 was written before that migration took place, otherwise their migration from Cassius would not have been the only migration mentioned. Although we do not know exactly when these two migrations of the Philistines took place, both biblical and Egyptian records suggest that the two came rather close together. The Egyptian records indicate that the Philistines (Pulasati) were a formidable force there, threatening Rameses III (1202–1171 B.C.). The biblical record indicates that at the time of Samson, Samuel, and Saul, the Philistines were already a strong nation with formidable military power. This development of the Philistines in Canaan must be explained by the addition of large numbers of their people from their original homeland. This leads us to the conclusion that Genesis 10:14 could not have been written later than the time of Samuel and Saul.

A second factor that has bearing on the date of the writing of the Table of Nations deals with Tyre, but this well-known Phoenician city is not mentioned. Sidon, however, is mentioned and this was a well-known city by the year 1400 B.C. The fact that other Phoenician cities like Arka, Arvad, and Zemar are mentioned, strongly suggests that the omission of Tyre has special significance.

It is known that Tyre arose to prominence long after Sidon did. The logical conclusion is that at this writing, Tyre, although it did exist, was as yet not considered of any importance among the Phoenician cities. Tyre came into prominence during the tenth and ninth centuries B.C. Witness to this is the relationships that David and Solomon had with this city. From this it would appear that Genesis 10:15–19 was written before the time of David.

A third factor that sheds light on this matter deals with Ophir. If Van Gelderen's assumption that Ophir was of Elamite origin is correct, then the name Ophir in Genesis 10:29 cannot have been written before 1300 B.C. Furthermore, since these Elamites are mentioned among the Joktanites they must have become a part of this line of descendants. Although this may have taken some time, Van Gelderen is confident that this must have taken place well before the time of Solomon.

When all of this data is considered, there is a strong indication that this Table of Nations was written at the time we have ascribed to the writing of the entire Pentateuch, namely during the reign of Saul or, at the latest, during the early days of David's reign. (See our discussion of the date of the Pentateuch in the Introduction.)

Professor Van Gelderen, however, suggests that this Table of Nations underwent some changes at a later time. He thinks that this may have been during the time of King Hezekiah. He points to Proverbs 25:1, which suggests that Hezekiah appointed a group of scholars who gathered some of the scattered proverbs of Solomon. Van Gelderen then suggests that this same group of scholars could also have devoted study to other sections of the Old Testament. Some of the material in Genesis 10, which he feels may have been altered at the time of Hezekiah, is the classification of the Japhethites in verse 2. As we have observed, this classification is not geographically oriented. Just what standard was used for this classification is hard to determine. Professor Van Gelderen, however, points out that Gomer (the Cimmerians) is mentioned first. He points out that the Cimmerians were very prominent among the Japhethites during the time of Hezekiah. This can be explained by the fact that it was just at this time that the so-called Cimmerian migration took place. They relocated in large numbers from the north shore of the Black Sea, which had been their homeland, passing along the East Coast to the south and continuing until they overran all of Asia Minor. This Cimmerian migration must be dated from 720–710 B.C., which is the time of Hezekiah.

In the second place, Togarmah is mentioned in Genesis 10:3 as a subdivision of Gomer. As we have noted, this name appears as Tegerama in the 14th century B.C. and is presented as a people of Asia Minor by the Cimmerians.

In the third place, in Genesis 10:4, Javan, or the Greeks, includes several tribal groups outside the traditional territory of the Greeks. This wide expansion of the Greeks also points strongly to the time of Hezekiah.

There are two other factors that Van Gelderen points out. One deals with the classification of the Hamitic peoples in which Cush is given first place. Van Gelderen assumes that this refers to Ethiopia. As we have observed above, we consider this to be doubtful. Even so, Van Gelderen tries to explain this by pointing out that there was a time when Ethiopia controlled Egypt, and this would have been during the time of Hezekiah.

Van Gelderen's final point is that the proper Hebrew name, Rehoboth Ir, in verse 11, refers to a Hebrew colony, namely the ten tribes who were exiled into Assyria. This would place this reference in the Table of Nations after 722 B.C. and once again would point to the time of Hezekiah. We are in disagreement with this conclusion. As mentioned above, we are convinced that this Hebrew name was formed by the writer of Scripture and literally means "the city square," and this is also expressed in the Assyrian name Rebit-Ninua. Of course, all bases for making this a Hebrew colony then fall away.

We have no real objection to acknowledging the possibility that there was some editorial correction of the Pentateuch after the final redaction in the time of Saul or the early days of David. As we have pointed out in our Introduction, whether such later editorial changes were actually made is another question altogether. Professor Van Gelderen himself acknowledges that his theory of a final redaction during the time of Hezekiah is purely a hypothesis. He acknowledges that newer discoveries may cast an entirely different light on some of the problems that presently seem to reside in the text.

We are convinced that besides the objections that have already been raised against the identification of Cush with Ethiopia and the interpretation of Rehoboth-Ir, we have some difficulties with the interpretation of the prominence given to Gomer among the Japhethites and Cush among the Hamitic people. The question that immediately presents itself is, "Why not take the same position with respect to the Semitic group with its prominent mention of Asshur?" Certainly Assyria played an important role during the time of Hezekiah. We need think only of the captivity of the ten tribes and the siege of Jerusalem by Sennacherib. Why, then, should we think of a purely geographic classification in this case?

With respect to the subordination of some groups under others we stand before problems of such magnitude that we do well to reserve all judgment. In general our knowledge of the lands and peoples of the ancient world is still so limited and incomplete that we cannot with any degree of certainty establish historical evidence for either an acceptance of the record of Genesis 10 or a critical rejection of it. The possibility that the Table of Nations as it was originally transcribed by the writer of the Pentateuch underwent some editorial changes at a later date we are willing to accept. Most certainly it must be acknowledged that the last word has by no means been spoken about this chapter. We can certainly believe that continued research and excavation will cast significant light on this important section of Holy Scripture.

8. *The Tower of Babel and the Confusion of Speech* (11:1-9)

We are now told how this new humanity, which originally was one people, became the many nations and tribes described in chapter 10. As we remarked earlier, the many varied groups of people were distinguished from each other by differences of language. It is not until chapter 11, however, that the occasion that produced these many languages is described.

This section is ascribed to the "J" source by those who insist on dividing the sources. This is not too surprising since the name "Jahweh" is used no less than five times in these nine verses.

Within the circle of those who are committed to this division of sources there is, however, considerable difference of opinion regarding the unity of this passage. Some argue that the record of the building of a city comes from one source, while the account of the erection of a tower is taken from another record. Their arguments run somewhat as follows.

(1) It is argued that in verse 5 we are told that the Lord "came down" to the earth and that consequently the words of the Lord recorded in verses 6 and 7 were spoken on the earth. But in verse 7 the Lord said, "Come, let us go down. . . ." This, it is claimed, is a contradiction that requires two distinct sources. It is granted that we face some difficulty with these statements. The liberal scholars have decided that this difficulty can be resolved only by ascribing this material to an original narrative that was basically polytheistic. Verse 5, then, would tell us how one of the gods was sent to earth to investigate what was going on; verse 6 would include the report of his findings in the councils of heaven; and verse 7 would then constitute the advice of this one god to his fellow gods. The original polytheistic character of this passage, it is claimed, was erased, either in the handing down of the oral tradition, or in the actual writing of the narrative, by making the messenger of the gods "the LORD" Himself. It should go without saying that such a resolution of the difficulty is purely hypothetical and has no basis in the sacred text.

But is this difficulty actually so serious? It is obvious that we are dealing with anthropomorphism in verses 5-7. As such, the sequence of events can easily be visualized as follows. The Lord, after the investigation He made in verse 5, returns to heaven, and thereupon determines, on the basis of His evaluation of mankind's activity, to go down and put an end to this project that mankind has undertaken (vv. 6 and 7). The silence of the passage about God's return to heaven is really quite inconsequential. Hebrew narration, on the one hand, is apt to repeat elements which we, in our modern, western style of writing, would not consider repeating. On the other hand, the Hebrew narrator might well omit details that we would consider to be required to make the narrative complete. Obviously, the Hebrew mind simply assumes that the reader will fill in these details.

Another solution that has been suggested is that verse 5 presents the Lord as approaching the scene to see the tower that was being built. Then, in verse 7, we are told that He actually came down to earth. This interpretation is, however, rather artificial. It is far more natural to accept the fact that verse 6 assumes that the Lord returned to heaven. One thing is sure, the entire narrative is strongly anthropomorphic, and in keeping with this a symbolical returning to heaven would be altogether natural. God is, after all, omnipresent.

(2) Another alleged basis for multiple sources is that there are two motives given for building the tower—that they might make a name for themselves, and that they might avoid being scattered over the face of the earth. It should be observed that these two statements appear in the same verse (v. 4), and that there is no real conflict between them. Actually, the one was the means for achieving the other. This becomes obvious when we translate the word "name" as "memorial." This is obviously the meaning of the word in 2 Samuel 8:13. There we are told that David received a "memorial" after he returned from battle. The word simply cannot be translated "name." He acquired this "name" in the thick of the battle, not after he returned home. So, also, this tower can be seen as a memorial monument which would, in turn, serve to keep the people together.

(3) It has also been argued that the material used for building was of two kinds, and that this suggests two distinct sources. But this is the rankest kind of distortion of the text. In both instances the same word is used in the original Hebrew and it means "brick."

(4) It has also been claimed that the two parts of verse 8 don't fit together too well, so, of course, this means two sources. We are told that if the people were scattered over the whole earth, they would not be able to continue to build the tower. But this is a childish argument. The two parts of the verse can readily be blended together. God scattered the people, and in that way He brought the construction of the tower to a halt. If these two concepts were really so difficult to relate, this would certainly have been evident to the writer and the redactor and it would have been simple to merely invert the order of the two statements.

(5) Finally, it has been argued that, since there is mention of the building of a city *and* the building of a tower, this suggests two sources. Just why the fact that two events are recorded as happening at approximately

the same time should require two distinct sources is not at all clear. On this assumption we would have to seek multiple sources for almost every historical record in the Bible, and in secular history as well.

With considerable justification Professor Bohl has described these efforts toward dividing the sources as a "superfluous exercise in clever ingenuity."

11:1 *Now the whole world had one language and a common speech.*

As we move into the record, we are immediately told that the entire humanity spoke the same language during the period immediately after the Deluge. The assumption, of course, is that this was also true before the Deluge. Here, again as in 9:19 and 10:25, we have the word "earth" to describe the population of the earth. The matter of a single language is brought into focus at the outset because the narrative that is about to unfold deals with the confusion of languages.

11:2 *As men moved eastward, they found a plain in Shinar and settled there.*

The account is actually introduced with a statement which locates the descendants of Noah in the Plain of Shinar. No mention is made of when they made this their central location. Some have claimed that they moved to this area soon after the Deluge, but there is no evidence to support this claim.

The land of Shinar is actually Babylonia (see 10:10). In this connection we probably should think primarily of southern Babylonia.

Now, the text says that the people moved "eastward." Interpreters are sharply divided about the meaning of this statement. The original actually says "from the east." Some interpreters insist that this must be taken literally and that these people moved from the east into the area of Babylonia. They then proceed to the assumption that the cradle of civilization was somewhere in mid-Asia, possibly even in India. But this is in conflict with the previous record, since the Ark came to rest on the mountains of Ararat (Gen. 8:4). This is to the north of Babylonia, rather than to the east.

The Catholic scholar, Heinisch, advanced a theory that when the people left Ararat they didn't go directly to Babylonia, but first roamed around in an easterly direction. Then, later, they came from Elam, which lay east of the Tigris, thus from the east, to Babylonia.

It must be recognized, however, that the Hebrew expression "from the east" or "out of the east" does not always, and probably not even primarily, mean "from an easterly direction." It is generally used to designate a place to the east of a given place or person in question. A good example of this use is given in Genesis 12:8, where we are told that Abraham pitched his tent toward the hills east of Bethel, "with Bethel on (from) the west and Ai on (from) the east." Here the same preposition is used. It clearly indicates that his location had Bethel to the west and Ai to the east, with his location between these two cities. At the same time it was located to the east (in an easterly direction) from Bethel.

Genesis 12:8, thus, clearly indicates that the term "out of the east," in Hebrew usage, can mean "in an easterly direction." It depends entirely on the perspective from which the direction is indicated. In the same way, in the case of the descendants of Noah, it depends on what the point of origin was from which their migration is described. There can be no doubt, thus, that the text implies that they migrated in an easterly direction from where they had been. This is the understanding of a majority of interpreters as well.

Someone can still take issue with this on the basis of Genesis 8:4. It could be argued that Babylonia lies somewhat to the south of Ararat and therefore, if it is to be geographically correct, the direction should be "southeast." But Hebrew narrators never give directions with such modern, western precision. They simply designate the primary direction and, therefore, the migration from Ararat to Babylonia is adequately described as "to the east."

In the land of Shinar, that is Babylonia, these people who had been living in a mountainous area found a fertile plain or valley. We should probably think of an area where alluvial deposits had formed a broad valley in the lower drainage of the great rivers, the Tigris and the Euphrates. It is even conceivable that such a plain had been greatly extended as a consequence of the Deluge. Here then the descendants of Noah found an ideal area for the development of their new civilization. It was an area that naturally attracted them to make this their homeland.

11:3 *They said to each other, "Come, let's make bricks and bake them thoroughly." They used brick instead of stone, and tar instead of mortar.*

But there was also another factor that attracted them to this area. It seems that there was an abundance of clay available, and this led to the making of bricks for their construction efforts. It was in this area that the making of bricks by baking available clay in ovens was first developed. This discovery is described in typical Hebrew narrative style. It is declared that the people said to each other, "Come, let's make bricks and bake them thoroughly.'' Here then a new material for constructing homes and public buildings was developed. It would appear that the antideluvian people used only natural stone for erecting their buildings. The developing civilization in the Plain of Shinar was characterized by the discovery of making bricks.

In order to fasten these bricks to each other, and thus erect firm buildings, still another substance was needed to serve as mortar. Once again, the Plain of Shinar provided such a substance in a pitch-like asphalt that was discovered there. This was a dark-brown substance, found near the surface, as a by-product of the subterranean oil deposits. This asphalt, then, was used as mortar to hold the bricks together. Thus a whole new method of erecting buildings was developed.

11:4 *Then they said, ''Come, let us build ourselves a city, with a tower that reaches to the heavens, so that we may make a name for ourselves and not be scattered over the face of the whole earth.''*

We are now told about the plan conceived by the people to build a city and a tower. In this way they hoped to establish a great monument that would keep the populace from scattering over the entire face of the earth. We need not read this as though this decision was made as soon as the successful making of bricks was discovered. It should, rather, be considered as a natural development as they gradually began to recognize and take pride in their skill in erecting substantial buildings.

It should also be noted that the scattering that they determined to avoid had become a real possibility. This suggests, in turn, that the population had increased to such an extent that their rural life style was putting pressure on the space available in the Plain of Shinar.

Thus the narrative moves along through various time periods. Verse 2 describes the time when the Deluge had been relegated to the past and civilization began to move forward again. Verse 3 points to a later time, since it would be difficult to conceive of the discovery of the process of making bricks as taking place immediately after the Deluge. This development came after the people had migrated to and settled in the Plain of Shinar. Verse 4 transports us to an even later time when the population had increased considerably and their proficiency in erecting buildings had been further developed.

The expression concerning the tower that it would ''reach to heaven'' raises the question whether this must be taken literally or figuratively. Even if the people of that time thought of it as a literal possibility, it probably should be seen as a determination to build a tower of great height, probably equal to the height of the distant mountains. There certainly is no evidence here that the people actually intended to "storm the gates of heaven." Their purpose is clearly expressed in that they wanted a central point of reference that could be seen by all. This would then serve to point the way back to the center of their civilization, no matter how far they might have wandered from that point. It was an obvious determination to avoid being scattered widely over the earth.

This purpose was in conflict with God's plan for mankind. At the time of creation God had specifically ordered that humanity was to be fruitful and "fill the earth." This was repeated at the time they left the ark (Gen. 1:28; 9:1). Mankind was not to congregate in one small area, such as the Plain of Shinar, but was to spread over the whole earth and fill it. They now had determined to disobey this order and to crowd into one place. With conscious intent they decided to reject the purpose of God's blessing. And since they had now discovered a means for achieving their God-defying intention, they ventured forth on their program of achieving their own desires and thereby of nullifying God's expressed command.

11:5 *But the LORD came down to see the city and the tower that the men were building.*

The activity of humanity, of course, did not escape God's all-knowing attention. This is stated in a human form of speech. We are told that "the LORD came down to see" what mankind was doing. Such anthropomorphisms certainly do not imply a limited, human concept of God. It is no more than a mode of speaking about God and His activities. What we are told, then, in this "God came down to see," is that God was fully aware of what mankind was about.

It should be noted that the expression, "that the men were building," can also be read, "that the men had built." Normally the Hebrew form would be so read and many interpreters render it thus. The form used here indicates completed action. Verse 8, however, suggests that the work was still far from completed. God's intervention prevented it from being finished. This raises the question about the verb form in verse 5 which normally denotes completed action. It is obvious that we are dealing here with a subtle distinction in Hebrew usage which our language cannot express. What the inspired writer is saying is that, when God considered what mankind was doing, this in itself sealed its termination. Men were still working busily, full of enthusiasm for their unholy plan, but when God took account of what was going on, it was as good as ended. This, then, explains the use of a verb form denoting completed action, even while the project was still continuing.

11:6, 7 *The LORD said, "If as one people speaking the same language they have begun to do this, then nothing they plan to do will be impossible for them. Come, let us go down and confuse their language so they will not understand each other."*

Over against man's efforts to thwart God's purposes, God now responds with a manifestation of His almighty power whereby He achieves His goal and at the same time blasts man's efforts into ruins (cf. Ps. 2:4). The key to this unholy venture on the part of humanity lay in their common language. The fact that they all spoke one language enabled them to collaborate in their plans and to cooperate in their activities. The unity of language held them together in one place and in a common effort. Once that unity of language was broken, all of man's boasted schemes would be defused in one swoop. And so the Lord confused their speech. Suddenly they could no longer communicate with each other. Immediately their whole plan lay in a shambles.

The Lord could not allow humanity to continue in the course they had set for themselves. It was not only a matter of preventing mankind from thwarting His purpose that they should fill the earth. It was also a matter of halting the increasing pride and boldness of mankind, should their God-defying effort prove successful. Had this not been checked, mankind would have pursued this course further and further to their own downfall and destruction. Thus God's action in halting this rebellious effort was not only a matter of punishment, but it was also an act of mercy. God prevented mankind from pursuing a self-destructive course of rebellion against their creator.

"Let us go down" is also anthropomorphic. God is omnipresent and does not have to go to a certain location in order to carry on an activity there. The meaning is simply that God took action at that place where mankind had congregated and developed their bold schemes. (See our comment regarding this under v. 5.) With respect to the use of the plural form, "let *us*," see our discussion of the plural usage for the being of God under 1:26 and 3:22. Here, again, we have a reference to the Trinity, in that God is revealed as existing in a plurality in unity.

11:8 *So the LORD scattered them from there over all the earth, and they stopped building the city.*

By confusing their speech God scattered mankind from their central location in the Plain of Shinar. Thus, God's decree that the earth should be filled was carried out. The ambitious construction program undertaken by humanity remained unfinished.

11:9 *That is why it was called Babel—because there the* LORD *confused the language of the whole world. From there the* LORD *scattered them over the face of the whole earth.*

A comment about the name "Babel" is added in this verse. This has caused a veritable flood of discussion, much of it critical of the Holy Scriptures. Many have argued that here is an instance of error in the Scripture since it ascribes a mistaken meaning to a word. The argument goes something like this. "Babel" should actually read "babylon" which means "the gate of god," and thus the word means something different from the meaning given in Scripture. But considerable caution should be exercised when making dogmatic statements about the exact meaning of ancient words. It is not at all certain that the name "Babel" should actually read "Babylon." It is possible that this was a kind of popular etymology that had no connection with the true meaning of the word used. It should be observed, for instance, that in the Babylonian language there is a word that appears as "babal" that means "scattered." It is possible that this could be the origin of the term "Babel" in this passage. Another reasonable possibility would be that the word originated from the Hebrew verb *bālal,* which means "to confuse."

But all of this is really unimportant. It may well be questioned whether the biblical text actually means to say anything about the etymology of the word "Babel." A careful reading of the text indicates only that the name of the city was "Babel," and that this was a suitable name because that was where the Lord confused the language of mankind. That the Hebrew word *balal* happens to mean "confuse," still does not prove that the author is establishing an etymological connection here. It could very well be a typical Hebrew play on words, so common in Hebrew narrative style. It would then be similar to the play on words in which Abigail indulged (1 Sam. 25:25). In referring to her husband Nabal, she singles out a Hebrew word that has the same sound but which actually means "fool." So she says, "He is just like his name—his name is 'fool' and 'folly' goes with him." But this certainly does not imply that the name Nabal meant "fool." Certainly no father would name his son "fool." Abigail simply indulged in a subtle play on words in connection with the sound of the name of her husband. In our view, that is precisely what the writer of Genesis does with respect to the name of the city of Babel. The source of that name is not at issue here. The writer simply plays on that name and says that this name was suitable since it was there that the Lord "confused" mankind's speech. To now press this play on words into a technical etymological study on the origin of the word "Babel" is wholly facetious.

That the narrative recounted here by the inspired writer is presented as history is beyond question. Exegetically it must be agreed that the intent of the author was to describe an actual event. Even so, there are many interpreters who deny the historicity of the building of the tower and the confusion of languages. They accept it only as a myth or a saga. Some of these scholars will admit that there is some historical fact underlying the narrative. But there are few who are willing to accept the account as given in Scripture as historical reality. It can be seen, in this connection, that the point of view from which one approaches the Bible is of utmost importance. When one acknowledges the Scriptures to be the very word of God in its entirety, then everything that is contained in the Scripture is accepted without any doubts. Then the narrative of the Tower of Babel and the confusion of speech can also be readily accepted as describing actual events. When, on the other hand, one does not accept the divine authority of Scripture, the way is opened for all kinds of critical questions regarding the truth of that which is recorded.

It is of considerable interest that many interpreters have emphasized the extensive ruins of enormous building projects that have been discovered in the area of Babel. There are especially two sites that have been considered to be possible ruins of the Tower of Babel.

The first site is an old tower, Eoeriminanki, at the Nebo temple Ezida in Borsippa. This city is located on the west bank of the Euphrates, a short distance to the southwest of ancient Babel. This structure, which was built of brick and used asphalt for mortar, still is some seven stories high. Regarding this tower the well-known King Nebuchadnezzar said that it had been started by an earlier king and brought to a height of 42 cubits. But it had never been completed. Later it had fallen into ruins and then he, Nebuchadnezzar, restored it and installed the pinnacle that had previously been lacking. This was accepted as the Tower of Babel by the Jewish tradition. The well-known historian, Flavius Josephus, ascribes the original construction to Nimrod. As a result, even today these ruins, which still reach a height of 46 meters (about 151 feet), bear the name "Birs Nimrod."

Another site that has been ascribed to this structure, and probably with greater justification, is the tower of Etemenanki, of the Temple of Marduk, Esagila, in Babel itself. This is in the northern section of the city on the eastern bank of the Euphrates. Regarding this tower there is also a Babylonian tradition that its base was constructed in ancient times but that its top was never completed. Several kings later added to this tower. It was finally completed during the reigns of Nabopolasser and his son Nebuchadnezzar. Xerxes destroyed it and Alexander the Great had the debris cleaned up so that it could be rebuilt. Alexander, however, died before the reconstruction of the tower was accomplished. Today the ruins of the tower can still be seen as they were left by Alexander's workmen, but nothing remains of the original spectacular structure.

It is difficult to determine which of these two sites actually marks the location of the original Tower of Babel. It is possible that it may have been neither of these two sites, and that the ruins of the original Tower of Babel can no longer be identified. Moreover, this is of no great consequence. The acceptability of the biblical narrative certainly does not depend on being able to identify, in our day, the ruins of this ancient structure.

One other point that is brought into consideration in this connection is the extent of the tradition of a similar event among other peoples. It is generally agreed that such a tradition does not appear among the Babylonians. Among some other peoples there are traditions that have some similarity to the Genesis narrative, but usually these similarities are found in only one element of the account.

The saga that comes closest to the biblical narrative is found in India. There we find a tradition about a huge tree by which people hoped to climb into heaven. However, this tree was smashed by the gods and its branches were scattered over the whole earth. The Greeks had a myth about two brothers who were giants. They planned to stack several mountains on top of each other and in this way to storm heaven. They were struck down by the chief god. The Greeks also had a tradition that all peoples at one time had one language. Later the languages were confused and this explains the variety of languages on the earth. Among the Greeks there was, however, no connection between the two narratives.

The Persians ascribe the multiplicity of languages to the evil god Ahriman, who taught the people thirty different languages and in this way brought about a conflict and disunity among people. There is no reference here to a building effort, except that this took place during the reign of a king who was renowned as a builder of cities.

There are also some traditions that come closer to the biblical narrative but these have obviously been influenced by Jewish and Christian accounts. Such an account is found in Armenian writings which speak of a generation of giants who proposed to build a high tower. But a violent wind destroyed the structure and also cast strange words among the people which caused disunity and confusion. This saga appears first in the writings of the Armenian historian, Moses of Chorene, in the 5th century A.D. It is generally accepted that it was influenced by the spread of the biblical narrative by the Jewish dispersion. The presentation about a violent wind that destroyed a tower is also found earlier in the Book of Jubilees 10:26.

The same thing is true of a saga found in Korea. According to this account, people originally had one language, but at the time of the building of a tower by which they tried to reach heaven, their language was confused. This saga, however, first appears in the writings of a monk-like sect of the 17th century A.D. It was obviously influenced by Christian missionaries who brought the Bible to Korea before that time.

We cannot be equally certain about the origins of some of the traditions in Central America. In Mexico a saga was discovered about the building of a tower by a giant named Xelhuaz, after the Deluge. In this case the gods cast down fire on the tower. There the confusion of speech appears as follows. At the time of the Deluge only one man, Coxcox, was spared. All of his children were mute, but they were taught by a dove to speak. They learned to speak so differently, however, that they could not understand each other. As a consequence they scattered in different directions. From Yucatan comes the saga about a grandson of the only survivor of the Deluge who was present at the building of an enormous house which, on orders from his grandfather, would reach from earth to heaven. In the area where the great house was built, each people would be given their own language. Whether these are original, ancient folk traditions or later adaptations of Christian and biblical influences cannot be definitely determined. The latter, however, remains a real possibility. We would do well, in the light of the evidence, not to conclude too hastily that there is a common tradition among other peoples regarding the Tower of Babel and the confusion of speech, similar to the common tradition regarding the Deluge. It is possible that there are some minor traces of such a common tradition but more than that cannot be established.

A question of far greater importance, in this connection, is whether the science of linguistics supports or contests the record of Genesis 11:1-9. It has been pointed out, for instance, that new languages develop only over long periods of time. Naturally, this concept would call the Genesis account into serious question. It should be remembered, however, that the Genesis account does not pretend to describe the normal development of a new language in a given part of the world. It deals, rather, with a miraculous intervention on the part of God by which, at one moment, God established what later could have continued to develop through more normal processes.

Now, it can be insisted that some do not believe in such a miraculous intervention on God's part. But, that such an act of God in confusing man's speech is impossible cannot be determined by scientific evidence. Roman Catholic scholars have generally yielded to this argument that new languages can develop only over long periods of time. They, then, interpose a long space of time between verses 7 and 8, during which the descendants of Noah spread out from the Plain of Shinar in different groups. Each of these groups, then, in the course of time supposedly developed its own language. But this approach clearly reverses the order of the biblical narrative, which specifies that the confusion of speech took place first and that this in turn caused the scattering of the various groups.

A more serious objection that has been raised against the Genesis record of the confusion of speech is that the original unity of all languages cannot be substantiated. The differences between languages are so great that many are convinced it is unthinkable that all of these languages should originally have stemmed from one source. Even conservative Bible scholars, who accept the biblical record, have acknowledged that the study of linguistics in the ancient languages does not substantiate the fact that all languages originally came from a common language. However, they also insist that these studies do not disprove this either. In other words, our acceptance of the historical reality of one original language is not dependent on linguistic studies but rests solely on the authority of Scripture itself.

Even so, although such a venture has not proved completely successful, there have been scholars from time to time who, on the basis of comparative linguistic studies, have produced some significant evidence to support the theory that all languages may well have sprung from one original source language. Many interesting discoveries have been made in this regard.

A famous Assyriologist made the amazing discovery that there is a clear relationship between the languages of some of the native people in Central and South America and some of the Islands, on the one hand, and the ancient Sumerian and Egyptian languages, on the other. This scholar, who formerly had considered the account in Genesis 11:1–9 to be no more than a myth, came to the conclusion that the biblical narrative is more credible than had been supposed. One significant factor in this connection is that the Sumerian language is the oldest known language. Further, it was this language that was spoken in ancient times in the plain of the Tigris and Euphrates Rivers. We do not mean to imply that the original language of mankind was Sumerian, but it certainly is significant that it was precisely this language with which this relationship was discovered. As far as our present understanding goes, Sumerian would be the most apt to reveal certain root words from which the words in other languages could have developed. The fact that it was there that a relationship was discovered with languages spoken by native peoples on the other side of the world is certainly of more than passing interest.

Several Roman Catholic scholars hold that the confusion of languages affected only part of humanity, as, for instance, the Semitic people or possibly even only part of those. They arrive at this conclusion on much the same basis as is used to support the theory that the Deluge covered only part of the earth. The term, "the whole world" in verses 1 and 9 referred, then, only to the population of a limited area. But this interpretation does not do justice to the biblical narrative regarding the Tower of Babel and the confusion of languages. Even if the Deluge did submerge only part of the earth with water, the Scripture clearly states that *all* human beings, with the exception only of Noah and his family, were destroyed. Thus, when after the Deluge it refers to "the whole world," this must refer to the entire new humanity which developed from the descendants of Noah.

9. *From Shem to Abram* (11:10–26)

11:10–26 *This is the account of Shem.*

Two years after the flood, when Shem was 100 years old, he became the father of Arphaxad. And after he became the father of Arphaxad, Shem lived 500 years and had other sons and daughters.

When Arphaxad had lived 35 years, he became the father of Shelah. And after he became the father of Shelah, Arphaxad lived 403 years and had other sons and daughters.

When Shelah had lived 30 years, he became the father of Eber. And after he became the father of Eber, Shelah lived 403 years and had other sons and daughters.

When Eber had lived 34 years, he became the father of Peleg. And after he became the father of Peleg, Eber lived 430 years and had other sons and daughters.

When Peleg had lived 30 years, he became the father of Reu. And after he became the father of Reu, Peleg lived 209 years and had other sons and daughters.

When Reu had lived 32 years, he became the father of Serug. And after he became the father of Serug, Reu lived 207 years and had other sons and daughters.

When Serug had lived 30 years, he became the father of Nahor. And after he became the father of Nahor, Serug lived 200 years and had other sons and daughters.

When Nahor had lived 29 years, he became the father of Terah. And after he became the father of Terah, Nahor lived 119 years and had other sons and daughters.

After Terah had lived 70 years, he became the father of Abram, Nahor and Haran.

This section manifests much similarity to the register of the descendants of Adam in chapter 5. Consequently, those who divide the sources ascribe this section, as chapter 5, to "P." The main difference between the two lists is that chapter 11 does not give the total life span. This can, of course, be readily calculated by adding the numbers that are given.

In seeking an explanation for this omission it has been argued that "P" is characterized by a strict, consistent scheme of details. It is then argued that the omission of some of these details where would imply that "P" considered this family tree to be of less importance than the one listed in chapter 5. This conclusion is not only without foundation but it is also in conflict with the entire purpose of this genealogy. The sole purpose of this present listing is to point out the line that leads to Abraham, the father of the people of Israel. This passage clearly indicates that this claim for uniformity in "P" is not as well established as the critics would like to believe.

It has also been pointed out that here there are only 9 generations from Shem to Terah, while there were 10 generations from Adam to Noah. It is then argued that including 10 generations must be normative and therefore this present list must also be stretched to 10. Some have argued that the original genealogy ran from Noah to Terah. Some have counted Abram as number 10. Some have followed the Septuagint and have inserted Cainan between Arphaxad and Shelah. But the whole assumption that this genealogy must total 10 generations is facetious. If Shem, Ham, and Japheth are included in chapter 5, that list actually includes 11. Moreover, the genealogy in the Septuagint certainly is not original since it gives the same figures for Cainan as those for Shelah.

We want to repeat here what we observed in our Introduction to chapter 5. The occurrence of lists of generations is no argument in favor of a specific "source." It only indicates that the redactor of the Pentateuch had a certain predilection for such lists. We also point out again that these genealogies undoubtedly were based on ancient written records that were available when the Pentateuch was written. This is especially obvious in chapter 5, where the redactor took over such a document with title and all. Even though this is not quite as evident here in chapter 11, there is no reason to doubt that here also the author took over data from a written tradition that was available to him. This would explain both the similarities and the differences between these two chapters. Simply put, the author used two different sources.

This genealogy begins with a heading, "This is the account of Shem." It is obvious that this is not intended to be a repetition of 10:21–31. The end of this list makes it clear that the author of this record intends to point out how this genealogy of Shem leads to Abram. The next section of the book deals with the history of Abram and here the stage is set for that history.

How the statement, ''Two years after the flood, when Shem was 100 years old, he became the father of Arphaxad'' is to be harmonized with what is stated in 5:32 and 7:6, has been discussed in our treatment of 5:32. We refer you to that discussion. Undoubtedly the names that are given in this register of generations are intended to be personal names. This is evident from the constant repetition of their ages when their sons were born and the number of years they lived after that. Some of these names, however, such as Arphaxad and Eber, also were names of tribes and nations.

Efforts have been made to explain each of these names. This has been somewhat less than successful, however. It has been suggested that Shelah could refer to Methuselah (5:25); that Reu could be a shortened form of Reuel, Moses' father-in-law (Exod. 2:18) and means ''friend of God''; that Nahor could be tied in with Akkadian personal names such as Nachiri and Nachuru; that Terah could be related to Akkadian names such as Tarkonazi and Tarkoedaraba; and that Serug could be connected with the Akkadian Saroegi, the name of a district in northern Syria near the city of Haran. All of this is, however, completely uncertain. The only conclusion that has good grounds is the interpretation of the name Peleg as ''divided'' (see our interpretation of 10:25).

That it was the author's intent to give a complete list of persons in precise genealogical succession from Shem to Abram must be emphatically denied. The scriptural objections to such an interpretation have been discussed in our introduction to chapter 6, and our interpretation of 9:28–29. At the same time, we should point out that the numbers given in the Samaritan Pentateuch and in the Septuagint, just as was the case in chapter 5, differ from those in the Hebrew text. In this case both of these texts arrive at a considerably higher total. The chart below gives a clear overview of these differences.

	HEBREW TEXT		SEPTUAGINT		SAMARITAN PENTATEUCH	
	Age when son was born	Remaining years of life	Age when son was born	Remaining years of life	Age when son was born	Remaining years of life
Shem	100	500	100	500	100	500
Arphaxad	35	403	135	430	135	303
Cainan			130	330		

Genesis 11:10–26

	HEBREW TEXT		SEPTUAGINT		SAMARITAN PENTATEUCH	
	Age when son was born	Remaining years of life	Age when son was born	Remaining years of life	Age when son was born	Remaining years of life
Shelah	30	403	130	330	130	303
Eber	34	430	134	370	134	270
Peleg	30	209	130	209	130	109
Reu	32	207	132	207	132	107
Serug	30	200	130	200	130	100
Nahor	29	119	79	129	79	69
Terah	70	135	70	135	70	75

It is evident that the age at which a son is born, except for Shem and Terah, where they are the same as those in the Hebrew text, is consistently increased by 100, in the case of Nahor by 50. We need not discuss the other differences. It is obvious, however, that the number of years which separate Abram from the Deluge becomes significantly larger. It is increased from 292 to 942 years. The Septuagint, moreover, adds another 130 years by inserting Cainan, and thus arrives at a total of 1072 years.

Various reasons could be advanced for holding that the Hebrew text has the original numbers and that these have been altered in the Samaritan Pentateuch and the Septuagint, rather than the reverse. It is worthy of note that it is the age at which the son is conceived that is systematically raised, in one case by 100, and in the other by 50. It should also be noted that the Samaritan Pentateuch and the Septuagint agree in this, even though they have surprising differences in other areas. One cannot help but wonder whether these figures were arbitrarily raised because a span of 292 years from the Deluge to Abram was obviously too short. This was, then, an attempt, be it somewhat awkward, to remove this difficulty. The attempt was, however, quite unsatisfactory and seems completely arbitrary.

There is a far better way of resolving this difficulty. If we assume that these genealogies were not intended to be complete but simply were summary reviews which often skipped over one or more generations, there really is no problem. There is ample support for such an assumption in other parts of Scripture. Consequently it should be noted that using the genealogies to measure extended time spans is an exercise in futility.

In Ezra 7:1–5 we are given the genealogy of the priest and scribe named

Ezra. His ancestors are traced back to Aaron. This covers about 1000 years. But only 16 generations are listed and this is far too few to cover such a long period. There are, moreover, other discrepancies in Ezra's genealogy. Ezra is called the son of Seraiah. But this Seraiah was high priest when Jerusalem was destroyed by the Chaldeans in the year 586 B.C., which was approximately 150 years before Ezra came on the scene (see 2 Kings 25:18). From 1 Chronicles 6:14–15 we learn that Seraiah's son was named Jehozadak, but he is not even mentioned in Ezra's genealogy. If we compare Ezra 7:1–5 with 1 Chronicles 6:3–15, we discover that the latter passage mentions six names between Azariah and Meraioth that are not included in the Ezra list.

Another example in Scripture is the genealogy of our Savior, Jesus Christ, in Matthew 1:1–16. There we find at least two places where names have been omitted. In verse 8, between Joram and Uzziah, the names of the well-known kings Ahaziah, Joash, and Amaziah are omitted. Between Zerubbabel and Jesus several surprising omissions occur. Luke includes no less than nine additional names at this point alone.

It should be completely obvious, then, that it is not at all uncommon for biblical genealogies to be incomplete. The same thing is obviously true of the genealogy in our passage and therefore the time from Shem to Abram cannot be fixed on this basis.

It has been objected that such an assumption seems to imply that these records in Scripture are actually in error when they state that X was so old when he conceived Y and Y was so old when he conceived Z, etc. If we allow for gaps we are thereby declaring that these statements are in error.

In spite of this objection, the assumption made above is the only acceptable solution to the problems presented by the genealogies. All we can conclude is that the genealogy informs us only that X was so old when he conceived a son from whom Y was a direct descendant. How many generations are omitted and just at what points in the list they are omitted cannot be determined with any degree of accuracy. It should be recognized that even at the outset the list was obviously not complete. In the days of Peleg, the fourth generation from Shem—a little more than a century after the Deluge—the confusion of speech took place (10:25). But it is obviously improbable that mankind could have developed so rapidly in such a short space of time. A far longer period of time would be required to make the events recorded in Genesis 11:1–9 credible.

In summary, let it be said that the genealogies of Scripture were not given for the purpose of establishing accurate dates for specific historical events. Any attempt to use these passages for that purpose is doomed to failure and erroneous conclusions.

Part Two

The History of the Chosen People From the Call of Abram to the Death of Joseph (11:27–50:26)

1. *The Call of Abram* (11:27–12:9)

There is a sharp line of demarcation between Genesis 11:26 and 11:27. Genesis 1:1 to 11:26 gives us the history of humanity as a whole. Genesis 11:27 begins the history of a single family, chosen by God to receive the revelation of redemption. The universalism of the first period now gives way to the particularism which continues from this point to the close of the Old Testament.

In the first section of this second main division of the book, Genesis 11:27–12:9, the call of Abram is recorded. We are told about Abram's obedience to that call, which, in turn, brought him and his family into Canaan as a family of nomads.

This places before us the question of where Abram was residing when he received this call. According to 12:4 it appears as though this took place in Haran. But in Acts 7:2–3, Stephen specifically says, "The God of Glory appeared to our father Abram while he was still in Mesopotamia, before he lived in Haran. 'Leave your country and your people,' God said, 'and go to the land I will show you.'"

Moreover, in Genesis 15:7 God Himself says to Abram, "I am the LORD, who brought you out of Ur of the Chaldeans to give you this land. . . ." And in Nehemiah 9:7 we read, "You are the LORD God, who chose Abram and brought him out of Ur of the Chaldeans."

For this reason, some translators have rendered Genesis 12:1, "The

LORD *had* said to Abram.'' Giving this verb the pluperfect tense, which designates completed action in the past, is grammatically permissible. Even so, reading the verb as a simple past tense would appear to be a more natural reading.

It has further been pointed out that the manner in which 12:4–6 speaks of Abram's departure from Haran gives the impression that this must be seen as the consequence of God's call as it is given in 12:1. Besides, the call of God emphasizes the fact that Abram should leave not only his land and people, but also his ''father's household.'' It would be difficult to think of Abram leaving his ''father's household'' when he left Ur of the Chaldeans since his father, Terah, and his family came with him.

It should be noted that Stephen, in Acts 7, does not mention departing from his ''father's household,'' but only from his ''country and people.'' It would seem, then, that we should think of Abram's call as coming in two stages. First, he was called by God to leave ''his country and people'' in Ur of the Chaldeans. This he did when Terah's entire family moved from Ur to Haran. Then, later, he was called in Haran to leave his land and people and also his ''father's household.'' Stephen speaks of that first call. Genesis 12:1–3 describes the second. Then in Genesis 15:7 and Nehemiah 9:7 both are combined as one event.

Naturally, those who divide the sources give this matter a far different interpretation. They claim that this section, Genesis 11:27–12:9, was a mixture of pieces taken from both ''J'' and ''P.'' They ascribe 11:28–30; 12:1–4a, and 6–8 (9) to ''J.'' A few ascribe 12:9 to the redactor. Then 11:27, 31–32, and 12:4b and 5 are ascribed to ''P.'' Their argument goes as follows. There are, of course, certain distinguishing words that the critics normally place in one or other source. (See our Introduction to this commentary for our evaluation of this procedure.) They also call on the use of the name of God—''Jahweh''—as evidence, in 12:1, 4, 7–8. Further, it is claimed that the presence of lists of numbers and names is characteristic of ''P.'' None of these arguments needs further discussion at this point.

What does warrant our attention, however, is that these scholars insist that ''P'' gives Ur of the Chaldeans as Abram's home city, while ''J'' does not name such a city. This supposedly implies that ''J'' considered Abram's home city to be Haran. In reply to this argument, we point out that Ur is also mentioned in 15:7 and this passage is generally ascribed to ''J,'' because the name ''Jahweh'' appears there in 15:1, 2, 4, 6, 7, 8. To avoid this difficulty the critics claim that 15:7 must have been a later interpolation. Furthermore, the name Ur also appears in 11:28, which is also a ''J'' passage. But, it is claimed, there the name must have been inserted later.

All of this manipulation of the text of Scripture indicates how arbitrary this theory of two sources for this narrative really is. This is even recognized by some of the scholars who hold to the theory but acknowledge that, in this passage, the two sources cannot be consistently distinguished. Would it then not be far more responsible to simply drop the whole hypothesis of two sources in a passage such as this?

Biblical scholars have devoted considerable discussion to the question of whether Abram (and the other patriarchs—Isaac and Jacob) should be considered to be a historical person or not. Naturally, the issue is far different in this case than it was in the history presented in Genesis 1–11. Even if it is assumed that the first 11 chapters are myths, similar to those in Babylonia and Egypt and other countries, Genesis 12–50 obviously demands an altogether different viewpoint. To be sure, there are a few scholars who see the narratives of this section of Genesis as having no historical reality but as the product of mere poetic imagination. Some have considered the patriarchs to be no more than personifications of certain tribes, as mythological figures, and even as gods that were degenerated to the level of men.

Generally, however, even the liberal scholars have acknowledged the fact that a historical core must be recognized in these narratives. This core, they insist, has been greatly embellished by legendary elements. It is claimed that the actual historical facts have been idealized. Even so, there is a growing acknowledgment that there is a basic narrative here which must be accepted as actual history.

There certainly is much evidence for the historicity of this pre-Mosaic material. The keen historical sensitivity of the people of Israel, for instance, dictates that they would never base their national roots on material that could not be historically substantiated. They could just as well have begun their national history with the period of Moses and the conquest of Canaan. The very fact that the people of Israel, to this day, root their history so firmly in this pre-Mosaic period establishes the historicity of this material beyond all question or reasonable doubt.

It should be obvious, also, that if the narratives about the patriarchs were mere artful inventions, their content would have been far more embellished and idealized. Many of the details included in the narratives give them an unmistakable quality of historicity. Several of these will be pointed out as we treat them in the course of our interpretation. Mention could be made of the whole historical background in which the account of the patriarchs is set. There is complete accord between the events recorded in the lives of the patriarchs and the historical situation that is known to have existed during that period in history. We could also point to their names, which have a definite quality of genuineness rather than of artful invention.

Of course, we do not need these arguments to accept the historicity of Genesis 12-50 without reservations. These chapters are, without any question, part of the inspired Holy Scriptures, God's authoritative Word. As such, they are trustworthy and infallible in their entirety, in every detail. Even so, some of the arguments to which we have pointed above may have some value, especially in responding to those who deny the historicity of this biblical material.

It probably should be added here that accepting the historicity of the entire biblical narrative does not imply that we must ascribe the written record of these events to the patriarchs themselves or to one of their contemporaries. It is altogether possible, and even highly probable, that oral tradition preserved the many details of these events for a long time. The oral tradition could then have been put into writing at a later time, probably during the sojourn in Egypt. These oral and written records were then incorporated into the Book of Genesis by the inspired author, under the guidance of the Holy Spirit, to the extent that the heavenly Author deemed necessary.

Fixing the exact time in which this history of Abram took place presents some real difficulties. We have already referred to this at the close of our discussion on the Deluge (6:1-9:17). However, when Abram is dated, as is often done, at about 2000 B.C. this is not too far from being correct.

According to the Old Testament itself, there was a period of 480 years between the Exodus from Egypt and the building of the temple (1 Kings 6:1). Then there was a span of 430 years during which Israel stayed in Egypt (Exod. 12:40). To this we must add 130 years in the life of Jacob before his family moved to Egypt (Gen. 47:9), 60 years in the life of Isaac before his twin sons were born (Gen. 25:26), and 100 years in the life of Abram before the promised son, Isaac, was born (Gen. 21:5). Adding all of these figures together we arrive at a period of 1200 years that had lapsed between the birth of Abram and the building of the temple. This latter event can be accurately dated since it took place in the third year of Solomon's reign, which has been fixed as the year 969 B.C. (See the commentary in this series by Van Gelderen on 1 Kings 6:1.) This would then place the birth of Abram in the year 2169 B.C., and the year of his call from Haran in 2094 B.C. (Gen. 12:4).

Now this arrangement is not without some real difficulties that we should carefully consider. In the first place, there is other chronological data in the Old Testament that is difficult to harmonize with the 480-year figure of 1 Kings 6:1. When we add up the periods of oppression and deliverance that are recorded in the Book of Judges, we already arrive at a total of 410 years. If we add to this the 40 years of wilderness wanderings, the time needed for Joshua and his armies to conquer Canaan, the period of Samuel and Saul, and the 40 years of David's reign, we obviously arrive at a total of far more than 480 years before Solomon came to the throne. This difficulty cannot be resolved by juggling the given data or by rounding out numbers. One explanation that is plausible, however, is that it is possible that the periods of oppression and deliverance in the Book of Judges overlapped, with more than one of these events taking place simultaneously in different parts of the country.

A second difficulty is that Egyptian records make it hard to establish the date of the Exodus. Most scholars hold that this took place during the reign of Pharaoh Meren-Ptah (1234–1225 B.C.). But if this was the case the time span between the Exodus and the building of the temple would be reduced to a mere 260 years, which is far too short. It is better to think of the reign of Pharaoh Amenophis II (1447–1421 B.C.), which would then harmonize with the 480 years of 1 Kings 6:1.

A third difficulty is presented in Exodus 12:40. Paul says in Galatians 3:17 that the Law was given 430 years after the covenant with Abram. Thus he seems to include the period of the patriarchs, the entire sojourn in Egypt, and the first stage of the Exodus in that 430 years. But the Septuagint and the Samaritan Pentateuch offer a reading of Exodus 12:40 that also includes this entire period. It is rather tempting to accept this reading since this would also make the reference in Genesis 15:16, that the fourth generation would return to Canaan, more acceptable, especially if it is related to Exodus 6:15, 17, 19, and Numbers 26:59. This is what Greydanus does in his commentary on Galatians.

We are convinced, however, that this does not resolve our difficulty, since this reading permits only 215 years for Israel's stay in Egypt. This is obviously too short a time to allow for the amazing growth of Jacob's family into a great nation with a fighting force of 600,000 men (see Exod. 12:37). How we will deal with Genesis 15:16 and the other passages mentioned above will be taken up when we discuss the passages in question in the course of this commentary. It cannot be denied that Genesis 15:13 specifically mentions a stay in Egypt of 400 years. This can be accepted as a rounding off of the 430 years referred to in Exodus 12:40. It is interesting that the Septuagint uses the figure 435 years in the latter passage. Although this difference is rather inconsequential it does make it questionable whether Paul quoted from the Septuagint in this instance, as he often does in his quotations from the Old Testament. The difficulty really lies with an interpretation of Galatians 3:17, and that is not our main concern here. No satisfactory solution has as yet been offered, to our knowledge.

The fourth and last problem we face with dating Abraham is that we are not able to identify his contemporaries with certainty. We would have a very helpful indication of Abram's date, for instance, if we could positively identify the kings that are mentioned in Genesis 14:1, with evidence from secular history. But this has not been the case. It is not at all sure, for instance, that Amraphel, king of Shinar, is the same as Hammurabi of Babylon, as has often been suggested. Modern research has discovered that Hammurabi must be dated considerably later than was formerly supposed, probably as late as 1700 B.C.

After considering all of the data available to us, we have concluded that Abram lived approximately 2000 B.C. No specific date can be set on the basis of the evidence we have.

11:27, 28 *This is the account of Terah.*
Terah became the father of Abram, Nahor and Haran. And Haran became the father of Lot. While his father Terah was still alive, Haran died in Ur of the Chaldeans, in the land of his birth.

The statement that introduces this new section in the Book of Genesis is, "This is the account of Terah." This forms a heading for what follows. As the narrative proceeds, however, little is said about Terah. It actually is the story of Terah's son, Abram. We might well ask why the statement does not read, "This is the account of Abram." All we can say, in reply, is that this is not really a personal history of Abram that unfolds in the material before us. It is actually the history of God's chosen people, and this history begins with Terah and his family leaving their country and people.

After the heading, the three sons of Terah are again mentioned (see 11:26). Whether the order in which their names appear is any indication of their ages is completely uncertain, as it was in the case of the three sons of Noah. Some have concluded that Haran must be the oldest because Nahor married one of his daughters. This is not at all conclusive, however, since later we read that Abram's son Isaac married a granddaughter of Nahor. Some have even suggested that the three sons were triplets, but there is no more basis for that than there was for the same theory with respect to the sons of Noah.

Beyond this we are given few details about the family of Terah. We are told that his son Haran had a son named Lot. We are also told that Haran died at a comparatively young age, before the family moved from Ur of the Chaldeans.

The city of Ur was of some importance long before Babel became prominent. The ruins of this ancient city have been discovered in the sand hills of el-Muqayyar. This is located about half way between Bagdad and the Persian Gulf, a few hours southwest of the Euphrates River. The discoveries that were made there during the 1920s have produced much information about this ancient city, which dates back as far as 3700 B.C.

11:29, 30 *Abram and Nahor both married. The name of Abram's wife was Sarai, and the name of Nahor's wife was Milcah; she was the daughter of Haran, the father of both Milcah and Iscah. Now Sarai was barren; she had no children.*

The wives of the other two sons, Abram and Nahor, are also mentioned. It is interesting that Nahor's wife, Milcah, was the daughter of Haran. Thus we have a case of the marriage of an uncle and a niece. Although this type of union was later forbidden in the Mosaic Law, there are other instances of such marriages of blood relatives during this early history. Abram's wife, Sarai, was his half-sister, according to Genesis 20:12. Earlier we observed that such marriages were necessary in the early development of the human race (Gen. 4:17). Later, when the people multiplied, the need for such marriages no longer existed. In Leviticus 18 the laws against consanguinity are given and in the course of time a strong prejudice against such marriages developed, but in the days of Abram this was still considered to be acceptable, and even desirable. There was, for instance, a strong religious motivation for Isaac's marriage to his second cousin, Rebekah. The grievous idol worship that prevailed in Canaan made it impossible to find a wife for him among his people (Gen. 24:3). It should be stressed that such cases should never be used as precedents to justify consanguineous marriages in our day.

One interesting detail that is included here is a reference to Iscah, Milcah's sister. There have been some conjectures as to the reason for mentioning Haran's other daughter. The ancient Jewish rabbis suggested that this could be another name for Sarai, Abram's wife. Some Roman Catholic scholars have also adopted this view, but this is in conflict with what we are told in Genesis 20:12. Others have surmised that Iscah was the wife of Lot, but this is also without any foundation in the biblical text.

Then we are told that Sarai was barren. Later we read that the childlessness of Abram and Sarai became a matter of considerable significance. By way of contrast, we know that her sister-in-law, Milcah, did not share her situation, since we learn from Genesis 24:24 that Bethuel was her son and that he in turn was the father of Rebekah.

11:31 *Terah took his son Abram, his grandson Lot son of Haran, and his daughter-in-law Sarai, the wife of his son Abram, and together they set out from Ur of the Chaldeans to go to Canaan. But when they came to Haran, they settled there.*

The narration now moves to the departure from Ur of the Chaldeans. The migrating party consisted of Terah, Abram and Sarai, and Lot, Terah's grandson. No mention is made of Nahor at this point. From Genesis 24:10 we learn that Nahor also moved from Ur in Mesopotamia, but we are not told when he made this move.

What motivated Terah to move away from his land and people is not mentioned. We can assume, however, that God's call to Abram, mentioned in Acts 7:2–3, was the motivating factor. Whether there were other motivating factors that inspired this move is not revealed to us. If there were such factors, we may be sure that these also were under the controlling providence of God.

The ultimate goal of their migration was the land of Canaan. This is clear from Acts 7:3 and Genesis 12:1, even though this was not revealed to Abram at this time. In both passages mention is made of "the land I will show you." This also squares with Hebrews 11:8, where we are told that Abraham went out "even though he did not know where he was going." Evidently, at this point, while they were still in Ur of the Chaldeans, God did not give specific instructions as to where they were to go. The route of Terah's migration, although not by direct orders from God, certainly was influenced by God's providential guidance, and it brought Abram in the direction God wanted him to take. The statement "to go to Canaan" can also be read "to go in the direction of Canaan." Some have suggested that this does not express Terah's own goal, but rather the direction in which God would providentially lead him and his family. We do not agree to this. The verb translated "set out from" indicates that Canaan was actually the objective Terah had in mind. A similar usage is found in Joshua 22:9; 1 Samuel 17:33; 1 Kings 11:22; 22:49; 2 Chronicles 20:36–37; Ezra 8:31; and Jeremiah 37:12. In each case it is clear that it is not only the direction taken that is indicated but also the specific goal that was sought.

Terah's plan, however, was not carried out. The travelers moved through the valley of the Euphrates River to the north. Then they probably planned to veer to the southeast and in that way reach the land of Canaan. But they didn't get any further than Haran, which was a prominent city in the northern part of Mesopotamia. The city was located on the left bank of the Balich River, which was a branch of the Euphrates, and was approximately halfway from Ur to Canaan. It was here that the family settled, because for some reason, the original plan of migrating to Canaan was changed. This makes it the more evident that God had not originally designated the land of Canaan as their appointed destinction. If He had, Abram would certainly have refused to compromise his "call" from God by stopping at Haran.

11:32 *Terah lived 205 years, and he died in Haran.*

The account continues with the record of Terah's death in Haran, at the age of 205. This is the last reference to him, and it is obvious that this took place many years after the events recorded in 12:1. According to 12:4, Abram was 75 years old when he left Haran; 11:26 tells us that he was born when Terah was 70 years old. This leaves a time span of 60 years, but this poses no real formal problem, for it should be noted that the Old Testament frequently gives a record of events that took place many years later than the event immediately in discussion. The biblical author plans to proceed with the narrative of Abram and so he gathers all the information about Terah into one record and brings that to a conclusion.

But this record about Terah's age at his death does present a real problem when we try to harmonize these facts with Stephen's statement in Acts 7:4 that Abram did not leave Haran until after his father Terah had died. Various attempts have been made to reconcile these two references— Genesis 11:26–32 and 12:4, and Acts 7:4. Some have suggested that Abram should be considered to be Terah's youngest son, as much as 60 years younger than his oldest brother. This seems most unlikely. Others have accepted the reading of the Samaritan Pentateuch, which itself apparently tried to reconcile these two passages by giving Terah's age at his death as 145. But this is in conflict with both the Hebrew text and the Septuagint. Obviously, what Stephen did was simply to accept a Jewish tradition that was widely accepted in his day. This had also been recorded by the famous Jewish scholar, Philo of Alexandria. This tradition held that Abram remained in Haran until after his father died. It was obviously based on a superficial reading of the events recorded in Genesis, without taking careful account of the time spans that were involved in that record.

12:1–3 *The Lord had said to Abram, "Leave your country, your people and your father's household and go to the land I will show you.*

"I will make you into a great nation and I will bless you; I will make your name great, and you will be a blessing. I will bless those who bless you, and whoever curses you I will curse; and all peoples on earth will be blessed through you."

These verses follow directly on 11:31 and do not actually start a new stage in the narrative. We are now told that it was in Haran that Abram received God's call to leave his land and his people, and now his "father's household" is also included. Once again he must take his leave from his established location. After moving there from Ur with his father and his family and adopting this as his homeland through an extended stay, he is once again called upon to move. This time he is also told to break with his family ties. He was to leave his "father's household" and go to an unknown land that God would show him. Thus, he was to make his departure and then await God's directions with respect to the destination of his journey.

This "call" of God included a rich promise, however. Abram was promised that his descendants would become a great nation, a new people, a peculiar people whose entire history would originate with him. This promise required a strong accepting faith on Abram's part because, from a human point of view, there was no likelihood this would be realized. Abram had no children; Sarai was barren (11:30). This promise also included a special blessing and honor in the declaration, "I will make your name great."

The second part of the promise included the declaration that Abram would be a blessing to others, even to all peoples of the earth. This promise actually comes in the form of an imperative, "Be a blessing." Abram was to become the personification of God's blessing to his fellow men. This is further explained in verse 3, "I will bless those who bless you, and whoever curses you I will curse."

This latter statement needs some elucidation. What God declared is that His attitude toward Abram's fellow men would be determined by their attitude toward Abram. Those who acted favorably toward Abram would win the favor of God. Those whose inclination to Abram was hostile and evil would come under the curse of God. This clearly indicated that Abram stood in a distinctive relationship to God. Abram was the friend of God, and he was chosen to enjoy a special fellowship with Him. This implied that the blessing and curse did not apply only to temporal matters. The area with which these dealt related to Abram's relationship to God and hence also to the relationship of Abram's fellow men to Abram's God. This blessing and curse dealt with God's favor or disfavor as it came into expression in their lives.

Still another factor included in God's promise is, "All peoples on earth will be blessed through you." This statement reveals even more clearly that the promise dealt with more than material blessings. It would be unthinkable that what God promised here was that all peoples on the earth would prosper materially through Abram.

Some interpreters read this statement, "In you shall all families of the earth bless themselves." In other words, they would consider and declare themselves fortunate. It probably would mean that anyone who enjoyed good fortune would be described as being as fortunate as Abram. But this is not what the text says. The translation "be blessed" is preferable because it sets forward the idea of "to be a blessing." It also corresponds more closely with the original declaration, "I will bless."

What, then, would be the blessing with which the whole of humanity would be blessed? In an absolute sense the blessing would be the opposite of the curse that came upon humanity as a consequence of the Fall. This blessing, therefore, is not merely a general blessing, but it amounts to a nullifying of the curse. This, in turn, is the fulfillment of the maternal promise given in Genesis 3:15. God promised Abram that the Protevangelium would be realized in him, that is, in his seed (note "a great nation" in v. 2). Abram would prepare the way and establish the line from which the "seed of the woman" would come. We must then assume that the patriarch was acquainted with the "maternal promise." How he acquired this knowledge, whether by oral tradition or in writing, we do not know.

12:4, 5 *So Abram left, as the Lord had told him; and Lot went with him. Abram was seventy-five years old when he set out from Haran. He took his wife, Sarai, his nephew Lot, all the possessions they had accumulated and the people they had acquired in Haran, and they set out for the land of Canaan, and they arrived there.*

Abram willingly obeyed God's call, and left his "father's household" in Haran. Only his wife, Sarai, and his nephew, Lot, accompanied him. He also took his business, those who worked for him, and his personal possessions.

With this entourage he migrated to Canaan. At the time he did not know that Canaan was to be his destination, as is clear from 12:1. (See also our comments under 11:31.) However, since he had to go somewhere, he resumed Terah's original plan and moved to the land of Canaan.

12:6 *Abram traveled through the land as far as the site of the great tree of Moreh at Shechem. The Canaanites were then in the land,*

When he arrived in Canaan he stopped first at Shechem. Near Shechem was the "great tree of Moreh," and this is where the traveling band set up camp. Ancient Shechem was the natural capital of Palestine. It lay a short distance east of Neapolis which is still a prominent city today. Shechem is mentioned in the Amarna Tablets and in some of the older Egyptian documents, and it played an important role during the time of the Judges. The ruins of the ancient city have been uncovered by various excavations.

Some interpreters claim that the term should read "the place" of Shechem. "The place," then, would refer to a holy place where the Canaanites carried on their idol worship. One scholar insists that the word "place" always refers to such centers of worship, but this is not correct. Genesis 18:24, just to mention one example, speaks of the city of Sodom as "the place."

With respect to "the tree of Moreh" we probably should understand this as a sacred tree or grove, and these were common among the Canaanites. Whether this must be seen as a proper name or merely as a designation of a specific location is difficult to determine. The Hebrew word *moreh* means "teacher" in a religious sense. It has also been translated "soothsayer." And it is also used in an adverbial form as "teaching" or "soothsaying." Thus it can be translated the "soothsayers' tree." The message of the soothsayer supposedly was received from the rustling of the leaves of the tree. If it is concluded from this that Abram acknowledged the sacred character of this tree, or that the inspired writer of this narrative accepted this pagan concept, we are reading something into the text that is not there. Here it simply designates a specific location where Abram camped. The same is probably true of a reference to "the soothsayers' tree" in Judges 9:37. It is not likely that the same tree is referred to in Genesis 35:4 and Judges 9:6.

This verse also tells us that the Canaanites occupied this land at that time, and some read this as indicating that the Canaanites were still there but had left by the time the account was written. It is then argued that this was written after Joshua and his armies conquered this land and drove the Canaanites out. Others take exactly the opposite view. They insist that it says that the Canaanites were already in the land. It would then imply that the people who occupied this land before the Canaanites took it over had already left by the time Abram arrived. Neither of these views has any basis in the sacred text. We are simply told who occupied this territory when Abram came on the scene.

12:7 *But the LORD appeared to Abram and said, "To your offspring I will give this land." So he built an altar there to the LORD, who had appeared to him.*

"But the LORD appeared to Abram." This is the first time in the Old Testament we are told that God "appeared" to someone. In Acts 7:2 Stephen mentions the fact that God had appeared to Abram in Ur of the Chaldeans also. Just what are we to understand by such a "theophany"? It is obvious that we must think of some kind of visible manifestation of God's presence. This manifestation does not come by way of a dream or a vision so that we should think of a subjective, spiritual revelation. There was definitely an objective reality that could be seen and recognized. This is clear from the Hebrew presentation which actually means to appear to someone. It implies that a visible presence comes to the person receiving the revelation. Of course, we must maintain that God is a Spirit and as such cannot be recognized in visible form. Thus, it is not God Himself who is seen. That which is seen is a symbol or a representation of God's presence.

This appearance, as is usually the case, was accompanied by a spoken message. Thus, Abram saw with his eyes and heard with his ears a special revelation from God. "To your offspring I will give this land." Here we have the fulfillment of the promise given in 12:1 (cf. Acts 7:3), "the land I will show you." Abram now is informed that this land, the land of Canaan, was the designated place where he must establish his residence. This was the land that God would give to Abram's descendants. This land, which Abram seemed to have reached by chance, was the land to which God had brought him by providential guidance.

Thereupon, Abram built an altar on this memorable spot. Earlier (Gen. 8:20) we read that Noah built an altar. Now we are told that Abram did the same thing, but it is added that he did so before "the LORD, who had appeared to him." Thus it is emphasized that Abram's great experience at this location was memorialized by the building of an altar.

12:8, 9 *From there he went on toward the hills east of Bethel and pitched his tent, with Bethel on the west and Ai on the east. There he built an altar to the LORD and called on the name of the LORD. Then Abram set out and continued toward the Negev.*

Abram did not stay at this precise location, however. He moved on to establish his camp in the hill country between Bethel and Ai. The inspired writer used the name Bethel even though the city was still known by the name Luz (see Gen. 28:19). Ai lay approximately 3 km. (about 2 miles) from Bethel. It is familiar from the narrative in Joshua 8:1-28.

Here Abram again built an altar. In addition, we are told that he "called on the name of the LORD." Thus he engaged in public worship (cf. Gen. 4:26), although this worship must be conceived of as very simple and elementary. Even so, Abram gathered his entire entourage together which, according to Genesis 14:14, was a considerable number of people, and led them in public prayers to God.

But even this was not to be Abram's permanent place of abode. According to verse 9, he moved still farther to the south.

2. *Abram in Egypt* (12:10-20)

Those who divide the sources ascribe this portion to "J." Even so, there are some who object that this section is not in full accord with other portions of Abram's history that have been ascribed to "J." There is a difference of opinion about which sections are primary and which sections are secondary, but there is no need for us to become involved in this debate. We should, however, deal with the claim that this section does not fit into its immediate context.

The main objection that has been raised against the placement of this section here is that Lot is not mentioned in any way. According to 12:4 and 13:5, Lot accompanied Abram on the entire journey. Genesis 13:1 does tell us that Lot was with Abram when they left Egypt. The critics, however, consider this to be an insertion. We would respond that it is altogether understandable that Lot should not be mentioned here because he played no part in the whole "adventure" of Abram and Sarai in Egypt. In the same way, Lot is not mentioned in Genesis 12:6–9 either.

12:10 *Now there was a famine in the land, and Abram went down to Egypt to live there for a while because the famine was severe.*

Abram had been in Canaan only a short time before he again faced a need to move, even if it would only be temporarily. A famine in the land of Canaan drove him and his whole tribe to Egypt, which was known as the breadbasket of the ancient world because of its abundant grain crops. This must have been no small trial for the patriarch. He had not yet gained possession of a square foot of the Promised Land when he was already facing a bitter disappointment. Because of the critical need for food, he had to leave the object of his long quest to once again take up his journey to find food.

12:11–13 *As he was about to enter Egypt, he said to his wife Sarai, "I know what a beautiful woman you are. When the Egyptians see you, they will say, 'This is his wife.' Then they will kill me but will let you live. Say you are my sister, so that I will be treated well for your sake and my life will be spared because of you."*

As Abram approached the borders of Egypt, he manifested a serious moral weakness. He was so overcome by fear that he urged his beautiful wife, Sarai, to tell a lie. This lie would place Sarai in a dangerous situation morally. Evidently, Sarai was a beautiful woman and was very attractive to men. Abram feared that when Sarai and he came to Egypt, men would be so attracted to her that they would readily dispose of her husband and take her for themselves. He therefore urged Sarai to pose as his sister, rather than his wife. Then if some man desired to have Sarai, Abram would not be endangered, but would be treated kindly to gain his favor.

Genesis 20:12 informs us that Sarai indeed was Abram's sister—that is,

his half sister. They had the same father but different mothers. What
Abram wanted her to say, then, was partially true. But it was only a half
truth and was intended to give a false impression. What Sarai was asked to
say was intended to give the impression that she was not Abram's wife;
therefore it was an actual lie. No attempts should be made to try to justify
or excuse what Abram did. This was an obvious sin. It was a violation of
the ninth commandment. Moreover, this falsehood could also be the occasion for a sin against the seventh commandment, and this was precisely
what resulted from this cowardly scheme.

12:14–16 *When Abram came to Egypt, the Egyptians saw that she was a very
beautiful woman. And when Pharaoh's officials saw her, they praised her to
Pharaoh, and she was taken into his palace. He treated Abram well for her sake,
and Abram acquired sheep and cattle, male and female donkeys, menservants and
maidservants, and camels.*

Sarai's physical beauty immediately caught the attention of the Egyptians. So general was the attention she received that it even came to the
attention of the pharaoh. Understandably, Pharaoh proceeded to take the
necessary steps to bring this new beauty into his harem. Abram had also
been correct in anticipating the consequences for himself. Because of
Pharaoh's interest in Sarai, Abram was showered with gifts—sheep and
cattle, donkeys, slaves, and camels.

"Pharaoh," in this case, is not a personal name but merely a title. For
this reason it should probably be read "the pharaoh." In Egyptian the word
meant "the great house" and thus referred to the palace in which Egyptian
royalty lived. It is worthy of note that the actual name of this pharaoh is not
given, nor is this done in other references in Genesis and Exodus. This is in
accord with ancient Egyptian practice, for they preferred not to use the
name of the pharaoh. Thus he was simply called "the pharaoh." It wasn't
until the 22nd dynasty was established by Shishak (see 1 Kings 11:40;
14:25) in approximately 945 B.C., that it became the practice to add the
name of the pharaoh. Thereupon we get Pharaoh Neco in 2 Kings 23:29,
33–35; Jeremiah 46:2, and in Jeremiah 44:30 we meet Pharaoh Hophra.

Another matter that demands our attention here is that the horse is not
included among the animals that were given to Abram. It is generally
accepted that horses were introduced to Egypt by the Hyksos, a people or
tribe of Asiatic origin that overran Egypt and maintained control of the
country for several centuries. They, supposedly, got the horse from the
Arians. Whether all of this can be historically established is not important
to us at this time. We do not know exactly when the Hyksos people took

over Egypt, but we do know that they were driven out by Pharaoh Amosis, founder of the 18th dynasty, at approximately 1580 B.C. We probably can assume then that Abram's sojourn in Egypt took place before the arrival of the Hyksos. By the time of Joseph's ascendancy in Egypt, horses were already in evidence (Gen. 47:17); thus it can be assumed that the Hyksos had taken over Egypt before the time of Joseph. We will return to this data when we take up the narrative of Joseph (cf. what is said in this regard in our introduction to ch. 39).

Some scholars have insisted that it is most unlikely that Sarai could be physically so attractive at the age of 65. This is the age that must be accepted on the basis of 12:4 and 17:17, for she was only ten years younger than Abram. Various attempts have been made to get around this alleged problem. The source splitters ascribe the ages given in the above passages to another source. Others look upon these figures as a later insertion. We must insist, however, that the text gives no basis for ascribing a younger age to Sarai. Nor is there any need for doing this. We certainly cannot manipulate the biblical text to make it concur with someone's theory about how old a woman can be and still be physically attractive to men. It should also be remembered that this narrative falls in a time when people lived to be much older than they do today. Abram lived to be 175 and Sarai 127. This would place her in the period of life approaching middle age. This was the age when these people normally had their children. Terah was 70 when he had his family and Isaac was 60. Certainly it is obvious that Sarai was no decrepit old lady at the age of 60. She may well have been in the full bloom of her womanhood.

In the final analysis, we once again come to the point that it is a matter of whether or not we accept the Bible. If we accept the biblical record regarding the ages people reached at that time, we have no difficulty with Sarai's physical attractiveness at the age of 60, or considerably later for that matter (see Gen. 20:2). Besides this, some scholars have pointed out that during this period of the 12th Egyptian dynasty, approximately 2000 B.C., the beauty of the light-skinned Asiatic women was especially prized by Egyptians, in contrast to their native dark-skinned women. The harems of the pharaohs were therefore abundantly supplied with Syrian women. Also, an ordinance has been discovered which specifies that the wife and children of any stranger who came to Egypt during this period in history could be taken over by the pharaoh without any problem.

12:17–20 *But the LORD inflicted serious diseases on Pharaoh and his household because of Abram's wife Sarai. So Pharaoh summoned Abram. "What have you done to me?" he said. "Why didn't you tell me she was your wife? Why did you* *say, 'She is my sister,' so that I took her to be my wife? Now then, here is your wife. Take her and go!'' Then Pharaoh gave orders about Abram to his men, and they sent him on his way, with his wife and everything he had.*

In this present situation, however, this could not be allowed. The Lord was watching over His chosen people. Even though Abram had forfeited his rights by his weak faith and his falsehood, God did not permit his wife to be taken from him. As a consequence of the pharaoh's action, the Lord brought a serious malady upon him and his family. It is not specified what the nature of this malady was. In any case, the king became aware that something was wrong. He conducted an investigation and learned that the beautiful woman he had added to his harem was actually a married woman. Just how he discovered this we are not told either. Abram was therefore called before the king and sternly rebuked by the Egyptian monarch, for he had placed the king in a serious moral dilemma by his falsehood. Abram's wife was returned to him, but he was ordered to leave Egypt immediately. He was given an escort to bring him, his wife, and his entire retinue safely across the border. The gifts Abram had received were not returned, for the pharaoh was obviously too proud to reclaim gifts he had once given.

There certainly was a marked contrast between the conduct of Abram in this instance and the unconditional obedience he demonstrated earlier when God called him to leave his fatherland. This makes it clear that the Bible does not hesitate to reveal that the heroes of faith were, in themselves, sinful men such as we are. Abram's unconditional obedience to God's call was therefore not an indication of his exceptional virtue. It was, rather, a manifestation of God's wonderful grace.

The inspired narrative informs us about this incident without making any comment about it. Some have interpreted this silence on the part of Scripture as an indication of tacit approval of what Abram had done. Quite to the contrary, the author expresses his disapproval by clearly recording Pharaoh's scathing denunciation of the patriarch, while Abram is not credited with any defense for his misconduct. We cannot but be impressed with the objectivity of the biblical narrative. There is no false glorification of the heroes of Scripture; there is a straightforward recording of the facts as they were, even when these facts place the person involved in an unfavorable light.

3. *Abram and Lot* (13:1–18)

This chapter is also ascribed to ''J,'' except for verses 6, 11c, and 12b, which are ascribed to ''P'' by those who split the sources. The argument goes as follows. Verse 6 would appear to be superfluous. The close of verse 11, supposedly, comes too late to be logically joined with the first part of the verse. And 12a also seems to be somewhat redundant. Some hold that verses 2–4 must be ascribed to a "redactor," while verses 14–17 must be seen as a later insertion into the text. We find that the grounds adduced for these claims are without any real substance.

13:1–4 *So Abram went up from Egypt to the Negev, with his wife and everything he had, and Lot went with him. Abram had become very wealthy in livestock and in silver and gold.*

From the Negev he went from place to place until he came to Bethel, to the place between Bethel and Ai where his tent had been earlier and where he had first built an altar. There Abram called on the name of the LORD.

The first verse begins by establishing a connection with what is recorded in chapter 12. We are told how Abram and his people and his possessions left Egypt. At this point specific mention is made of Lot as being part of the group. Many, with no justification, consider this to be a later insertion.

And so they came into the "southland" or the Negev. It should be noted that this was not an area that lay to the south of Egypt. It was actually an extended area in the southern part of the land of Canaan, and it stretched from the hills near Hebron to Kadesh. Abram retraced his steps through this territory, passing the same places where he had stopped when he first journeyed through the land (see Gen. 12:9). Finally he reached the place where he had settled before, between Bethel and Ai (Gen. 12:8). When he arrived there with his whole tribe, he again conducted a public worship service for his entire entourage.

In this connection, mention is made of Abram's great wealth, especially in livestock. This prepares the way for what is to follow.

13:5–7 *Now Lot, who was moving about with Abram, also had flocks and herds and tents. But the land could not support them while they stayed together, for their possessions were so great that they were not able to stay together. And quarreling arose between Abram's herdsmen and the herdsmen of Lot. The Canaanites and Perizzites were also living in the land at that time.*

Lot also had great possessions, with many flocks and herds. The area in which Abram and Lot settled was not large enough to provide adequate grazing pasture for the herds of both men. The consequences of this over-crowding could not be avoided. Soon there was strife between the herdsmen of the two families.

This strife, already regrettable in itself, could have other serious conse-quences as well. Abram and Lot had settled in an area that was not altogether unoccupied. They, in a sense, were taking this land from other peoples. As was mentioned in 12:6, the Canaanites were in the land. Besides the Canaanites, mention is here made of the Perizzites, and they are mentioned in Genesis 34:30; Judges 1:4–5; and Joshua 17:15. They are also included in various lists of peoples living in Canaan, such as in Genesis 15:19–21; Exodus 3:8, 17; 23:23; 33:2; Deuteronomy 7:1; 20:17; Joshua 3:10; 9:1; 11:3; 1 Kings 9:20, etc.

There is a widely held theory that the word "Perizzites" does not refer to a specific tribe or people. The word, it is claimed, is the same as the Hebrew word *Perāî* which means "rural people," in distinction from "city dwellers." In Deuteronomy 3:5 we read about the "unwalled villages" which were called *Perāî*. Similarly, in 1 Samuel 6:18 the term is translated "country villages." The theory then is that the Canaanites lived in fortified, established cities, while the Perizzites lived in the open country in scattered villages. In support of this theory our attention is called to the omission of the Perizzites from the descendants of Canaan in the Table of Nations in Genesis 10:15–19. Although this theory is very attractive, it cannot be correct. There can be no doubt that the word Canaanite refers to a tribe or a nation. Thus, when the word Perizzite is used beside it, we can hardly change its meaning to describe country dwellers in general, in distinction from city dwellers. But even more cogent is the inclusion of the Perizzites among the lists of tribes and nations who occupied the land of Canaan, mentioned above. Thus we must accept the fact that the Perizzites were indeed a tribal group living in Canaan, even though we know nothing further about them.

13:8–13 *So Abram said to Lot, "Let's not have any quarreling between you and me, or between your herdsmen and mine, for we are brothers. Is not the whole land before you? Let's part company. If you go to the left, I'll go to the right; if you go to the right, I'll go to the left."*

Lot looked up and saw that the whole plain of the Jordan was well watered, like the garden of the LORD, like the land of Egypt, toward Zoar. (This was before the LORD destroyed Sodom and Gomorrah.) So Lot chose for himself the whole plain of the Jordan and set out toward the east. The two men parted company: Abram lived in the land of Canaan, while Lot lived among the cities of the plain and pitched his tents near Sodom. Now the men of Sodom were wicked and were sinning greatly against the LORD.

Abram was fully aware of the danger that was presented by the strife between his herdsmen and those of Lot. The local residents could readily use this kind of division as an opportunity to attack them and drive them out. So Abram made the decision that he and Lot should part company.

Abram assumed a noble attitude as he gave his nephew the first choice of grazing lands. If Lot chose to go to the left he would go to the right and vice versa. Lot, who was less generous in his attitude, quickly chose the fertile plain of the Jordan. Thus he left the more mountainous area, which was characteristic of much of the land of Canaan, for Abram. The plain of the Jordan is called, in Hebrew, *kikkār,* which means "circle" or "surroundings." Here it indicates the area in southeastern Canaan, on both sides of the Jordan River, which was well watered and had fertile grazing land. In verse 12 this area is simply called "the kikkār" or "the plain."

Mention is made of the fertility of this plain "before the LORD destroyed Sodom and Gomorrah." This note, added by the inspired writer, clearly indicates that this was written after the destruction of the "cities of the plain." Thus, these words are properly given as a parenthesis. When "the plain" is further described, we are told that it was "like the garden of the LORD," which is a reference to Paradise. Further, we are told that it was "like the land of Egypt, toward Zoar." This refers to the eastern section of the Nile Delta, which was renowned for being well watered and very fertile. It is also described as such in the Egyptian papyri.

The soil of "the plain" was very rich but the residents of this area were known for their extreme wickedness. This is here briefly pointed out in preparation for what is to be recorded later (Gen. 18:16–19:29). This also tells us something about Lot's choice. His personal greed enabled him to see only superficial values and in consequence his choice turned out to be for his detriment rather than for his benefit.

The separation between Lot and Abram was apparently occasioned by the strife between their herdsmen, but it actually formed a significant link in the chain of God's plan and purpose for Abram. God had called Abram to leave his "country," his "people," and his "father's household." As long as Abram kept Lot with him, he still maintained a close tie with his "father's household." It was imperative that those ties be completely severed. It was Abram alone who was chosen to be the head of a special people of God who were to be the recipients of God's redemptive revelation.

13:14–17 *The LORD said to Abram after Lot had parted from him, "Lift up your eyes from where you are and look north and south, east and west. All the land that you see I will give to you and your offspring forever. I will make your offspring like the dust of the earth, so that if anyone could count the dust, then your offspring could be counted. Go, walk through the length and breadth of the land, for I am giving it to you."*

After Lot had moved out of Abram's domain, God repeated His promise that the land of Canaan would be given as an enduring possession to Abram and his offspring. It actually reads, "to Abram *in* his offspring" (12:7). To this is added a renewal of the promise of Genesis 12:2 that he would become "a great nation." This promise is now clothed in descriptive symbolism which pictured Abram's offspring as the "dust of the earth." Abram was also urged to inspect the entire land of Canaan because it would all be given to him and his offspring as a possession.

13:18 *So Abram moved his tents and went to live near the great trees of Mamre at Hebron, where he built an altar to the LORD.*

The chapter closes with the account of Abram moving to a more permanent place of residence near the city of Hebron, by the great trees of Mamre. According to Genesis 14:13, 24, Mamre was the head of one of the native tribes, and the grove of trees was named for him.

Just as Abram had done at Shechem (12:7) and between Bethel and Ai (12:8), he again built an altar to the Lord. Provision for the worship of God was of primary importance to the patriarch.

4. *Abram Goes to War* (14:1–24)

Genesis 14 is a very unusual chapter, for it presents a completely different picture of Abram and his lifestyle than any other part of the narrative offers. This is the only passage in which the patriarch is introduced as a man of military might. In this connection it is important to see Abram in total perspective.

To be sure, Abram appeared as a stranger in the Promised Land. Even so, we must not conceive of him as a poor, isolated wanderer. As was pointed out in 13:2, 6, Abram was very wealthy, especially in herds and flocks. As such, he also had many servants (see 12:5), who worked as herdsmen and in many other functions. Although the narrative is presented as the story of a family, Abram was more like the head of a sizeable desert tribe. So our present chapter reveals that, in an emergency, Abram could raise a formidable military force within his own camp.

Another striking feature of chapter 14 is that this is the only place in the entire narrative where Abram is called "the Hebrew" (v. 13). Naturally this name must be given a broader meaning here than we usually ascribe to it. Here the name cannot be identified with "Israelite" because that name is of later origin. To understand this broader use of the name "Hebrew," see our treatment of 10:21.

Another unusual aspect of this chapter is the use of many precise names.

There are the names of all the kings who went to war and the nations and cities they ruled. We also read the names of the places where the battles were fought, the route of pursuit, the names of Abram's associates, and the name of the priest-king of Salem.

Finally, this chapter frequently (actually five times) adds explanatory notes to what is recorded. In verse 2 and again in verse 8 we are told that "Bela" was later called "Zoar." In verse 3 we are informed that the Valley of Siddim later became the Salt Sea (the Dead Sea). In verse 7 we read that En Mishpat later became the familiar Kadesh. And in verse 17 "the Valley of Shaveh" is identified as the "King's Valley."

The advocates of the division of sources have failed to relate this chapter to any recognized source. They therefore ascribe this material to an unknown independent source. There is complete disagreement among these scholars as to when this material was formulated. Some hold that it must have been considerably earlier than the usually recognized sources such as "J" and "P." Others insist that it must be placed much later. Which of these views is accepted also influences the acceptance or rejection of the historicity of this passage. Those who hold to an early date accept that, in general, it records actual historical events. Those who favor the late date describe the chapter as no more than Jewish fantasy resulting from a Jewish tendency to glorify their great patriarch. This tendency led them to exalt him not only as a hero of religious faith but also as a military hero with great prowess. In this latter group there are some who will admit that the chapter does include some historical data, but they insist this history has been so mixed with unrealistic fantasy that it can only be classed as Jewish folklore of a very late date.

We will not discuss the historicity of this chapter at this time. In our detailed commentary that follows, we will discuss the validity of the specific objections that have been raised to the credibility of the narrative.

There is, however, one observation we should make at this point. The interpretation of this chapter as a very late product of Jewish fantasy, intended to glorify their patriarch, must be categorically rejected. Such an interpretation denies the divine authority and trustworthiness of Scripture. Furthermore, when we consider the nature of this chapter, it certainly appears highly unlikely that such a Jewish fantasy would have taken this form. The narrative simply does not read like Jewish fantasy. It reads like carefully recorded history.

The unique character of Genesis 14 leads us to the conclusion that we are dealing with an ancient document which may have been discovered in some archive. The biblical author then took it over and inserted it into his narrative. The many explanatory notes that appear in the chapter were probably from his own hand. By placing the new names beside the old ones, he sought to assist his readers by making the narrative more understandable. The surprising use of the name "Hebrew" for Abram suggests that the original document came from a source outside the chosen people who received God's revelation. When it was incorporated in Scripture, the author, under the guidance of the Holy Spirit, made some necessary corrections and additions for the sake of clarity. Thus it became an authentic part of the divine revelation—the Bible.

14:1, 2 *At this time Amraphel king of Shinar, Arioch king of Ellasar, Kedorlaomer king of Elam and Tidal king of Goiim went to war against Bera king of Sodom, Birsha king of Gomorrah, Shinab king of Admah, Shemeber king of Zeboiim, and the king of Bela (that is, Zoar).*

This chapter begins with the record of a great battle between four kings from outside Canaan and five city kings from the area where Lot had settled. We will consider the kings who are named here, individually.

The first is Amraphel. There was a time when he was generally identified with Hammurabi, the famous Babylonian king. The land of Shinar over which Amraphel ruled would then be Babylon. Thus, whenever the name Shinar appears in the Old Testament, this was accepted as being a reference to Babylon. We have given some discussion to this in our treatment of Genesis 10:10. However, in more recent times there have been some serious objections raised against identifying Amraphel with Hammurabi. The letter "l" appears in this name and does not appear in the Babylonian name. Moreover, recent discoveries have indicated that Hammurabi probably lived at a later date. Some scholars have therefore sought to identify Amraphel with Amorapil, who may have been the king of a territory known as Sanhar. This kingdom supposedly lay in northwestern Mesopotamia. However, we cannot be certain of the exact identification of this king and his realm.

The second king mentioned was Arioch, in Hebrew *Aryôk,* and in Babylonian *Eriako*. This name also appears in Daniel 2:14, as the captain of Nebuchadnezzar's bodyguard. Here he is called king of Ellasar, which probably can be identified with Larsa, a city on the lower Euphrates, near the city of Ur. For a time it served as headquarters for an important dynasty which tried to gain hegemony over all of Babylon. Not all scholars agree to this interpretation, however. Some feel that this should refer to a territory in northern Babylon.

The third king introduced is Kedorlaomer, king of Elam. There is no doubt about his name being Elamitish, for there were several Elamite kings whose names began with what is equivalent to "kedor." The last part of his name is the same as an Elamite goddess named "Lagamar." Up to the time of this writing, no information has been discovered about this king, but because of his prominence in this narrative, it is possible that newer excavations will unearth some information about this powerful Elamite king.

The fourth king is Tidal, king of Goiim or, as other translations have it, "king of the nations." In the Hethite records, this name appears in conjunction with five of their kings in the form of "Toedhal." It probably was equivalent to the word "Pharaoh" in Egypt, and one of these could have been a contemporary of Hammurabi. It has been suggested that the Hethites were split into various tribes or "nations," and if so, this king then controlled several of these tribal groups. Other scholars have suggested that he was a "vagabond king" who was able to win various Hethite tribes and provinces into his army, and consequently was called "king of the nations."

Although we cannot positively identify these four kings, we do have enough information to determine that we are dealing with actual historical figures. There certainly is no basis for reducing these names to the product of some later Jewish fantasy.

As we move on to the city kings of the plain of the Jordan, it would certainly be unreasonable to expect to be able to identify these comparatively minor rulers with any degree of certainty. It is difficult to establish such identity with respect to ancient kings of great renown who governed vast empires. When they ruled only one city or local area, and that for an undetermined time, probably very briefly, such an identification would be most unlikely.

What we can establish, however, is that these names have a genuine Palestinian character. Therefore, it is unlikely that they were the product of later fantasy. The name of the king of Bela (Zoar) is missing. Certainly, if all of these names were fictitional, there would be no reason for leaving one name out.

On the basis of the Arabic language, the name of Bera, king of Sodom, can be interpreted as "conqueror"; Birsha, king of Gomorrah, as "large man"; Shinab, king of Admah, as "health" or "beauty," or as "Sin (the moon god) is father"; Shemeber, king of Zeboiim, as "his name is mighty." Here again these names have been interpreted by some as products of fantasy and as such they become symbols of evil. But the structure of the names is such that this would require considerable alteration of the biblical text.

14:3 *All these latter kings joined forces in the Valley of Siddim (the Salt Sea).*

In verse 3 we are told how the five kings from the plain of the Jordan joined their armies to engage in a fight for freedom. The staging area was the Valley of Siddim. An interesting note is added when we are told that this Valley is the "Salt Sea," or the Dead Sea.

Critics have objected to this because they claim this implies that the Dead Sea did not exist during Abram's time. They argue that the water of the Jordan River that flows into what is now the Dead Sea, must have gone somewhere. It must be noted, however, that the statement, which is no more than a brief explanatory note, does not declare that the entire Dead Sea covered the Valley of Siddim. It can logically be read to indicate that the Dead Sea was already in existence but that at some later time it was enlarged and thus inundated part or all of what had been the Valley of Siddim. (See our interpretation of Gen. 19:24–25.)

14:4–7 *For twelve years they had been subject to Kedorlaomer, but in the thirteenth year they rebelled.*

In the fourteenth year, Kedorlaomer and the kings allied with him went out and defeated the Rephaites in Ashteroth Karnaim, the Zuzites in Ham, the Emites in Shaveh Kiriathaim and the Horites in the hill country of Seir, as far as El Paran near the desert. Then they turned back and went to En Mishpat (that is, Kadesh), and they conquered the whole territory of the Amalekites, as well as the Amorites who were living in Hazezon Tamar.

Here we are informed about the occasion for the great battle. The kings of the plain of the Jordan had been subject to the Elamite monarch, Kedorlaomer, for twelve years. They finally determined to throw off this yoke. The implication here is that Kedorlaomer was the dominant leader of the kings mentioned in verse 1a, even though his name is not mentioned first. He is given the primary position in verses 5 and 9. This agrees with what we know about this period of history from other sources. In Abram's time Elam was a great world power. While two dynasties were contending for power in Babylon, Elam was able to acquire controlling power in that part of the world, and this supremacy also extended over the territory of Canaan. This can be explained by understanding the importance of controlling the main trade route from the Euphrates, via Damascus, through the Jordan Valley, down to the Red Sea and Egypt. The city kings of the Jordan plain were useful accomplices for Elam in maintaining control of this life line.

It may seem strange that Elam and Babylon are presented here as allies when historically they were bitter rivals. But this need not surprise us. History is replete with examples of two nations, which at times were bitter enemies, joining forces as allies in a common cause at other times. Moreover, the reverse has also repeatedly been true.

The rebellion of the city kings called forth a strong expedition which intended to bring the entire area under firm control again. We need not picture this as though Kedorlaomer and the kings allied with him personally led this expedition. They undoubtedly entrusted this to military leaders who were under their orders. Ancient accounts of military victories customarily were written as though the kings themselves were present on the field of battle leading their victorious armies.

The powerful, well-armed expedition did not immediately move against the cities of the plain. This fact probably suggests that the uprising against the yoke of Elam had a far broader participation. It may well have included all of the western provinces. The first to be attacked were the Rephaites who, with the Zuzites and the Emites, were among the earliest inhabitants of Canaan known to us. The Rephaites were defeated at Ashteroth Karnaim, located east of the Sea of Galilee and thus also east of the Jordan River.

Next, the Zuzites were engaged in battle and were defeated at Ham, a place mentioned nowhere else in the Old Testament. It probably lay east of the Jordan also, somewhat south of the site of the first battle. Then came the Emites who were brought down at Shaveh Kiriathaim. This also was east of the Jordan, still farther south, just north of the Arnon River. This was the area later occupied by the Moabites.

The victorious army continued to move southward to attack the Horites in the hill country of Seir, which was the area later held by the Edomites. They pushed as far south as El Paran. Although we do not know its exact location it must have been near the northern part of the eastern bay of the Red Sea, now the Gulf of Aqaba. Some have identified it with the port city of Elath. It lies on the edge of the Wilderness of Paran, the high plateau between the Gulf of Aqaba and the Gulf of Suez.

At this point the great army changed direction and moved to the northwest until it came to En Mishpat, which was later known as Kadesh Barnea, on the southern border of Canaan. On this march the army ravaged the Amalekites, a Bedouin tribe that lived in the Wilderness of Paran. They also overran the Amorites at Hazezon Tamar, which lay on the west side of the Dead Sea, about halfway up the coast. This would indicate that they had bypassed Sodom if the traditional location of the Valley of Siddim at the south end of the Dead Sea is correct (Some scholars believe this valley was situated at the north end of the Dead Sea), but the invaders probably had good reasons for this maneuver. However these details are interpreted, it is obvious that the battle at Sodom was critically important.

14:8–12 *Then the king of Sodom, the king of Gomorrah, the king of Admah, the king of Zeboiim and the king of Bela (that is, Zoar) marched out and drew up their* *battle lines in the Valley of Siddim against Kedorlaomer king of Elam, Tidal king of Goiim, Amraphel king of Shinar and Arioch king of Ellasar–four kings against five. Now the Valley of Siddim was full of tar pits, and when the kings of Sodom and Gomorrah fled, some of the men fell into them and the rest fled to the hills. The four kings seized all the goods of Sodom and Gomorrah and all their food; then they went away. They also carried off Abram's nephew Lot and his possessions, since he was living in Sodom.*

We now come to the great battle against Sodom and the other cities of the plain. These did not wait for the invading force to attack, but went out to meet the invaders in the open field in a terrain of their own choosing. Their reasoning was obvious. The Valley of Siddim had many tar pits, and the local warriors knew this area and were confident that the invading forces would be impeded by this treacherous terrain.

The results of the battle, however, proved to the contrary. The Sodomites and their allies lost the battle and were put to flight. In their panic many of them fell into the tar pits while some of the survivors escaped into the mountains. The statement in verse 10 does not mean that the kings themselves fell into these pits. From verses 17 and 21 we learn that the king of Sodom, for one, survived the tragic defeat of his armies. The cities of Sodom and Gomorrah were conquered and plundered; thereupon the victorious hosts of Kedorlaomer retreated to the north, confident that they had totally subdued the rebellion. It is possible that their own losses may have been so heavy that they were incapable of further battle.

Among the many captives taken was Abram's nephew, Lot. This indicates clearly that Lot's choice of dwelling was not for his well-being but for his detriment and disgrace.

14:13–16 *One who had escaped came and reported this to Abram the Hebrew. Now Abram was living near the great trees of Mamre the Amorite, a brother of Eshcol and Aner, all of whom were allied with Abram. When Abram heard that his relative had been taken captive, he called out the 318 trained men born in his household and went in pursuit as far as Dan. During the night Abram divided his men to attack them and he routed them, pursuing them as far as Hobah, north of Damascus. He recovered all the goods and brought back his relative Lot and his possessions, together with the women and the other people.*

A survivor who managed to escape the conquering invaders brought tidings of what had happened to Abram. According to 13:18, Abram had now established his residence by the trees of Mamre, near the city of Hebron. Mamre was an Amorite, and he and his brothers Eshcol and Aner had formed a friendship alliance with Abram. These all probably were tribal chiefs, and as such they leagued together for mutual security.

Upon receiving the tidings, Abram immediately decided to launch a military mission in order to rescue his nephew Lot. In order to achieve his goal, he raised an army of as many men as he could muster. He called on his neighbors who had a special concern in this crisis since it was their fellow countrymen who had been ravaged at Hazezon Tamar. The word we have translated "allied" has caused much confusion among interpreters of this passage. We accept the theory that the word was borrowed from the Canaanites. In Egyptian texts the word is frequently used to refer to Canaanite and Syrian forces that were leagued together against the pharaohs. There the word definitely means "allies."

Abram also armed his own servants and slaves, those who were born in his extended household. There is considerable difference of opinion regarding the use of the conjunction here. Our translators have not included it. We point out, however, that verse 24 strongly suggests that Aner, Eshcol, and Mamre accompanied Abram on his mission. Verse 14, on the other hand, suggests that the 318 men were "born in [Abram's] household." We resolve this difficulty by supplying the conjunction "and." The passage would then read, "those who were allied with Abram, *and* those who were born in his household, 318 trained men. . . ."

One point on which the critics have seized is that there were only 318 men. They argue that such a small force could not possibly have routed the large victorious army of Kedorlaomer. In reply, it should be remembered that both in Scripture and in secular history there are many examples of small forces, under very special circumstances, winning spectacular victories over vastly superior forces. We need only think of Gideon (Judg. 7:16–22). At the same time it should be observed that 318 fighting men may not have been considered such a small force at that time in history. It has not been established, for that matter, that Kedorlaomer's fast-moving army was much larger than this. Many of the armies in ancient times were comparatively small by present-day standards. The Amarna Tablets tell about army divisions which numbered 40 to 50 men, and even 10 to 20 men. In the great battle of Megiddo, in 1479 B.C., the victorious Egyptian king counted 83 enemy soldiers killed and 340 captives taken. In one of the greatest battles of ancient times, between the forces of Egypt and the Hethite armies, at Kadesh in 1288 B.C., the entire Egyptian army numbered only 15,000 to 18,000 men, and only half of those took part in the battle. Even if we were to assume that Kedorlaomer's force was of that size, which is most unlikely, when we take into account the losses they must have sustained during their long campaign, losses which could not be replaced because of the distance from their homeland, the remaining force would have been seriously cut down and weakened. Abram, taking skilled advantage of every factor in his favor, could very well have routed the leftovers of the invading force with 318 well-trained men.

Since the forces of the enemy had a head start, Abram and his men had to pursue them the full length of the land of Canaan. They finally caught up with the retreating force in the area of Dan, in the far northern section of Palestine. Although the name "Dan" is of later origin, the inspired author used that name here rather than the name "Laish" which was in use during Abram's time. The name Dan became well-known later when Palestine was described as extending "from Dan to Beersheba."

When Abram reached the area where Kedorlaomer was camped, he divided his forces and struck in a surprise attack in the middle of the night. Descending on the camp from all directions gave the impression of a large attacking force. The result was total confusion and hasty flight for the enemy which had been caught completely off guard. Abram went in pursuit, all the way to Hobah, north of Damascus. The exact location of Hobah is not known, however. Abram succeeded in recapturing all the goods that had been plundered and also all the prisoners that had been taken, including his nephew Lot.

14:17 *After Abram returned from defeating Kedorlaomer and the kings allied with him, the king of Sodom came out to meet him in the Valley of Shaveh (that is, the King's Valley).*

The king of Sodom came out to meet the victorious patriarch to express his appreciation for his unexpected help. He met him in the area of Jerusalem in the Valley of Shaveh, which later was known as the King's Valley.

14:18–20 *Then Melchizedek king of Salem brought out bread and wine. He was priest of God Most High, and he blessed Abram, saying, "Blessed be Abram by God Most High, Creator of heaven and earth. And blessed be God Most High, who delivered your enemies into your hand." Then Abram gave him a tenth of everything.*

Abram met Melchizedek, who is first introduced as "king of Salem," at the same place. Salem is a shortened form for Jerusalem. Melchizedek came here to pay homage to Abram, and he brought wine and bread and blessed the patriarch for his victory. Many have questioned the historicity of Melchizedek, but there is little substance to their arguments.

The striking factor about Melchizedek is that he, as a Canaanite, is called "priest of God Most High." This suggests that he served the true and living God. According to verse 22, Abram also used the name "God Most High, Creator of heaven and earth" and then added the name

"Lord." This implies that Abram and Melchizedek served the same God. Thus, Melchizedek was an exception to the grossly pagan world of the Canaanites. In some way he had carried on the tradition from the time of Paradise when mankind recognized only one true God.

It is worthy of note that Melchizedek was king of Salem, and at the same time was a priest. This dual role need not surprise us, for there are other instances of this. Moses' father-in-law, Jethro, is called priest of Midian in Exodus 2:16 and 3:1, while he obviously also was the political ruler of one of the Midianite tribes.

The statement that he "gave him a tenth of everything" raises some sticky questions. The first question is, who was the giver and who was the recipient? The usual position is that Abram gave the tenth to Melchizedek, and this is confirmed by Hebrews 7:4. However, some scholars insist that Melchizedek gave a tenth to Abram since he considered Abram as priest and brought homage to him as his superior, but this is quite impossible. We read that Melchizedek brought wine and bread to Abram and his army for their refreshment after their long journey. It would make no sense to have him also bring, in addition to what he had already given, "a tenth of everything." Just what would be inferred by the term "of everything" of which he supposedly brought a tenth? It certainly makes far more sense to read this as an offering on Abram's part. This would then be Abram's response to Melchizedek's gift of bread and wine, and his pronouncement of blessing upon Abram. The "everything" of which a tenth was given would then be the spoils Abram had retrieved and returned.

It has been objected that, according to verse 23, Abram refused to accept any of the spoils for himself and that consequently he could not have given any to Melchizedek. But this is a complete misunderstanding of Abram's attitude. It is true Abram refused to keep any of the spoils for his own use, but while it was in his control he had full authority to dispose of it as he saw fit. The king of Sodom recognized Abram's right in this also (see v. 21). As such, Abram had the full freedom to give one tenth of all of it to Melchizedek.

The name Melchizedek also appears in Psalm 110:4 where the Word of God declares, "You are a priest forever, in the order of Melchizedek." The sudden and almost mysterious appearance of Melchizedek gives him a quality of timelessness, like a symbol of eternity. Thus his unique priesthood offers a figure of the eternal priesthood of Jesus Christ.

There is, of course, a far broader treatment of the priesthood of Melchizedek in Hebrews 6:20–7:21. This, in turn, ties in with the reference in Psalm 110:4. The Hebrews passage develops this concept of timelessness still further by stating that Melchizedek had neither father nor mother, was without genealogy and without beginning or end of days. It goes without saying that these words in Hebrews must not be read literally. What is intended is that the biblical record does not mention Melchizedek's parents or ancestry, nor does it give any information about his birth or his death. The mysterious way in which this man appears and disappears in the biblical narrative sets him apart from all other biblical personalities. This makes him uniquely fit to be a type of the Christ. "Like the Son of God, he remains a priest forever." In other words, Melchizedek stands in sacred history as a type of the Messiah, until the time when the fulfillment of all types appears in the person of Jesus Christ.

14:21–24 *The king of Sodom said to Abram, "Give me the people and keep the goods for yourself."*

But Abram said to the king of Sodom, "I have raised my hand to the LORD, God Most High, Creator of heaven and earth, and have taken an oath that I will accept nothing belonging to you, not even a thread or the thong of a sandal, so that you will never be able to say, 'I made Abram rich.' I will accept nothing but what my men have eaten and the share that belongs to the men who went with me—to Aner, Eshcol and Mamre. Let them have their share."

The narrator now returns to the king of Sodom. We probably should conceive of this as though the king was present when Abram met Melchizedek. The king proposed that Abram keep all the spoils that had been retrieved since this was his right by conquest. But he requested that the prisoners who had been rescued be returned to their homes. Abram, however, objected to this proposal. Under oath he declared that he would keep none of the spoils for himself. He would not offer anyone an occasion for making the claim, "I have made Abram rich." Only two exceptions are allowed. First of all, that portion of the spoils which was eaten by Abram's fighting men would not be returned. Secondly, Abram refused to make the decision regarding the disposition of the spoils for his confederates, Aner, Eshcol, and Mamre. He insisted that they should be free to make their own decision in this matter and be permitted to keep their share of the spoils if they so chose.

5. *Promise and Sign* (15:1–21)

According to those who divide the sources of the Pentateuch, Genesis 15 is composed of a combination of sources. There is, supposedly, a narrative taken from "J." This is then supplemented by various passages taken from "E." This latter source is dated approximately 750 B.C. and this would then be the first trace of it in Genesis. The grounds that are adduced for questioning the unity of this chapter run as follows:

1) It is pointed out that when God appears at the end of the chapter it is in the evening after sundown (vv. 12, 17); but according to verse 5 it was night and all the stars were visible in the heavens. In reply we would point out that what is overlooked by the critics is that the scene described in verse 5 occurred in a vision and as such it has no bearing whatsoever on the actual time of day. But even if the events of the entire chapter had actually been experienced, they could well have occurred over a period of two days. It would start with the night vision, then go on to a second revelation on the following day which continued until evening when darkness once again fell. Thus there is no evidence here of two separate records.

2) We are told by the critics that in verse 6 Abram's great faith is lauded, but in verse 8 he expresses serious doubts. In reply we observe that this reasoning completely overlooks the fluctuation that normally takes place in the life of the believer. It is perfectly normal for true believers to experience periods of doubt and question. These cycles often occur after the believer has reached a high point in his faith experience. Even so, there is a real question as to whether Abram actually expresses doubts in verse 8. All we have there is a request for a sign. This request is not rebuked by God but is readily granted.

3) It is pointed out that in verse 7 God introduces Himself to Abram as "the Lord." But in verse 2 it is evident that Abram already knew Him by that name. This objection carries no weight at all, for this formula appears over and over in Scripture. A few examples would be Exodus 20:2; Leviticus 18:2; Deuteronomy 5:6; Isaiah 43:3; 44:24; Jeremiah 17:10; Ezekiel 20:5; 39:22; Zechariah 10:6.

4) It is argued that God does not appear to Abram until verse 17. Consequently the words of God to Abram recorded in verses 13–16 come too early. But this obviously overlooks the specific purpose for which God appears (in v. 17), namely, for the ceremony of confirming the covenant (see our commentary in loco).

The adherents of the division of sources have considerable difficulty deciding how the various sections must be designated as being from "J" or from "E." Nearly every interpreter makes a different division of the material in the text, and these scholars actually admit their difficulty in this regard. Professor Bohl concludes that none of the many divisions that have been advanced is correct. We go one step farther and insist that there is no substantial ground for any division of the text at all.

15:1 *After this, the word of the Lord came to Abram in a vision: "Do not be afraid, Abram. I am your shield, your very great reward."*

The chapter begins by announcing a new revelation from God to Abram. Although the revelation consisted largely of words spoken by God, it came to Abram in the form of a vision. The distinguishing characteristic of vision, whether it be something seen or something heard, is that the subject receives the spiritual message without the normal use of his regular sensory experience.

What Abram heard God say in his vision was, "Do not be afraid, Abram. I am your shield, your very great reward." We need not assume that Abram was in a state of great fear at the time. His position as a stranger in a hostile environment was frightening in itself. The assurance that God was protecting him as a shield and that therefore he need not fear was certainly relevant to Abram's situation. The Lord also assured Abram that his faithfulness would be rewarded, that is, that he would be showered with God's blessings.

15:2, 3 *But Abram said, "O Sovereign Lord, what can you give me since I remain childless and the one who will inherit my estate is Eliezer of Damascus?" And Abram said, "You have given me no children; so a servant in my household will be my heir."*

Abram asked in reply, "O Sovereign Lord, what can you give me?" He wanted to know what the nature of that reward would be. Abram expected that the promises he had received (12:2–3; 12:7; 13:14–17) would be fulfilled. Thus far none of the blessings had been realized. He was still childless. Perhaps he would have to resort to making his trusted servant Eliezer (ch. 24) his heir.

The words we have translated "the one who will inherit my estate" have given interpreters some difficulty. It is generally thought that the text has been corrupted at this point. We agree with our translators that the Hebrew word, the meaning of which is obscure, refers to the heir of an estate.

15:4, 5 *Then the word of the Lord came to him: "This man will not be your heir, but a son coming from your own body will be your heir." He took him outside and said, "Look at the heavens and count the stars—if indeed you can count them." Then he said to him, "So shall your offspring be."*

The Lord replied that Abram's servant was not to become his heir but that Abram would have a son produced "from your own body." The Lord then took the patriarch out into the night, and asked him to look up at the myriads of stars. The Lord then renewed the promise, already given in 13:16, by using a new analogy. Abram's descendants would be as innumerable as the stars of the heavens. There is no need to insist that God literally took Abram out under the stars since we are dealing with a visionary experience. In his vision Abram was made aware of the countless stars even as God, also in vision, renewed His promises to Abram.

15:6 *Abram believed the LORD, and he credited it to him as righteousness.*

Even though the possibility that Abram could produce a child was growing more unlikely with each passing year, he continued to believe the promise of God. The verb used in Hebrew implies that he wholly put his trust in God. Moreover, the form of the verb indicates that this trust in God was not a momentary attitude at that time only. It was an enduring, constant trust that did not waver.

And God "credited it to him as righteousness." His faith, his childlike trust did not justify Abram, nor did it *make* him righteous. His believing trust was "credited to him" by God as righteousness. The faith of this sinful person placed him in a position where the Judge of heaven and earth declared him to be righteous.

This is the first time where these two concepts, faith and justification, are bound together in Scripture. Paul comes back to this in Romans 4:23 when he declares that the deliverance of the sinner is not "by works" but "by grace." (See also Gal. 3:6.) To be sure, Genesis 15:6 does not specifically state that Abram's faith should not be looked upon as a "work" that he accomplished in and of himself but was wrought by God through grace. Even so, the entire narrative makes this very clear. When we consider the scene in Egypt (12:10–20), in which Abram's own weakness is clearly presented, it becomes obvious that his faith could be made strong only by God's gracious power.

The concept that Abram was "justified by faith" is presented here as historical reality. It would be reasonable to assume, however, that God revealed to Abram that he was righteous before Him only through faith.

15:7 *He also said to him, "I am the LORD, who brought you out of Ur of the Chaldeans to give you this land to take possession of it."*

We now come to the record of a second revelation from God which, as we have already observed, probably was received on the following day. Here no mention is made of a vision. We must therefore think of this revelation as coming to Abram by direct revelation, but just how the message was communicated to him is not indicated. Shortly after that the patriarch was promised that the land of Canaan would become his inheritance. Since he could not occupy the entire land alone, or as a family unit, the promise definitely related to Abram's descendants. It was for this purpose that God had brought him out of Ur of the Chaldeans (see 12:7; 13:14–17).

15:8 *But Abram said, "O Sovereign LORD, how can I know that I will gain possession of it?"*

Abram asked how he could be certain that he would inherit the land. This constituted a request for some kind of sign or guarantee that the promise he had been given would indeed be realized (cf. Gideon in Judg. 6:17, 36–40, or Hezekiah in 2 Kings 20:8). Such a request need not be interpreted as an indication of unbelief or doubt. It was, rather, an expression of a longing to have the Word of God sealed. This longing on our part is fulfilled in the sacraments. It must be granted, however, that this longing was an indication of human weakness. Many of our liturgical orders for the sacraments speak of the sacraments as being provided because of our weakness.

15:9–11 *So the LORD said to him, "Bring me a heifer, a goat and a ram, each three years old, along with a dove and a young pigeon."*
Abram brought all these to him, cut them in two and arranged the halves opposite each other; the birds, however, he did not cut in half. Then birds of prey came down on the carcasses, but Abram drove them away.

God responded to Abram's request by giving him an order. He was to present certain animals as a sacrifice to the Lord. There can be no doubt that these sacrificial animals were to serve as a sign of the promise that God had made. Although this does not become clear until later in the narrative, Abram must have realized this from the outset. This is evident from the unusual way he handled these sacrificial animals. The animals specified were a calf, a goat, and a ram, and each was to be three years old. In addition Abram was to provide a dove and a young pigeon. The animals were cut in two and the two halves were placed over against each other. The birds were not split, and probably were placed one on each side of the entire display. It is obvious that here we are not dealing with a dream or a vision but the fact that Abram actually carried out the instructions he received from God. This becomes even more evident when we are given the added detail that birds of prey came upon the carcasses and Abram had to drive them away.

15:12 *As the sun was setting, Abram fell into a deep sleep, and a thick and dreadful darkness came over him.*

We probably should allow for the passing of some time during which Abram watched over the scene and tried to keep the birds of prey away. As the day advanced and the sun was setting, Abram fell into a deep sleep. Just what is indicated by this deep sleep? Some have interpreted this as a special means of revelation. We, however, consider this to have been ordinary sleep that overcame Abram since he was tired from all his exertion.

While Abram was asleep a dreadful thing happened. A "thick . . . darkness" came over him. Many scholars are convinced that this is an insertion into the text. This is possible because to assert that a sleeping man is frightened by a "thick darkness" hardly makes sense. This fear or dread he experienced probably should be seen as a dream or a nightmare. It often happens that when a person has been extremely overwrought during the day, as Abram certainly had been, he has dreams or nightmares during the ensuing night.

15:13–16 *Then the Lord said to him, "Know for certain that your descendants will be strangers in a country not their own, and they will be enslaved and mistreated four hundred years. But I will punish the nation they serve as slaves, and afterward they will come out with great possessions. You, however, will go to your fathers in peace and be buried at a good old age. In the fourth generation your descendants will come back here, for the sin of the Amorites has not yet reached its full measure."*

Again we have a spoken message from God. How this message came to Abram is not mentioned. He could have been awakened by whatever frightened him and then God could have spoken to him directly. He could also have received this revelation via a dream. The importance, however, lies in the content of God's message.

Abram is now told that his descendants would go into Egypt and would be oppressed there for 400 years. The 400-year figure is obviously a round number, for in Exodus 12:40 we are told that Israel was in Egypt 430 years. (See also our introduction to the section on the call of Abram.) It should be remembered that the oppression did not start immediately after Jacob and his family arrived in Egypt. At first they were treated kindly for Joseph's sake. Thus the time reference given here must be seen as approximate only. The period of oppression was to be terminated by the judgments that God would bring on the oppressor. Thereafter Abram's descendants would leave Egypt, greatly enriched.

Thus God reveals to Abram how the promise he had received would be fulfilled. It would be "through suffering to glory," although Abram himself would not experience this suffering. He would have a peaceful old age and then would die. It would be the fourth generation of his descendants who would go through this experience and would be given the land of Canaan as a possession. This would not happen without a great conflict. The inhabitants of Canaan would defend their land, but Abram's descendants would be empowered by God to be victorious and conquer the land.

The long delay would, in part, serve to enable Abram's descendants to multiply into a great nation. But there was also another factor to be considered. We read that "the sin of the Amorites had not yet reached its full measure." When the level of their sin reached a point where God had to pour out His judgment upon them, this would be the time when the land would be given to Abram's descendants in God's providing grace.

The reference to "the fourth generation" presents some problems. It appears to be intended to coincide with the 400 years. Exodus 6:15–19 and Numbers 26:57–59 also suggest that there were four generations from Levi to Moses. Just as is the case in genealogies, the practice of counting generations was obviously not intended to be chronologically exact since several generations were freely omitted. So here also four generations is a loosely used term to coincide with 400 years.

15:17 *When the sun had set and darkness had fallen, a smoking fire pot with a blazing torch appeared and passed between the pieces.*

This verse refers to a later time in the same day. The sun had set and darkness had fallen. In typical Eastern narrative style, the author graphically tells about what "appeared." It was a "smoking fire pot with a blazing torch." The Hebrew literally calls them "an oven of smoke and a torch of fire." We probably should not think of two separate objects but a fire pot from which the burning torch came forth. This oven obviously was movable since it passed between the two sections of the sacrificial animals Abram had laid out. Just how are we to conceive of this mysterious appearance?

When we turn to Jeremiah 34:18, we receive some definite light on the meaning of this display. There we are told that a covenant was made and a ceremony was instituted to confirm the terms of the covenant. A calf was slaughtered and the two halves of the carcass were placed side by side. Then the two parties entering into covenant passed between the two halves of the slain animal. The symbolism obviously was that if either party was to break the covenant he would perish just like that animal. The smoking and flaming oven serves the same purpose here and was intended to be the sign Abram had requested. God confirmed this covenant by using the ceremony commonly used at that time for sealing covenants. The burning oven then would be a symbol of the presence of God.

It should be noted that God Himself performed this ceremony. In this way He sealed to His "friend" the fact that his descendants would inherit the land of Canaan. As we observed in connection with Genesis 12:7, the "appearance" (theophany) of God was not actually God Himself, but was a symbol of His presence. It should be noted also that it was only the oven that passed between the pieces of the sacrifice and not Abram himself. This points to the one-sided nature of the covenant that God makes with a person. This "monopluric" nature of God's covenant with human beings is also evident in God's covenant with Noah (Gen. 6:18; 9:8ff.). The covenant is indeed an agreement between two parties since this is the nature of a covenant. But the two parties are by no means equal since one of them is God Himself. Thus Abram must accept God's promise and His guarantee in complete faith.

15:18–21 *On that day the L*ORD *made a covenant with Abram and said, "To your descendants I give this land, from the river of Egypt to the great river, the Euphrates–the land of the Kenites, Kenizzites, Kadmonites, Hittites, Perizzites, Rephaites, Amorites, Canaanites, Girgashites and Jebusites."*

In the light of the above, it is clear that verse 18 does not introduce a new concept. This is merely a recapitulation of what had transpired, as described in the preceding verses. "On that day," then, refers to the day on which the above-mentioned events occurred.

It is worthy of note that the Hebrew word for the making of a covenant is the word which means "to cut." This undoubtedly refers to the cutting up of the sacrificial animal which symbolized the covenant agreement. Other terms that are used for establishing a covenant are "to set upright" in Genesis 6:18 and 9:8, and "to give" in Genesis 9:12.

At this point the specifics of the promise that was sealed to Abram in this covenant are spelled out. This promise had been announced in verse 7, and then Abram asked for a sign. Now God specifies the boundaries of the "land" that Abram's descendants would inherit.

This detailed description of the "land" certainly is not a superfluous insertion, as some scholars have claimed. On the basis of the promise given in verse 7, Abram could have assumed that the "land" would include the ground on which he stood and its immediate surrounding territory. Abram had to be informed regarding the size of the "land" they would occupy and possess, especially in view of the promise of the innumerable descendants he was to produce. He had been given some indication of this at the time he separated from Lot. At that time God had told him to "lift up [his] eyes" in all directions in order to view the land that God would give him as an inheritance (Gen. 13:14–15). In our present passage, the extent of the land is more specifically designated. We should not think of this, however, as a precise delineation of exact boundaries. Only the global dimensions of the land are given.

The land of promise was to extend from "the river of Egypt," the Nile, to the Euphrates. There is no reason to try to make the "river of Egypt" some lesser stream which ran closer to where the southern boundary of Canaan later fell. This description is not intended to identify precise boundaries. The listing of the tribes that occupied the land at that time does offer some more specific boundaries, but these, without exception, were peoples who lived in the actual land of Canaan or its immediate borders.

The Kenites originally lived a little to the south of Palestine but later established their territory in what became the land of Judea (Judg. 1:18). The Kenizzites settled in the southern part of Canaan. This can be deduced from the fact that Caleb, who received Hebron as his inheritance, was called a Kenizzite in Joshua 14:13–14. The Kadmonites are mentioned only here. Presumably they settled a little further east. The Hittites lived in the area of Hebron (see Gen. 23:3ff.). The Perizzites were discussed under Genesis 13:5–7. The Rephaites were discussed under Genesis 14:4–7. The Amorites occupied part of the area east of the Jordan (see Deut. 3:8; 4:47; 31:4; Josh. 2:10; 9:10), and the hills of West Jordan (Num. 13:29). The Canaanites occupied the plains of that area. The Girgashites are mentioned more often among the peoples of Canaan (Deut. 7:1; Josh. 3:10; 24:11), but we have no indication of their exact location. The Jebusites lived in the area of Jerusalem (Josh. 15:8, 63; Judg. 1:21; 19:10–11).

Naturally, we cannot claim that this is an exhaustive list of all the tribes who occupied the land of Canaan. The Hivites, for example, are mentioned in other references and they are not included here. What we have here, then, is a global description of the tribes and people which serves to give the impression that it was an extensive area. Abram's descendants would inherit a large territory, an area that now was occupied by many different peoples.

6. *Hagar and Ishmael* (16:1–16)

This chapter is, for the most part, ascribed to "J." A few verses, 1a, 3, 15, and 16, have been ascribed to "P" by those who divide the sources of the Pentateuch. The reason given for ascribing these latter verses to "P" is that they provide some chronological details and this is supposed to be characteristic of "P." It does seem to be a bit ridiculous to assume that

"P" is the only source capable of offering some chronological material.

Another argument that is used to justify the plurality of sources is that verse 3 seems to break the flow of the narrative from verse 2 to verse 4. A careful reading of this portion, however, indicates that the narrative flows logically just as it is. Sarai first discussed her plan with her husband and, after he agreed, she proceeded to put it into effect by giving her slave to Abram as a wife. When Abram consummated marital relations with Hagar she became pregnant. Thus the narrative moves along naturally.

A final argument used by the source splitters is that there is a conflict between verses 11 and 15. First it is suggested, they insist, that Hagar named her son Ishmael, and later it is Abram who named the child. Once again, we reply that the narrative is consistent. God revealed the name to Hagar before the child was born. After she gave birth to him she undoubtedly informed Abram of the revelation she had received. Abram performed the father's duty of legally naming the child and he concurred with the revelation that had been given.

16:1–3 *Now Sarai, Abram's wife, had borne him no children. But she had an Egyptian maidservant named Hagar; so she said to Abram, "The Lord has kept me from having children. Go, sleep with my maidservant; perhaps I can build a family through her."*

Abram agreed to what Sarai said. So after Abram had been living in Canaan ten years, Sarai his wife took her Egyptian maidservant Hagar and gave her to her husband to be his wife.

The chapter begins by pointing out that, in spite of God's promise that they would have countless descendants, Abram and Sarai remained childless. Sarai was the one who was finally overcome with a sense of hopelessness, so she began to consider other possibilities for bringing a child into their family. She had an Egyptian servant girl, named Hagar, who could have been given to her at the time of their experience in Egypt, described in Genesis 12:15ff. She proposed that this slave girl become Abram's secondary wife in the hope that in this way children might be produced which technically could be considered as hers. This arrangement was in accord with the practice and the culture of that day. This is evident from a regulation in the Code of Hammurabi that provided for just such an eventuality. (We have a similar instance in Gen. 30:3 and 9.) Sarai used the expression, "perhaps I can build a family through her." This figure implies that the family was like a building in which the children were building blocks. The same expression is used by Rachel in 30:3 (cf. also Deut. 25:9 and Ruth 4:11).

Abram was weak enough to go along with his wife's proposal, but to declare that Abram also had doubts about God's promise being fulfilled would be going too far. All we can say is that he went along with Sarai's proposal. Thus, ten years after his arrival in Canaan, Abram enters into a secondary marriage with Hagar and proceeds to have marital relations with her.

16:4 *He slept with Hagar, and she conceived.*
When she knew she was pregnant, she began to despise her mistress.

The plan was effective and Hagar promptly became pregnant by Abram. When the former slave realized she was pregnant, she expressed her womanly pride by flaunting her condition in a spirit of disdain for Sarai, her childless mistress.

16:5, 6 *Then Sarai said to Abram, "You are responsible for the wrong I am suffering. I put my servant in your arms, and now that she knows she is pregnant, she despises me. May the LORD judge between you and me."*
"Your servant is in your hands," Abram said. "Do with her whatever you think best." Then Sarai mistreated Hagar; so she fled from her.

This was too much for Sarai to accept, so she reproached her husband and charged him with responsibility for the entire situation. She even called on God to judge between them. But Abram, eager to keep peace in the family, gave her a free hand in dealing with her slave girl as she saw fit. Sarai availed herself of this freedom and harshly tried to put the pregnant girl in her place as a slave. Hagar, thereupon, escaped Sarai's oppression by fleeing from Abram's camp.

16:7–9 *The angel of the LORD found Hagar near a spring in the desert; it was the spring that is beside the road to Shur. And he said, "Hagar, servant of Sarai, where have you come from, and where are you going?"*
"I'm running away from my mistress Sarai," she answered.
Then the angel of the LORD told her, "Go back to your mistress and submit to her."

But this did not end the matter. The angel of the Lord appeared to the fleeing Hagar while she was resting near a spring in the desert. The angel urged her to return to her mistress and to submit to her. The location of this encounter with the angel is further described as being "beside the road to Shur," and according to Genesis 25:18 and 1 Samuel 15:7, this was near the border of Egypt. It would appear that Hagar intended to return to her homeland. The reference to "the spring" suggests that this was a well-known spring where desert travelers often stopped for refreshment. We need not assume, however, that this spring was near Shur and the Egyptian border. The lonely, fleeing girl, already obviously pregnant, probably had not traveled very far before the angel urged her to return (see also v. 14). Thus the encounter with the angel also served for her own protection. It would be for her own welfare to return to Abram's home rather than to continue on this strenuous journey in her present condition.

This is the first reference to an angel in Scripture. The word actually means "envoy" or "messenger." There is good reason, however, in this case, not to think of this as one of the created angels. There are similar references to "the angel of the LORD" in 1 Kings 19:5; 2 Chronicles 32:21; Psalms 8:5; 91:11; 103:20; 104:4; 148:2; Daniel 3:28; 6:22; Mathew 4:11; 13:41; 25:31; Luke 2:13, 15; Hebrews 1:4ff., etc. This "angel of the LORD" spoke as if He himself was God. Moreover, in verse 13 he is referred to as "the LORD." Hagar called him "the God who sees me." It has been objected that it is not unusual for a messenger to speak as though he actually was the one he represented. In this case it would be quite natural for the "angel" to speak as though "God" were speaking. Certainly the prophets often brought their message from God in the first person. Even so, no prophet is ever called "God" or "the LORD." It would appear, therefore, that this reference to "the angel of the LORD" indicates more than a mere heavenly messenger. This "messenger" must be seen as a special manifestation of the being of God Himself. Christian exegesis, therefore, with considerable justification, has related this manifestation of God to the Second Person of the Holy Trinity. At the same time, it must be remembered that we do not have a clear revelation here of the divine Logos. That must await the incarnation of Jesus.

16:10–12 *The angel added, "I will so increase your descendants that they will be too numerous to count."*

The angel of the LORD also said to her:

"You are now with child and you will have a son. You shall name him Ishmael, for the LORD has heard of your misery.

He will be a wild donkey of a man; his hand will be against everyone and everyone's hand against him, and he will live in hostility toward all his brothers."

The angel of the Lord added a promise to His exhortation to Hagar to return to Sarai. First of all, Hagar was promised that she would have countless descendants. Second, she was assured that the child she was carrying within her body would be born. It would be a son and he was to be named Ishmael, which means "God hears." This name was to serve as a memorial to the incident at hand, since God had "heard" the cry of her misery. Even though Hagar was not without fault in this entire episode, God was merciful to her and showed her the way out of her troubles.

In addition, the angel gave her a characterization of the son she was to bring forth. This characterization was to fit not only her son, Ishmael, but also his descendants. He was to be like a wild donkey, roaming free in the hills. Furthermore, he would be in conflict with the peoples surrounding him and his descendants. And their enemies would not be able to drive Abram's descendants out of the land.

Some critics have insisted that this promise of countless descendants could hardly have come before the child was born. They therefore consider verse 10 to be a later interpolation. This view, however, is the result of looking at this material from a Western perspective which demands a logical progression of a narrative, but this is not the case with Eastern narrators. In this connection we can point out the fact that Abram was promised that he would become a great nation even before he was promised a son and long before that son was born (Gen. 12:2; 13:16; 15:4). It certainly was of greatest importance to Hagar, in her present desperate situation, to be assured that she would have many descendants. She must have been aware of the promise to Abram that Sarai hoped to see realized through her. And now it looked like she would perish here in the desert. So she is not only told to return, but she is also assured that she too will have countless descendants.

16:13, 14 *She gave this name to the L*ORD *who spoke to her: "You are the God who sees me," for she said, "I have now seen the One who sees me." That is why the well was called Beer Lahai Roi; it is still there, between Kadesh and Bered.*

After hearing the message of the angel of the Lord, Hagar concluded that God Himself had spoken to her. This probably was not clear to her when she first was asked, "Where did you come from and where are you going?" But now, having received the entire message, she addressed the messenger as "You are the [One] who sees me." Thus she acknowledged Him as the all-seeing God.

The remainder of this passage produces some difficulty. The exact meaning of the original text is not clear, but the best interpretation of this line probably is that it forms an expression of wonderment on Hagar's part. Thus it could read, "Have I really seen the One who sees me?" Some interpreters claim that the text was corrupted at this point and that she actually said, "Have I actually seen God and remained alive?" This reading, however, would require too many changes in the text to make it credible.

As a consequence of her statement, the well at which the incident took place was called "Beer Lahai Roi"—the Well of the Living God, or, the God who sees me. The location is given, more specifically, as being between Kadesh (Kadesh Barnea) and Bered. Although the exact location of Bered is not known, it probably lay to the west of Kadesh. This would confirm what we said under verse 7, that Hagar had not yet traveled very far from Canaan.

16:15, 16 *So Hagar bore Abram a son, and Abram gave the name Ishmael to the son she had borne. Abram was eighty-six years old when Hagar bore him Ishmael.*

Although we are not specifically told that Hagar obeyed the command of the messenger, it is implied. We are told that Hagar bore Abram a son who was named Ishmael, and Abram was now 86 years old. The events of 16:1–3 took place ten years after he arrived in Canaan. In 12:4 we are told that he was 75 when he arrived there. Add a year for the conception of the child and we arrive at the age of 86 when Ishmael was born.

7. *The Renewal of the Covenant and the Institution of Circumcision* (17:1–27)

Those who divide the sources see in Genesis 17 a parallel to chapter 15. While chapter 15 was ascribed to "J," chapter 17 is generally ascribed to "P." It is argued that there are certain words used here that are characteristic of "P," such as the name "Elohim" for God. It is claimed, moreover, that the chronological data in verses 1, 17, 24, and 25, as well as the broad style of the narrative, also point to "P." We will not go into a detailed critique of this position at this point. We do want to point out, however, that the name "Jahweh" is used in verse 1, and this is supposed to be characteristic of "J." The critics try to avoid this by charging that this was slipped in later by the redactor.

We hold that chapter 15 and chapter 17 cannot be considered to be parallel passages or doublets because even though both chapters speak of the covenant that God made with Abraham and both include some of the terms of that covenant, there are also some significant differences. In chapter 15 the sealing of the covenant was effected by the theophany passing between the sections of the sacrificial animals. There is no trace of this in chapter 17. In chapter 15 this sign was given in answer to Abram's request for assurance. This also is omitted in chapter 17. In chapter 17 the covenant was related to the rite of circumcision and this is not mentioned in chapter 15. Chapter 17 also introduces the changes of the names of Abram and Sarai, and these are not mentioned earlier.

Furthermore, both of these chapters include references that strongly suggest that we are dealing with two distinct incidents that took place on different occasions. In 17:1 and 24 Abram's age is given as 99 years. Although chapter 15 does not specifically mention his age, we can establish the fact that Abram was only 85 at that time by comparing 12:4 and 16:3. We realize, of course, that those who divide sources will simply reply that this indicates that these chapters come from different sources. But no substantial basis for this conclusion has been adduced. Even if we set aside these chronological data, the fact remains that in chapter 17 Ishmael was already on the scene (vv. 18, 23, 25), while in chapter 15 he had not yet been born. His birth is recorded in chapter 16 and that chapter is ascribed to "J" as is chapter 15. Thus the textual evidence strongly suggests that we should not look on this as one event presented from two different perspectives, but as two distinctly different events, separated by a considerable space of time.

The similarities between the two chapters are easily explained. After God first made His covenant with Abram, He returned to this concept frequently to confirm and reemphasize it. It would be strange indeed if in the entire hsitory of Abram there would be only one reference to this covenant that had such monumental significance in the progress of God's revelation of redemption. It should not surprise us, moreover, that the content of the covenantal promise has some similarities in these two references. We have already seen some repetition of this promise in 12:2, 7; 13:14–16; 15:5–7. God is not changeable. His promises, once given, stand forever.

17:1, 2 *When Abram was ninety-nine years old, the Lord appeared to him and said, "I am God Almighty; walk before me and be blameless. I will confirm my covenant between me and you and will greatly increase your numbers."*

When Ishmael was 13 years old, Abram received another "appearance" from God. We have already discussed this concept of theophany under 12:7. Once again the "appearance" was accompanied by an audible voice. "I am God Almighty," was the name with which the messenger identified Himself. The Hebrew word is *El Shaddai.* The derivation and meaning of *Shaddai* are uncertain, but "the Almighty" seems to be the best translation. (Cf. Isa. 13:6 and Joel 1:15.)

God, as the almighty one, began His message to Abram with a command, "Walk before me and be blameless." The Hebrew uses the term that means "walk before my eyes." God required that Abram live a life that was pleasing to Him, in order that he need not fear being seen by His holy eyes.

The Lord then proceeded directly to a renewal of the promise of countless descendants that had previously been presented as one of the terms of the covenant (see ch. 15). Abram was now reassured of that covenant, and the promises it included were repeated.

Abram had been waiting for the fulfillment of those promises for many years. By all human standards, each passing year made the realization of what had been promised more unlikely. By now, in fact, it was humanly impossible. It is undoubtedly for that reason that God began His message with the self-designation, "I am God Almighty." What is impossible with man is possible with God, for from what follows, it is evident that God was telling Abram that the time for the realization of what had been promised was near at hand. Thus the purpose of this "appearance" of God was to announce to Abram that the reality, for which he had waited so long, would soon be experienced.

17:3–6 *Abram fell facedown, and God said to him, "As for me, this is my covenant with you: You will be the father of many nations. No longer will you be called Abram; your name will be Abraham, for I have made you a father of many nations. I will make you very fruitful; I will make nations of you, and kings will come from you.*

When Abram saw the "appearance" and heard God's voice, he cast himself to the earth in humble worship. God continued to reassure Abram of the covenant promise by indicating that his descendants would include "many nations." A special emphasis was placed on "*my* covenant" in order to give force and significance to the fact that the covenant was established by the "Almighty God."

The concept of "many nations" must be seen from the perspective of both Abram's physical descendants and his spiritual offspring. The addition of the reference to "kings" who would descend from Abram strongly suggests that we should think of tribes and peoples such as the Ishmaelites, the peoples who would descend from the children Abram would have by Keturah (Gen. 25:1–4), and the Edomites who also were descendants from Abram and became a separate people.

But, in a broader sense, there is also a reference here to Abram's spiritual descendants who would share in benefits of the covenant as ultimately centered in Christ. In Genesis 12:3 God had declared that "all nations" of the earth would be blessed in Abram. This promise was now enforced by the name given to Abram. From now on he would be called Abraham.

The name Abram appears nowhere else in Scripture in this form, but the name could be a shortened form of Abiram. We have a similar shortening of a name in the case of Abner from Abiner (see 1 Sam. 14:50, 51; 17:55, 57; 20:25). We probably have a similar usage in the name Absalom, taken from Abishalom (see 2 Sam. 3:3ff.; 1 Kings 15:2, 10). The name Abiram means "exalted father." The name appears in this form in Numbers 16:1; 1 Kings 16:34. In Babylonian the name has been found as Abarama and Abi-ramu.

That the name Abraham is merely a lengthened form of Abram, as some claim, is not likely. Even so it is difficult to explain the name Abraham etymologically. It is possible also that it relates to an Arabic word *rueham* which means "a great number." Perhaps there also was an ancient Hebrew word such as *raham* meaning "multitude." Then the word Abraham could be readily interpreted as "father of a multitude," which was what God promised to the patriarch.

17:7 *I will establish my covenant as an everlasting covenant between me and you and your descendants after you for the generations to come, to be your God and the God of your descendants after you.*

The statement in verse 7 is of fundamental importance for the whole of religion, man's relationship with God. Here we have the basic formula of the covenant God made with Abraham. That covenant not only involved Abraham as an individual person, but it also included his descendants. Moreover, the significance of this revelation is not limited to Abraham and his immediate descendants, but it became a formula for all of God's special relationships with humanity. Here it was applied to Abraham, and that in the age of particularism. On Pentecost when the church became universal, Peter took over this concept as well (Acts 2:39). Further, when Paul preached the gospel to the Gentiles the same concept was introduced (Acts 16:31).

Thus we can understand the term "everlasting covenant" in its fullest sense. To be sure, in the Old Testament the word "forever" does not always imply what we sometimes read into it today. For example, kings were addressed with the wish, "O king, live forever" (1 Kings 1:31; Neh. 2:3; Dan. 2:4; 3:9; 5:10; 6:6, 21). This, of course, implied only that the king was wished a long reign. But here the term implies that the covenant would carry through in all the generations to come.

Another statement with special significance in the formulation of God's covenant with Abraham is, "to be your God and the God of your descendants after you." This established the very essence of the covenant relationship. God not only gave many gifts of grace but He also gave *Himself* to His covenant people. And this indicates the true reality of the covenant blessing. God's covenant people would not only be blessed by God but they would possess God as their own God. This included the fullness of the blessing that was promised in the "maternal promise." In the promised Deliverer, God, as it were, gave Himself back to His chosen people.

17:8 *The whole land of Canaan, where you are now an alien, I will give as an everlasting possession to you and your descendants after you; and I will be their God."*

To this promise of far-reaching spiritual blessings there was now added a renewal of the promise that Abraham would possess the land of Canaan. (See 12:7; 13:15; 15:7, 18–21.) This land, in which he had lived as an alien, would become the everlasting possession of him and his descendants. Just how the word "everlasting" must be interpreted in this instance cannot be determined from the text. We do know from later history, however, that Israel was punished for its sins by being driven out of this land. This *conditional* nature of the promise was also implied in the Mosaic law in Leviticus 26:33–35; Deuteronomy 4:26–28; 28:63–68; and in the prophets in Hosea 9:17 and Amos 9:9, etc.

At the close of this more temporal part of the covenant promise, we again read, "and I will be their God." The special relationship of Abraham's descendants to God remained the primary aspect of the covenant promise and the temporal blessings were to be completely dependent on the continuation of that relationship. When Abraham's descendants broke that relationship to God by their disobedience they thereby also forfeited the temporal blessings.

17:9–14 *Then God said to Abraham, "As for you, you must keep my covenant, you and your descendants after you for the generations to come. This is my covenant with you and your descendants after you, the covenant you are to keep: Every male among you shall be circumcised. You are to undergo circumcision, and it will be the sign of the covenant between me and you. For the generations to come every male among you who is eight days old must be circumcised, including those born in your household or bought with money from a foreigner–those who are not your offspring. Whether born in your household or bought with your money, they must be circumcised. My covenant in your flesh is to be an everlasting covenant. Any uncircumcised male, who has not been circumcised in the flesh, will be cut off from his people; he has broken my covenant."*

The promise to Abraham and his descendants came in the form of a covenant which also placed definite responsibilities upon them. In verse 4 we read, "As for me, this is my covenant with you." Now we have the other side of the covenant announced in, "As for you, you must keep my covenant." This reveals the very nature of the covenant. Although it was one-sided in the sense that God set up all the terms, there were two parties in this covenant, as there are in every covenant. (See our treatment of Gen. 15:17.) One of the particular responsibilities placed on Abraham and his descendants involved the rite of circumcision. Every male child was to be administered this rite at the age of eight days. This was to include all the boys born into the household, children of slaves as well as those of the master of the house. Even those who were bought with money from a foreigner were to be included. Anyone who did not keep this rite would thereby be excluded from God's covenant people.

It is worthy of note that the rite of circumcision was by no means limited to the immediate descendants of Abraham. It was also practiced by the Ishmaelites and the Edomites (cf. Jer. 9:25, 26). It was also found among the Ammonites. All of these may well have acquired the practice from the line of Abraham, or, in the case of the Ammonites, from Lot. But the practice has also been found among the Egyptians, as is clear from the passage in Jeremiah and also from Ezekiel 31:18; 32:19, as well as from the records of secular historians. Besides, it has been evidenced by the discovery of some of the Egyptian mummies. It was also practiced among the Phoenicians and has even been discovered among various tribes in Africa and South America and the Islands of the South Pacific. In these distant places the practice certainly had no connection with the descendants of Abraham. Consequently, we cannot escape the conclusion that God did not establish the rite of circumcision as an entirely new practice but that He took over an existing practice and designated this as the sign of the covenant.

17:15, 16 *God also said to Abraham, "As for Sarai your wife, you are no longer to call her Sarai; her name will be Sarah. I will bless her and will surely give you a son by her. I will bless her so that she will be the mother of nations; kings of peoples will come from her."*

Just as Abram was to change his name to Abraham, so Sarai was to be called Sarah. There is no real difference in meaning, but Sarai is the older form of the feminine ending while Sarah is the newer form. Both words mean "heroic" or "heroine." The newer form was probably introduced in order to give fresh emphasis to the meaning of Sarah's name. This change in name for Abraham's wife focuses on that part of the covenant promise which declared that she would give birth to a child. The promises regarding Abraham's descendants, their numbers, and their significance in God's plan of redemption, were to be fulfilled through Sarah. She was to play a crucial role in the entire covenant fulfillment. Her descendants were to become "nations." Her offspring would include "kings." She was indeed to become a "heroine" as her name indicated.

17:17, 18 *Abraham fell facedown; he laughed and said to himself, "Will a son be born to a man a hundred years old? Will Sarah bear a child at the age of ninety?" And Abraham said to God, "If only Ishmael might live under your blessing!"*

There is considerable difference of opinion as to whether these verses indicate that Abraham's attitude was one of unbelief or one of joyous amazement. Even though Calvin and several other conservative scholars accept the latter interpretation, we question whether this is really justified. Both the question that Abraham asked of himself and the request he uttered regarding Ishmael strongly suggest that Abraham was not ready to accept the possibility that Sarah would indeed give birth to a child. Certainly a man who was 100 years old (he uses a round number) could not possibly become the father of a child by a woman who was 90 years old. Abraham would have been satisfied if God would have graciously spared and blessed Ishmael, his son by the slave girl, Hagar.

Some have even suggested that the prospect of having a child by Sarah would pose a threat to Abraham's relationship to Ishmael, who was also his flesh and blood. Actually, then, this would be seen as a plea in behalf of the well-being of Ishmael. But this interpretation seems a bit too contrived. The same is true of an interpretation offered by some Jewish scholars, that this was merely an expression of Abraham's modesty. They argue that this was not an expression of doubt but rather one of being overwhelmed by what God had announced. His words must then be read as being a bit facetious. We would consider it not at all unreasonable to accept the fact that the faith of the great hero of faith was momentarily overcome by a measure of disbelief. We would then remind ourselves of certain inadequacies that came to the surface in Abraham's attitudes on other occasions also, such as are recorded in Genesis 12:11–13 and 16:2–4.

17:19–21 *Then God said, "Yes, but your wife Sarah will bear you a son, and you will call him Isaac. I will establish my covenant with him as an everlasting covenant for his descendants after him. And as for Ishmael, I have heard you: I will surely bless him; I will make him fruitful and will greatly increase his numbers. He* *will be the father of twelve rulers, and I will make him into a great nation. But my covenant I will establish with Isaac, whom Sarah will bear to you by this time next year.''*

God replied to Abraham by assuring him that he indeed would have a child by Sarah. He should not doubt this because it would happen within a year. The child was to be named Isaac (Hebrew—*Yishāq*) which means "he laughs" or "one laughs." This does not necessarily imply that the child would be given this name because Abraham had laughed. The meaning would rather be that this child, as the child of promise, would bring great joy and happiness. The inspired writer did engage in a bit of wordplay, however, which is a favorite figure of speech among the ancient Israelites. He refers to Abraham's laughter in the immediate context of this reference to the name Isaac. (See also Gen. 18:12–15.)

The child that was to be born would be the child of promise. He was to be the one in whom the covenant promises were to be fulfilled. At last the time had come that had been announced to Abraham years before while he was still in Haran (12:2, 3). The promise was about to be realized.

Naturally, we wonder why God made Abraham wait so long for the fulfillment of the promise. Undoubtedly He wanted to reveal something to Abraham and to His people of all time. They must know, beyond all question and all doubt, that God's promises are absolutely trustworthy. No matter how impossible the fulfillment of these promises might appear from human perspectives, God would do the impossible and keep His promises. Abraham's history reveals with unmistakable clarity that God's word is always trustworthy. God fulfills His promises, not because they are reasonable, by human standards, but because God is God and His Word is true and absolutely reliable.

Abraham's plea in behalf of Ishmael also was to be answered. Although the covenant that God had made with Abraham would not directly involve Ishmael, this son of the patriarch would also receive a blessing. He too would have many descendants and would produce a great people. His descendants would also include "rulers," no less than twelve in fact. In this connection, see Genesis 25:16.

17:22 *When he had finished speaking with Abraham, God went up from him.*

At this point the verbal revelation ended and consequently the "appearance" of God also came to an end. This is described by the statement, "God went up from him." This expression again indicates that the "appearance" of God involved something that was externally visible, as we observed in 12:7. Although we are told that God ''went up,'' this refers only to this ''appearance'' of God since God Himself has no visible form that can be limited in space. (See Deut. 4:12, 15.)

17:23–27 *On that very day Abraham took his son Ishmael and all those born in his household or bought with his money, every male in his household, and circumcised them, as God told him. Abraham was ninety-nine years old when he was circumcised, and his son Ishmael was thirteen; Abraham and his son Ishmael were both circumcised on that same day. And every male in Abraham's household, including those born in his household or bought from a foreigner, was circumcised with him.*

Finally, we are told that Abraham immediately followed the divine injunction and administered the rite of circumcision to himself, to his son Ishmael, and to all the males of his household. Once again we are told that Abraham was 99 years old, while Ishmael had reached the age of 13.